D1986899

Protecting Nature

Protecting Nature

Organizations and Networks in Europe and the USA

Edited by

C.S.A. (Kris) van Koppen

Wageningen University, The Netherlands

and

William T. Markham

University of North Carolina at Greensboro, USA

Edward Elgar

Cheltenham, UK • Northampton, MA, USA

© C.S.A. van Koppen and William T. Markham 2007

All rights reserved. No part of this publication may be reproduced, stored in a retrieval system or transmitted in any form or by any means, electronic, mechanical or photocopying, recording, or otherwise without the prior permission of the publisher.

Published by
Edward Elgar Publishing Limited
Glensanda House
Montpellier Parade
Cheltenham
Glos GL50 1UA
UK

Edward Elgar Publishing, Inc.
William Pratt House
9 Dewey Court
Northampton
Massachusetts 01060
USA

Staats- u. Universitäts-
bibliothek Bremen
Ausgeschieden
Staats- und Universitätsbibliothek Bremen
15.09.25 DM
TE 5223

A catalogue record for this book
is available from the British Library

Library of Congress Cataloging in Publication Data
Protecting nature : organizations and networks in Europe and the USA /
edited by C.S.A. (Kris) van Koppen and William T. Markham.
p. cm.
Includes bibliographical references and index.
1. Nature conservation—Europe—Societies, etc.—Directories. 2. Nature conservation—United States—Societies, etc.—Directories. I. Koppen, C.S.A. van, 1953– II. Markham, William T., 1946–

QH77.E9P76 2007
333.7206'04—dc22

2007029866

ISBN 978 1 84542 970 6

Printed and bound in Great Britain by MPG Books Ltd, Bodmin, Cornwall

Contents

Contributors

Magnus Boström, Stockholm University and Södertörn University College, Sweden

Cécilia Claeys-Mekdade, Université de la Méditerranée, France

Piotr Gliński, Polish Academy of Science and University of Bialystok, Poland

Marie Jacqué, Université de la Méditerranée, France

Małgorzata Koziarek, Polish Academy of Science, Poland

William T. Markham, University of North Carolina at Greensboro, USA

Angela G. Mertig, Middle Tennessee State University, USA

Giorgio Osti, University of Trieste, Italy

Christopher Rootes, University of Kent at Canterbury, UK

Ørnulf Seippel, Institute for Social Research, Oslo, and Norwegian University for Science and Technology, Trondheim, Norway

C.S.A. (Kris) van Koppen, Wageningen University and Utrecht University, The Netherlands

Abbreviations

CHAPTER 1

EEB	European Environmental Bureau
EU	European Union
IUCN	International Union for the Conservation of Nature and Natural Resources, now World Conservation Union
NGO	non-governmental organization
NSM	new social movement
SMO	social movement organization
UNEP	United Nations Environmental Programme
UNESCO	United Nations Educational, Scientific, and Cultural Organization
WWF	World Wildlife Fund, now World Wide Fund for Nature

ENGLAND

BBC	British Broadcasting Corporation
BP	British Petroleum
BTCV	British Trust for Conservation Volunteers
CAFOD	Catholic Agency for Overseas Development
CND	Campaign for Nuclear Disarmament
CoEnCo	Committee (now Council) for Environmental Conservation
CPRE	Council for the Preservation of Rural England, later Council for the Protection of Rural England, now Campaign to Protect Rural England
DfID	Department for International Development
EC	European Commission
EEB	European Environmental Bureau
EMO	environmental movement organizations
EU	European Union
FoE	Friends of the Earth
GBP	pound sterling
GM	genetically modified

GMO	genetically modified organism
LWT	Lincolnshire Wildlife Trust
MP	Member of Parliament
NC	Nature Conservancy
NT	National Trust
RSNC	Royal Society for Nature Conservation
RSPB	Royal Society for the Protection of Birds
RSPCA	Royal Society for the Prevention of Cruelty to Animals
RSWT	Royal Society of Wildlife Trusts
SCC	Stop Climate Chaos
SSSI	site of special scientific interest
UK	United Kingdom (of Great Britain and Northern Ireland)
UNCED	United Nations Conference on Environment and Development
WT	Woodland Trust
WWE	Who's Who in the Environment
WWF	World Wildlife Fund, now World Wide Fund for Nature

FRANCE

CAF	Club Alpin Français (French Alpine Club)
CNRS	Centre National de la Recherche Scientifique (National Centre for Scientific Research)
DATAR	Direction de l'Aménagement du Territoire et de l'Action Régionale (Regional Development and Regional Action Agency)
FFSPN	Federation Française des Sociétés de Protection de la Nature (French Federation of Nature Conservation Societies)
FNE	France Nature Environnement (Nature and Environment Federation)
FRAPNA	Fédération Rhône Alpes de Protection de la Nature (Nature Protection of Rhône Alpes Federation)
INRA	Institut National de Recherche Agronomique (National Institute for Agronomic Research)
LPO	Ligue de Protection des Oiseaux (League for the Protection of Birds)
MEDD	Ministère de l'Ecologie et du Developpement Durable (Ministry for Ecology and Sustainable Development)

SNA	Société Nationale d'Acclimatation (National Acclimatization Society)
SNPN	Société Nationale de Protection de la Nature (National Society for Nature Protection)
SZA	Société Zoologique d'Acclimatation (Zoological Acclimatization Society)
TCF	Touring Club de France (Touring Club of France)
WWF	World Wildlife Fund, later World Wide Fund for Nature

GERMANY

BBU	Bundesverband Bürgerinitiativen (Federal Alliance of Citizens' Initiatives for Environmental Protection)
BfV	Bund für Vogelschutz (League for Bird Protection)
BH	Bund Heimatschutz (League for Homeland Protection)
BIs	Bürgerinitiativen (citizens' initiatives)
BN	Bund Naturschutz in Bayern (Bavarian League for Nature Protection)
BUND	Bund Umwelt und Naturschutz Deutschland (League for Environment and Nature Protection in Germany)
DNR	Deutscher Naturschutz Ring (German Nature Protection League)
GNU	Gesellschaft für Natur und Umwelt (Society for Nature and Environment)
NABU	Naturschutzbund Deutschland (German Nature Protection League)
SPD	Social Democratic Party
WWF	World Wide Fund for Nature

ITALY

LAV	Lega Antivivisezione (Antivivisection League)
LIPU	Lega Italiana per la Protezione degli Uccelli (Italian League for the Protection of Birds)
IUCN	International Union for the Conservation of Nature and Natural Resources, now World Conservation Union
IUPN	International Union for the Protection of Nature
WWF	World Wide Fund for Nature

NETHERLANDS

IFAW-NL	Stichting IFAW Nederland (International Fund for Animal Welfare Netherlands)
IVN	Instituut voor Natuurbeschermingseducatie (Association for Environmental Education)
KNNV	Koninklijke Nederlandse Natuurhistorische Vereniging (Royal Dutch Society for the Study of Wildlife)
NEN	National Ecological Network
NJN	Nederlandse Jeugdbond voor Natuurstudie (Dutch Youth Organization for Nature Studies)
WNF	Wereld Natuur Fonds (World Wide Fund for Nature)

NORWAY

DN	Direktoratet for naturforvaltning (Directorate for Nature Management)
FIOH	Framtiden i våre hender (The Future in our Hands)
FoEN	Friends of the Earth, Norway
GEL	Grønt hverdagsliv (Green Everyday Life)
NJFF	Norges jeger- og fiskerforbund (Norwegian Association of Hunters and Anglers)
NMT	Den norske turistforening (Norwegian Mountain Touring Association)
NOAH	NOAH – for dyrs rettigheter (NOAH – For Animal Rights)
NOU	Norske offentlige utredninger (Official Norwegian Report)
NSC	Norges Naturvernforbund (Norwegian Society for the Conservation of Nature)
NY	Natur og ungdom (Nature and Youth)
SNM	Samarbeidsgruppene for natur- og miljøvern (Cooperation Groups for Nature and Environmental Protection)

POLAND

CEE	Central and Eastern Europe
EU	European Union

InE	Instytut na rzecz Ekorozwoju (Institute for Sustainable Development)
IUCN	International Union for the Conservation of Nature and Natural Resources, now World Conservation Union
KOO	Komitet Ochrony Orłów (Committee for Eagle Protection)
LOP	Liga Ochrony Przyrody (League for the Conservation of Nature)
OTOP	Ogólnopolskie Towarzystwo Ochrony Ptaków (National Bird Protection Society)
PTOP	Północnopodlaskie Towarzystwo Ochrony Ptaków (North Podlasian Bird Protection Society)
UNDP	United Nations Development Programme
WWF	World Wide Fund for Nature

SWEDEN

FoE	Miljöförbundet Jordens Vänner (Friends of the Earth)
FSC	Forest Stewardship Council
IUCN	International Union for the Conservation of Nature and Natural Resources, now World Conservation Union
KF	Kooperativa Förbundet (Cooperative Union and Wholesale Society)
KVA	Kungliga Vetenskapsakademien (Royal Swedish Academy of Sciences)
KVAN	KVAs Naturskyddskommitté (KVA's committee for nature conservation)
LO	Landsorganisationen i Sverige (Swedish Trade Union Confederation)
PEFC	Programme for the Endorsement of Forest Certification
SEPA	Naturvårdsverket (Swedish Environmental Protection Agency)
SfH	Samfundet för Hembygdsvård (Swedish Homestead Society)
SMO	social movement organization
SOF	Sveriges Ornitologiska Förening (Swedish Association for Ornithologists)
SSNC	Svenska Naturskyddsföreningen (Swedish Society for Nature Conservation)
STF	Svenska Turistföreningen (Swedish Tourist Club)
WWF	World Wide Fund for Nature

Acknowledgements

This book began as a conversation between the editors at the International Sociological Association's 2002 World Congress of Sociology about their overlapping research interests. Several months later we decided to invite the authors of five of the country chapters included in this book to join us in presenting papers about nature protection in their countries at the 2003 conference of the European Sociological Association (ESA). The idea for the book originated there. The next year, all but one of the members of this same group had the opportunity to participate in a panel discussion on nature protection at an International Sociological Association conference in Gorizia, Italy. The conference, which was jointly cosponsored by the Institute for Sociology at the University of Gorizia, the Department of Human Science at the University of Trieste, and the Italian Sociological Association, also afforded us the opportunity to critique one another's papers from the ESA conference and set directions for the book. The 2005 meeting of the European Consortium for Political Research provided an opportunity for three of us to meet again and two of us to present much-revised papers. The 2005 ESA conference provided us a last chance to meet as a group and an opportunity to meet our Polish co-authors, who, along with Angela Mertig, were recruited to write their chapters after the meeting in Gorizia. This is how academic life is supposed to work, and we are grateful to the organizers and sponsors of all of these meetings for nurturing our endeavour.

We are grateful too to the other members of the original 'gang of eight', Magnus Boström, Cécilia Claeys-Mekdade and Marie Jacqué, Giorgio Osti, Chris Rootes and Ørnulf Seippel, who helped to shape this project from the beginning, stuck with us through its extended gestation period, and patiently revised their papers time after time as we worked to create a common framework for analysis. Equal credit belongs to Piotr Gliński and Małgorzata Koziarek and to Angela Mertig, who agreed to join us after the project was under way, willingly shaped their chapters to fit seamlessly into an already ongoing project, and invariably responded quickly to our requests for quick turnaround. This book would not have been possible without the dedication and cooperative spirit of these fine colleagues.

We are grateful to Wageningen University's Environmental Policy Group for supporting Kris van Koppen in dedicating substantial parts of his time to this book. A much-appreciated invitation to Bill Markham from the Environmental Policy Group, with funding from the Wageningen Institute for Environment and Climate Research, allowed us to work closely together during the autumn of 2005, and the support of Steve Kroll-Smith and the Sociology Department at UNC–Greensboro made it possible for Bill to accept the opportunity. Both of us are grateful to the Environmental Policy Group for providing a pleasant and supportive working environment, and Bill is indebted to the Fulbright Commission for the time away from his regular duties provided by a 2004 Fulbright Fellowship, and to Angelika Wolf, who sponsored his visit at the University of Duisburg–Essen.

Brian Boylston, Bill's Research Assistant, carefully and accurately proofread almost every chapter and checked references. We also benefited greatly from the help and support of Chris Rootes, who carefully read and commented on several drafts of the final chapter and coined the title of the book. Needless to say, the work of editing and writing inevitably extended far beyond our usual office hours. Therefore we are also much indebted to the two people who put up with our many hours in our respective upstairs studies in the USA and the Netherlands, Peggy and Stella.

Bill Markham and Kris van Koppen,
Greensboro and Wageningen,
31 March 2007

1. Nature protection in nine countries: a framework for analysis

William T. Markham and C.S.A. (Kris) van Koppen

This book is about organizations and networks created by citizens of Western societies to protect nature. We focus on them because the story of nature protection in these societies is largely their story. Nature protection organizations and networks were among the first national-level, non-governmental organizations (NGOs) in these societies, and they have survived over a century of wars, dictatorships, depressions and political turmoil. At times, they have participated in social movements that counted nature protection among their goals – including most recently the environmental movement; however, they have also promoted nature protection when it ranked far down the public agenda. Although nature protection advocates have often called on the state for support, and the state has occasionally taken the initiative in this area, nature protection has always been propelled, in large measure, by non-governmental organizations, networks and discourses.

Nature protection remains a vital endeavour today. The environmental movements of the 1960s and 1970s and the subsequent institutionalization of environmentalism did change the context in which nature protection groups operate, but nature protection was neither fully assimilated nor shunted aside by environmentalism. Instead, nature protection groups gained support, and many broadened their agendas to incorporate new themes, while new environmental organizations typically accorded nature protection a prominent role. Today, even as concern about pollution and resource depletion appears to be waning in many nations, nature protection organizations and networks continue to display remarkable vitality and, in some cases, spectacular growth. Indeed, organizations with nature protection as a key goal are among the largest organizations concerned with environmental issues. They include groups as diverse as bird protection organizations, organizations advocating for national parks and nature protection areas, and organizations working to save ecosystems and impressive species in faraway lands. In many nations, they are deeply embedded in the institutions of civil society, and many are linked to international NGOs, such as the World Wide Fund for Nature (WWF), that are among the largest in the world.

Because of their long history and key roles, nature protection organizations and networks in Western nations invite historical and comparative analysis, but this has been largely absent. Instead, social scientists (e.g. Diani 1995; Oswald von Nell-Breuning-Institut 1996; Brulle 2000) have often viewed nature protection as an old-fashioned, limited manifestation of environmentalism that has been largely supplanted by struggles against pollution, environmental injustice and nuclear power. Research on environmental activism is important, and some of it (e.g. Van der Heijden et al. 1992; Rootes 2003) is comparative and relevant to our concerns; however, it often neglects nature protection in favour of more dramatic movements and events. Other recent work on environmental NGOs (e.g. Mol 1995; Jänicke et al. 1999) emphasizes not nature protection, but reforms centred around ecological modernization and new forms of governance.

Nature protection organizations and networks may also have been neglected because they do not fit standard social science taxonomies well (Lake 1998). They can be viewed as voluntary associations, interest groups, social movement organizations, or components of civil society, and they lend themselves to analysis from the standpoints of diverse theoretical perspectives, disciplines and national traditions (Markham 2006).

This book represents a collaborative effort by 11 sociologists to give nature protection organizations and networks the prominence they deserve. It addresses key questions about such organizations: Why do citizens support nature protection organizations? What strategies do they employ, and how do they choose among alternative goals and strategies? What roles do they play in society, and how effectively do they play them? We address these questions through a comparative study of nature protection groups in nine Western nations: Sweden, Norway, England, Poland, Germany, the Netherlands, France, Italy and the USA. Although differences in the concrete circumstances in the nine societies and the information available necessitate some differences in coverage, the authors committed themselves to use a common approach designed to facilitate comparisons. Because we view organized efforts by citizens to protect nature as important in their own right, each chapter places them at the centre of the analysis. We believe that much can be learned by examining nature protection in different historical periods and that present-day organizations cannot be understood apart from their historical context, so we compare nature protection organizations and networks not only across nations, but also across historical periods. We believe that nature protection groups must be understood in context. Therefore each chapter examines how economic structures, government, ideologies and culture, other social movements, the support base for nature protection, and social change have influenced the goals, structures and strategies of nature protection groups. Finally, we agreed that each chapter should be strongly grounded in research, that theories should be used as aids to interpretation rather than straitjackets, and that multiple perspectives should be employed as appropriate.

Investigating this relatively unexplored terrain required (1) clear definitions of nature protection, nature protection organizations and nature protection networks, (2) selection of a balanced set of national cases, and (3) an examination of which theories might best illuminate these organizations and networks. This chapter thus provides some initial guidelines to help demarcate the terrain we shall explore. In the process, we hope to convey the rationale for our fascination with nature protection in Western societies.

NATURE PROTECTION, NATURE PROTECTION ORGANIZATIONS AND NATURE PROTECTION NETWORKS

Core Spheres of Nature Protection

Many studies (for instance, McKibben 1999; MacNaghten and Urry 1998; Price 1999; Whiteside 2002) examine the meaning of 'nature'. They show clearly that what people define as 'nature' and 'wilderness' varies over time and place, and that it often has significant emotional, cultural, political and moral connotations (see also Neumann 1998). Guided by these studies and by previous research, we identify three core themes that surface repeatedly in discussions of nature protection in Western societies: (1) protection of wilderness; (2) protection of cultural landscapes; and (3) protection of 'wild' animals and plants. These three central foci are illustrated by the overlapping circles at the centre of Figure 1.1.

Wilderness untouched by human activity has all but disappeared from the earth, but pockets of relatively undisturbed nature remain in many Western nations, and larger areas exist in some. How undisturbed an area must be in order to be called wilderness is a matter of social and cultural definition, but the fact that what a Western European calls wilderness might seem tame to an Alaskan should not distract us from the shared core of meaning. Nature protection, as understood in Western nations, almost invariably includes a concern with protecting relatively untouched areas.

Particularly in densely settled European nations, nature protection has also focused on protecting traditional and scenic rural landscapes of cultivated fields, hedgerows, woodlots and managed forests. We use the term

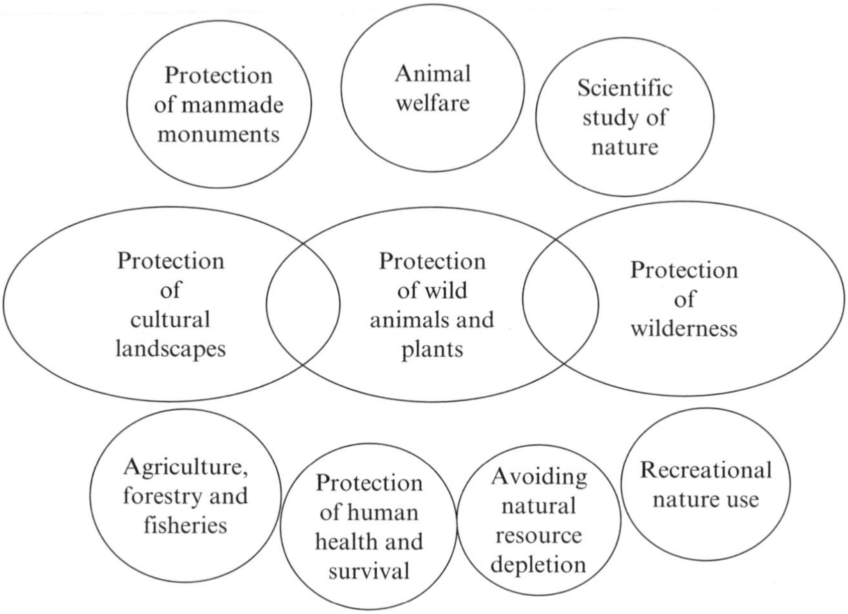

Figure 1.1 Core spheres of nature protection and related spheres of action

'cultural landscapes' to describe this vision of nature because it emphasizes that such 'nature' is a product of human activity. Parklands and county estates purposefully maintained to conform to cultural images of natural beauty are also included here, but golf courses, playing fields, and other areas created for active recreational use are not. This concept of nature is less widespread in North America than in Europe (Lange 2000), but efforts by land preservation groups to preserve scenic farmland show that it exists there as well. The specific types of landscapes seen as worthy of protection vary across place and time, but once again there is a shared core of meaning.

Nature protection in Western societies also frequently focuses on wild animals and plants, that is, on species that have not been modified by breeding and domestication and do not live in captivity. The circle for wild animals and plants in Figure 1.1 overlaps both wilderness and cultural landscapes, but it is not coextensive with them because such species also live in areas that are neither wilderness nor cultural landscapes. These include cities, recreational areas, and agricultural lands that would not qualify as cultural landscapes.

These core spheres of nature protection are reflected in the various types of protected areas distinguished by the IUCN (Box 1.1). Category I represents wilderness strictly protected from human intervention. In category IV species protection is central. In categories II, III and V, varying degrees of human intervention are allowed, and category V matches the concept of 'cultural landscape' especially well (Pimbert and Pretty 1995).

Goals of Nature Protection Organizations and Networks

Some organizations or networks in each of the nations included here focus primarily or exclusively on protecting wilderness, cultural landscapes, and wild animals or plants or some combination of the three. We reserve the terms 'nature protection organization' and 'nature protection network' for them; however, each nation also has organizations or networks that pursue nature protection as secondary to other goals. Figure 1.1 displays the most common of these other goals in the circles arrayed around the three core spheres of nature protection. We have positioned each near the nature protection goals with which it is most commonly associated, although no fully adequate representation is possible in two-dimensional space. The most common combination involves organizations or networks that couple nature protection goals with an emphasis on human health and survival and/or natural resource conservation. We refer to such groups as environmental organizations or networks. Organizations or networks that focus on one or both of these goals but lack an emphasis on nature protection are also commonly called environmental groups, but we have not included them in this book.

Other organizations and networks combine nature protection, usually protection of cultural landscapes, with protection of historic, manmade structures. A less common combination unites nature protection – almost always the protection of wild animals – with protection of domestic animals. A fourth combination joins scientific interest in nature with efforts to protect it. Traditionally referred to in English as 'natural history', it focuses on cataloguing and describing species and their habitats. Professional researchers have always been involved in this work, but amateur researchers have always outnumbered them. Other groups bring together nature protection and efforts to maintain viable or sustainable agriculture, forestry, or fisheries. Finally, numerous groups unite nature protection with efforts to maintain conditions necessary for recreation in nature. The activities involved include fishing, hunting, hiking, canoeing and country walking.

A complete treatment of nature protection groups must thus encompass not only nature protection organizations and networks in the strictest sense, but also groups where nature protection shares the stage with other goals. We used two criteria to determine which organizations and networks of the latter type to emphasize: (1) the significance of nature protection goals for the

BOX 1.1 IUCN (WORLD CONSERVATION UNION) PROTECTED AREAS MANAGEMENT CATEGORIES

Category Ia: Strict nature reserve/wilderness protection area managed mainly for science or wilderness protection – an area of land and/or sea possessing some outstanding or representative ecosystems, geological or physiological features and/or species, available primarily for scientific research and/or environmental monitoring.

Category Ib: Wilderness area: protected area managed mainly for wilderness protection – large area of unmodified or slightly modified land and/or sea, retaining its natural characteristics and influence, without permanent or significant habitation, which is protected and managed to preserve its natural condition.

Category II: National park: protected area managed mainly for ecosystem protection and recreation – natural area of land and/or sea designated to (a) protect the ecological integrity of one or more ecosystems for present and future generations, (b) exclude exploitation or occupation inimical to the purposes of designation of the area and (c) provide a foundation for spiritual, scientific, educational, recreational and visitor opportunities, all of which must be environmentally and culturally compatible.

Category III: Natural monument: protected area managed mainly for conservation of specific natural features – area containing specific natural or natural/cultural feature(s) of outstanding or unique value because of their inherent rarity, representativeness or aesthetic qualities or cultural significance.

Category IV: Habitat/species management area: protected area managed mainly for conservation through management intervention – area of land and/or sea subject to active intervention for management purposes so as to ensure the maintenance of habitats to meet the requirements of specific species.

Category V: Protected landscape/seascape: protected area managed mainly for landscape/seascape conservation or recreation – area of land, with coast or sea as appropriate, where the interaction of people and nature over time has produced an area of distinct character with significant aesthetic, ecological and/or cultural value, and often with high biological diversity. Safeguarding the integrity of this traditional interaction is vital to the protection, maintenance and evolution of such an area.

Category VI: Managed resource protected area: protected area managed mainly for the sustainable use of natural resources – area containing predominantly unmodified natural systems, managed to ensure long-term protection and maintenance of biological diversity, while also providing a sustainable flow of natural products and services to meet community needs.

Source: IUCN (1994).

group's mission and (2) the group's size and influence. Where national organizations are branches of international organizations such as Greenpeace or the WWF, we applied these criteria to the national branch, not to the international organization as a whole.

Structures and Strategies of Nature Protection Organizations and Networks

We use the term 'nature protection organization' to refer to groups that are relatively formally organized; ordinarily, they have a constitution or bylaws that formally describe their goals and structure, the duties of leaders, employees and members, and the method of leadership selection (Hall 2002). Their members are individuals, not other organizations. Organizations that fit this definition vary along a wide variety of dimensions, including: (1) whether the highest level of organization is local, national or international, and whether there are chapters at lower levels; (2) the extent to which policy making and leader selection are democratic; (3) the degree of reliance on paid professionals versus volunteers to accomplish tasks; and (4) the extent to which a group's financial support comes from individual supporters, donations from business or foundations, government subsidies, contracts with government or business, revenues from their publications, and sales of products or services to individuals.

By networks, we mean loosely organized groupings whose members are independent nature protection groups or organizations. Networks are usually created to exchange information, coordinate the activities of member groups, and provide mutual assistance (Diani and McAdam 2003). Networks vary structurally in important ways, including: (1) whether their members are informally organized local nature protection groups, formally structured organizations, or both; (2) whether they are geographically based (i.e. national, regional or local), include only groups with a specific goal, or both; and (3) whether individuals can also be direct members.

Organizations and networks with nature protection goals employ a wide array of specific strategies, but we can distinguish four general approaches. The first is lobbying government to place specific areas under protection – sometimes after acquiring them – or implement other measures (e.g. controlling hunting or animal trade or reducing pollution) to protect nature. Lobbying often involves building alliances with specific government agencies and other organizations. A second strategy is protests to attract media attention and influence public opinion or politics. Third, many nature protection groups seek to educate citizens about nature and nature protection. Some educational activities involve simply providing information; others use group activities, such as excursions in nature, to build solidarity among supporters and attract new ones. Some educational activities are directed to a broad audience, while others are aimed at specific groups. A fourth strategy is acquisition and/or management of nature reserves for the public good.

The wide variety of structures, goals and strategies means that there is no such thing as 'the' typical nature protection organization. In fact, exploring the causes and consequences of this variation is one of the chief goals of this book.

THE NATIONS STUDIED

The decision to focus this book on Western nations rather than including countries elsewhere was a carefully considered one. There are, to be sure, major nature protection challenges throughout the world, and nature protection organizations and networks in Western countries exist within the broader context of international nature protection. Nevertheless, it is our premise that nature protection organizations and networks in the developed nations of Europe and North America are of signal importance and interest in their own right.

Several arguments support this premise. First, nature protection organizations occupy a special place in the civil societies of most Western nations. They were among the earliest significant NGOs in these societies, and they have a long record of public support and accomplishment. They provide opportunities for citizens interested in nature protection to work together, influence politics, and acquire and manage nature protection areas, and they have sometimes functioned as components of social movements. Second, as demonstrated below, nature protection is deeply rooted in

Western culture. Third, models and practices of nature protection from Western countries have a strong impact on efforts elsewhere, and the nature protection problems of some rapidly developing societies may soon come to approximate those of Western nations. Finally, Western nations vary enough in the nature protection challenges they face, in their political, economic and cultural contexts, and in the structure, goals and strategies of their nature protection groups to allow fruitful comparisons and useful generalizations. At the same time, they are similar enough to keep this first effort to make comparisons and formulate generalizations from being overwhelmed by the enormous variation that exists worldwide.

We have purposefully selected eight European nations with a wide range of cultural traditions, population densities and geographical characteristics. Seven, stretching from Norway and Sweden in the North to Italy in the South, lie in Western Europe, but we extended our range into Central Europe to include Poland, a Western nation that exemplifies the era of socialist control and a new course today towards European integration. The chapter on Germany also briefly considers Poland's former socialist neighbour, the German Democratic Republic. We included the USA as representative of North America because of its distinct history and cultural and political traditions and its worldwide influence. We further illustrate the range of variation below by exploring the major contextual factors – geographic, cultural, economic and political – that vary among our countries and may influence the goals, structures and strategies of nature protection groups.

Biogeographical and Demographic Contexts

Differences in geography and demographics may influence the structure, goals and strategies of organizations with nature protection goals. Our sample countries vary considerably in these respects, and some nations also have great variation within their borders.

One salient feature is simply the kinds of 'nature' that are available to protect. Some of the nations studied retain large and relatively undisturbed wilderness areas. Norwegians and Americans can thus, if they choose, focus on saving remote mountain areas where wolves still roam, while citizens of very densely populated areas may have to content themselves with protecting traditional agricultural landscapes that harbour beloved bird species. Other differences involve the availability of natural resources, forests, hydropower, coal etc. While the sheer availability of these resources does not guarantee conflicts over their extraction and use, their absence precludes such conflicts.

Also potentially influential are the extent of urbanization and ongoing demographic changes in the countryside. In densely populated areas, cultural landscapes and wild animals and plants come under pressure from urban sprawl and urban pollution. Where depopulation is occurring, on the other hand, preservation of traditional cultural landscapes and opportunities to create new nature reserves or wild areas may become important.

Nature protection goals and activities are moulded by such variation, which itself is subject to change over time. Because this study is also historical, we can compare not only societies today, but also periods when wilderness was disappearing, cultural landscapes were changing, and urbanization was occurring.

Cultural Contexts

Nature protection issues are not, however, simply 'given' by geography or population. They are constructed by human actors who 'frame' them in specific ways (Hannigan 1995). The history of Western views of nature protection is thus also a cultural history of changing sensibilities toward animals, plants, wilderness and landscapes. Understandings of nature have been affected, for example, by urbanization and industrialization, which separated employment from winning a living from soil, forests and domestic animals, and increased leisure time. Cultural trends, such as increases in the popularity of pets, the expansion of ornamental gardening from the upper and upper-middle classes to other strata, and the emergence of associations and laws for animal welfare have signalled changing views of nature (Thomas 1993), and views of cultural landscapes and wilderness have been mediated by poetry, music and the works of landscape painters. Painters such as Ruisdael and Constable introduced urban elites to the beauty of the countryside, and the romantic Rocky Mountain wilderness paintings of Bierstadt offered Americans and Europeans a window on wild nature (Bazarov 1981; Honour 1981; Schama 1995). As Schama expressed it, 'Landscapes are culture before they are nature; constructs of the imagination projected onto wood and rock' (Schama 1995, p. 61).

Representations of nature in literature and art often transcend national boundaries, but there can also be marked differences in cultural interpretations of nature. As pointed out above, nature protection can be centred on protection of wilderness, wild animals and plants, or cultural landscapes, and preservation of cultural artefacts, such as traditional building styles and ruins, can be seen either as part and parcel of nature conservation or as a distinct activity. Tracking the influence of cultural change and variations in national cultures on conceptions of nature and nature protection and examining how culture interacts with the underlying 'plate tectonics' of geography and demography constitutes another important focus of this book.

Economic and Political Contexts

All the nations in our study have industrialized, capitalist economies, although they industrialized at different times. Most are now undergoing processes of deindustrialization and service sector growth, although at different rates. Several have significant agricultural or resource extraction sectors, and some display considerable regional variation in economic structure. Differences in the economic bases of nations or regions, as well as changes over time, might well be associated with differing nature protection issues and differing amounts of conflict between nature protection and economic interests. Conflicts between resource extraction industries and nature protection, for example, typically revolve around establishing nature protection areas, instituting sustainable production practices, and reducing the damage resulting from mining, logging and similar industries. Industrial firms, by contrast, are more likely to produce emissions that threaten forests, rivers, or other ecosystems and may resist controls on these emissions. Service sector industries are least likely to resist nature protection proposals; however, regardless of industry, if firms become convinced that sustainable production and ecological modernization allow them to protect nature without harming their competitive position, conflicts over regulations to protect nature should diminish (Mol 1995). Businesses may also support nature protection efforts in order to burnish their images or out of genuine concern, and even industrial firms sometimes contribute to efforts to protect wild species, as these seldom threaten their interests (Dalton 1994; Bosso 1995).

Historically some of the nations in our study experienced fascist or state socialist regimes, allowing comparisons of how groups with nature protection goals functioned under these political systems. Today all are democratically governed, but political systems do differ. Some tend towards pluralism, a system in which numerous independent interest groups work to influence politics, interest groups frequently form temporary coalitions on particular issues, and political decisions are generally compromises reflecting the relative influence of the groups involved (Dahl 1961; Petracca 1992b). Other political systems lean towards neo-corporatism. Here major interest groups, especially business and labour, are encouraged by government to organize as large national associations. Such associations enjoy privileged access to decision-making circles, where decisions are reached through compromise and consensus, and they are invited to cooperate in policy implementation. They may also receive government financial support; however, they are expected to accept the decisions reached and persuade their members to follow them (Schmitter and Lehmbruch 1979; Lehmbruch and Schmitter 1982; Wilson 1990). We explore the likely implications of these differing systems for nature protection groups in the section on interest group theories below.

More concrete differences in the organization and functioning of political systems may also be consequential. For example, in federal states, where decision making is decentralized, interest groups have considerable incentive to form regional branches, while those in unitary states might be more effective by focusing on the national level (van der Heijden 1997; Dryzek et al. 2003). Interest groups in nations with legal systems that provide many opportunities to appeal unfavourable government decisions may have more incentive to develop expertise and activity in this area (van der Heijden 1997; Stein 2003), and nature protection groups in societies where government plays the major role in acquiring and managing nature reserves face a different situation than those elsewhere. The question of how the organization of the state affects nature protection organizations and networks resurfaces repeatedly in the chapters that follow.

POLICY ARRANGEMENTS AND NATURE PROTECTION ORGANIZATIONS AT INTERNATIONAL LEVELS

This book's emphasis on comparing nature protection in Western nation-states should not blind us to the crucial importance of international nature protection efforts and their effects on national-level nature protection organizations and networks. Demographic, cultural, economic and political factors at the national level are increasingly influenced by globalization and international cooperations, and international nature protection organizations and networks are prominent players on the international stage. Here it is possible only to highlight key international structures and developments. We begin with an overview of international environmental governance, followed by a look at the most important international environmental NGOs.

All the nations in our sample are members of international political organizations such as the International Whaling Commission and signatories of nature protection treaties and conventions, such as the Convention on Biological Diversity, the Convention on International Trade in Endangered Species, and the Ramsar Convention for the protection of wetlands (van Kersbergen and van Waarden 2004). Nature protection organizations and networks played significant roles in bringing about virtually all of these agreements, and the agreements, in turn, have significant impacts on national-level nature protection efforts.

Nature protection organizations and networks also cooperate with two United Nations organizations involved in nature protection, UNEP (the United Nations Environmental Programme) and UNESCO (the United Nations Educational, Scientific, and Cultural Organization). However, the most influential international nature protection organization is probably the IUCN (World Conservation Union), founded in 1948. The IUCN has always cooperated closely with governmental agencies, but, in fact, it is a hybrid organization. Its membership includes 81 states, 109 governmental agencies, and some 800 NGOs (IUCN 2006). It is best known for spearheading the international movement for nature parks and protected areas (Swanson 1997). Along with the UNEP, it played a major role in preparing the Rio Convention on Biological Diversity (Suplie 1995).

For eight of our nations, the most important supra-state organization is the European Union (EU). Environmental policy has become a major domain of EU activity, and over 200 EU directives and regulations require member states to pass and enforce environmental legislation, including legislation to protect flora and fauna (Rucht 1997; Sbragia 2000; Roose 2002; Hey 2004). The two most important EU directives concerning nature protection are the Bird Directive (Directive 79/409) and the Habitats Directive (Directive 92/43/EEC). They call for conservation of the natural habitats of endangered plant and animal species. Each EU member state is obliged to designate sites for the protection of the species listed under the Directives and provide legally binding measures for their protection. The areas designated to comply with the two Directives constitute the 'Natura 2000' network, and the Directives call for measures, such as the protection of ecological corridors and stepping-stones, to combine the Natura 2000 areas in a Europe-wide network (Coffey and Richartz 2003).

EU directives have given strong impetus to national nature protection, but their impact depends partly on pre-existing nature protection policies. For the older member states, the Directives have meant significant modifications of existing regulations, sometimes accompanied by controversy. For new member states, such as Poland, EU accession has required that regulations and Natura 2000 areas be established very quickly.

The EU has also supplemented the nature protection groups' resources in several ways. It has provided substantial funds for their nature protection projects, and nature protection organizations and networks have been involved in EU consultations, such as drafting lists of Habitat Directive areas. Finally, nature protection groups can turn to the European Court of Justice when governmental authorities in their country fail to fulfil their obligations.

International Nature Protection Organizations

International organizations and networks constitute an increasingly important contextual factor for national nature protection groups, and some national nature protection organizations are branches of international ones. Moreover, the work of international nature protection organizations and networks has contributed to the internationalization of nature protection policy. Efforts by the IUCN and WWF, for example, prepared the ground for several international nature protection conventions. In addition to the IUCN, the organizations described below are among the most important.

The World Wide Fund for Nature

The World Wide Fund for Nature (WWF), known originally – and still in the USA – as the World Wildlife Fund, is the largest, best-known international nature protection organization. It was founded in the UK in 1961 by scientists, prominent conservationists, wealthy donors and political elites who wanted to develop a vehicle to raise money for projects to protect wildlife throughout the world. The donors provided the working capital to fund administrative expenses, but funding for WWF projects comes mainly from public and corporate donations. WWF's national branches are independent organizations, but they cooperate closely with the international organization and support it financially. In its early years, WWF devoted itself mainly to establishing wildlife reserves and protecting impressive species in less developed countries. Later, it realized that this strategy was not fully adequate and moved toward protecting entire ecosystems and providing economically viable options for local citizens who might otherwise destroy wildlife. In recent years, WWF has also embraced the concept of sustainable development and launched campaigns against worldwide threats to wildlife such as climate change; however, it continues its highly visible efforts to protect large impressive species (Haag 1986; Dalton 1994; Denton 1993; Wapner 1996).

With almost five million supporters and 4000 employees, WWF is the largest international environmental organization. It has independent branches in 30 nations and offices in over 20 more. Its total income worldwide was almost €390 000 000 (WWF International 2006a, 2006b).

Greenpeace

Greenpeace originated in Canadian-based protests against US nuclear testing. Branches formed almost immediately in the USA and several European countries, and Greenpeace International was organized in 1979 to coordinate their efforts. Greenpeace International quickly broadened its agenda to include environmental and nature protection issues, such as industrial emissions and whaling. It is, therefore, best classified as an environmental organization, not a pure nature protection organization.

Greenpeace's trademark is staging spectacular actions in which it presents itself as a morally indignant David risking life and limb to point up environmental abuses and challenge selfish and callous Goliaths. Greenpeace activists have sailed ships into nuclear testing zones, driven rubber rafts between whalers and whales, and climbed smokestacks of polluting industries to hang banners calling attention to problems. These actions are professionally planned and executed media events designed to raise public consciousness about environmental issues and pressure businesses or government to change. They are well publicized by Greenpeace's professional press office. In general, its actions focus on problems that are easy to understand and report. Greenpeace also conducts research to highlight environmental problems, commissions scientific reports, sponsors demonstration projects of ecologically sound technologies, and lobbies national governments and international government agencies (Rucht 1995; Wapner 1996; Brand et al. 1997).

The combined income of Greenpeace International and all of its chapters in 2004 was over €162 000 000. As of 2002, it claimed about 2.8 million donors worldwide. Greenpeace has offices in 41 nations, although only 27 are full fledged national chapters (Greenpeace International 2006a, 2006b). National chapters of Greenpeace are bound to the international organization by a strict contract, and major protests must be cleared with the international headquarters, which controls the allocation of ships and equipment, and operates the international press office (Rucht 1995; Flechner 1999). Greenpeace has a small Brussels office charged with keeping Greenpeace International and its European chapters informed about European developments and representing Greenpeace positions to the EU (Rucht 1997; Webster 1998; Roose 2002).

Friends of the Earth

Friends of the Earth is a federation of over 70 national environmental organizations. It originated in 1969 as an offshoot of the US Sierra Club and was soon joined by sister organizations in Britain, Sweden and France. It has emerged in recent years as a strong opponent of globalization and industrialized agriculture, and a strong advocate for grass-roots democracy, locally based economies, biodiversity, and environmental justice in relations between industrialized and less developed countries. It is therefore best classified as an environmental network (Dowie 1995; Jordan and Maloney 1997; Friends of the Earth International 2001, 2005).

Friends of the Earth International claims about 1.5 million members. It is organized as a network of autonomous organizations, many of which existed before joining it. Its comparatively small budget of about €1 200 000 comes primarily from government and foundation grants for specific projects (Friends of the Earth International 2005; Doherty 2006). It maintains an office in Brussels to lobby the EU and supply its members with information (Roose 2002).

The European Environmental Bureau

The European Environmental Bureau (EEB) is a network of environmental and nature protection organizations set up in 1974 by 25 national-level environmental organizations to lobby the EU and keep its member organizations informed of EU policy. The EU's Environmental Directorate prefers input from multinational networks over input from national-level organizations, and the EEB has always received part of its financial support from the Directorate and enjoyed substantial access to it (Hey and Brendle 1994; Sbragia 2000; Rootes 2004). At present, the EEB has 143 member groups (European Environmental Bureau 2006). It works in numerous environmental policy areas and has working groups comprising EEB staff and representatives from the member organizations for most of them; however, its own staff is small. The EEB's governing board comprises one member from each EU nation, plus Norway (Webster 1998; Roose 2002).

Other organizations

Many other international organizations and networks are active in nature protection. BirdLife International, for example, is a well-funded and -organized network, which gathers information and provides it to its affiliates, coordinates their efforts, and lobbies the EU and other international bodies (Webster 1998; Roose 2002). Conservation International and the Rainforest Alliance are US-based international organizations that focus on biodiversity 'hotspots' in developing countries. Like the major organizations describe above, their influence on national nature protection groups receives attention in the chapters that follow.

THEORETICAL APPROACHES TO NATURE PROTECTION

One reason for the neglect of nature protection organizations and networks in past research is the difficulty of situating them theoretically. Nature protection groups have generally been inclined towards work within the system, and their constituencies often include persons from privileged strata; however, they also have numerous supporters from other classes and grass-roots groups, and they have occasionally adopted more radical goals and confrontational strategies. No existing theoretical approach captures all of this diversity, so nature protection groups have been analysed variously as interest groups, social movements, civil society associations, and voluntary associations. This book privileges none of these approaches. Instead, the authors use varying theoretical frames, depending on the focus of analysis and the country under investigation. This section sets the stage for subsequent chapters with a brief overview of the major theoretical approaches to nature protection. As a heuristic, we classify them according to whether and how they address three key questions: (1) Why do people join nature protection organizations? (2) Why do nature protection organizations choose the goals, structures and strategies they do? (3) What roles do nature protection organizations play in society?

Why People Join Nature Protection Organizations

To understand nature protection organizations and networks, we must first explore why people choose to invest effort and energy in protecting nature. This is by no means a simple question, and answers have been proposed from many disciplinary perspectives.

The free-rider hypothesis and its critics

Discussions of why people contribute funds or volunteer work to nature protection groups often begin with the free-rider problem. According to Olson's (1965; see also Jordan and Maloney 1997) well-known formalization, free riding is likely when large organizations attempt to mobilize large numbers of people to work to produce collective goods – benefits that can be enjoyed by all citizens – or to influence government or business to produce them. Were they purely rational actors, citizens would refrain from contributing to such groups because: (a) the fruits of any successful efforts by the organization can be enjoyed equally by those who contributed nothing, and (b) no one individual's contribution has much impact on whether the group reaches its goals. Many people do behave as Olson predicted, but hundreds of thousands do join nature protection organizations and networks. How can this be explained?

First, while some citizens seek to protect nature so that they can personally enjoy its use (e.g. for outdoor recreation), decisions to support nature protection are often expressions of deeply held moral or emotional sentiments towards nature. That is, many supporters of nature protection groups wish to preserve nature for future generations and for its own sake (Hargrove 1989; Takacs 1996; Felbinger 2005). For such persons the first of the two reasons for withholding support cited above is largely irrelevant.

Second, calculations of whether one's contributions to nature protection groups have a significant impact on their success may not be made on completely rational grounds. Supporters may assess their contributions as more important to the groups' success than is realistic, and fundraising campaigns are likely to do all they can to promote this misapprehension by using strategies such as emphasizing 'collective bads', the damage to nature that will result if something is not done immediately (Jordan and Maloney 1997; Felbinger 2005). More prosperous supporters may view the costs of their financial contributions as too small to warrant elaborate cost–benefit analysis (Diekmann and Preisendörfer 1998), and supporters who are morally committed to the cause may be disinclined to make such calculations in the first place. For them, supporting nature protection groups may be perceived as a moral or normative obligation, and doing so may also provide them with the 'warm glow' that comes from doing the 'right thing'. For some supporters, membership in nature protection groups may also serve as a way of reinforcing a valued identity as nature lovers (Mount 1996; Felbinger 2005).

Finally, supporters of nature protection organizations and networks may find their participation rewarding in other ways. The nature protection groups themselves may offer 'selective incentives' (e.g. subscriptions to member magazines or opportunities to join 'outings') that are available only to members. Joining a nature protection group may provide social contacts or – if the group is prestigious – social status; volunteer work may help volunteers acquire skills or career qualifications, and leadership in such groups may provide political influence. Questionnaire studies suggest that such motivations are typically of less importance to supporters than commitment to the group's goals, but they may well provide additional incentives to participate for some and be decisive for a few (Smith 1994; Jordan and Maloney 1997; Shaiko 1999; Felbinger 2005).

The biophilia hypothesis

Why so many individuals desire to protect nature in the first place has been the subject of much debate in literature from philosophy, sociology, psychology and biology. One commonly used set of approaches (e.g. Kahn and Kellert 2002) is rooted in environmental or ecological psychology and evolutionary biology. Attention restoration theory, for example, argues that modern society puts individuals under mental strain by forcing them to constantly pay attention to a multitude of stimuli. To recover from the resulting fatigue, restorative environments are needed (Kaplan and Kaplan 2005). Nature is the restorative environment *par excellence*, an indispensable way to compensate for the stresses of modern life.

Other authors relate human affection for natural landscapes to the evolutionary roots of *Homo sapiens* as a dweller of the African savannah landscape (e.g. Orians and Heerwagen 1992). The most widely known theoretical claim of this type, however, is the biophilia hypothesis introduced by E.O. Wilson (1984; see also Kellert and Wilson 1993). It asserts that positive values attached to the natural world 'reflect affinities for nature that presumably have proven adaptive in human evolution' (Kellert 2002, p. 129). The expression of these values is shaped by learning, culture and experience, and varies greatly across individuals and groups, but 'this variability and its healthy expression are . . . biologically limited and bounded' (ibid.).

The Arcadian tradition

Regardless of whether one accepts the premise that humans are psychologically or biologically programmed to care about nature, it is clear that culture plays a key role in shaping sentiments toward nature. Beginning with this assumption, the 'Arcadian tradition' approach links individual motives and values regarding nature protection in Western societies to broad social, economic and cultural trends (Van Koppen 2000, 2002). Drawing on the cultural history research of Worster (1985), Hargrove (1989), Thomas (1993), Schama (1995) and others, it links Western views of nature to aesthetic, moral and other cultural values that emerged in parallel to the modernization of Western society and were articulated in their modern forms by Romanticism. Landscape painting, natural history, recreation in nature, and care for animals and plants are typical expressions of this tradition, which, since the Industrial Revolution, has spread from urban elites to broader categories of citizens, propelled by increasing income and leisure opportunities, and a growing separation from nature in daily work (see section on the cultural context of nature protection above).

According to this view, the key motives for citizens' efforts to protect nature are to be found in this 'profound shift in sensibilities' towards plants, animals and landscapes (Thomas 1993, p. 15). In many ways, this shift complements increased efficiency in the use of nature as a resource for production in modern society. It thus constitutes an inherent 'undercurrent' of modernization, which was already thematized by Horkheimer and Adorno as the 'dialectic of enlightenment' (Horkheimer and Adorno 1971[1947]). By placing valuation of nature for its non-use values at centre stage, the Arcadian tradition hypothesis helps to explain why nature protection has assumed such a central and persistent place in Western societies. How values like these influence motivation to support nature protection and how nature protection groups succeed in attracting supporters thus becomes a key question for exploration in this study.

Goals, Structures and Strategies of Nature Protection Organizations and Networks

Understanding nature protection organizations and networks requires knowing more than why people support them. We also need to know why such groups choose the goals, strategies and structures that they do, and how they interact with the state and other social actors. Interest group theories, theories of organizations, and theories of social movements all offer important insights into these questions.

Interest group theory

According to interest group theory, people with shared interests frequently set up organized interest groups to work within the political system to influence political decisions and their implementation. They accomplish this by (1) lobbying or testifying before legislators and government agencies, (2) mobilizing citizens to sign petitions or contact the authorities, (3) conducting public information campaigns, (4) influencing election outcomes through campaign contributions and voter mobilization, and (5) staging occasional protests to influence politicians or public opinion (Wilson 1990; Walker 1991; Petracca 1992a). Interest group theories are most applicable to organizations and networks that emphasize such activities. They are less relevant to organizations and networks that rely mainly on confrontation or those that focus on non-political activities, such as acquisition of nature reserves or environmental education of children.

In addition to investigating how organizations recruit individual supporters and donors, researchers have noted the importance of funding from foundations, wealthy private donors, and even government in initiating and sustaining interest groups (Godwin 1988; Jordan and Maloney 1997; Shaiko 1999; Bosso 2005). Although some scholars decry interest groups as undermining democracy by giving voice only to well-resourced 'special interests', others emphasize their positive contributions. These include clarifying and bundling needs and discontents that might otherwise remain unarticulated and ensuring that they are recognized by the political system. Nature protection organizations and networks can clearly be considered in this light (Berry 1984; Rucht 1993).

Interest group theorists have also examined how political systems incorporate interest groups into their functioning. The most commonly used models are the pluralist and neo-corporatist approaches already described briefly above.

Pluralist theory, developed mainly in the USA, sees interest groups as competing with one another for political influence, which they gain by mobilizing supporters and funds and using them skilfully. Some groups have more such resources than others, but ordinarily no single group has enough influence to reach all of its objectives. Proposals advanced by one group frequently work to the detriment of others, and the more extreme the plan, the greater the resources other groups can mobilize to resist it.

Therefore most decisions are compromises fought out within the political system. Interest groups can increase their influence by forming coalitions with other groups, but groups with nothing at stake generally avoid taking sides (Dahl 1961; Petracca 1992b).

Pluralist systems make it easy for nature protection organizations and networks to participate in politics, but they are typically relatively uninfluential organizations whose main power resource is their broad base of public support. Accomplishing their more ambitious goals – saving large areas or crusades against climate change or ocean pollution – may therefore require strong allies to overcome the resistance such proposals evoke. The most likely allies are interest groups representing the various interests shown in Figure 1.1 above. Unless they can find powerful allies, nature protection organizations and networks may have to settle for what they can accomplish through conventional interest group strategies or turn to mass mobilization or protest to gain influence.

The neo-corporatist model best fits societies such as Sweden and the Netherlands, where broad sectors of society, especially business and labour, are organized as powerful associations. These associations are deeply intertwined with government, which recognizes them as speaking for their sectors and includes them in deliberations about key decisions. In return, they must be willing to compromise and to persuade the individuals and organizations in their sector to accept decisions reached in these negotiations. Government may support the interest groups financially and allocate responsibility for carrying out important tasks to them (Schmitter and Lehmbruch 1979; Lehmbruch and Schmitter 1982; Wilson 1990).

In comparison to business or labour, nature protection groups are typically among the weaker actors in neo-corporatist systems. They are, therefore, at risk of being excluded altogether if their demands are too radical. Ensuring participation is likely to require considerable willingness to compromise. Corporatist systems might work to the advantage of nature protection organizations if they succeeded in gaining access to decision-making circles, but they would then come under pressure to form a single organization or umbrella association. Where nature protection organizations and networks are excluded from decision making, they might experience difficulty influencing government and have to move towards protest outside the system or choose to emphasize other goals.

Organization theory

Many branches of organization theory focus mainly on business firms and government agencies, but two theories from this literature, open systems theory and the neo-institutional approach, have considerable potential for analysing organizations with nature protection goals.

Open systems models (Thompson 1967; Katz and Kahn 1978) highlight the effects of organizations' social contexts on their goals, structures and strategies. Specifically, they suggest that an organization's behaviour is influenced not only by its general social and cultural milieu, but also by the preferences and behaviour of (1) individuals and organizations from which it acquires key resources, (2) organizations with which it competes or cooperates, (3) government agencies or other organizations authorized to regulate it, and (4) groups that oppose it.

Organizations with nature protection goals, like other organizations, combine the resources they obtain from employees, volunteers, donors and other organizations to produce various outputs, including public education, lobbying, purchase or care of nature reserves, and protests. An organization's activities affect and are observed by other actors in its environment. Depending on the favourableness of their evaluations, they decide whether to provide it with 'generalized media of exchange' (Parsons 1970): (1) money, including private donations or government grants; (2) legitimacy, i.e. its entitlement to exist and pursue its activities; (3) prestige, including especially its reputation for effectiveness; and (4) influence. The more of these resources an organization commands, the more easily it can procure additional inputs and continue its work.

When organizations with the same objectives compete, they become subject to comparisons by potential members, donors, sponsors and government agencies. Unfortunately, goals and strategies that win approval from some of these evaluators may reduce support or stir opposition from others. Selection of goals and strategies under such circumstances is no small challenge, and there are diverging interpretations of how organizations deal with these dilemmas. The resource dependence approach (Pfeffer and Salancik 1978) sees organizations as strategically adopting goals and strategies that allow them to obtain key resources without hopelessly offending other constituencies. The population ecology model, by contrast, suggests that organizations' capacity to adapt and respond planfully to their environments is quite limited; consequently, when an organization's social context changes radically, it is more likely to be superseded by new organizations than to adapt successfully (Hannan and Freeman 1977).

Viewing organizations with nature protection goals as institutions (Zucker 1983; DiMaggio and Powell 1991) provides additional insights into how they choose goals and strategies. Organizations are institutionalized when they are governed by shared assumptions and normative standards that prescribe specific roles, goals and activities as appropriate for them. Operating within these parameters increases their legitimacy and provides them with agreed-upon solutions for vexing strategy problems. The goals, modes of operation, myths and rituals of organizations with nature protection goals – like those of other organizations – can become infused with symbolic significance, especially for supporters who are strongly vested in the organization (Trice and Beyer 1993). Retaining these supporters' loyalty and commitment can then require swearing allegiance to these goals and strategies (Perrow 1993).

Because such expectations are based, in part, on organizational history, the neo-institutional approach views organizations as innately conservative. Innovations are likely to diffuse widely only when they come to be defined as normal practice by peer organizations, oversight agencies and professional associations (Zucker 1983; Dalton 1994). Consequently, organizations with similar goals often display institutional isomorphism. Particularly in uncertain environments, organizations tend to mimic one another (Powell and DiMaggio 1991) and to come under pressure to conform to commonly accepted models of operation (Meyer and Rowan 1977). This argument contrasts with the resource dependence approach, which suggests that organizations might differentiate their goals and strategies to attract support. Examining how nature protection organizations as organizations adapt or fail to adapt successfully to their complex and changing environments in ways that keep needed resources flowing is a core theme of this book.

Social movements

Sociologists and political scientists have frequently viewed environmental organizations and networks as components of social movements. Definitions of social movements vary widely; however, much of the literature focuses on movements that mobilize their supporters for confrontation and protest to bring about major change in political or economic systems (McAdam et al. 1988; Diani 1992; Markham 2006). Nature protection organizations and networks have seldom mounted such movements alone; however, nature protection has fairly frequently emerged as one goal among others in broader social movements. At least three social movement theories can be brought to bear on nature protection movements: resource mobilization; social constructionism and framing; and theories of new social movements. Subsequent chapters explore the conditions under which nature protection advocates have mounted independent nature protection movements or allied themselves with other movements and the factors that determine the success of such movements.

Resource mobilization theory (Klandermans 1986; McAdam et al. 1988; Jenkins 1983), developed in the USA during the 1970s and 1980s, focuses attention on social movement organizations (SMOs), the relatively formalized, permanent organizations that emerge as key actors in most long-lived social movements. According to the theory, grievances and desires for change, such as the desire to protect nature, are ubiquitous in society. Therefore the rise of movements is best explained not by popular discontent or desire for change, but by the activities of 'social movement entrepreneurs', who assemble the necessary financial resources and public support to build SMOs, including nature protection organizations and networks. Although financial support from individual donors and volunteers can be important for SMOs, the resource mobilization approach emphasizes the importance of obtaining financial support from other sources, including foundations, wealthy individuals and government, and it sees SMOs as in competition for needed resources.

According to resource mobilization theory, social movements are most likely to succeed when they explicate the problem to be solved and strategies for solving it in ways that attract broad support without hopelessly alienating powerful opponents. In this respect, they resemble 'social constructionist' accounts of environmentalism (e.g. Hannigan 1995) and related theories of 'framing' from the social movements literature (Snow 1986; Gamson 1992). These theories argue that people do not automatically consider conditions such as destruction of nature to be problems. Consequently, social movements must develop ideologies and ways of 'framing' problems that persuade media and the general public to define specific situations as 'problems' in need of solution. Arguments for nature protection, for example, can be 'framed' in terms of the need to preserve nature as a basis for human life, to preserve ecosystems for their own sake, or to protect beloved species or landscapes. Successful frames resonate with the public and attract supporters because they fit well into existing cognitive frameworks, portray problems in graphic and understandable ways, or evoke emotions.

New social movement theory was developed, primarily in Europe, as an effort to account for the rise of new social movements (NSMs), including the student, peace, feminist and environmental movements, during the 1960s and 1970s (Klandermans 1986; Brand et al. 1986; Beuchler 1995). These movements were 'new' in several respects: (1) they were not as directly focused as older movements on gaining economic advantage or political power; indeed some eschewed success and progress as defined by the dominant culture in favour of pursuing new post-material or ecological values; (2) NSMs typically sought to bring about social change not only through political action, but also by lifestyle changes; and (3) active participation in NSMs became the basis for important personal and group identities, such as 'feminist' or 'environmentalist'. The applicability of NSM theory to nature protection is less clear than its applicability to environmentalism because nature protection efforts began long before the 1960s and because nature protection also appeals to segments of the population that were little affected by the value changes cited by NSM theory. Nature protection advocates did, of course, have to adapt to the rise of the environmental movement, and there is some emerging evidence that they may now have to cope with its decline (Blühdorn 2000).

The Role of Nature Protection Organizations and Networks in Society

Nature protection organizations and networks deserve attention not only for their own sake, but also because of their roles in the larger society. They play an important role in the civil societies of Western nations, and they are part and parcel of ongoing changes in the economic and political organization of these societies.

Civil society

Civil society comprises 'areas of social life . . . which are organized by private or voluntary arrangements between individuals and groups outside of the direct control of the state' (Held 1995, p. 181). Theorists of civil society (e.g. Putnam 2000; Salamon and Anheier 1997) typically argue that neo-liberal democracies with market economies function best when they have well-developed civil societies. Especially important for the success of civil society are civic associations, 'the array of institutions and organizations in and through which individuals or groups can pursue their own projects independently of the direct organization of the state or of economic collectivities' (Held 1995, p. 181). These include groups as diverse as amateur sports leagues, hobby clubs, self-help groups, neighbourhood associations, charitable associations and public interest lobby groups.

According to theories of civil society, civic associations serve at least five important functions for society. First, they build social capital, the network of overlapping memberships that binds citizens to one another and society (Putnam 2000). Second, they meet needs not met by the market economy or the state, and they may deliver services on behalf of the state (Weisbrod 1986; Zimmer 1996; Deakin 2001). Third, civil society supplements markets and the formal democratic structures of the state in societal goal setting, self-regulation and correction by providing additional mechanisms for public participation and checking government and business power (Held 1995; Skocpol 2003; Habermas 1992). Fourth, civil society organizations help to educate citizens about social problems and political issues. Finally, organizations of civil society contribute to the development of skills in self-government and democratic citizenship (Fung 2003; Skocpol 2003; Habermas 1992).

Nature protection organizations and networks fit well under the rubric of civil society associations. They have worked for over a century to limit the destruction of nature, preserve wilderness and cultural landscapes, educate the public, and influence government and business. They work in an area where market institutions often produce undesired risks and externalities, fail to produce socially valued amenities, and fail to preserve valued resources (Beck, 1986; Schnaiberg and Gould 1994). They mediate among citizens, government and business, and impact legislation and public policy, both through protests and through partnerships with government and business. Finally, they have responsibility for managing substantial amounts of public space, some of which they have procured with their own resources. It is less clear that nature protection organizations have effectively fulfilled the role of facilitating civil participation and stimulating political dialogue, as many have elitist tendencies, and some provide for little democratic input. On the other hand, many do have strong programmes of public education (Dowie 1995; Brulle 2000; Dekker 2002).

Ecological modernization and risk society

Also potentially relevant to understanding the place of nature protection organizations and networks in society is a group of recent theories, almost exclusively of Northern European origin, that focus on ecological and political modernization. These theories consider environmental risks to be one of the driving factors in a further 'modernization of modernity' (Mol 1995, p. 37), which is engendering transformations in political and economic structures that make it possible to achieve environmental sustainability without abandoning modern, industrialized society.

There are two major variants of this approach. Ecological modernization theory describes an ongoing shift in social structure involving the emergence of a new sphere of ecological rationality in society, which will stand alongside and influence the economic and political spheres. The emergence of this sphere is associated with the emergence of new technologies, monitoring systems, policy arrangements and management procedures that allow major improvements in the efficiency of production and drastic reductions in environmental damage (Spaargaren and Mol 1992; Mol 1995). Beck's theory of the risk society, on the other hand, stresses how threats from new technologies and environmental risks have undermined public trust in the state and science. He argues that coping with such problems requires deliberative arrangements that go beyond the nation-state. These new political arrangements, called 'subpolitics', include consumer action and NGO–company alliances to minimize environmental damage (Beck 1986).

Both ecological modernization and risk society theory foresee a somewhat reduced role for the nation-state in the future, coupled with increasingly important roles for NGOs, civil society, and supranational and sub-national governmental bodies. These changes are summarized by the term 'multilevel governance' (Van Tatenhove et al. 2000). 'Hybrid arrangements', combining state, market and civil society actors, are also expected to expand their role in managing environmental problems (Spaargaren et al. 2006). Furthermore, against the backdrop of the globalization of production, consumption and environmental issues, global civil society organizations and networks are destined to be of crucial importance in environmental governance (Lipschutz and Mayer 1996; Wapner 1996; Vig and Axelrod 1999; Held 2004).

Clearly, such expectations fit well with the roles that international nature protection organizations such as Greenpeace and WWF aspire to fulfil (Wapner 1996), and IUCN is an apt illustration of a hybrid organization bringing together states and NGOs. It is less clear that nature protection organizations in the narrower sense contribute to the type of structural political changes that Beck and ecological modernization theory hypothesize, for nature protection organizations have typically been very cautious about interfering with political structures (Van Koppen 2003); however, this may vary from nation to nation.

CONCLUSION

This chapter has provided a conceptual framework for analysing nature protection organizations and networks, as well as an overview of theories that help explain the motivational bases for nature protection activism, the goals, structures and strategies of nature protection organizations and networks, and the contributions of nature protection organizations to societies at large. While this chapter provides an orienting framework for the chapters that follow, it does not, and indeed could not, encompass their full empirical and theoretical diversity. Although all the authors agreed to write chapters that fit within the parameters described above, our aim in planning the book and in this introduction has been to set the stage for the chapters that follow, not to dictate their details. Variations across nations in the histories and present-day contexts of nature protection, the amount and kinds of information available, and national sociological traditions, as well as the differing theoretical orientations of the authors, thus make for both uniformity and diversity across chapters. We view this as a strength, not a weakness, for the resulting chapters provide not only a plethora of useful substantive comparisons, but also a wealth of hunches and insights for further exploration. In the final chapter we make a number of comparisons that seem to us especially significant among the country chapters, but individual readers will no doubt want to make their own, and the following chapters suggest numerous avenues for further enquiry.

REFERENCES

Bazarov, Konstantin (1981), *Landscape Painting*, London: Octopus Books.
Beck, Ulrich (1986), *Risikogesellschaft: Auf dem Weg in eine andere Moderne*, Frankfurt am Main: Suhrkamp.
Berry, Jeffrey M. (1984), *The Interest Group Society*, Boston, MA: Little Brown.
Beuchler, Steven M. (1995), 'New Social Movement Theories', *The Sociological Quarterly*, **36**, 441–64.
Blühdorn, Ingolflur (2000), *Post-Ecologist Politics, Social Theory, and the Abdication of the Ecologist Paradigm*, London: Routledge.
Bosso, Christopher J. (1995), 'The Color of Money: Environmental Groups and the Pathologies of Fundraising', in Allan J. Cigler and Burdett A. Loomis (eds), *Interest Group Politics*, Washington, DC: Congressional Quarterly Press, pp. 101–30.
Bosso, Christopher (2005), *Environment, Inc.: From Grassroots to Beltway*, Lawrence, KA: University of Kansas Press.
Brand, Karl-Werner, Klaus Eder and Angelika Poferl (1997), *Ökologische Kommunikation in Deutschland*, Opladen: Westdeutscher Verlag.
Brand, Karl-Werner, Detlef Büsser and Dieter Rucht (1986), *Aufbruch in eine andere Gesellschaft: Neue Soziale Bewegungnen in der Bundesrepublik*, Frankfurt: Campus Verlag.
Brulle, Robert J. (2000), *Agency, Democracy, and Nature*, Cambridge, MA: MIT Press.
Coffey, Clare and Saskia Richartz (2003), 'The EU Habitats Directive: Generating Strong Responses', London: IEEP, www.ecologic.de/download/projekte/850-899/890/in-depth/eu_habitats_directive.pdf, accessed 8 July 2006.
Dahl, Robert A. (1961), *Who Governs?*, New Haven, CT: Yale University Press.
Dalton, Russell (1994), *The Green Rainbow: Environmental Groups in Western Europe*, New Haven, CT: Yale University Press.
Deakin, Nicholas (2001), *In Search of Civil Society*, Basingstoke, UK: Palgrave.
Dekker, P. (2002), *De Oplossing van de Civil Society*, Den Haag: Sociaal en Cultureel Planbureau.
Denton, Peter (1993), *World Wide Fund for Nature*, Watford, UK: Exley.
Diani, Mario (1992), 'The Concept of Social Movement', *The Sociological Review*, **40** (1), 1–25.
Diani, Mario (1995), *Green Networks: A Structural Analysis of the Italian Environmental Movement*, Edinburgh: Edinburgh University Press.
Diani, Mario and Paolo R. Donati (1999), 'Organizational Change in Western European Environmental Groups: A Framework for Analysis', *Environmental Politics*, **8**, 13–34.
Diani, Mario and Doug McAdam (2003), *Social Movements and Networks: Relational Approaches to Collective Action*, Oxford: Oxford University Press.
Diekmann, Andreas and Peter Preisendörfer (1998), 'Umweltbewußtsein und Umweltverhalten in Low und High-cost Situations', *Zeitschrift für Soziologie*, **27** (6), 438–53.
DiMaggio, Paul J. and Walter W. Powell (1991), 'Introduction', in Walter W. Powell and Paul J. DiMaggio (eds), *The New Institutionalism in Organizational Analysis*, Chicago, IL: University of Chicago Press, pp. 1–38.
Doherty, Brian (2006), 'Friends of the Earth International: Negotiating a transnational identity', *Environmental Politics*, **15** (5), 860–80.
Dowie, Mark (1995), *Losing Ground: American Environmentalism at the Close of the Twentieth Century*, Cambridge, MA: MIT Press.

Dryzek, John S. et al. (2003), *Green States and Social Movements*, New York: Oxford University Press.
European Environmental Bureau (2006), http://www.eeb.org/, accessed 9 June.
Felbinger, Doris (2005), *Ego oder Öko?*, Berlin: Logos Verlag.
Flechner, Ralf (1999), 'Die Greenpeace-Gruppen vor Ort', in Ernst Kister, Heinz-Herbert Noll and Eckhard Priller (eds), *Perspektiven Gesellschaftlichen Zusammenhalts: Empirische Befünde, Praxiserfahrungen, Meßkonzepte*, Berlin: Edition Sigma, pp. 371–6.
Friends of the Earth International (2001), *Sparks of Hope: Fires of Resistance: FOEI Celebrates the Sustainable Path Forward*, Amsterdam: Friends of the Earth International Secretariat.
Friends of the Earth International (2005), *Annual Report 2004: Friends of the Earth International*, Brussels: Friends of the Earth International.
Fung, Archon (2003), 'Associations and Democracy: Between Hopes and Realities', *Annual Review of Sociology*, **29**, 515–39.
Gamson, William A. (1992), 'The Social Psychology of Collective Action', in Aldon D. Morris and Carol McClurg Mueller (eds), *Frontiers in Social Movement Theory*, New Haven, CT: Yale University Press, pp. 53–76.
Godwin, R. Kenneth (1988), *One Billion Dollars of Influence*, Chatham, NJ: Chatham House.
Greenpeace International (2006a), *Greenpeace Annual Report 2005*, Amsterdam: Greenpeace International.
Greenpeace International (2006b), http://www.greenpeace.org/international/, accessed 9 June.
Haag, Dietrich W. (1986), 'Die Umweltstiftung WWF-Deutschland', in Rolf Hauer et al. (eds), *Lebensbilder Deutscher Stiftungen*, Vol. 5, Tübingen: I.C.B. Mohr, pp. 471–82.
Habermas, Jürgen (1992), *Faktizität und Geltung: Beiträge zur Diskurstheorie des Rechts und des demokratischen Rechtsstaats*, Frankfurt am Main: Suhrkamp.
Hall, Richard (2002), *Organizations: Structures, Processes, and Outcomes*, Upper Saddle River, NJ: Prentice-Hall.
Hannan, Michael T. and John Freeman (1977), 'The Population Ecology of Organizations', *American Journal of Sociology*, **82** (5), 955–64.
Hannigan, J.A. (1995), *Environmental Sociology: A Social Constructionist Perspective*, London: Routledge.
Hargrove, E.C. (1989), *Foundations of Environmental Ethics*, Englewood Cliffs, NJ: Prentice-Hall.
Held, David (1995), *Democracy and the Global Order*, Cambridge: Polity Press.
Held, David (2004), *Global Covenant: The Social Democratic Alternative to the Washington Consensus*, Cambridge: Polity Press.
Hey, Christian (2004), 'Die Europäische Politik im Europa der 25', in Günter Altner et al. (eds), *Jahrbuch Ökologie 2005*, Munich: Verlag C.H. Beck, pp. 11–25.
Hey, Christian and Uwe Brendle (1994), *Umweltverbände und EG: Strategien, Kulturen, und Organisationsformen*, Opladen: Westdeutscher Verlag.
Honour, Hugh (1981), *Romanticism*, Harmondsworth, UK: Penguin Books.
Horkheimer, Max and Theodor W. Adorno (1971), *Dialektik der Aufklärung*, Frankfurt am Main: Fischer [original publication 1947].
IUCN (1994), *Guidelines for Protected Area Management Categories*, Gland, Switzerland and Cambridge, UK: IUCN and the World Conservation Monitoring Centre.

IUCN (2006), IUCN Membership List June 2006, http://www.iucn.org/members/Documents/membersList.pdf.

Jänicke, Martin, Philip Kunig and Michael Stitzel (1999), *Umweltpolitik*, Bonn: Verlag J.H.W. Dietz Nachf.

Jenkins, J. Craig (1983), 'Resource Mobilization Theory and the Study of Social Movements', *Annual Review of Sociology*, **9**, 527–53.

Jordan, Grant and William Maloney (1997), *The Protest Business? Mobilizing Campaign Groups*, Manchester: Manchester University Press.

Kahn, Peter and Stephen R. Kellert (eds) (2002), *Children and Nature*, Cambridge, MA: MIT Press.

Kaplan, Rachel and Stephen Kaplan (2005), 'Preference, Restoration, and Meaningful Action in the Context of Nearby Nature', in Peggy F. Barlett (ed.), *Urban Place. Reconnecting with the Natural World*, Cambridge, MA: MIT Press, pp. 271–98.

Katz, Daniel and Robert L. Kahn (1978), *The Social Psychology of Organizations*, New York: Wiley.

Kellert, Stephen R. (2002), 'Experiencing Nature: Affective, Cognitive, and Evaluative Development in Children', in Peter Kahn and Stephen R. Kellert (eds), *Children and Nature*, Cambridge, MA: MIT Press, pp. 117–51.

Kellert, S.R. and E.O. Wilson (1993), *The Biophilia Hypothesis*, Washington, DC: Island Press.

Klandermans, Bert (1986), 'New Social Movements and Resource Mobilization: The European and the American Approach', *International Journal of Mass Emergencies and Disasters*, **4** (2), 13–37.

Lake, Beate (1998), 'NPO im Spannungsfeld von Solidarität und Wettbewerb', in Rupert Graf Strachwitz (ed.), *Dritter Sektor – Dritte Kraft: Versuch einer Standortbissimung*, Stuttgart: RAABE, pp. 447–62.

Lange, Ulrich (2000), 'Rahmbedingungen des Naturschutzes in den USA und in Deutschland: Ein Vergleich', in Use Wegener and Hermann Behrens (eds), *Naturschutz in Vereinigten Deutschland*, Berlin: Verlag für Wissenschaft und Forschung, pp. 23–37.

Lehmbruch, Gerhard and Phillippe C. Schmitter (eds) (1982), *Patterns of Corporatist Policy Making*, Beverly Hills, CA: Sage.

Lipschutz, R.D. and J. Mayer (1996), *Global Civil Society and Global Environmental Governance*, Albany NY: SUNY.

MacNaghten, P. and J. Urry (1998), *Contested Natures*, London: Sage.

Markham, William T. (2006), 'Competing Models for the Analysis of Environmental Organizations: A Comparison and Assessment', paper presented at the World Congress of Sociology, Durban, South Africa, July.

McAdam, Doug, John D. McCarthy and Mayer N. Zald (1988), 'Social Movements', in Neil Smelser (ed.), *Handbook of Sociology*, Newbury Park, CA: Sage, pp. 695–737.

McKibben, Bill (1999), *The End of Nature*, New York: Anchor Books.

Meyer, John W. and Brian Rowan (1977), 'Institutionalized Organizations: Formal Structure as Myth and Ceremony', *American Journal of Sociology*, **83** (2), 340–63.

Mol, Arthur P.J. (1995), *The Refinement of Production: Ecological Modernisation and the Chemical Industry*, Utrecht: Van Arkel.

Mount, Joan (1996), 'Why Donors Give', *Nonprofit Management and Leadership*, **7** (1), 3–14.

Neumann, R.P. (1998), *Imposing Wilderness. Struggles over Livelihood and Nature Preservation in Africa*, Berkeley, CA: University of California Press.
Olson, Mancur Jr (1965), *The Logic of Collective Action*, Cambridge, MA: Harvard University Press.
Orians, G.H. and J.H. Heerwagen (1992), 'Evolved Responses to Landscapes', in J.H. Barkow, L. Cosmides and J. Tooby (eds), *The Adapted Mind: Evolutionary Psychology and the Generation of Culture*, New York: Oxford University Press, pp. 555–79.
Oswald von Nell-Breuning-Institut (1996), *Die Rolle der Umweltverbände in den Demokratischen und Umweltethischen Lernprozessen der Gesellschaft*, Stuttgart: Metzler-Poeschel.
Parsons, Talcott (1970), 'Some Problems of General Theory', in J.C. McKinney and E.A. Tiryakian (eds), *Theoretical Sociology: Perspectives and Developments*, New York: Appleton-Century-Crofts, pp. 28–68.
Perrow, Charles (1993), *Complex Organizations: A Critical Essay*, New York: McGraw-Hill.
Petracca, Mark P. (ed.) (1992a), *The Politics of Interests*, Boulder, CO: Westview.
Petracca, Mark P. (1992b), 'The Rediscovery of Interest Group Politics', in Mark P. Petracca (ed.), *The Politics of Interests*, Boulder, CO: Westview, pp. 3–31.
Pfeffer, Jeffrey and Gerald R. Salancik (1978), *The External Control of Organizations: A Resource Dependence Perspective*, New York: Harper and Row.
Pimbert, Michel P. and Jules N. Pretty (1995), 'Parks, People and Professionals. Putting "Participation" into Protected Area Management', in Krishna B. Ghimire and Michel P. Pimbert (eds), *Social Change and Conservation*, London: Earthscan.
Powell, Walter W. and Paul J. DiMaggio (eds) (1991), *The New Institutionalism in Organizational Analysis*, Chicago, IL: University of Chicago Press.
Price, Jennifer (1999), *Flight Maps. Adventures with Nature in Modern America*, New York: Basic Books.
Putnam, Robert D. (2000), *Bowling Alone: The Collapse and Revival of American Community*, New York: Simon and Schuster.
Roose, Jochen (2002), *Die Europäisierung von Umweltorganisationen: Die Umweltbewegung auf dem Langen Weg nach Brüssel*, Opladen: Westdeutscher Verlag.
Rootes, Christopher (ed.) (2003), *Environmental Protest in Western Europe*, Oxford: Oxford University Press.
Rootes, Christopher (2004), 'Is There a European Environmental Movement?', in John Barry, Brian Baxter and Richard Dunphy (eds), *Europe, Globalization and the Challenge of Sustainability*, London: Routledge, pp. 47–72.
Rucht, Dieter (1993), 'Parteien, Verbände und Bewegungen als Systeme Politischer Interessenvermittlung', in Oskar Niedermayer and Richard Stoss (eds), *Stand und Perspektiven der Parteienforschung in Deutschland*, Opladen: Westdeutscher Verlag, pp. 251–75.
Rucht, Dieter (1995), 'Ecological Protest as Calculated Lawbreaking: Greenpeace and Earth First! in Comparative Perspective', in Wolfgang Rüdig (ed.), *Green Politics Three*, Edinburgh: Edinburgh University Press, pp. 66–89.
Rucht, Dieter (1997), 'Limits to Mobilization: Environmental Policy for the European Union', in Jackie Smith, Charles Chatfield and Ron Pagnucco (eds), *Transnational Social Movements and Global Politics*, Syracuse, NY: Syracuse University Press, pp. 195–213.

Salamon, Lester and Helmut Anheier (1997), *Defining the Non-Profit Sector: A Cross-national Analysis*, Manchester: Manchester University Press.
Sbragia, Alberta M. (2000), 'Environmental Policy: Economic Constraints and External Pressures', in Helen Wallace and William Wallace (eds), *Policy Making in the European Union*, New York: Oxford University Press, pp. 293–316.
Schama, Simon (1995), *Landscape and Memory*, London: HarperCollins.
Schmitter, Philippe C. and Gerhard Lehmbruch (eds) (1979), *Trends toward Corporatist Intermediation*, Beverly Hills, CA: Sage.
Schnaiberg, Allan and Kenneth Gould (1994), *Environment and Society: The Enduring Conflict*, New York: St Martin's Press.
Shaiko, Ronald H. (1999), *Voices and Echoes for the Environment: Public Interest Representation in the 1990s and Beyond*, New York: Columbia University Press.
Skocpol, Theda (2003), *Diminished Democracy: From Membership to Management in American Civil Life*, Norman, OK: University of Oklahoma Press.
Smith, David Horton (1994), 'Determinants of Voluntary Association Participation and Volunteering: A Literature Review', *Nonprofit and Voluntary Sector Quarterly*, **23** (3), 243–63.
Snow, David A. (1986), 'Frame Alignment Processes, Micromobilization, and Movement Participation', *American Sociological Review*, **51** (5), 464–81.
Spaargaren, Gert and Arthur P.J. Mol (1992), 'Sociology, Environment, and Modernity: Ecological Modernization as a Theory of Social Change', *Society and Natural Resources*, **5**, 323–44.
Spaargaren, Gert, Arthur P.J. Mol and Hans Bruyninckx (2006), 'Introduction', in Gert Spaargaren, Arthur P.J. Mol and Frederick H. Buttel (eds), *Governing Environmental Flows. Global Challenges to Social Theory*, Cambridge, MA: MIT Press, pp. 1–36.
Stein, Tine (2003), *Interessenvertretung der Nature in den USA: Mit Vergleichendem Blick auf die Deutsche Rechtslage*, Baden-Baden: Nomos.
Suplie, J. (1995), *'Streit auf Noahs Arche'. Zur Genese der Biodiversitäts-Konvention*, Berlin: WZB.
Swanson, T. (1997), *Global Action for Biodiversity*, London: Earthscan.
Takacs, D. (1996), *The Idea of Biodiversity. Philosophies of Paradise*, Baltimore, MD: Johns Hopkins University Press.
Tarrow, Sidney (1991), *Struggle, Politics, and Reform: Collective Action, Social Movements, and Cycles of Protest*, Ithaca, NY: Center for International Studies, Cornell University.
Thomas, Keith (1993), *Man and the Natural World: Changing Attitudes in England 1500–1800*, London: Penguin Books.
Thompson, James D. (1967), *Organizations in Action*, New York: McGraw-Hill.
Trice, Harrison M. and Janice M. Beyer (1993), *The Cultures of Work Organizations*, Englewood Cliffs, NJ: Prentice-Hall.
Van der Heijden, Hein-Anton, Ruud Koopmans and Marco G. Giugini (1992), 'The West European Environmental Movement', in *Research in Social Movements, Conflict and Change, Supplement 2*, Greenwood, CT: JAI, pp. 1–40.
Van der Heijden, Hein-Anton (1997), 'Political Opportunity Structure and the Institutionalization of the Environmental Movement', *Environmental Politics*, **6** (4), 25–50.
Van Kersbergen, Kees and Frans van Waarden (2004), 'Governance as a Bridge between Disciplines', *European Journal of Political Research*, **43** (2), 143–71.

Van Koppen, C.S.A. (Kris) (2000), 'Resource, Arcadia, Lifeworld: Nature Concepts in Environmental Sociology', *Sociologia Ruralis*, **40** (3), 300–318.

Van Koppen, C.S.A. (Kris) (2002), *Echte Natuur. Een Sociaatheoretisch onderzoek naar Natuurwaardering en Natuurbescherming in de Moderne Samenleving*, Wageningen: Dissertation Wageningen University.

Van Koppen, C.S.A. (Kris) (2003), 'Ecological Modernisation and Nature Conservation', *International Journal of Environment and Sustainable Development*, **2** (3), 305–23.

Van Tatenhove, Jan, Bas Arts and Pieter Leroy (eds) (2000), *Political Modernisation and the Environment. The Renewal of Environmental Policy Arrangements*, Dordrecht: Kluwer Academic Publishers.

Vig, Norman J. and Regina S. Axelrod (eds) (1999), *The Global Environment: Institutions, Law, and Policy*, Washington, DC: CQ Press.

Walker, Jack L. (1991), *Mobilizing Interest Groups in America*, Ann Arbor, MI: University of Michigan Press.

Wapner, Paul (1996), *Environmental Activism and World Civic Politics*, Albany, NY: SUNY Press.

Webster, Ruth (1998), 'Environmental Collective Action: Stable Patterns of Cooperation and Issue Alliances at the European Level', in Justin Greenwood and Mark Aspenwall (eds), *Collective Action in the European Union*, London: Routledge, pp. 176–96.

Weisbrod, Burton Allen (1986), *The Nonprofit Economy*, Cambridge, MA: Harvard University Press.

Whiteside, K.H. (2002), *Divided Natures. French Contributions to Political Ecology*, Cambridge, MA: MIT Press.

Wilson, E.O. (1984), *Biophilia*, Cambridge, MA: Harvard University Press.

Wilson, Graham K. (1990), *Interest Groups*, Oxford: Basil Blackwell.

Worster, Donald (1985), *Nature's Economy: A History of Ecological Ideas*, Cambridge: Cambridge University Press.

WWF International (2006a), *Working Together: WWF Annual Review 2006*, Gland, Switzerland: WWF International.

WWF International (2006b), http://www.panda.org, accessed 8 June.

Zimmer, Annette (1996), *Vereine: Basiselement der Demokratie*, Opladen: Leske + Budrich.

Zucker, Lynne G. (1983), 'Organizations as Institutions', in Samuel B. Bacharach (ed.), *Research in the Sociology of Organizations*, Vol. 2, Greenwich, CT: JAI, pp. 1–48.

2. Nature protection organizations in England[1]

Christopher Rootes

HISTORICAL OVERVIEW

Beginnings

Human activity has dramatically altered the natural environment of England[2] during the past 6000 years. Conservation measures were introduced in the thirteenth century to permit regeneration of game species hunted for sport. By the sixteenth century, increasing population and changing agricultural practices led to the contraction of English forests, inspiring measures to protect a vital national resource. Nevertheless, by the end of the seventeenth century, half the country was given over to agriculture, and destruction of habitat had reduced many native species to the verge of extinction.

From the eighteenth century, the Industrial Revolution accelerated human impacts on nature, factories and mills concentrated people in industrial towns, and more efficient firearms enabled hunters and gamekeepers to increase their take. Reacting against the ravages of industrialization, Romantics celebrated natural landscapes. Pollution of air and water excited both protests and the 1863 Alkali and 1875 Public Health Acts. Civic initiatives created urban parks, and the idealization of the countryside took root.

At the same time, scientific investigation and exploration enhanced understanding of the natural world. Natural history societies came and went, and only in the late nineteenth century did a conservation movement emerge. An elite rather than a mass movement, which saw legislation as the instrument of nature protection, its success owed less to generally 'enlightened attitudes than . . . the influential positions of many of those who championed the cause' (Evans 1997, p. 34). The first local by-laws protecting plants were enacted in 1888, but most early legislation aimed to protect birds. The Sea Birds Preservation Act 1869 was followed by more inclusive Wild Birds Protection Acts, but their effectiveness was undermined by loopholes, derisory penalties, and scientific and public indifference.

During the nineteenth century, nature study groups, focused upon field studies, became divorced from increasingly professionalized science, but amateurs founded influential conservation organizations. The Society for the Prevention of Cruelty to Animals (later RSPCA), established in 1824, was active in some early wildlife campaigns. The Commons Preservation Society (1865), concerned to protect public access to open land, succeeded in preserving London's commons. Specialized societies proliferated, but the first nationwide association concerned with all forms of wildlife was the Selborne Society for the Protection of Birds, Plants and Pleasant Places (1885).

England's three largest conservation organizations all date from the late nineteenth or early twentieth centuries. The Society for the Protection of Birds (later RSPB) emerged in 1889 from the campaign against the trade in feathers for ladies' fashion. Its royal charter, granted in 1904, envisaged its acquisition of nature reserves, but early activity focused upon the employment of watchers to protect endangered birds. The National Trust for Places of Historic Interest or Natural Beauty (NT) (1895) grew from the Lake District Defence Society and the Commons Preservation Society, which had been frustrated by the latter's inability to buy the land it sought to protect. Not only could the NT buy land, but the National Trust Act of 1907 empowered it to declare its property inalienable, gave it protection from compulsory purchase, and thereby encouraged owners to give it property. The third major association, the Society for the Promotion of Nature Reserves (1912), the ancestor of the present Royal Society for Wildlife Trusts, did not itself intend to own land, but compiled lists of areas deserving protection and raised money to purchase sites to be entrusted to the care of others.

The Interwar Years

The interwar years saw the passing of four further bird protection Acts, and in 1930 the RSPB acquired its first reserves. In 1926 the first regional wildlife trust was established in Norfolk, and by 1941 it was managing 15 reserves (Evans 1997, p. 52).

If the prewar period was dominated by initiatives of resourceful, socially and politically well-connected individuals enjoying royal or aristocratic patronage and endorsement, the inter-war years saw the formation of new groups drawing upon a broader base, among them the Council for the Preservation of Rural England (CPRE), the Pedestrians' Association and the Ramblers' Association. While the latter two groups supported demands of an increasingly urbanized population for access to the countryside,

CPRE aimed to protect it from unplanned urbanization resulting from an unprecedented wave of house building, extension of urban railways, and the advent of the automobile. A countryside made unprecedentedly accessible was visibly threatened by its popularity.

An umbrella group, CPRE conjoined 40 bodies, including the NT, the Royal Institute of British Architects, the Royal Automobile Club, the County Council Association, the Society for the Preservation of Ancient Buildings and the Central Landowners' Association. Funded by architects and planners, CPRE campaigned for the creation of areas of special protection, including national parks, and the extension of planning controls to the countryside. Its distinctive task was to lobby decision makers, not to duplicate the more practical work of members. Largely because its leaders were 'pillars of society' (Lowe and Goyder 1983, p. 37), CPRE's impact was immediate; its pressure for universal rural planning resulted in the Town and Country Planning Act 1932 and the Restriction of Ribbon Development Act 1935.

The 1939–45 war caused immeasurable damage to the natural environment. Mobilization for total war required the exploitation of forests and the destruction of meadow and woodland to maximize agricultural production and extraction of mineral resources. These pressures continued into the period of postwar reconstruction. Only very slowly did awareness of what had been (often pointlessly) lost stimulate a revival of public interest.

Postwar Reconstruction

Elites continued, even during the war, to devise plans for national parks. Conflicts divided recreationists from conservationists, but the postwar Labour government's enthusiasm for planning had advantages. Realizing many of CPRE's ambitions, the Town and Country Planning Act 1947 established the modern, comprehensive land use planning system. CPRE also campaigned successfully for the designation of 'green belts' around towns and cities. Other legislation established the Nature Conservancy (NC) in 1948, and the 1949 National Parks and Access to the Countryside Act confirmed the NC's duties to provide scientific advice on the conservation of natural flora and fauna, manage and maintain nature reserves, and develop relevant research. The NC designated sites of special scientific interest (SSSI), became a statutory consultee in planning and development matters, and presided over a network of national nature reserves. The Act also envisaged the designation of Areas of Outstanding Natural Beauty and National Parks, the first of which – in the Peak and Lake Districts – were created in 1951. Disappointingly, these designations delivered little practical protection, and the 1947 Agriculture Act encouraged an agricultural boom that accelerated destruction of the natural environment.

The postwar years saw the formation of a variety of more specialized nature protection associations, including the Wildfowl Trust, the Herpetological Society, the Mammal Society and the Conservation Corps. The RSPB formed a film unit, and the BBC a natural history unit. Meanwhile cheap colour reproduction made available an increasing supply of attractive guide books. Increasingly evident river pollution and the catastrophic London smog of 1952 encouraged new protective legislation, and alarms were raised about indiscriminate pesticide use.

The 1960s and Beyond

The pace of development in nature protection legislation and policy increased from the 1960s onwards. International conventions encouraged protection of neglected wetlands, and the European Commission's assumption of competence in environmental matters – described in Chapter 1 – provided new links, new comparisons, and new opportunities for lobbying and leverage, as well as opportunities of redress through the European Court of Justice. British organizations played disproportionately large roles in the European Environmental Bureau (EEB), established to represent environmentalism to the EC.

The cumulative effect of more than a century of piecemeal legislation had given England an elaborate but fragmented legal apparatus for nature protection (Garner 2000, ch. 8). The first comprehensive attempt to protect wild plants, passed in 1975, was restricted to rare and endangered species (Evans 1997, pp. 148–51). The 1981 Wildlife and Countryside Act responded to demands of an increasingly politically aware movement and sought to give European levels of protection to English natural habitats (ibid., p. 164), but its teeth were drawn by vested interests, and SSSIs continued to be destroyed at an alarming rate. The 1990 Environmental Protection Act created English Nature from the Nature Conservancy, with responsibility for identifying and designating SSSIs that in 2000 covered 7 per cent of England, and creating nature reserves (Garner 2000, p. 159). From 1991, a government-funded Countryside Stewardship programme sought to reconcile economic exploitation of the countryside with conservation. The 1995 Environment Act created an Environment Agency, merging the existing regulatory bodies for industrial pollution, water and waste.

Labour came to power in 1997. It promised to 'put the environment at the centre of government' and created the Department of the Environment, Transport and the Regions, perhaps the most powerful and comprehensive environment department in the world. Evidently learning from its predecessor's calamitous transport strategy, the Labour government restrained road building and accepted a moratorium on the commercial planting of GM (genetically modified) crops. Fulfilling a long-held aspiration to break the power of vested agricultural interests, but also to bridge the long-criticized gulf between nature protection and agricultural policies, in 2001 it created the Department of the Environment, Food and Rural Affairs. However, the Countryside Agency, created in 1999 by the merger of the Countryside and Rural Development Commissions, was swiftly perceived to be a failure, and in 2006 conservation and amenity functions were merged in a new body, Natural England, designed to complement the Environment Agency and the Forestry Commission. The Ramblers' long-standing aim – the 'right to roam' across open uncultivated countryside – was fully implemented in 2005.

The Emergence of the Modern Environmental Movement

The 1960s and 1970s saw the emergence of the modern mass environmental movement (Rawcliffe 1998, pp. 15–16). This period of increased organizational innovation began with the launch of the World Wildlife Fund (WWF) in 1961. Although enjoying royal patronage and relying on wealthy individuals for initial funding, WWF-UK began with an appeal for members in the pages of a popular tabloid newspaper and was a mass membership organization from the outset.

Cooperation and division of labour have always characterized British environmentalism (Lowe and Goyder 1983), but increasing awareness of the need to connect diverse concerns and the growing number of organizations stimulated the formation of a Committee (later Council) for Environmental Conservation (CoEnCo) in 1969 to promote a common approach.

During this period, environmentalists widened their action repertoire to embrace the more moderate forms of direct action. Friends of the Earth (FoE) and, especially, Greenpeace skilfully exploited opportunities offered by mass media coverage of symbolic protests to put pressure upon corporations and government. The conservation movement mostly looked askance at such 'improper' publicity seeking (Evans 1997, p. 104). Yet, in addition to their high-profile antinuclear campaigns, FoE and Greenpeace launched major campaigns on nature protection issues. Frustration over the weakness of the Nature Conservancy, as well as a desire to escape the straitjacket of charitable status, encouraged the formation in 1980 of Wildlife Link to coordinate the activities of organizations as diverse as RSPB, RSNC, WWF, FoE and Greenpeace. Enjoying direct access to civil servants and regular meetings with ministers, Wildlife Link greatly increased the political influence of the movement. If conservation organizations were wary of alienating supporters they assumed to be socially and politically conservative, they were nevertheless influenced by the rise of the new campaigning organizations, and they gradually came to see the value of high-profile public campaigns as adjuncts to more traditional lobbying.

Growth and Consolidation

The 1960s also introduced a period of dramatic growth in the numbers of environmental groups, their members and supporters (see Table 2.1). Growth was not, however, evenly distributed. Between 1971 and 1981, membership of the longest-established and largest organizations, NT and RSPB, grew fourfold. Between 1981 and 1991, it doubled again, and it continued increasing through the 1990s. During the 1970s and 1980s, however, the most spectacular growth occurred in the newest and most activist organizations, FoE and Greenpeace, but whereas their growth levelled off in the 1990s, the Wildlife Trusts and the Woodland Trust continued to grow strongly.[3]

From 1991, a new generation of environmental 'disorganizations' emerged, most notably Earth First! They were no less concerned than their

Table 2.1 Membership of selected nature protection and environmental organisations (1971–2005) (thousands)

	1971	1981	1991	2002	2005
National Trust (NT)	278	1046	2152	3000	3400
Royal Society for the Protection of Birds (RSPB)	98	441	852	1020	1042
Wildlife Trusts[1]	64	142	233	413	560
World Wide Fund for Nature (WWF)	12	60	227	320	330
Woodland Trust[2]	–	20	63	115	147
Council for the Protection of Rural England/Campaign to Protect Rural England (CPRE)	21	29	45	59	60
Ramblers' Association	22	37	87	137	143
Friends of the Earth (FoE)	1	18	111	119	100
Greenpeace	–	30	312	224	221

Notes:
[1] Includes The Royal Society for Nature Conservation/Royal Society for Wildlife Trusts.
[2] Figure for 1981 from Evans (1997, p. 197).

Sources: Adapted from Haezewindt (2003) and supplemented with information supplied by the organizations themselves or drawn from their websites.

predecessors with protecting nature, but more radically critical of capitalist consumerism and more committed to mass participation in direct action. Just as the popularity and campaigning successes of FoE and Greenpeace had enhanced others' opportunities for successful lobbying, so environmental organizations gained leverage from the 'radical flank' effect the new radicals provided (Rawcliffe 1998, p. 24; cf. p. 180).

It would be a mistake to see these phases as marking linear progress from nature protection through environmentalism to radical ecologism. In each period, new nature protection organizations and networks have formed, and new 'environmental' and 'ecological' organizations have embraced protection of the natural environment. Differences are more often of strategy, tactics and organizational ethos than of attitudes to nature, and even among 'traditional' nature protection organizations there is considerable diversity.

The emergence of new international agenda with the Rio Earth Summit (UNCED) of 1992 encouraged collaboration among and beyond conservation and environmental organizations. WWF and FoE collaborated in preparations for the summit, and recognition of shortcomings of coordination among British NGOs in the UNCED process encouraged subsequent cooperation with aid, trade and humanitarian organizations such as Oxfam (Rawcliffe 1998, p. 212; Rootes and Saunders 2007).

Collaboration was not always easy. Following UNCED, the broadly inclusive Real World Coalition sought to promote sustainable development, but its agenda was increasingly formulated as one of social justice and, even before its formal launch in 1996, RSPB, CPRE, the Wildlife Trusts and Greenpeace disengaged. RSPB's director remarked that, although 'common principles across the development and environment organisations' were desirable, she 'just could not sell it' to her members (Rawcliffe 1998, p. 214). Thus an enduring fault line emerged between WWF and FoE, which have become increasingly concerned with social justice issues (Rootes 2006), and organizations such as RSPB and CPRE, which have stuck to a narrower nature protection agenda – RSPB citing the strategic need to maintain its focus upon birds (Rawcliffe 1998, pp. 229–30) and CPRE its need to deploy limited resources in specialized areas where it might have most effect.

NATURE PROTECTION ORGANIZATIONS AND THE ENVIRONMENTAL MOVEMENT

In 1998 almost 20 per cent of Britons claimed membership of one or more environmental organizations (Johnston and Jowell 1999, p. 183), and in

2000, the combined membership of the 11 major environmental organizations listed in the official statistical digest, *Social Trends*, totalled 5.5 million. Of these, most – and all the largest – are nature protection organizations (see Table 2.2).

These large organizations are, however, only part of an extraordinarily rich and complex movement. Some idea of its range and organizational complexity can be gained from entries in the Environment Council's database, *Who's Who in the Environment? (WWE)*(1999). During 1999–2000, all the national environmental movement organizations listed in *WWE* were surveyed. Covering 144 organizations, this is the most comprehensive survey of environmental movement organizations in Britain to date (Rootes and Miller 2000).

Among the concerns listed by environmental organizations in *WWE*, nature protection emerged the clear leader. Wildlife habitats ranked first (41 per cent), followed by farming, fishing and forestry (30 per cent); parks, reserves and landscapes were listed by 13 per cent and flora and fauna by 11 per cent. The built environment was a middle-ranking concern (12 per cent). In response to the survey, the main fields of activity reported were environmental education (62 per cent) and nature conservation (55 per cent).

Brief profiles of the more important nature protection organizations illustrate some of their diversity. Organizations are selected on the basis of their size, reputed influence within and beyond the movement, and/or their importance in practical conservation work.

LEADING NATURE PROTECTION ORGANIZATIONS

The National Trust

> '*for ever, for everyone*' (www.nationaltrust.org.uk, 2 September 2005)

The NT, created to acquire and protect threatened coastline, countryside and buildings, is the largest, best-resourced organization concerned with nature protection. In 2005 it had 3.4 million members and 43 000 volunteers. More than 12 million people visited its pay-for-entry properties in 2004, and an estimated 50 million its other properties. It protects and opens to the public over 300 historic houses, castles and gardens, including entire villages, 49 industrial monuments and mills, over 700 miles of coastline and over 250 000 hectares of countryside, beaches and coastline, as well as diverse collections of artefacts. Its activities include education, and it spends over GBP 160 million a year on conservation. Perhaps indicative of

Table 2.2 Leading British national nature protection and conservation organizations (2005)

	Year founded in UK	Members/donor supporters (thousands)	Income/budget (million GBPs)	Staff size	Local groups	Manage property or reserves	Focus
RSPB	1889	1042	63	1500	175[1]	yes (190)	Birds and their habitat; nature reserves
National Trust	1895	3400	315	>4000	>60[2]	yes	Landscapes and historic buildings
Wildlife Trusts*	1912	560	*	>1500	47	yes (>2200)	Wildlife and habitat, nature reserves
CPRE	1926	60	3	50	200	no	Countryside, land use planning
BTCV	1959	0.365[3]	23	588	no[4]	no[5]	Community conservation projects
WWF-UK	1961	330	39	290	200[6]	not in UK	Conservation, Sustainable Development Overseas
Friends of the Earth (England, Wales & Northern Ireland)	1971	100	9[7]	159	200	no	Environmental protection, social justice
Woodland	1972	147	21	223	no	yes	Woodland

Trust							(preservation and new planting)
Greenpeace UK	1977	221[8]	11[9]	100	102	no	Environmental protection (esp. marine), nuclear
Wildlife & Countryside Link**	1980	35 organizations (including all of above except BTCV)					

Notes:
* Umbrella organization representing autonomous local/regional groups.
** Umbrella organization linking autonomous member organizations.
Staff numbers include part-time staff, where separately declared as such, as 0.5 of full-time.

1 Plus 110 youth groups.
2 Plus >40 property-based groups of 'friends' or 'volunteers'.
3 BTCV has only 365 'members' with voting rights, but according to its website 'supports 140,000 volunteers'.
4 BTCV 'supports 2,225 local community groups' but these are not BTCV groups as such.
5 BTCV assists with management of various projects but does not manage property or reserves of its own.
6 Estimated for 2002.
7 Includes GBP 3.8 million for FoE Trust.
8 Includes 8000 'active supporters' who assist in delivery of Greenpeace campaigns.
9 Figure for 2004; includes GBP 1.9 million for Greenpeace Environmental Trust.

Sources: Haezewindt (2003); annual reports, websites and information supplied by organizations themselves.

its relationship with the public, 'visits and holidays' precede 'conservation, heritage and learning' on its website.

A charity independent of government, NT derives income from membership fees, donations and legacies, and its commercial operations. It is governed by a council of 52, half elected by members, half nominated by other organizations, only half of which are primarily nature protection organizations. Membership subscriptions, NT's largest source of income, amounted to GBP 90 million in 2004–5. Although one million people have been NT members for more than ten years, turnover is high. The benefit of free admission to Trust properties attracts new members, but many do not renew.

Less prominent in campaigns than its resources might suggest, NT is sometimes referred to as 'the sleeping giant of the British environmental movement'. The 2001 appointment of Fiona Reynolds, former Director of CPRE and the Women's Unit at the Cabinet Office, as Executive Director was seen as symbolizing a commitment to a higher, more political profile, but NT remains politically almost invisible. Though claiming to be 'committed to influencing the management of the whole environment, through development of best practice on our own land and also through advocacy of "green" solutions', NT is coy about its advocacy role. Under 'Policy and campaigns', its website (www.nationaltrust.org.uk, 2 September 2005) merely acknowledges the need to influence policy and cites the relevance of its experience. NT's account of its own history is, save for a few cases in which it attempted to preserve its property from threatened development, not a list of campaigns but a record of acquisitions, membership growth and organizational restructuring.

NT's responsibilities for the management and conservation of the properties and land it owns weigh heavy, and, because they are so extensive, NT has the responsibility and resources to be a beacon of best practice. Moreover, its size means that it is routinely consulted on conservation matters and has the capacity to respond. It sees little need to campaign more publicly in order to defend its interests.

The Royal Society for the Protection of Birds

> '*For birds, for people, for ever*' (www.rspb.org.uk, 2 September 2005)

RSPB claims to be the largest voluntary conservation organization in Europe, with over one million members, 12 regional offices and an annual income exceeding GBP 60 million. It manages 160 reserves covering more than 102 000 hectares.

The mix and range of RSPB's campaigns have changed over time. In the late 1970s and early 1980s, it expanded its interests in habitat conservation, began to take a more active stance towards government, and embraced the concept of biodiversity. Recognizing that there was little use putting great effort into conservation projects in the UK while key habitats were being destroyed along migratory routes elsewhere, RSPB was in 1992 instrumental in setting up Birdlife International, which it supports by an annual contribution of over GBP 1 million, as well as giving funds directly to various overseas projects. RSPB has thus evolved from a strictly national bird protection organization into one increasingly concerned with global environmental change. It was keenly involved with the 2002 World Summit on Sustainable Development.

In 2000, RSPB's three broad themes were agriculture, climate change and strengthening wildlife protection laws. In 2003 – in addition to opposing a mooted airport at Cliffe on the North Kent marshes, an important habitat for migratory wading birds – RSPB's headline campaigns included reform of the EC's Common Agricultural Policy, the protection of marine life, support for EC proposals to impose upon polluters the costs of cleanup, and the promotion of solar energy. By 2005, however, RSPB had returned to a narrower focus upon birds.

RSPB seeks to be 'positive and constructive', to provide realistic and well-researched solutions through 'problem solving partnerships' and forging broad alliances. Actively involved in the government's roundtable on sustainable development, RSPB played an important role alongside government in key international environmental forums, and was lead organization in the government's Biodiversity Challenge Group.

RSPB has always been a membership organization, but it is essentially a closed oligarchy, governed by a ruling council elected by a 'paper membership' who provide resources but can only influence policy by their exit. RSPB has been described as a 'third age body' whose members tend to be 'slightly right of centre, over 50 and rather blue stocking' (Conder interview 2000). Recognizing the limitations of this, RSPB has attempted to attract younger members, but fears that a younger constituency might drive away traditional members, particularly if the young should favour more radical campaigning. RSPB is wary of protest, no longer sees its main work as lobbying, and is focused upon practical measures to preserve wild birds and their habitat.

Its size gives RSPB the resources to buy or generate expertise. Its emphasis on being science-driven gives it standing and eases communication with science-based state agencies, which RSPB sees as partners in the pursuit of biodiversity and sustainability. Local groups provide volunteers for practical conservation work, and, although RSPB rarely tries to mobilize members, it encouraged over 300 000 objections against an airport at Cliffe and contributed 1500 protesters to the November 2006 Climate Chaos march in London.

The Wildlife Trusts

> '*an environment richer in wildlife for everyone*' (www.wildlifetrusts.org, 14 August 2006)

The Wildlife Trusts is a partnership of 47 local Wildlife Trusts. With more than 600 000 members, including 100 000 juniors, it is the largest charity exclusively dedicated to conserving all habitats and species. It campaigns to protect wildlife and natural heritage and promotes greater public appreciation of wildlife. Collectively, the Trusts manage more than 2200 reserves covering over 80 000 hectares. The Royal Society of Wildlife Trusts (RSWT), an independent charity, acts as an umbrella group for the local Trusts. Drawing on funds provided by the national lottery, a major waste company and a construction company, it provides more than GBP 20 million annually in grants to support local, regional and national projects. Because the Wildlife Trusts is decentralized, its character is best understood by examining one member of its network of regional Trusts.

Lincolnshire Wildlife Trust (LWT) has 22 000 members and 45–50 staff. Active volunteers assist with management of its reserves, but it is not a grass-roots organization; its agenda is set by senior officers, though thematically focused teams enable volunteers to have some input into policy (LWT interview 2003).

LWT rarely becomes directly involved in local planning issues but sometimes provides advice to supporters in local disputes. In such cases, LWT often feels constrained to stick to scientific evidence, even if this means failing to support local campaigners. Yet, in a modest way, confronted with unwelcome developments, it plays a 'radical flank' role for more constrained statutory consultees, compared with whom LWT has 'less power but more options' (LWT interview 2003).

LWT does not employ radical tactics, but it sometimes tries to mobilize members to write to MPs. It sees the Environment Agency as a partner and enjoys an increasingly satisfactory relationship with it. Familiar with the criticism that it focuses narrowly on wildlife, LWT tries 'hard to look at projects holistically rather than just seeing the wildlife benefit' 'because we understand the . . . need . . . to look at the wider . . . economic and social benefits' (LWT interview 2003).

WWF-UK

> '*for a living planet*' (wwf.org.uk, 2 September 2005)

By the end of the 1970s, WWF had changed from a small fundraising organization focused on endangered species and habitat destruction into an international institution concerned with conservation issues more generally (see Chapter 1). In 1990, a new mission and strategy reiterated WWF-UK's commitment to nature conservation and classified its work as: the preservation of biological diversity; promoting sustainable use of resources; and reducing wasteful consumption and pollution. It also aimed to decentralize decision making and increase cooperation with local people in areas where it has projects. Its five-year strategic plan (2000) described its mission as: 'action to protect the environment for the benefit of people and nature'. WWF has thus tried to strike a balance between protecting ecosystems and meeting economic needs of local communities. In so doing, it has incurred the wrath of some more strictly preservationist wildlife and animal welfare groups.

WWF has no reserves in the UK; approximately 70 per cent of its expenditures are grants for projects abroad. In Britain, WWF was active in the 1990s in campaigns to preserve peatlands, combat transport pollution and protect biodiversity. It promoted sustainable forestry and ethical investment, sponsored a conference on poverty and the environment, and partnered Channel 4, Oxfam and Voluntary Service Overseas in a North–South television project to mark the millennium by linking viewers in eight countries on the Greenwich meridian.

WWF-UK was initially a science-led organization but, as its campaigning broadened, by the mid-1990s staff were being 'appointed less on the basis of scientific merit and more in terms of policy familiarity' (Szerszynski 1995, p. 35). Another indicator of change was its appointment of Jonathon Porritt, former Director of FoE and Green Party candidate, as a trustee. Moreover, WWF assisted other, more radical groups, donating money towards the purchase of Greenpeace's first *Rainbow Warrior* and funding anti-road protests (Rawcliffe 1998, p. 138), as well as claiming to have 'nurtured hundreds of smaller conservation organisations' (WWF-UK 2001, p. 2).

WWF has collaborated with other British organizations on a variety of campaigns, working closely with RSPB on the EU Water Framework and Habitats Directives, lobbying the European Parliament against the advice of the Commission, which had been pressured by industry not to include strong environmental protection measures. Despite occasional differences, WWF has enjoyed excellent standing with government, was invited to be part of the official British delegation to the 1992 Earth Summit, and was described by Michael Meacher, UK Environment Minister (1997–2003), as 'his alternative civil service' (White interview 2000).

WWF acknowledges its similarities with RSPB but sees RSPB as

> rather too civil servant-like, . . . staid, . . . traditional. Although we're seen as being responsible, moderate, conservative with a small 'c', challenging but nonthreatening, we are still more able to . . . I won't say bite, but certainly snap a bit . . .. But . . . we're hugely respected. All our research shows that WWF is

> respected because we're scientifically based and . . . an organization whose information can be trusted. (White interview 2000)

Like RSPB, WWF had been nervous of alienating its supporters, whom it presumed to be narrowly interested in nature protection; however, following the appointment of a new director in 1998, it undertook a 'corporate review', which included a survey of audience perceptions. The results reassured WWF that it should be covering a wide range of issues.

> If you put a continuum of environmentalism from . . . animal welfare at one end to full blown sustainable . . . development at the other, and said 'where are WWF on that continuum?', we thought we were much towards the conservation end. [Our supporters] think we're . . . in the middle and want us to move even more towards the development . . . end. (White interview 2000)

Since Rio, WWF has worked to form a common agenda among groups working on development and environment. In 1993, it collaborated with Action Aid, CAFOD (Catholic Agency for Overseas Development), Oxfam, Christian Aid, Save the Children and FoE to produce a report calling for fundamental changes in foreign and domestic aid policy (Rawcliffe 1998, p. 217). WWF sees embracing sustainable development as a logical outcome of its analysis of the means of promoting its original objectives. Although WWF-UK spokesmen in 2000 described conservation of species as 'still the core of our business', in 2000–2002 it spent less than one-sixth of its grants budget on 'species' (WWF-UK Financial Report, 2001–2002). By contrast, it spent about one-third of its grants budget on 'levers for long term change' (a portfolio including education and information), an International Development Policy programme in conjunction with CARE International, and preparations for the 2002 World Summit on Sustainable Development. The major growth in grant expenditures – from GBP 660 000 in 2000–2001 to GBP 3.6 million in 2004–2005 – has been on 'freshwater', a portfolio of projects, mostly in less developed countries but including the UK, aimed at rejuvenating rivers, bringing people better access to clean water and improving fishing. In 2003–2004, just 8 per cent of all WWF's charitable expenditure was on 'species', and it had launched major campaigns on chemicals and health and for sustainable housing (WWF-UK Annual Reviews, 2003–2004, 2004–2005). It also highlights its partnerships with aid charities and the Department for International Development (DfID) to tackle the 'greatest threats to the environment: poverty and overconsumption' (Annual Review, 2003–2004, p. 3). Climate change has brought new urgency and a somewhat different focus. 'WWF views climate change as the single greatest threat facing the planet and has been saying so for 10 years. . . . we have all joined the list of endangered species' (WWF-UK Annual Report, 2004–2005, p. 3).

WWF-UK has increasingly formed partnerships with corporations. From 2000 to 2005, the fastest-rising source of its income was corporate donations and sponsorships. A mere 0.25 per cent of income in 2000–2001, these constituted 15 per cent in 2004–5, exceeding income from aid agencies and government grants. Castigated for accepting commercial donations, WWF insists that partnerships with companies do not inhibit it from criticizing its partners but provide opportunities 'for dialogue and progress' (WWF-UK Report and Financial Statements, 2003–2004, p. 7).

Campaign to Protect Rural England

> *'people who care passionately about our countryside and campaign for it to be protected and enhanced for the benefit of everyone'* (www.cpre.org.uk, 28 October 2006)

CPRE is a registered charity, operating as a network. Over 200 district groups, a branch in every county and a national office make CPRE a powerful combination of effective local action and strong national campaigning. The national organization has 50 salaried staff; a small number work at regional level servicing nine regional groups.

As well as highlighting problems and threats to the countryside, CPRE conducts research, canvasses opinion and advocates solutions. 'Through reasoned argument, we seek to influence decision makers at every level . . . We also try to influence opinion formers at every level – from local weekly newspapers to national broadcasters. We often work in partnership with other bodies at local and national level' (www.cpre.org.uk, 19 September 2003). CPRE works against: unnecessary building on greenfields; road, airport and port developments that destroy the countryside; degradation of landscapes and habitats by intensive farming; and pollution – including light and noise – in rural areas. CPRE encourages: urban regeneration; protection of quiet country lanes; alternatives to road building; locally grown and marketed foods; and sustainable management of woods, forests and farmland. Concern with sustainable development and to protect rural areas from population influx leads CPRE to campaign to improve the quality of life in towns and cities (www.cpre.org.uk, 19 September 2003).

In the early 1980s, CPRE became a more publicly visible campaigning organization, adopting a broader environmental critique and more sophisticated and outspoken methods of working that contrasted with 'the old ways of quiet words in decision makers' ears and gentle reminders over civilized lunches'. To long-established parliamentary lobbying it added hard-edged media campaigns. The membership was centralized, allowing expansion of its London office into a professional campaigning body (Szerszynski 1995, p. 19). This new style was exemplified when CPRE became a principal objector at the Sizewell Nuclear Inquiry (Rawcliffe 1998, p. 26). Since 2004, arguing for the necessity of strategic planning to protect landscapes and quality of life, CPRE has campaigned against government proposals to relax planning constraints and remove rights of public consultation and against massive expansion of housing in eastern England. Yet CPRE's campaigning scarcely marks it as an anti-establishment organization; its patron is Her Majesty the Queen.

CPRE is a very focused, successful lobbying organization with insider status and strong channels of communication to policy makers. 'Ministers never refuse to meet CPRE' (Conder interview 2000). Despite its decentralized network structure, CPRE is essentially officer-led. National staff recommend decisions to the Executive Committee, which rarely opposes them.

CPRE has been well served by a succession of able, high-profile directors, beginning with Robin Grove-White (1981–87), who later joined the board of Greenpeace UK. 'Robin always used to characterize us as a guerrilla group. He said "be flexible. . . . Don't pretend you're an expert. . . . just pick out the one or two things that are going to make the big issue – make the biggest change"' (Conder interview 2000). Fiona Reynolds, who served from 1991 to 1998, was a key player in the drive to bring green issues from the margins to the mainstream. Reportedly a friend of Tony Blair (Rawcliffe 1998, p. 94), she left CPRE for the Cabinet Office, and later became Director of the NT. The skills of its directors and its connections have enabled CPRE to punch above its weight; civil servants often treat CPRE staff as allies and speak to them 'professional to professional' as people mutually committed to making the planning system work. The high regard in which CPRE national officers are held does not, however, necessarily extend to local branches, whose members are often accused of obstructing all development (Murdoch 2003, n. 6). Yet CPRE relies on its branch structure to stimulate grass-roots activity to effect change at local level.

> the thing that really distinguishes CPRE . . . is the national–local strength. You cannot deliver something like planning policy just at national level. You have got to have branches scrutinizing local plans and structure plans and getting involved at local level. (Fiona Reynolds 1994, quoted in Rawcliffe 1998, p. 91)

As Murdoch (2003, p. 14) puts it:

> CPRE's national office has been successful at disseminating a professional approach to environmental campaigning throughout the organization . . . In broad terms, this approach tends to support national policy perspectives. Yet, CPRE cannot go too far in this process of 'nationalization' for . . . national perspectives

> need to be interpreted in the light of local circumstances . . . Thus, . . . the 'national' and the 'local' need to be constantly calibrated against one another . . .

Indeed, consultants commissioned to advise on membership recruitment in 1995 reported that prospective members were suspicious of national institutions and recommended that CPRE present itself as 'a local body which has strong national backup' (Conder interview 2000).

Despite these strengths, membership has scarcely risen in recent years, and in 2000, members' average age was 63, with almost half living in rural areas. Members are well informed and used to managing things and taking responsibility. According to one consultant, 'on the one hand your average CPRE member is the most establishment of any group, but on the other hand, of all the groups I surveyed, they were the most suspicious of authority'. Nevertheless, CPRE members 'don't like the word "activist". They hate it. It's something to do with Greenpeace and CND [Campaign for Nuclear Disarmament] . . . They didn't like the word "campaign" ten years ago. . . . But . . . they're now campaigners' (Conder interview 2000).

CPRE's relatively small size may encourage cooperation with others. Its closest allies are its sister organizations in Scotland and Wales, but it is also a member of several formal and informal alliances. During the 1990s, it collaborated in campaigns with a broad range of organizations, including RSPB, WWF and FoE, participated in the government's Urban Task Force and roundtable on Sustainable Development, and chaired a government committee on rural transport policy. Very active in the EEB in the 1990s, CPRE has since largely forsaken regular alliances with other European organizations in favour of temporary alliances for clear campaign goals.

The Woodland Trust

> '*the UK's leading conservation charity dedicated to protection of our native woodland heritage*' (www.woodlandtrust.org.uk, 23 August 2007)

The Woodland Trust (WT) protects over 1100 sites covering 19 000 hectares, ranging from nationally and internationally important sites to small urban and village woods. Nearly 350 of its sites contain ancient woodland, and it protects over 110 Sites of Special Scientific Interest. The WT has also created 3200 hectares of new native woodland (www.woodlandtrust.org.uk, 28 October 2006). The fastest-growing major nature protection organization, it is only nominally a membership organization; its governing body is appointed by invitation, not elected. Two-thirds of its annual income comes from supporters and the public as bequests, membership subscriptions and donations; grants, some tied to particular conservation projects, account for about 15 per cent.

To maintain its high profile, some 15 per cent of the WT's expenditure is on fundraising, appeals and membership. Although focused determinedly upon woodland, it has joined campaigns with others and encourages green energy.

Friends of the Earth

> '*making life better for people by inspiring solutions to environmental problems*' (www.foe.co.uk, 28 October 2006)

Determined to be free to take political positions and avoid the constraints of charitable status, FoE was set up in England in 1971 as a limited company. It became a grass-roots, mass membership organization almost by accident. As the central organization grew and was organized into specialized campaign departments, local groups demanded greater say, and in 1981 they, in alliance with national office staff, challenged the leadership (Lamb 1996, pp. 97–9). The resolution of this dispute shaped FoE's constitutional structure and identity, and although active members of local groups comprise only a small minority of its 100 000 members, FoE has become a notably decentralized organization. By 2000, ten of 17 members of its board of directors were elected through local groups. Although its Local Groups Conference is more an opportunity for national officers to educate local groups than vice versa, local activists are often consulted where their expertise is relevant. Local groups have remained largely autonomous, though many are networked into national campaigns coordinated by national officers. Although FoE officers attempt to set campaign priorities based upon expert, science-based advice, they are acutely aware of members' local and often scientifically questionable concerns. FoE's campaign agendas are, consequently, products of compromise (FoE interview 2003).

Generally considered the vanguard of the new environmentalism and sharply distinct from traditional nature protection organizations, FoE was, in fact, 'the first environmental pressure group in the UK to start campaigns for whales, endangered species and tropical rainforests, and against acid rain, ozone depletion and climate change' (www.foe.co.uk, 25 March 2005). From the mid-1980s, FoE broadened its portfolio to include such issues as economy and health, and became increasingly involved in campaigns to promote human rights and economic development in the global South. This reflected the views of members and supporters who, FoE's research suggested, were often members or supporters of groups such as Amnesty International or Oxfam, but not necessarily of other environmental groups (FoE interview 2003; cf. Jordan and Maloney 1997). But according to its director, the broadening of its agenda and range of contacts in government was also a response to past success on classic environmental issues (Juniper interview 2000).

Although FoE has sought to engage government agencies, it does not seek ongoing partnerships with them in implementing environmental policy. It regards itself instead as 'a campaigning organisation' whose job 'is to raise the standards' that others are charged to implement (FoE interview 2003).

FoE is at the core of the network of British environmental organizations. Although linked to a wide variety of organizations more exclusively focused upon nature protection, its considerable interaction with other groups increasingly extends beyond environmental organizations to include aid and development charities and organized labour. These linkages help set FoE's agenda, which is also increasingly influenced by links through FoE International, a federation of autonomous national organizations from over 70 countries from both North and South (Doherty 2006). Such links have also encouraged its embrace of domestic social justice issues. Following the example of FoE Scotland, FoE (England, Wales and Northern Ireland) embarked upon a community development initiative in an economically deprived, heavily polluted area of northeast England, and in 2003 it adopted a five-year action plan to integrate sustainability and biodiversity with environmental justice.

For some members, this was controversial. The 'burning question' at the 2003 local groups conference was whether this new focus upon environmental justice and 'tackling the corporates' placed at risk campaigns on themes such as forests and biodiversity. Officers assured delegates that those issues 'would remain key to FoE, albeit in the context of justice issues' (James 2003, p. 16).

Greenpeace

> '*For a positive change through action. We defend the natural world and promote peace*' (http://greenpeace.org.uk/about, 18 June 2007)

Greenpeace UK emerged when activists who were frustrated by FoE's preoccupation with arguing its case at the public inquiry into the nuclear operations at Windscale sought a vehicle for direct action. Despite a shaky start, Greenpeace UK became a singularly successful protest organization, spectacularly adroit at exploiting media attention to put pressure on governments and corporations.

Though not generally considered a nature protection organization, Greenpeace has a long history of campaigning on such issues both in Britain and transnationally. Indeed, with its iconic campaigns against whaling and sealing, Greenpeace is perhaps the best-known advocate of marine conservation, and its campaign priorities in 2005–6 were to stop climate change by choosing clean energy, defend oceans and save ancient forests (www.greenpeace.org.uk, 1 November 2006). Its domestic campaigns oppose nuclear energy and GMOs on grounds of both nature protection and public safety.

Greenpeace is not a mass membership organization, and its structure is designed to ensure the autonomy of its governing elite. Though famous for acting alone and prizing its autonomy, it has cooperated in *ad hoc* campaigns with FoE and WWF, and with direct action groups opposing GMOs. The frequency and scope of these collaborations appear to have increased. Senior Greenpeace officers meet regularly with leaders of other environmental organizations, and specialist campaigners frequently contact their counterparts in other groups. However, although Greenpeace has readily lent its name to joint press releases with other groups, it has been less active in joint campaigns and has stood aloof from protracted involvement in elaborate discussions of campaign agenda (Lamb 1996, p. 187).

Because it envisages the fundamental reinvention of business to ensure sustainability, Greenpeace has offered constructive advice even to its famous adversaries, Shell and BP, on their shift toward renewable energy, and it collaborated with an electricity utility to establish the UK's first major offshore wind farm. Greenpeace appointed its first Scientific Director in 1989, and its commitment to research has earned it increasing respect from government and industry. Nevertheless, Greenpeace remains primarily a campaigning organization committed to non-violent direct action and to 'bearing witness', and it is an influential member of the nature protection network.

British Trust for Conservation Volunteers

> '*to create a more sustainable future by inspiring people and improving places*' (www.btcv.org.uk, 6 September 2005)

Many nature protection organizations do not engage in high-profile campaigning, recruiting and fundraising, but instead undertake practical conservation work. Many of these are local, but, among national organizations, BTCV stands out. BTCV originated in the Conservation Corps, which was established in 1959 to involve volunteers in practical conservation work (Evans 1997, pp. 90–91). During the 1980s, BTCV's focus shifted to include the urban environment and community action. Working on many projects, with funding from a wide range of foundations, BTCV was the largest recipient of funding in the government's Millennium Volunteers programme.

BTCV's vision is 'a better environment where people are valued, included and involved' (www.btcv.org.uk, 6 September 2005). In 2005, it had nine regional offices in England, 134 local offices, 514 full-time and 148 part-time employees, and 300 unpaid volunteer officers supporting volunteers taking practical action to improve their urban and rural environments. The main sources of its GBP 23 million income were grants, government training schemes, conservation projects and donations. According to its membership secretary (personal communication, 18 September 2006), 'BTCV works with over 340,000 volunteers, 4,500 community groups in over 20,000 places across the whole of the UK'.

BTCV may, as it claims, be recognized as 'a key player in the delivery of programmes that deliver biodiversity and help people to care for their environment' (www.btcv.org.uk, 6 September 2005), but in our 2000 survey no national environmental organization named BTCV among the most important groups with which they collaborated. Consistent with its focus upon practical conservation and education, BTCV spends 80 per cent of its income on charitable activities and conservation, and just 1.4 per cent on fundraising and publicity, a much lower proportion than other, better-known and better-networked organizations.

NETWORKS

The environmental movement is a network of organizations and activists engaged in collective action to protect the environment. Within that, nature protection organizations might be considered a distinct sector, even a distinct movement. The only systematic survey of the British environmental movement in the 1980s concluded that organizations tended to have network links either with a few 'core' organizations, or with others in their own thematic sector (Lowe and Goyder 1983). That, however, was before the new campaigning organizations consolidated their positions. Our survey (Rootes and Miller 2000) revealed no clear separation between nature protection and general environmental organizations, even if the former tend to perform more specialized functions and to have narrower thematic concerns, while the latter, especially FoE, play key networking roles.

We asked the organizations we surveyed which were the most important groups with which they regularly cooperated. Respondents nominated 57 different environmental organizations, as well as an assortment of others. Table 2.3 reports the numbers of nominations received by kind and, within

Table 2.3 British environmental organizations and their networks: organizations nominated as most important collaborators by kind of nominator

Nominated organizations	Nominations received by kind of nominating organization	
	Environmental movement organizations (N = 58)	Animal welfare organizations (N = 6)
Environmental movement organizations (EMOs) (total)	128	5
FoE	18	0
WWF	10	1
Greenpeace	9	0
Wildlife and Countryside Link	7	1
CPRE	6	1
RSPB	6	0
Soil Association	4	1
Transport 2000	4	0
Wildlife Trusts	4	0
New Economics Foundation	3	0
National Trust	3	0
Other EMOs	54	1
Animal welfare organizations	4	11
Government (total)	37	1
State agencies	18	1
Local government	10	0
Environment department	6	0
Community groups	18	0
Business	10	0
Human rights/development organizations	10	0
Academic/education	6	0
Professional organizations	5	0
Farming groups	4	0

Source: TEA survey (Rootes and Miller 2000).

each category, the number of nominations received by the organizations most frequently named.

FoE received most nominations, followed by WWF, Greenpeace, Wildlife and Countryside Link, CPRE and RSPB. The Wildlife Trusts were nominated only four times, NT only three times, and groups concerned with the conservation of buildings not at all. Animal welfare organizations were scarcely less marginal. State agencies, however, were mentioned more often than all but the leading environmental movement organizations.

Analysis of who nominated whom as being among their five most important collaborators reveals a degree of specialization in the network. Although FoE, Greenpeace, WWF, Wildlife and Countryside Link and RSPB were central, a large number of smaller organizations were only loosely linked to the core or to one another. Secondary 'organic' and 'transport' networks emerged, but direct action groups such as Earth First! appeared marginal, and animal welfare groups especially so.

Respondents were also asked to indicate with which of nine major UK and European environmental organizations they had exchanged information and/or expertise and, second, cooperated in campaigns during the preceding 12 months. Again, FoE, WWF and Greenpeace appeared central, with CPRE also often named. No other organization was listed as a partner more than rarely. Not surprisingly, collaboration in campaigns was less common. Here FoE led WWF, Greenpeace and CPRE by some distance.

Of the six organizations that Lowe and Goyder listed as the core of the movement – CPRE, FoE, RSPB, NT, CoEnCo (now the Environment Council) and the Civic Trust – only the first three appeared to be at or near the core of the network in 2000. NT appeared marginal, and the latter two did not appear at all. Both Greenpeace, marginal in the early 1980s, and WWF, then identified as a non-core species protection organization, have moved to positions more central to the network than RSPB and CPRE. In a movement in which nature protection is still the predominant concern, the distinction between broadly environmental and narrowly nature protection organizations has thus been eroded.

Centrality to the network is not, however, an infallible indicator of influence upon public policy or of importance to practical nature protection. Large organizations such as NT and the Wildlife Trusts, though marginal to the network, are influential in their own right. Their size gives them opportunities of direct access to civil servants and ministers not enjoyed by smaller organizations acting individually, and they play at best modest roles in broad campaign networks.

CONCLUSION

Nature protection organizations in England are diverse and variously networked to other organizations in their own and cognate issue domains. Wildlife and Countryside Link (www.wcl.org.uk), whose 36 members include all the major nature protection organizations except BTCV, has since 1980 acted as an umbrella organization to coordinate their lobbying and campaigning, but informal, *ad hoc* and bilateral cooperation has continued to grow. Although some division of labour continues, especially among the smaller organizations, collaborative campaigns are now the norm, and the range of issues they embrace increasingly extends beyond nature protection to human well-being and social justice. It is thus significant that FoE, despite being a relatively small organization, should appear central to the environmental network, for FoE has an exceptionally broad remit, grass-roots base and strong international links, and has proceeded furthest in the embrace of social justice.

The network is the emergent organizational form of the movement, and there are numerous specialized networks. Airport Watch links local campaigns that bring together diverse coalitions struggling against airport expansion (Saunders 2005). Roadblock! (www.roadblock.org.uk) performs a similar function for campaigners against new and expanded roads, and there is an embryonic network of anti-incinerator campaigners. All these campaigns transcend the environmental/nature protection distinction, and it is noteworthy that it is generally FoE rather than the larger, better-resourced, unambiguously nature protection organizations that has taken the lead. If the latter are growing when FoE and Greenpeace are not, they are for the most part principally managers and custodians of their growing numbers of reserves and estates. Only occasionally do they initiate campaigns.

Many smaller nature protection organizations are relatively specialized, and they are more likely than the small number of generalist environmental campaigning organizations to have relatively specialized networks. Their size also affects their involvement in international networks; because their resources are limited and the foci of their agenda local or national, they are more likely to develop temporary alliances with like-minded organizations in other countries than to invest in formal and permanent transnational alliances.

The increasingly transnational agenda of environmentalism affects how conservation organizations see themselves and justify their positions. FoE and WWF now employ the concept of sustainable development to promote a reformist agenda in which the environment cannot be isolated from a wider range of human concerns (Rootes 2006). Together they have reframed the agenda of the movement; they and several other environmental organizations, including RSPB and Greenpeace, signed up to Make Poverty History and/or the Trade Justice Movement (Rootes and Saunders 2007). Others followed only cautiously – or not at all – but they nevertheless operate in a milieu where the conventional wisdom holds that nature protection has an ineradicably human dimension. If the global justice movement overlaps with the environmental movement rather than simply transcending it, there are signs of reciprocation. The 'Stop Climate Chaos' (SCC) coalition, launched on 1 September 2005 (www.stopclimatechaos.org), includes a number of aid and development charities as well as most of the larger environmental and nature protection organizations.

The receptivity of narrowly nature protection organizations to the agenda-setting efforts of more activist, campaigning organizations is only partly a tribute to the energy, increased professionalism and scientific credibility of the latter. It also reflects broader changes in a British society that has become less deferential and more participatory as it has become better educated and more affluent, changes reflected in increased rates of participation in demonstrations and consumer boycotts more than in any consistent rise of direct action. Even more striking is the increasing approval accorded to those who take principled action even where it is beyond the law. Thus citizens would not condemn and courts would not convict activists who, in the name of environmental protection, destroyed GM crops (Rootes 2003).

Nature protection organizations have not leapt aboard the activist bandwagon in response to these trends, but they have become less nervous about being judged guilty by association. The relaxation of charity law since 1995 has helped; registered charities no longer fear that campaigning publicly for policy changes will jeopardize their charitable status. Emboldened by the results of surveys of their supporters, they have become more audacious in extending their agenda beyond traditional core issues. All these changes have facilitated alliance building across the broad spectrum of the movement with the result that nature protection organizations now sit relatively comfortably in a complex web of organizations whose activities range all the way from lobbying and research to campaigning and practical conservation.

Challenges remain. The perennial threats of economic development to the natural environment are exacerbated as governments become persuaded of the urgency of infrastructure improvement and house building. Since the 1990s, developers have repeatedly demanded – and governments have several times proposed – revisions of planning laws to remove obstructions to speedy decisions and development, even in areas of outstanding natural beauty or special scientific interest. In order more effectively to resist, nature protection organizations have had to propose practicable alternatives, and so have been drawn closer to organizations for which sustainable development has been more central. Demands for new housing, and megaprojects such as the Olympic Games complex, with its promise of social and economic regeneration of deprived parts of London, or new nuclear power stations to maintain energy supplies in a post-carbon Britain, all raise social justice issues that nature protection organizations ignore at their peril. Climate change and sustainable development thus appear not as marginal issues, but as the unifying frames by which nature protection organizations might best hope to retain influence.

NOTES

1. This chapter is partly based on the TEA (Transformation of Environmental Activism) project (EC Directorate General Research contract no.: ENV4-CT97-0514) (www.kent.ac.uk/sspssr/TEA.html). The profiles of RSPB, WWF, CPRE and of FoE and Greenpeace draw upon dossiers assembled by Debbie Adams and Ben Seel respectively. Those of FoE and WWF draw upon Rootes (2006) and of CPRE upon Rootes (2005). I am indebted to Debbie Adams, Sandy Miller and Ben Seel for assistance with collection and/or analysis of data in the course of that project, to Julie Barnett for permission to use material from interviews she conducted in 2003 as part of our project 'Working with Special Interest Groups' contracted by the Environment Agency, and to Clare Saunders and Neil Carter for comments.
2. England, by far the largest and most populous country of the UK, is juridically, politically and socially distinct from Scotland, Northern Ireland and Wales. Because the legislative contexts and constellations of nature protection organizations differ from one country to another, the following account deals with England alone, even though some organizations also operate in other parts of the UK.
3. An organization's self-reported membership numbers are only one, variably reliable, indicator of its vitality and influence. There is no audited register, and 'member' means different things to different groups. Some count all donors and volunteers as members; others restrict 'membership' to formal subscribers. Organizations that provide services are more likely precisely to enumerate their members because members must pay dues to receive benefits, whereas advocacy organizations may be quite cavalier about 'membership' because whatever benefits they supply are not usually confined to formal subscribers. Moreover, the size of an organization's membership generally reflects the effort and resources devoted to recruitment, and both advocacy groups and practical conservation organizations have, from the 1990s, tended to concentrate resources on their core, substantive activities rather than on chasing ever larger numbers of 'paper members'.

REFERENCES

Doherty, Brian (2006), 'Friends of the Earth International: Negotiating a Transnational Identity', *Environmental Politics*, **15** (5), 860–80.

Environment Council (1999), *Who's Who in the Environment?*, London: The Environment Council.

Evans, David (1997), *A History of Nature Conservation in Britain*, 2nd edn, London: Routledge.
Garner, Robert (2000), *Environmental Politics: Britain, Europe and the Global Environment*, 2nd edn, Basingstoke, UK: Macmillan; New York: St Martin's Press.
Haezewindt, Paul (2003), 'Investing in Each Other and the Community: The Role of Social Capital', in Carol Summerfield and Penny Babb (eds), *Social Trends*, **33**, London: The Stationery Office (for Office of National Statistics), pp. 19–27.
James, Myra (2003), 'Local Groups, Conference 2003', *FoE Yorkshire & Humber and North East Newsletter*, Winter, p. 16.
Johnston, M. and R. Jowell (1999), 'Social Capital and the Social Fabric', in R. Jowell, J. Curtice, A. Park, K. Thompson, with L. Jarvis, C. Bromley and N. Stratford (eds), *British Social Attitudes: the 16th Report*, Aldershot, UK: Ashgate, pp. 179–200.
Jordan, Grant and William Maloney (1997), *The Protest Business? Mobilizing Campaign Groups*, Manchester: Manchester University Press.
Lamb, Robert (1996), *Promising the Earth*, London and New York: Routledge.
Lowe, Phillip and Jane Goyder (1983), *Environmental Groups in British Politics*, London: Allen and Unwin.
Murdoch, Jonathon (2003), 'Mediating the "National" and the "Local" in the Environmental Policy Process: A Case Study of the CPRE', paper presented to ESRC Democracy and Participation conference, University of Essex, Colchester, January.
Rawcliffe, Peter (1998), *Environmental Pressure Groups in Transition*, Manchester: Manchester University Press.
Rootes, Christopher (2003), 'The Resurgence of Protest and the Revitalization of British Democracy', in Pedro Ibarra (ed.), *Social Movements and Democracy*, New York: Palgrave Macmillan, pp. 137–68.
Rootes, Christopher (2005), 'A Limited Transnationalization?: The British Environmental Movement', in Donatella della Porta and Sidney Tarrow (eds), *Transnational Protest and Global Activism*, Lanham, MD: Rowman and Littlefield, pp. 21–43.
Rootes, Christopher (2006), 'Facing South? British Environmental Movement Organisations and the Challenge of Globalisation', *Environmental Politics*, **15** (5), 768–86.
Rootes, Christopher and Alexander Miller (2000), 'The British Environmental Movement: Organisational Field and Network of Organisations', paper presented at ECPR Joint Sessions, Copenhagen, 14–19 April.
Rootes, Christopher and Clare Saunders (2007), 'The Global Justice Movement in Britain', in D. della Porta (ed.), *The Global Justice Movement*, Boulder, CO: Paradigm.
Saunders, Clare (2005), 'Collaboration, Competition and Conflict: Social Movement and Interaction Dynamics of London's Environmental Movement', PhD thesis, School of Social Policy, Sociology and Social Research, University of Kent at Canterbury.
Szerszynski, Bron (1995), 'Framing and Communicating Environmental Issues Part 2, Entering the Stage: Strategies of Environmental Communication in the UK', Report to Commission of the European Communities, DG XII, SEER PL 210943.

Interviews

Conder interview, David Conder, CPRE, 8 June 2000.
FoE Senior Local Campaigns Officer interview, 2003.
LWT (Lincolnshire Wildlife Trust) interview, 2003.
Juniper interview, Tony Juniper, FoE, March 2000.
White interview, Stuart White, WWF-UK, 26 July 2000.

3. Nature protection associations in France

Cécilia Claeys-Mekdade and Marie Jacqué

The first French law dealing specifically with nature protection dates only to July 1976, but its adoption reflected efforts by organizations with nature protection goals extending back for more than a century. Born during the nineteenth century, French nature protection was characterized for many years by an elite constituency and a view of nature centred around natural history research, aesthetic enjoyment of nature, and nature's economic utility. It pursued nature conservation in the context of a society characterized by centralized state control of regional development. After the Second World War, associations developed in earlier periods faced a new situation, characterized by a growing middle class and the emergence of an environmental movement and new competitors. They adapted by modifying their structures and forms of action and increased their memberships, but they remained focused on nature conservation campaigns based on scientific knowledge. More recently organizations with nature protection goals have professionalized, increased their skills and know-how, and become recognized spokesmen for nature in the public sphere. They have also become direct and indirect participants in the implementation of nature protection laws, management of nature protection areas, and environmental education.

This chapter presents a chronological analysis of nature protection efforts in France. It emphasizes three main perspectives: (1) the impact of the social class of nature protection advocates on the goals and structure of nature protection efforts; (2) the relationship between associations that promote nature protection and the state; and (3) the key role of science, experts and professionalization. The theme of social class is characteristic of French theoretical work through the early 1990s. Bourdieu's school (Chamboredon 1985; Kalaora 1988), Touraine's team (Touraine et al. 1980), and Mendras's students (Picon 1979; Aspe 1991), for example, all point to the role of the rising middle classes in the redefinition of nature's symbolic meaning and uses after the Second World War. The roles of experts and scientists were seen in the context of class conflicts over nature.

More recently, the widely known and cited 'sociology of translation' proposed by Bruno Latour and Michel Callon subordinates the social class approach to a microsociological view focusing on individuals' skills and actors' networks (Callon et al. 2001; Latour 1999). It suggests a focus on networks of nature protection organizations and their relationship to the state.

This chapter first summarizes the origins of French nature protection in the mid-nineteenth century. We then examine the profound transformations in the nature protection local organizations between 1960 and 1980, which reflected the structural and ideological transformations of French society as a whole. The third section presents an analysis of the contemporary nature protection organizations and networks, and their relation to environmental organizations and networks.

NATURE PROTECTION IN FRANCE BEFORE 1960

1850–1914: the Meeting between Scientific and Aesthetic Views of Nature

Today's nature protection associations are the heirs of late nineteenth-century learned societies, the first French organizations to concern themselves with nature protection. These societies emphasized a scientific approach to nature – natural history – which remains a part of their approach today. However, science alone did not drive the early nature protection movement. The nature protection associations also arose out of a combination of the economic, political and ideological changes that French society was experiencing during the late nineteenth century.

On 10 February 1854, Isidore Geoffroy Saint Hilaire, a member of the French Academy of Science and Professor at the Muséum National d'Histoire Naturelle, founded the Société Zoologique d'Acclimatation (SZA) [Zoological Acclimatization Society], the first learned society to emphasize collection of specimens of various species. By 1856, the SZA had 1200 members. It was composed of recognized scientists, naturalist travellers, eminent personalities, artists and politicians (Raffin and Ricou 1985).

Learned societies were also founded in provincial areas. Like the SZA, they centred their efforts on the development of a scientific approach to nature and the dissemination of scientific knowledge about it. The amateur members of these societies – including eminent local citizens such as pharmacists, primary school teachers, doctors and members of the clergy – were the first advocates of nature protection. 'Amateur naturalists identify flora of their canton, experienced amateurs identify flora of the *Départements* or regions, and the professional botanists in the capital centralize this information and deduce from it the areas of distribution of species, genera and families' (Drouin 1991, p. 66, authors' translation). These societies concerned themselves with nature protection, but they did not aim solely at protecting nature or focus on France alone. Instead, one of their major goals was to bring back from the colonies birds, mammals and plants that might have economic or ornamental use, introduce them into France, and study their adaptation to France. Many of these animals and plants can be seen in French gardens and zoos today.

During the nineteenth century, the learned societies were centred around Muséums d'Histoire Naturelle in cities such as Marseille, Bordeaux, Nantes, Lyon and Grenoble. The museums served as the headquarters of the societies, gathered together scientists' and travellers' private collections, and made them available to the public. While the learned natural history societies were dominant in the nature protection initiatives of the late nineteenth and early twentieth centuries, they found it difficult to gain popular recognition of their work and mass dissemination of their ideas, and their memberships remained very small. In 1909, the SZA had only 2500 members, whereas its Swiss equivalent had 30 000.

The growth of the learned societies was closely intertwined with economic and political developments. During this period, the power of the bourgeoisie, and in particular the intellectual bourgeoisie – France's intellectual and artistic elite – was rising. On the political side, the Third Republic (1871–1914) was seeking legitimacy through government activism, which was seen as a way to unify the nation. Abroad, it sought to demonstrate the power of France by showing the wealth that it could draw from its colonies. Domestically it sought to strengthen the French nation through measures such as road building, railway construction, mountain reforestation and flood control. Like colonialism, this policy was meant to strengthen economic growth, in particular the growth of the industrial sector, which, in turn, benefited the bourgeoisie. This economic and political context set the stage for the strong influence of national-level decisions over regional development and for cooperative efforts between the state and nature protection associations.

The growing interest in nature in nineteenth-century France was also encouraged by the intellectual and artistic elite's growing interest in nature's 'major attractions'. The development of bourgeois tourism began during France's Second Empire (1830). With it came visits to landscapes of natural beauty. Fontainebleau Forest, near Paris, for example, developed into an area for hiking and leisure, particularly for nature tourism associations that were founded near the end of the nineteenth century.

The elite's visits to nature also had a strong cultural and aesthetic dimension (Micoud 1991). This viewpoint was reflected in developments in art and literature. For example, the so-called 'Barbizon school', a school of painting that developed out of opposition to the Académie's classicism, was noted for its paintings of nature in the Fontainebleau Forest. In literature, George Sand, Albert de Musset and Jules Michelet, to name a few, produced Romantic literature that described Fontainebleau Forest as a 'source of joy and of aesthetic delectation' (Kalaora 1988). This artistic movement was supported by the nineteenth century's rising industrial *petite bourgeoisie*.

The first nature conservation measures in France resulted from a convergence of these trends: the policy of centralized state control of regional development, particularly in mountainous areas, and the elite's appropriation of nature's major attractions for its own recreational and aesthetic purposes. The nature conservation policy put in place in the early twentieth century prefigured the later work of forestry engineers engaged in reforestation and other projects in mountainous areas; however, voluntary associations also played a role. The Club Alpin Français (CAF) and the Touring Club de France (TCF), founded respectively in 1874 and 1890, were especially important. These associations, with a membership composed of members of the *grande bourgeoisie* – the urban elite of civil servants, artists, scientists, dignitaries and politicians, and relevant government agencies – contributed not only to the appreciation of natural sites, but especially to efforts to protect 'natural monuments', such as scenic mountainous areas. In the perception of the CAF and TCF, these landscapes provided a 'pleasant perspective' (Williams 1977) which satisfied the 'curiosity for the beholder's eye looking for the picturesque and the exotic' (Kalaora and Savoye 1985, p. 11). Their perspective, based on the idea of 'nature as spectacle', was thus as much aesthetic as naturalist.

From 1900 onwards, associations that advocated the scientific and aesthetic protection of scenic areas worked jointly for the creation of biological reserves. Although initially based on mountain tourism, the elite and aesthetic approach to nature taken by these associations set the trend and set standards for the definition of natural areas. For example, although it retained 'Alpine' in its name, the Club Alpin Français soon began to operate in other localities that corresponded to its conception of 'outstanding nature'. The CAF and TCF were joined in 1904 by the Société Nationale de Protection des Paysages et des Colonies (National Society for the Protection of Landscapes and of Colonies). It was founded because of a new republican government after the SZA became the Société Nationale d'Acclimatation (SNA) (National Acclimatization Society). The new association aimed at protection of natural areas throughout the whole of France. In 1913, the TCF and the CAF created the Association des Parcs Nationaux de France et des Colonies (National Parks of France and of the Colonies Association), which aimed to promote the establishment of national Nature Reserve Parks inspired by American models.

This first period culminated in 1914 with the creation of France's first nature reserve park, in Oisans (in the Alps), an area that is now part of the Ecrins National Park. However, most of the first protectionist actions worked to the detriment of the local people because they forced out self-sufficient farming in favour of an aesthetic presentation of areas.

The Interwar Period: Specialization of Nature Protection Associations

The development of natural history associations after the First World War was marked by a stronger focus on efforts to protect fauna and flora. The SNA, for example, abandoned efforts to introduce non-native species and began to promote protection of native species. The Ligue de Protection des Oiseaux (LPO) (League for the Protection of Birds) was founded in 1912 as a specialized offshoot of the SNA. In 1923, the SNA, the LPO and the Society for the Protection of Landscapes organized the International Nature Conservation Congress, which had a noticeable political impact in France: several laws regulating hunting and fishing in France and the colonies were passed between 1924 and 1930, and several additional nature reserves (including the Camargue in Provence, and Néouvielle in the Pyrenees) were created between 1927 and 1936.

The strong influence of members of learned societies and tourism associations in the political world led the associations to focus primarily on lobbying for government actions to protect nature. Even though the organizations failed to mobilize a large number of members and activists – probably due ironically to their elite social composition – their members were well positioned to engage in lobbying. Their prestigious social positions helped them to exert effective pressure on the political authorities to create reserves and provide protection for specific sites with interesting flora and fauna.

The creation of the Camargue zoological and botanical reserve is a particularly good example of this approach. Bernard Picon (1979) shows how creation of this reserve was a solution to the continuing conflict between the Alais-Froges company (engaged in industrial extraction of salt in the south-west Camargue) and the large agricultural landowners of the north-west.

> The . . . idea of creating the reserve arose in 1926–1927 from the friendship between Mr Dubreuil, vice-chairman of the *Société d'acclimatation*, Mr Boyaud, assistant administrator of the *Alais-Froges-Camargue* company, and Mr Azaria, administrator of the latter. Faithful to the aims of the SNA, Mr Dubreuil proposed to create a reserve of land owned by *Alais-Froges-Camargue* in the Camargue which it did not use at the time for its industrial activity. (Caffarelli, J., quoted in Picon 1979, p. 94)

The goal of this reserve was to maintain the land in its natural state and to use it for scientific purposes. This plan represented a compromise between scientists, who wanted to protect an area of great wildlife potential, and economic interests, which wanted to set aside areas that might be useful for salt mining in the future. It was made possible by the close connections between the owners of the salt-mining company and the members of the Société Nationale d'Acclimatation.

The establishment of nature protection areas provided a model for the protection of nature in France that took concrete shape in an Act of Parliament on the 'protection of natural monuments and of sites of artistic, historical, scientific, legendary or picturesque character' dated 2 May 1930. This Act gives a real status to the natural areas; however, it never had concrete effects.

The Second World War and its Aftermath

During the period of German control of France, the puppet Vichy regime, led by Maréchal Pétain, suspended the vast majority of organizations, thus placing nature protection activity in a dormant state. The regime itself emphasized nature development through glorification of France's agricultural and rural heritage, so nature protection during this period took on a very strong political complexion.

In the aftermath of the Second World War, French natural history societies had few members in comparison to their European neighbours, and their efforts to accumulate descriptive scientific knowledge about species, which had previously provided much of the impetus for nature protection, became much less important. This reorientation was associated with the growth of new scientific approaches and the institutionalization of research into nature. The scientists and urban elites, who had constituted the majority of the members of the natural history associations, now refocused their attention on scientific activity within the universities and at public research centres such as the CNRS (Centre National de la Recherche Scientifique) and INRA (Institut National de Recherche Agronomique). Scientific ecology and field experimentation displaced natural history and specimen collection, and a number of the learned societies reoriented their interests in this direction. The result was a partial decoupling of scientific interest in nature from nature protection. The activity of scientists now centred on scientific research and ecology. Scientists continued to take part in nature protection associations by working for the dissemination and popularization of natural history, aiming to win over a widened audience and to create awareness of the question of nature conservation, and they cooperated with them episodically to argue for creation of a reserve or a nature park.

Nature Conservation Meets Environmentalism: Democratization, Structuring and Institutionalization (1960–80)

The 1960s marked a turning point in the history of France's nature protection associations. Previously the concern of a learned elite, nature protection became democratized and transformed, as nature protection organizations experienced profound transformations in membership composition, forms of action and ideology. The events of 'May 68' accelerated this transformation and led the older organizations to adapt themselves to the emerging environmental movement.

Popularization and recruitment policy

During the 1960s, national organizations, such as the SNA and LPO, initiated efforts to address a wider audience and win broader support. In an effort to broaden its appeal, the SNA renamed itself the SNPN (Société Nationale de Protection de la Nature) (National Society for Nature Protection) in 1961. The associations' efforts to spread their message involved both dissemination of more information about nature and a new vision of the natural sciences and nature protection, which displaced the old anthropocentric point of view in favour of a biocentric view. Their efforts also dovetailed with new developments in education. After 1970, new school textbooks replaced the former natural history approach, which had been based on human-centred useful/harmful distinctions, with the study of biology, and later life sciences and earth sciences. These approaches gave precedence to ecosystemic approaches (Lambert 1999).

The elite and scientifically oriented natural history associations had been centred in Paris and major provincial cities, but their membership now became more broadly based and diverse. Beginning in the 1950s, local nature protection associations were set up in provincial areas. As a result of the restructuring of French society during the post-Second World War boom period known as the 'Trente Glorieuses' (the Thirty Glorious Years), efforts to open and democratize the learned societies fell on fertile ground, for this social transformation had created the 'new middle classes'. They provided a new pool of potential nature protection supporters. The 1960s thus saw a convergence between the former elite organizations and the growing middle classes, who were in search of ideals and of social identity (Vergès 1986).

Denis Buhot (1985) has closely analysed this evolution using the example of an ornithological association. Until after the Second World War, ornithology was characterized by its links with the cage breeding and acclimatization of birds and by hunting by the bourgeois upper middle classes. However, by the 1960s, the bourgeois ornithologist–hunter had lost his prestige, and the collection and hunting of birds was viewed as morally unacceptable (Buhot 1985).

As a result of these changes, the notion of nature protection, which had previously been secondary to the human-centred useful/harmful categorization, acquired a new dimension. Species were now to be protected not just to satisfy the curiosity of a few learned enthusiasts and scientists or because of the economic benefits they could bring, but to protect nature as a shared common heritage. By redefining nature as *res communis*, the nature protection associations that replaced the old learned societies were adopting a symbolically important moral value. This new morality of nature protection, which is characteristic of the middle classes, excluded the predatory appropriation and economic exploitation of nature (Chamboredon 1985).

Why did this convergence between the new middle classes and the nature conservation associations occur? Denis Buhot's survey of members of an ornithological association – mainly citizens from the intellectual middle classes (teachers, members of medical professions, social workers, etc.) – led him to emphasize the compensatory benefit of valuing nature protection for its own sake. For the new middle class, advocating nature protection had the benefits of 'at least ensuring moral superiority' and allowing one 'to live the lack of social mobility with dignity' (Buhot 1985, p. 106). The natural heritage, which the middle classes could not appropriate materially due to a lack of significant economic capital, was thus transformed into a common heritage that could be appropriated symbolically, so long as one adhered to the cultural codes of this new orientation to nature. In this respect, the intellectual middle classes, which are particularly rich in cultural capital, set the standards (Picon 1979; Chamboredon 1985; Aspe 1991).

The changing class composition of nature conservation organizations also had much to do with the spatial reconfiguration of the class structures of French society, for in their search for quality of life, the new middle classes became the main players in the 'urban exodus', deserting town centres for the suburbs and exurbs. The post-1968 communal living experiments were only the most visible part of this change. More symbolically significant was the fact that 1975 was the first year when the population of predominantly rural areas increased, albeit gradually, after several centuries of decline (Bessy-Pietri et al. 2000).

Against this background, the core membership of the nature protection associations shifted from the urban elite to the suburban and rural middle classes of France's provincial areas. This change gave an increasingly strong voice to the typically anti-Parisian attitude of the provinces and brought about major changes in the organizational structures and modes of operation of the associations. Figures such as those who had originally founded and developed the learned societies were not active in renewed and reoriented organizations, e.g. the SNA/SNPN. They were called on only to contribute their scientific expertise to the organizations' publications. The emblematic players of the nature conservation movement were now more frequently housed in political and ministerial bodies, such as the nature conservation agencies, where they used their influence to affect public policies through steps such as calling for the creation of a Ministry of the Environment.

Structuring of organizations and their position in relation to new social movements

These same social changes that had provided the nature protection associations with a new pool of potential members and boosted their previously declining memberships also gave rise to new social movements (Touraine et al. 1980), which simultaneously nurtured, renewed and competed with nature protection.

The 'cultural revolution' of 'May 68' (Mendras 1988) highlighted and accelerated social changes that were already taking place. They involved the mobilization of both workers and students, raising both traditional working-class claims and some very new ones. The leftist and ecologist, regionalist and pacifist youth (Mendras 1988) who took to the streets denounced both the archaic nature of traditional French society and the evils of galloping modernization.

These events brought ecology into politics (Touraine et al. 1980), and nature protection played a role in the leftward trend of the 1970s as one of the elements in the anti-capitalist and anti-technocratic position. In comparison to other issues, the nature protection movement did not occupy a leading role, but in the anti-nuclear campaigns and in various conflicts concerning regional development, France's traditionally strong central state, supported by the scientific and technical legitimacy of its major engineering institutions (Muller 1992), found itself facing an opposition that combined local nature protection associations, newly developing environmental associations and local residents' associations. Some trade unions were also involved, but unions were often uneasy with these new issues (Duclos 1980).

New associations concerned with environmental problems were founded in France as part of the post-1968 movement, but they were oriented more towards new environmental issues than to nature protection. Examples include Survive, founded by a group of scientists critical of the scientific establishment, which later became Survivre et vivre (Survive and Live), and Les amis de la terre, the French branch of the Friends of the Earth. In the anti-nuclear campaigns, critiques of modernity and 'return-to-nature' communal living experiments of the time, concerns about the health and welfare of human beings and the ills of society were dominant, and these 'environmental' issues proved more in tune with the times than older models of nature protection. As Pierre Jacquiot (2000) points out, environmental associations were also more involved than older nature protection groups in the 'great struggles' of the 1970s. On the other hand, the new environmental organizations also drew attention to the question of the consequences of pollution on natural environments.

The Green movement soon moved into the political field and, more concretely, the electoral field. Even before the founding of what was to become the Verts (Green Party), the anthropologist and ecologist René Dumont stood in the presidential elections in April 1974, and received no fewer than 337 800 votes (Sainteny 1991). Based on the momentum of his candidacy, France's first Green political organization at the national level was founded at the Montargis conference in June 1974.

Although nature protection did not occupy centre stage, this period was nevertheless highly significant for the nature protection associations. Between the end of the 1960s and the middle of the 1980s, many new local associations for protection of flora and fauna were created. In 1968, the nature protection groups sought to unify their forces around the country by forming the Federation Française des Sociétés de Protection de la Nature (FFSPN). Its first years were mainly devoted to increasing its membership to cover the whole of France and creating regional associations (Charvolin 1993). From 1968 to 1975, the number of organizations affiliated to the FFSPN increased from 21 to 100. In 1968 alone, 14 regional Départements were formed;[1] they numbered more than 55 in 1975 (Charvolin 1993). This federation of associations was viewed by its founders as a flexible structure, leaving a large role for local initiative. This flexibility enabled the federation to group together very diverse associations.

Although it represented a 'minimalist form of coordination', the FFSPN did increase the visibility of France's nature protection movement. Through the FFSPN, nature protection groups, which had previously been denigrated as 'defenders of little birds' by the central state administration, attained national visibility, giving increased weight to their arguments (Charvolin 1993). From then on, dialogue with the administration could open and develop, starting a move towards French-style institutionalization.

Meanwhile national societies, such as the SNPN and LPO, moved towards redefining themselves as nature protection organizations. They also focused on the popularization of natural history, for example, through the creation of the *Courrier de la nature* magazine in 1961. The policy of opening natural history societies to the public described above and redefining their goals proved fruitful. The SNPN had 2500 members in 1969 and 7000 in 1971.

The Paradoxical Relationship between the French State and Nature Protection Organizations

Relations between nature conservation organizations and the French state during the 1970s and 1980s often had a paradoxical character. Although the associations often sought cooperation with the state, they also often opposed it, campaigning against regional development plans, particularly those proposed by DATAR (Direction de l'Aménagement du Territoire et de l'Action Régionale), the Regional Development and Regional Action Agency created in 1963. They also campaigned for stricter application of administrative rules (particularly those regarding protection of coastal areas or pollution control) than desired by the state itself (Barthélémy 2000).

This paradoxical outcome resulted from the contradictory way in which the French state dealt with nature. It typically favoured the construction of costly infrastructure and facilities – particularly the development of transport systems and energy production – to increase the country's economic production. However, since the nineteenth century, it has also played an important role in nature management, which it views in terms of the conservation of natural resources (Kalaora and Savoye 1985) and the regulation of polluting activities, mainly for health reasons.

Until the 1970s, the state's approach to nature had remained fragmented and largely subservient to other concerns. The creation of France's first Ministry of the Environment in 1971 was thus, in part, a response to demands of environmental and nature protection organizations for more attention to environmental issues (Charvolin 1993; Lascoumes 1994). The new ministry was intended to unify state actions in favour of nature and the environment. Although this 'Ministry of the Impossible' (Poujade 1975) did act as a central interlocutor for nature conservation associations, it encountered resistance from other, longer-established and more powerful ministries, and had minimal influence. Although theoretically in charge of developing public policies for nature conservation, the Ministry lacked efficient administrative tools to do so until 1991. Consequently, it was marginalized at the political and legislative levels.

In an effort to better cope with the contradictory role of the state, DATAR had implemented a new land designation system during the 1960s, which was intended to promote regional specialization. Certain localities were to be dedicated to mass tourism, others to industrial production, and still others to nature conservation. Areas designated for the most complete protection, such as nature reserves or national parks, were to be walled off by forbidding any type of activity within them, while economic development areas gave free rein to urban development.

This approach was quickly contested by the local nature protection groups. Opposition to the extension of urban tourism and industrial areas led associations in these zones to demand greater protection of rural areas endangered by these activities. In September 1966, on the initiative of DATAR, a conference was organized in the province of Lurs to propose a status for rural areas that the policy had left relatively 'undefined' – neither entirely natural nor completely exploitable. One result of this conference was a proposal to establish 'Regional Nature Parks *à la française*'. This involved a reversal of the then current conception of the development of rural areas. The regional nature parks created between 1969 and 1977 had typically been areas of high ecological value, while areas whose economic and social composition did not make it possible to apply the very restrictive rules regarding National Parks did not qualify (Picon 1979). The first French law on nature conservation passed in July 1976, by contrast, clearly defined the role of the Regional Nature Parks as an instrument for protecting spaces and landscapes in order to ensure a harmonious balance of the population residing in urban and rural environments.

The process for establishing Regional Nature Parks included the active involvement of local community associations. In most cases, the associations were in charge of the project, including development of proposals for parks and highlighting of the important ecological, cultural and heritage characteristics of the sites. By 1977, responding to the demands of associations for the protection of rural areas, there were 22 Regional Nature Parks located throughout France.

RECENT DEVELOPMENTS AND PROSPECTS

During the 1990s, the structure, goals and activities of nature conservation organizations experienced profound transformations along a number of dimensions.

Networks, Expertise and Citizen Education

One such change involved the diverse organizations concerned with nature conservation and environment in a new role: partnering with regional and local government bodies to implement new participative processes to manage the environment. This change was, in large measure, as a result of the decentralization of French government administration in recent years.

The implementation of many laws and the financing of their implementation has become primarily the responsibility of local authorities (*régions, départements, municipalités*), and this applies also to nature conservation activities, such as management of *parcs naturels régionaux* (Regional Nature Parks) and public education campaigns. The implementation of these public policies, which had previously been carried out by the centralized state agencies, was gradually transferred to locally based NGOs. They thus became the agents of public policy implementation, dealing with social exclusion and poverty, training excluded people, management of natural and rural space, and campaigns to raise environmental awareness. New actors were sought out by local governments to function not only as activists–experts, but also as professionals responsible for policy implementation. The knowledge they deployed to this end was more technical than scientific or political.

Local Organization Networks in France: from Nature to Environment

By the mid-1980s, many new nature protection and environmental organizations had been founded, older scholarly societies, such as the SNPN and the LPO, had moved nature protection to the top of their agendas, and membership in nature protection and environmental organizations had increased considerably. Precisely delimiting and defining the present-day nature protection movement is, nevertheless, a difficult exercise (Fabiani 1998). Earlier attempts at typological classification have proposed distinctions between 'nature protection activists', who emphasize protection of nature in the strict sense, and 'environmentalists', who are more concerned with the conservation of environments, ecosystems, and the bases for human life (Lascoumes 1994). However, it is clear that organizations and networks in both categories often have nature protection goals. Today, 144 associations concerned with protecting nature, the environment and/or the quality of life are officially certified by the MEDD (Ministry for Ecology and Sustainable Development). Those listed in Table 3.1 are among the most important.

The Fédération France Nature Environnement (Nature and Environment Federation) (FNE) now includes 3000 members' groups. This organization, formerly called the FFSPN, is France's largest federation of nature conservation and environmental organizations. Compared to its German counterpart, the German Nature Protection Ring, it is a relatively weak organization (Jacquiot 2000), and relationships among its member organizations are also relatively weak, existing mainly during episodic joint campaigns at the local level.

The FNE was formed originally by local groups that came together to form a federation. This federative model represents a compromise between

Table 3.1 Main nature and environmental protection associations in France

Name	Date Founded	Members	Ties to other organizations	Level of action
Nature and Environment Federation (FNE)	1968	3000 local and national organizations representing 300 000 individuals	Local organizations	Local and national
League for the Protection of Birds	1912	33 000 members	Representative of Bird Life International in France since 1993	Local, national and international
National Society for Nature Protection	1855	20 000	Local reserves and organizations	Local and national
Friends of the Earth	1970	24 local groups representing 1500 members	Friends of the Earth	International and national
Greenpeace	1977–1987 / since 1989	80 000 supporters	Greenpeace-International	National and international
WWF	1971	100 000 supporters	WWF-International	International and national
Nature and School	1983	230 members and 32 local networks representing 1200 member (organizations and individuals)	Local organizations	Local and national

two principles underlying the social organization of French society: (1) community, which corresponds to a sense of already belonging to a local group; and (2) society, which corresponds to membership in an association based on a social contract (Ion 1997). The French republican model of governance has tilted historically towards the latter principle; that is, it idealized the principle of national integration and denigrated regional communities, as evidenced by the 1901 law authorizing and certifying associations' structures, which was written to favour national associations. However, in practice, the French association system continues to display tension between the competing principles, and – in contrast to associations in the realms of social activity, leisure and politics – nature protection groups are more anchored in local than national issues, and they most often mobilize on interests related to locality rather than to the nation (Aspe 1991).

In line with this emphasis, the FNE is strongest at the local and regional levels. Each of the 22 *régions administratives* in France has at least one federation of local associations affiliated with the FNE. These federations represent the FNE on the regional level, especially in negotiations with the local authorities. The FNE, in turn, represents them on the national and international levels, again mainly in dealings with the state or international agencies. Examples of large regional nature protection association include Alsace Nature, Bretagne vivante (Living Brittany) and FRAPNA (Fédération Rhône Alpes de Protection de la Nature). The regional federations bring together a diverse set of local associations. Natural history associations, nature protection associations, residents' associations, environmental associations, and associations for improvement of the quality of life all coexist in these regional networks.

Alsace Nature, for example, groups together environmental and nature protection activists, unifying their demands for nature conservation. During the 1980s, it became a unifying force for local associations in Alsace, presenting a unified image of the local nature conservation movement on the regional level. Its activities include participation in conferences, working with schoolchildren, and representing environmental and nature protection interests to environment management agencies – national or regional commissions organized by the national government or by local and regional authorities. They address such issues as regional development, water management, agriculture and forestry, energy, waste, transport, nature protection, air quality, quarries and industries.

Following the example of Alsace Nature, other regional federations were created in regions where nature and environmental protection activism was well established. Most of these were regions with emblematic natural areas, where there were pre-existing networks of nature protection groups, representatives of nature protection areas, and government authorities.

The FNE now comprises 150 regional federations, plus 29 national associations and 3000 individuals, representing altogether 300 000 members. The local and regional dimension of the associations' action is partly related to the expansion of their focus during the 1970s and 1980s from nature protection *per se* to environmentalism. This is why the 1989 name change name from FFSPN (French Federation of Nature Conservation Societies) to FNE (Nature and Environment Federation) is so significant. It implies that nature conservation can no longer be considered as simply saving particular species, but includes the overall protection of the environment.

The change from nature to environmental protection was mirrored by a shift from national to local activity. Nature protection efforts during the first half of the twentieth century were based on seeking intervention by the national state as a guarantor of the protection of local areas. The environmental movement, by contrast, mobilized people mainly around local issues, becoming an 'affair between the locality and the middle classes' (Aspe 1991, p. 207). Localism also strongly influences the nature protection and environmental associations' strategies with regard to government. Their actions today are aimed mainly at governmental authorities, especially at the local or regional levels, which are seen as opponents or as intermediaries, depending on the local conditions. The importance of the international level is typically acknowledged in principle but neglected in practice.

Indeed, international nature protection and environmental organizations, such as Greenpeace and WWF, have proved poorly adapted to French conditions and have enjoyed very modest success. Greenpeace France, which was established in 1977, has struggled to adapt to French nationalism and to the environmental movement's traditions of localism and disinterest in international activity. Despite attracting considerable media publicity and affiliating with the FNE, Greenpeace initially attracted only a few dozen members. Membership in the USA and many European countries grew rapidly during the 1980s, but Greenpeace France reached a peak of only 7000 supporters in 1985. Following the *Rainbow Warrior* affair in 1985,[2] the number of supporters dropped to 2500, and the French branch had to suspend operations between 1987 and 1989.

Since the late 1990s, Greenpeace has marginally improved its position. Bucking an international trend of membership losses, it grew from 25 000 supporters in 1996 to 80 000 today. However, this count includes people who only make an occasional donation, which does not equate with the membership statistics of traditional French associations. Furthermore, Greenpeace France has boosted its membership by organizing proactive membership recruiting campaigns, employing young people, often with temporary contracts, to recruit members on the streets and in public places.

Created in 1973, WWF France was officially recognized as a public interest organization in 2004. Its annual activity report claims 100 000 'donors', who by their donations or purchase of merchandise support the WWF. Within France, WWF acts primarily as a lobby group. It follows a two-pronged strategy: (1) public education campaigns and (2) actions aimed at influential actors in the nature conservation domain, including agencies that administer nature reserves, politicians, industrialists and foundations.

Apart from tensions between Greenpeace and the French population over French nuclear tests, there are other reasons for the relatively weak position of Greenpeace and WWF in France. Neither organization's sphere of action corresponds well to the local emphasis of French nature protection efforts. Instead, organizations such as Greenpeace or WWF rely heavily on highly publicized campaigns to raise international public awareness of environmental problems and influence events at the international level. Their approach is thus far removed from the characteristic French pattern.

Emerging Partnerships with the State and Professionalization

As a result of changes described above, some nature conservation organizations developed during the 1990s into partners with local government, particularly in the concrete implementation of nature protection policies. They are now heavily involved in managing natural sites, regional development, and organization of programmes to separate waste at source, as well as public awareness campaigns and environmental education. The LPO is a good example. Although it continues to carry out a considerable amount of voluntary and activist work, it has been transformed in a major way since the 1980s. Today it has 33 000 members and 400 paid staff. It is involved not only in the protection of birds by conservation programmes, but also in numerous tasks delegated to it by the state and local and regional authorities. These include management of nature reserves and bird sanctuaries, public education, and work with schoolchildren. Similarly, the FNE's regional federations are involved in the conception and dissemination of teaching resources. Teaching resources designed by the FRAPNA such as *La rivière m'a dit* (The river told me) or *La forêt m'a dit* (The forest told me) are now distributed throughout France. These management and educational activities are funded mainly by local and regional authorities, which enlist the assistance of local associations in implementing public policies as part of the obligations that they must meet since decentralization.

This new relationship between the local authorities and associations is resulting in considerable professionalization. Jobs now on offer with the associations include 'nature study facilitator', 'education manager', 'nature reserve technician', 'curator', and 'study and expert assessment officer'. They require professional skills in the management of nature and the environment. Their employees are young, highly qualified and trained in life sciences, environmental sciences and geography. For them, protection of nature and environment means use of technical skills acquired through education, not just volunteer activism.

From Protest to Participation: from Militant to Expert

Since the 1990s, relationships between groups working for nature protection and the state have taken on new forms centred around the development of public consultative procedures. As organizations and networks for the protection of nature and environment evolved into a dynamic, effective opposition force, their growing strength was reflected in the increasing number of legal actions they initiated. On the national level, for questions of urban development alone, legal actions increased from 2600 in 1978 to 6300 in 1986, and they numbered more than 10 000 a year during the 1990s (Segaud 1998). It must have seemed to the authorities that there was no longer a single locality in France where an association was not ready to mobilize against development plans, and where an association did not exist, there was often the capacity to create one for the occasion. Along with other factors, these legal challenges provided the impetus for the development of public consultative procedures, which, in turn, provided an avenue for avoiding conflicts that the government was no longer certain of winning (Blatrix 2000).

The response to this crisis was the development during the 1990s of a legal framework that encouraged public consultation and – depending on the scale and cost of the development project[3] – sometimes made it obligatory (Müller 1992; Chambat and Fourniau 2001). While these procedures are perceived by jurists as a means of giving a voice to the diversity and multiplicity of opinions in the local population, experience has shown that most participants are spokespersons of associations. Public consultative procedures thus introduced an additional avenue for participative democracy in which association spokespersons act as intermediaries between the authorities and the local population (Blatrix 2000; Claeys-Mekdade 2003).

Participation by nature protection groups in these consultations has become increasingly dominated by two types of experts. First, activists acquire know-how they can transfer from one project to the next in opposing projects through participative processes. They learn how to work with the administrative machinery, they form contact networks with local or even national elected representatives, and they acquire basic legal knowledge that enables them to increase their association's field of action (Claeys-Mekdade 2003). Second, the associations have developed scientific expertise, mainly in the life sciences. Such experts are especially prevalent in the nature protection associations.

The nature protection groups are active in opposing state development plans, and they almost always participate in public consultative procedures, but they avoid taking politicized and explicitly militant positions, preferring to present themselves as the spokespersons of scientific knowledge. In so doing, they attempt to counter official experts with their own alternative empirical knowledge. When state experts present reports about the technical feasibility of a development project from geological, hydrological, or seismic points of view, nature conservation associations respond with inventories of flora and fauna, endemic species and biodiversity.

Whether they are voluntary workers or full-time staff, most of the local nature protection association supporters who are involved in expert research and assessment have had basic scientific training, mainly in the life sciences. Others have acquired empirical knowledge of their locality through amateur observation of nature. Reflecting this difference, the local organizations' work in generating expert studies and assessments draws on both these types of knowledge. That is, they present hands-on knowledge as a complement – or sometimes a counterweight – to academic knowledge that can be too theoretical and too far removed from the reality on the ground. In this battle between different forms of expertise, official experts with competencies and arguments based on a technocratic and academic conception of science are often opposed by community association experts with competencies and arguments also based on an empirical conception of knowledge, but valuing hands-on ground experience and local knowledge.

This double competence of the nature protection organizations equips them well to be central actors in the Natura 2000 network, for they are familiar both with participative process and local natural history (Alphandéry et al. 2003). More broadly, the increasing influence of European policies, as well as decisions of the European court, appear favourable to the nature protection organizations, their arguments and their actions. One typical recent example involved a sustained and hard-fought conflict between bird hunters and nature protection organizations. During the last decade, the European court, honouring the claim of the nature protection organizations, actually restricted hunting periods. This example demonstrates that, even though local embeddedness is one of the main characteristics of French nature protection organizations, they are not always isolated. In fact, they have been able to mobilize European resources and international resources effectively. The appropriation of new concepts from abroad is also evident. Even within basically local actions, French nature protection organizations can mobilize concepts developed far away, such as the notions of sustainable development from the 1987 Bruntland Report and from the 1992 Rio Declaration.

Educational Activism of Nature Protection Organizations

According to Jean-Pierre Chibret, the development of professional expertise in environmental communication and environmental education is among the indicators of the end of the natural history model of nature protection, 'which was entirely centred in a project by amateur scientists who tended to devote most of their association activity to collecting naturalist information, processing it and publishing it in book form' (Chibret 1995, p. 36). Today, professionally planned and conducted public awareness and information campaigns have replaced simple popularization of natural history research, and professionally developed teaching resources have replaced scientific brochures. The knowledge conveyed in this context is no longer mere description of natural habitats and species. It is based on concepts that are not derived from scientific research, but from knowledge of specific measures to solve environmental problems.

One aspect of this development is the involvement of community associations in 'pedagogical activism', which emerged as the associations professionalized (Jacqué 2003). According to this approach, the transformation of the individual's ways of thinking and acting is a new means of political action on behalf of nature protection and the environment. Educational programmes and materials for schools are now developed by salaried professionals, who hope to resolve environmental issues by training and educating young people. Nature and environment educators and facilitators work in schools to help children experience nature and better understand recycling via field trips, games, use of educational information packs, etc. Activities such as nature study field trips, which had long been reserved for voluntary workers and activists, have thus been transformed into professionally conducted activities for schoolchildren.

This new area of activity implies a profound transformation of the local nature protection association, their demands, their activists, and their forms of action. It incorporates them into networks not involved in nature conservation *per se*, but in environmental education for social change. The first such network was Ecole et Nature, which was created in 1983 by a few dozen teachers and popular education activists concerned with ecology. It has since emerged as a key network, which promotes a very activist discourse, project-based teaching, and sustainable development. It has been largely responsible for initiating education on nature and the environment, and its work partly structures the work of the staff of nature conservation associations. Its educational information pack *Rouletaboul* (Roll your bowl) is about waste and alludes to the scarab beetle, which rolls its excrement. Another pack, *Ricoche* (Bounce), is about water.

CONCLUSION

Nature protection efforts in France began with elite natural history organizations engaged mainly in assembling specimens and compendiums of various species. From the 1960s on, with the rise of the environmental movement, a shift toward a new middle-class membership went hand in hand with a move toward democratization and institutionalization of nature protection; however, nature protection organizations remained basically volunteer associations. Since the end of the 1990s, however, these organizations have professionalized by providing their services to local governments.

French nature protection organizations are typically local and specialized; that is, they are related to a specific environment, species or territory. The local character of nature protection efforts defines both the scope and the extent of the actions that nature protection associations carry out and their relations with political authorities. Although there is indeed a network of nature conservation associations covering the whole of France, nature protection can hardly be seen as possessing a formally organized and hierarchical structure with identifiable spokespersons.

As opposed to the model in the English-speaking world, the legitimacy of nature protection in France remains rooted in grass-roots activist involvement and practical knowledge of the situation on the ground, and nature conservation organizations in France draw their legitimacy from their relationships with other local associations and with political authorities at the local level. This unique characteristic of France's nature protection movement helps to explain the difficult and slow integration of international nature conservation associations such as WWF or Greenpeace into France. These associations carry out mainly publicity-attracting and fundraising campaigns at the national and international levels rather than being involved in local areas, which is more characteristic of French nature protection associations. Consequently, interventions carried out by organizations such a Greenpeace or WWF, which are based on major communication campaigns and 'media impact', have found very little echo in local mobilization in France.

The traditional French nature conservation movement remains more concerned with continuing to perform its management and conservation role in the framework of local natural spaces, rather than stimulating more widespread social movement mobilization. It is for this reason that the France Nature Environnement (FNE), which is emblematic of this French-style form of organization, cannot function as a unified, coherent voice of the nature protection associations. This weakness, which is at times both openly affirmed and concealed, is a key feature of the French nature conservation movement.

The legitimized role of nature protection organizations in France today continues to lie in their scientific and technical competencies in the field of ecology. Their main activities include the following: management of natural reserves and protected sites; implementation of directives such as Natura 2000; and involvement in monitoring committees on contamination and waste. In addition to these activities, the organizations carry out educational activities of nature discovery or environmental consciousness, raising issues such as water contamination and waste management.

The evolution undergone by local nature protection organizations leads to a paradoxical situation. They maintain a high rate of membership by middle and upper intellectual classes who participate in the nature discovery and observation activities offered by these associations. At the same time, their discourse is professionalizing, and nature protection is becoming mainly a technical management issue. In this context, the protest discourse about nature and environment protection is left today to the non-specialized organizations, such as Greenpeace, which act primarily at the national and international levels.

NOTES

1. Note that metropolitan France is composed of 95 areas known as *Dèpartements*.
2. On 10 July 1985, the *Rainbow Warrior*, a ship belonging to Greepeace, sank in Auckland harbour in New Zealand following two explosions under the hull of the boat. Greenpeace had planned to sail it to the Polynesian atoll, Mururoa, to protest against a French nuclear test. French agents, however, launched a secret operation aiming at scuttling this expedition. France's responsibility for the crime was established by a judgment of the International Court of Justice.
3. In particular, the Bianco Circular dated 15 December 1992 and the Barnier Act dated 2 February 1995.

REFERENCES

Alphandéry, Pierre, Jean-Paul Billaud, Christian Deverre, Agnès Fortier, Perrot Nathalie and Florence Pinton (2003), *Local Scenes of Dialogue around Nature. French Construction of the Network Natura 2000*, Paris: Ministère de l'Ecologie et du Développement Durable, IFB, Institut Français de la biodiversité.

Aspe, Chantal (ed.) (1991), 'L'Environnement: Une Histoire Entre les Couches Moyennes et la Localité', *Chercheurs d'eau en Méditerranée*, Paris: Le Félin, pp. 191–213.

Barthélémy, Martine (2000), *Associations, Un nouvel âge de la participation?*, Paris: Presse Sciences Po.

Bessy-Pietri, Pascale, Mohamed Hilal and Bertrand Schmitt (2000), 'Recensement de la population 1999. Evolutions contrastées du rural', *INSEE Première*, **726**, July.

Blatrix, Cécile (2000), *La 'Démocratie Participative' de Mai 68 aux Mobilisations anti-TGV. Processus de Consolidation d'Institutions Sociales Émergentes*, thèse pour l'obtention du Doctorat en Science Politique soutenue à Université Paris I, January.

Buhot, Denis (1985), 'Classes Moyennes et Transformation d'un Loisir de Nature: Le Cas d'une Association Ornithologique', in Anne Cadoret (ed.), *Protection de la Nature, Histoire et Idéologie*: de la Nature à l'Environnement, Paris: L'Harmattan, pp. 94–107.

Caffarelli, J. de (1966), 'Histoire de la réserve de Camargue', *Le Courrier de la Nature*, **35**, 57, quoted by Bernard Picon, *L'Espace et le Temps en Camargue*, Actes Sud, 1979, p. 94.

Callon, Michel, Pierre Lascoumes and Yues Barthe (2001), *Agir dans un Monde Incertain. Essai sur la Démocratie Technique*, Paris: Seuil.

Chambat, Pierre and Jean-Michel Fourniau (2001), 'Débat Public et Participation Démocratique', in Serge Vallemont (ed.), *Le Débat Public: Une Réforme dans l'Etat*, Paris: LGDJ, pp. 9–38.

Chamboredon, Jean-Claude (1985), 'La Naturalisation de la Campagne: Une autre Manière de Cultiver les Simples?', in Anne Cadoret (ed.), *Protection de la Nature, Histoire et Idéologie: de la Nature à l'Environnement*, Paris: L'Harmattan, pp. 138–51.

Charvolin, Florian (1993), *L'Invention de l'Environnement. Les Pratiques Documentaires dAgrégation à l'Origine du Ministère de la Protection de la Nature et de l'Environnement*, thèse sous double sceau pour les doctorats de science politique de l'IEP de Grenoble, et de socio-économie de l'innovation de l'école des Mines de Paris.

Claeys-Mekdade, Cécilia (2003), *Le Lien Politique à l'Épreuve de l'Environnement. Expériences Camarguaises*, Brussels: Peter Lang, P.I.E.

Chibret, René-Piéerre (1995), 'Les Réseaux d'Associations de Défense de l'Environnement, L'Avergne', in F. Agostini, R. Chibret, J. Fabiani and B. Maresca (eds), *La Dynamique du Mouvement Associatif dans le Secteur de l'Environnement. Etat de la question et Monographies Régionales*, Paris: CREDOC, vol. 3, pp. 22–46.

Drouin, Jean-Marc (1991), *L'Écologie et son Histoire, Réinventer la Nature*, Paris: Desclée de Brouwer.

Duclos, Denis (1980), 'Classe ouvrière et environnement', *Sociologie du Travail*, **22** (3), 324–45.

Fabiani, Jean-Louis (1988), 'Commentaire', *Dossiers de L'Environment de L'INRA*, **17**, 27–9.

Lambert, Serge (1999), 'Quand l'écologie et la biologie s'appelaient histoire ou sciences naturelles. Application aux. animaux utiles ou nuisibles', *Courrier de l'environement de l'INRA* (38), November, 23–40.

Ion, Jacques (1997), *La Fin des Militants?*, Paris: L'Atelier, Editions Ouvrières.

Jacqué, Marie (2003), 'La formation de l'écocitoyen', *Communication*, **74**, Ed. du Seuil, 103–15.

Jacquiot, Philippe (2000), 'La Normalisation de l'Écologisme: Comparaison des Associations Vertes en France et en Allemagne', in Jean Paul Bozonnet and Jacques Jakubec (eds), *L'Écologisme à l'Aube du XXI°Siècle. De la Rupture à la Banalisation?*, Geneva: Georg Editeur, pp. 149–81.

Kalaora, Bernard (1988), *Le Musée Vert, Radiographie du Loisir en Forêt*, Paris: L'Harmattan.

Kalaora, Bernard and Alain Savoye (1985), 'La Protection des Régions de Montagne au 19ème Siècle: Forestiers Sociaux contre Forestiers Étatistes', in Anne Cadoret (ed.), *Protection de la Nature, Histoire et Idéologie: de la Nature à l'Environnement*, Paris: L'Harmattan, pp. 6–23.

Lascoumes, Pierre (1994), *L'Éco-pouvoir. Environnements et Politiques, Les Associations au Risque de la Démocratie Participative*, Paris: La Découverte.
Latour, Bruno (1999), *Les Politiques de la Nature, Ou Comment Faire entrer les Sciences en Démocratie*, Paris: La Découverte.
Mendras, Henri (1988), *La Seconde Révolution Française, 1965–1984*, Paris: Gallimard.
Micoud, André (1991), 'La Production Symbolique des Lieux Exemplaires', in André Micoud (ed.), *Des Hauts Lieux – La Construction Sociale de L' Exemplarité*, Lyon: CNRS, pp. 7–15.
Müller, Pierre (1992), 'Entre le local et l'Europe, la crise du modèle français de politiques publiques', *Revue Française de Sciences Politiques*, **42** (2), 79–94.
Picon, Bernard (1979), *L'Espace et le Temps en Camargue*, Arles: Actes sud.
Poujade, R. (1975), *Le Ministère de l'Impossible*, Paris: Calmann-Lévy.
Raffin, Jean-Pierre and Georges Ricou (1985), 'Le Lien entre les Scientifiques et les Associations de Protection de la Nature: Approche Historique', in Anne Cadoret (ed.), *Protection de la Nature, Histoire et Idéologie: de la Nature à l'Environnement*, Paris: L'Harmattan, pp. 61–74.
Sainteny, Guillaume (1991), *Les Verts, Que sais-je?*, Paris: Presses Universitaires de France.
Segaud, Marion (1998), 'Entre Publics et Usagers, la Concertation', in Club des Maîtres d'Ouvrages d'Opérations Complexes (ed.), *L'Aménagement Urbain face à la Crise de la Ville*, La Tour d'Aigues: L'Aube, pp. 173–91.
Touraine, Alain, Zsuzsa Hegedus, François Dubet and Michel Wieviorka (1980), *La Prophétie anti-Nucléaire*, Paris: Le Seuil.
Vergès, Pierre (1986), 'Approche Localisée des Classes Socials', *L'Esprit des Lieux*, Paris: CNRS, pp. 277–90.
Williams, Raymond (1977), 'Plaisantes, Perspectives. Invention du Paysage et Abolition du Paysan', *Actes de la Recherche en Sciences Sociales*, **17–18**, 29–36.

4. Nature protection in Germany: persistence and change in a turbulent century[1]

William T. Markham

Germany is a country of celebrated beauty with an impressive array of natural landscapes, celebrated in German poetry and beloved by generations of hikers. Yet since the nineteenth century, Germany has also been a densely settled, industrial land, so it is not surprising that German nature protection organizations have a long history and strong contemporary presence. This chapter examines these organizations' histories and present-day goals, structures and strategies in the context of the economic, cultural and political contexts that have shaped them. The narrative invites reflection on the durability of the impulse to protect nature, nature protection's broad appeal, and the ease with which it has melded with various other ideologies and movements. It also identifies key tensions characteristic of nature protection efforts: tensions between national-level political action and practical nature protection projects conducted locally, struggles over how closely to affiliate with other social movements, and arguments over confrontational versus cooperative strategies.

HISTORY OF NATURE PROTECTION IN GERMANY

Among the nations covered in this volume, Germany has perhaps the most varied and dramatic history of nature protection, affected by world wars, runaway inflation and depression, National Socialism, postwar reconstruction, socialist rule in East Germany, and the confrontational social movements of the 1970s and 1980s.

Nature Protection before 1933

Isolated efforts to protect scenic areas, such as the Siebengebirge, an area of scenic hills, cliffs and ruins along the Rhine, date to the mid-1800s

(Dominick 1992; Gröning and Wolschke-Bulmahn 1998); however, national nature protection organizations first appeared at the end of the nineteenth century in the context of far-reaching changes resulting from population growth, industrialization and urbanization. They produced both threats to nature and social discontent that could be mobilized to support efforts to protect it.

The most obvious threats occurred near the new mines and factories. In areas such as the Ruhr valley, entire landscapes were transformed from rural to industrial, emissions polluted the air and water, and explosive urban growth outran local governments' ability to manage urban waste. Numerous efforts to combat these problems ensued, but these focused more on human well-being and property damage than protecting nature, and their success was limited by capitalist political power, a dominant ideology that equated industrialization with progress, and deficiencies of the law-making and enforcement apparatus. Amelioration involved half-measures, such as taller smokestacks and improved disposal of human waste, and no national-level organizations emerged (Wey 1982; Dominick 1992; Gröning and Wolschke-Bulmahn 1998).

The effects of industrialization extended well beyond cities. Railroads were built along scenic rivers, dams turned valleys into lakes, power transmission lines bisected forests, and railroads brought mass tourism to formerly isolated areas. The changes affected not just these relatively pristine areas, but also the cultural landscapes of forests and fields that many Germans thought of as nature. Rationalized forestry transformed forests into monotonous monocultures, and landowners removed hedges and woodlots, combined small fields into larger ones, straightened roads, drained wetlands, and channelized streams, threatening many familiar species (Dominick 1992; Knaut 1993). These changes evoked strong opposition and calls for nature protection from several quarters.

For many critics, advocacy of nature protection was part of a broader critique of industrialization and urbanization. For some of these – advocates of urban beautification, rural communes and romantic hikers – it was a secondary objective; however, for others – well-educated intellectuals, aristocrats, and small business owners who had lost status in Germany's transformation – nature protection became a cornerstone of opposition to modernization. They were attracted to the ideas of intellectuals such as Ernst Rudorff, who railed against the destruction of nature and the replacement of rural *Gemeinschaften* and traditional class relations with anomic cities and an urban proletariat (Knaut 1993).

Rudorff's calls for nature protection were based mainly on aesthetics and sentiment, but for another group, led by Hugo Conwentz, a biologist and museum director, science was the heart of the matter. In 1906, Conwentz parlayed authorship of a report on nature protection into a job as Director of Prussia's new Office for the Protection of Natural Monuments. Prussia was Germany's largest *Land*, so his efforts attracted notice. Arguing that budget realities and a lack of large wilderness areas made creating national parks like those in the USA unrealistic, Conwentz focused instead on protecting *Naturdenkmäler* (natural monuments): geological formations, small populations of animals or plants – including sometimes even a single tree – and micro-ecosystems that were important due to their scientific significance, uniqueness, endangered status or beauty.

Conwentz set out to save *Naturdenkmäler* through a programme that included speeches, publications, inventories and efforts to place them under legal protection. To assist with this effort, he set up a network of volunteer regional committees and also promoted new legislation, such as 1902 and 1907 laws limiting outdoor advertising; however, neither the committees nor Conwentz's Office had the staff, financial resources, or authority to vigorously enforce the laws, and there was no money for significant land purchases (Knaut 1993; Milnik 2003).

Other nature protection advocates worked to protect nature simply for its own sake. Some were motivated by empathy for birds and appreciation of their beauty, while others focused on preserving scenic landscapes, such as the Lüneberg Heath and the Alps. They too were drawn mainly from the educated middle class, especially government officials and teachers, and from the aristocracy (Dominick 1992; Gröning and Wolschke-Bulmahn 1998; Wöbse 2003).

A final set of nature protection advocates came from the urban working class. They based their arguments on scattered passages in Marx and the writings of Bebels, which included destruction of nature among the sins of capitalism and sometimes displayed a good grasp of ecological principles. And at the practical level, the Social Democrats sometimes introduced environmental legislation in the Reichstag, even if their pre-eminent goal always remained a larger share of the pie (Hannigan 1995).

At the turn of the twentieth century, three key organizations with nature protection goals emerged from this social context. The first, the Bund Heimatschutz[2] (BH) (League for Homeland Protection) was founded in 1904 by Rudorff and like-minded supporters. They viewed nature protection as an integral part of Heimatschutz, which also included protecting cultural landscapes, architectural styles, local customs and dialects. The BH attracted socially conservative intellectuals, aristocrats, landowners, architects and government officials. Its founders intended it to absorb existing local and regional groups, but they resisted, and it grew rapidly only after reconstituting itself as a national umbrella organization. The BH promoted its objectives through lectures and slideshows, publications, museums and efforts to introduce Heimatschutz into school curricula. It also engaged in behind-the-scenes lobbying. Defeats in several early battles, most notably a highly publicized but unsuccessful effort to prevent damming the upper Rhine, strengthened the voice of the compromisers among its leaders, and the BH often settled for improvements that would make new facilities fit better into the landscape. It sometimes mounted arguments for nature protection that would pass scientific muster today, but its predominant line of argument was aesthetic and sentimental. Over the BH's first three decades, nature protection gradually lost ground to other aspects of Heimatschutz, especially preservation of traditional architecture, and it rarely participated in efforts to control urban pollution (Wey 1982; Knaut 1993).

The Bund für Vogelschutz (BfV) (League for Bird Protection) was founded in 1899. Under the skilful leadership of Lina Hähnle, the hard-working, charismatic wife of a prominent industrialist, it quickly emerged as Germany's largest, most influential bird protection organization. Its success rested on limiting its goals to protection of birds and their habitats, avoiding ideological extremes or political entanglements, active solicitation of a broad membership base via lectures and slideshows, and the very low dues made possible by support from the Hähnles and other donors. Its core supporters were birdwatchers, teachers, ornithologists, government officials and aristocrats; few were working class. The BfV purchased, leased and maintained bird sanctuaries, sold nest boxes and birdfood, and solicited pledges to forego feathered fashions. It circulated petitions and lobbied behind the scenes for bird protection laws, but it was rarely confrontational (May 1999; Wöbse 2003).

The Naturfreunde (Friends of Nature) was established in Vienna in 1895 as a workers' alternative to middle-class hiking and nature study organizations. Like similar workers' organizations, it was intended to complement unions and political parties by educating workers, enriching their lives, and providing an alternative to crowded apartments and taverns. The Friends of Nature spread throughout Europe, and in the early 1920s the German branch, the largest, was authorized to set up a national headquarters and board of directors; however, during the late 1920s, a bitter split between the Social Democratic and Communist Parties led to heated conflict within the German branch. After the communists took over some groups, the nominally non-partisan leadership expelled them, costing the organization about half its 100 000 members.

The Friends of Nature's major activity was nature hikes, but there were interest groups for activities such as photography, natural history and canoeing. A network of 'Friends of Nature houses' provided places to rest between hikes, peruse a small library, or pursue hobbies. Nature study and efforts to prevent landowners from closing hiking paths were important concerns of the Friends of Nature from the beginning, and in 1910 nature protection became an official goal, albeit never the top priority. The organization's publications complained of land enclosures and destruction of nature by capitalist profiteers, and it lobbied government and protested against logging scenic forests, railroad construction in scenic areas, strip mining, river channelization and wetlands drainage. It also argued for creation of nature protection areas and worked to educate tourists about nature protection (Wunderer 1991; Zimmer 1984; Erdmann and Zimmer 1991). Its goals and activities clearly demonstrated the appeal of nature protection across ideological and class lines.

Two other nature protection organizations from this period warrant mention. The Verein Naturpark (Nature Protection Park Association) was founded in 1909 to promote parks for nature protection. It grew rapidly and eventually succeeded in combining government subsidies with its own fundraising to establish Germany's first large park in the Lüneberg Heath; however, the high cost of land blocked development of additional parks for many years (Dominick 1992; Gröning and Wolschke-Bulmahn 1998).

The Bund Naturschutz in Bayern (BN) (Bavarian League for Nature Protection), Germany's most visible regional nature protection organization, was founded in 1913. The membership included many teachers, professors, foresters and state officials, but the BN failed to achieve a large or diverse membership. It nevertheless undertook an ambitious programme to protect scenic and ecologically sensitive areas from road building, quarrying, and construction of power stations and tourist facilities by persuading government to designate them as protected areas. Within the limits of its scant resources, it also purchased or leased such areas, and it set up patrols to monitor sensitive mountain areas. The BN also published a magazine and worked to educate tourists, the public and schoolchildren about nature protection by distributing educational materials. Its approach was generally cooperative, not confrontational, and it rarely addressed industrial pollution (Hoplitschek 1984; Dominick 1992; Wolf 1996).

Environmental Protection under National Socialism

During the post-First World War period, Germany was plagued by massive hyperinflation, depression and legislative gridlock resulting from conflicts among its numerous and contentious parties. Hitler's promises to restore prosperity, order and national pride resonated with many, and his promise to rebuild Germany as a unified *Volksgemeinschaft* rooted in the peasantry proved especially appealing to some more reactionary supporters of nature protection – as did Nazi ideologist Walther Darré's set phrase, '*Blut und Boden*' (blood and soil). The racist, anti-urban Darré viewed Germany's rural communities, rooted in their native soil, as the nation's strength (Bergmann 1970; Dominick 1992).

Even nature protection advocates with reservations about the Nazis hoped that the new government would move German nature protection forward, and during its early years, the National Socialist government compiled a noteworthy record. As Minister of Agriculture, Darré worked to strengthen traditional farming, promote organic farming, and fight erosion, and the new government overcame legislative gridlock with a flood of new legislation and regulations. These included progressive hunting, forest protection, and homeland protection laws and implementing regulations for a plant and animal protection law already long on the books. City parks were built and upgraded, new nature protection areas designated, and reforestation programmes begun. Most importantly, Göring, as Minister of Forests, pushed through a long-delayed nature protection law. It called for protecting animals, plants and natural areas of unusual beauty, rarity, distinctiveness, or scientific significance, and charged the authorities with inventorying them. It barred factories, waste dumps, railroads, power lines, and billboards from ecologically sensitive areas and required government agencies to consult with the nature protection authorities before implementing building plans that might threaten nature. It also allowed the authorities to seize property and limit land use. Finally, it transformed the Prussian nature protection office into a German national office.

In the long run, however, Nazi nature protection proved less impressive than the early legislative record. Efforts to revive the economy and increase Germany's military power led to intensive lumbering, draining and cultivation of wetlands, and construction of new motorways, factories, and military facilities. These steps proved hard to square with nature protection, even after the regime appointed a landscape architect to ensure that the motorways fitted into their natural surroundings. The number of new nature protection areas was, in fact, much smaller than stated in official documents, and the nature protection law included exemptions for the army, transportation rights of way, and 'vital' economic programmes. Responsibility for advising local authorities about nature protection remained in the hands of volunteers, and enforcement of nature protection laws was underfunded and understaffed. As war preparations intensified, nature protection was increasingly neglected. Later it was all but ignored (Dominick 1992; Gröning and Wolschke-Bulmahn 1987; Radkau and Uekötter 2003).

Nazi rule created a new situation for organizations with nature protection goals. The government disbanded the left-leaning Friends of Nature and seized its property. The remaining organizations experienced '*Gleichschaltung*', literally, the setting of all switches in the same direction. Their leaders, goals and policies were now dictated or approved by the state.

The nature protection organizations acceded to these requirements with varying enthusiasm. The League for Homeland Protection was the most positive. Nazi ideology resonated strongly with some of its members, including its first president, an early convert to National Socialism. It welcomed the new nature and homeland protection legislation and government support for its work, but it sometimes found state control a burden and struggled to protect its autonomy (Dominick 1992; Speitkamp 1988). The relatively apolitical leaders of the BfV and BN kept any reservations they had about the Nazis to themselves. The fulsome praise for Hitler's accomplishments in their publications was probably in part simply expedient, but their delight with the new nature protection law was genuine. Like the BH, the BfV and BN profited from government subsidies and support, and the BfV was authorized to absorb smaller bird protection groups and establish chapters in conquered territories slated to become part of Germany (Dominick 1992; May 1999; Hoplitschek 1984; Wolf 1996).

Nature Protection in West Germany during the Postwar Years

The Second World War left Germany a shattered land administered by occupying armies. Rebuilding the economy, infrastructure and political institutions, not nature protection, was the top priority. As postwar rebuilding evolved into the 'economic miracle' of the 1950s and 1960s, West Germans continued to focus more on economic growth and enjoying their prosperity than on the resulting threats to nature.

State nature protection offices resumed their work in West Germany after the war; however, due to the low priority of nature protection, old patterns of understaffing, underbudgeting and weak enforcement reappeared. Interest in nature protection did begin to increase by the late 1950s, especially in the form of arguments for *Landschaftspflege* (regional planning and care of the landscape); however, concrete accomplishments were relatively few (Wey 1982; Dominick 1992; Chaney 1996).

The postwar period also brought a reshuffling of nature protection's support base. The defeat of the Nazis undermined the reactionary critique of modernization, discrediting the ideological basis of this branch of nature protection (Dominick 1992). Right-wing ecology did not disappear (Geden 1999), but its appeal was limited. Support for a separate workers' nature protection movement was undermined by the diminishing rigidity of class boundaries, the Social Democratic Party's (SPD's) self-redefinition as a party of the moderate left, and the unions' emphasis on economic growth (Krüger 2000). Consequently, nature protection found itself neither allied with wider social movements nor strong enough to function as an independent movement. It was forced to function instead as an interest group with modest support.

The prewar organizations were, nevertheless, eager to resume operations. They peppered the occupation authorities with applications to reincorporate and re-establish contacts across occupation zones. These efforts testify to their core members' strong commitment to both nature protection and their organizations, for they faced many obstacles: lack of funds, destroyed or lost records, and the burden of their collaboration with a discredited regime. The occupation authorities in the West chose not to stand in the way, so long as they purged leaders who had embraced National Socialism too eagerly (Dominick 1992).

The League for Bird Protection and the Bavarian League survived the war, but both were greatly weakened. Lacking better alternatives, both returned to prewar goals and strategies. The BfV did not regain its prewar membership until the mid-1960s, and diminished public interest, an ageing membership, and a reorganization that strengthened its regional units at the expense of the national organization made it less influential than before the war (May 1999; Wöbse 2003). The BN emerged from the war with only half its prewar membership and a staff of one, and many local chapters had dissolved. It required two decades to reach its former membership (Hoplitschek 1984; Wolf 1996).

The BH also survived the war, and the Friends of Nature was quickly re-established, but, in a changed world, both drifted away from nature protection. Abandoning nature protection as an official goal, the BH focused increasingly on preserving the customs and architecture of the past (Fischer 1994), while the Friends of Nature struggled to reclaim its confiscated property and find a unified voice. In subsequent decades, it functioned variously as a politically uninvolved hikers' federation, an ally of the SPD and unions, and a part of the far left, anti-nuclear and countercultural movements. Nature protection was only one aspect of a multifaceted and shifting agenda (Zimmer 1984; Erdmann and Zimmer 1991).

Despite these difficulties, nature protection did not fade away. In fact, three new organizations emerged during the postwar years. The Schutzgemeinschaft Deutscher Wald (German Forest Protection Association) was founded in 1947 to combat the unsustainable exploitation of German forests for fuel and reparations revenue. Its membership included many foresters and government employees, and its major activities were public education and lobbying (Dominick 1992; Bergstedt 1998).

The Deutscher Naturschutz Ring (DNR) (German Nature Protection Ring) was founded in 1950 by 15 local and regional nature protection organizations with support from government nature protection offices. Its founders believed that a single umbrella organization could exert more political influence than individual organizations, while government officials hoped that having a single negotiating partner would simplify things and help to balance negotiations with labour and business.

By the late 1960s, the DNR had over one hundred member organizations with about two million members, but its decision to seek the largest possible number of member groups caused numerous problems. Its member groups included not only nature protection organizations such as the BfV, but also organizations of nature users, such as hunters and anglers, and organizations with only limited interest in nature protection, such as the youth hostel association. Consequently, the DNR generally had to settle for inoffensive goals on which its diverse membership could reach consensus. The member groups proved unwilling to cede much power to the DNR or fund it adequately, so it remained underfunded, understaffed and highly dependent on small government subsidies. Although it logged significant accomplishments in areas such as integrating nature protection into school curricula, it failed to become a unified, effective advocate for nature in the political system (Leonhard 1986; Hey and Brendle 1994).

The third new organization, the German branch of the Worldwide Fund for Nature, was founded in 1963. During its early years, it functioned – under the leadership of a relatively inactive board full of wealthy donors and prominent politicians – mainly to raise funds for its international partner's projects in less developed countries. WWF, a foundation with a self-perpetuating board, had no voting members, only donors (Haag 1986; Bergstedt 1998).

Nature Protection and Confrontational Environmentalism

Germany's economic miracle helped to build a stable polity, but the environmental effects were less positive. By the late 1960s, the Rhine was experiencing massive fish kills and episodically covered with foam. Visible pollution hung over industrial areas such as the Ruhr (Wey 1982; Dominick 1992). The SPD/Liberal government elected in 1969 moved quickly to ameliorate these problems, passing new laws in areas such as solid waste disposal and air and water pollution, and setting up advisory panels and bureaus to formulate policy, enforce the laws and conduct research. Its programme targeted mainly human health and well-being, but much of the new legislation also benefited nature (Müller 1986).

Increasing public interest in environmental problems manifested itself in the same period in the form of many new Bürgerinitiativen (BIs) (citizens' initiatives) with environmental goals. They were part of a broader movement seeking increased citizen participation in local policy decisions, which included BIs with diverse types of goals. The environmental BIs most often emphasized human health or well-being – addressing issues such as air and water pollution, highway construction, traffic and energy; however, their work often benefited nature indirectly, and some were founded specifically to protect nature from construction projects or to establish nature reserves and parks. BIs were generally less tightly structured and shorter lived than the nature protection organizations, and their national organizations were loose networks, like the Bundesverband Bürgerinitiativen (BBU) (Federal Alliance of Citizens' Initiatives for Environmental Protection) (Mayer-Tasch 1985; Markham 2005).

New environmental legislation and the BIs were just two among many factors that ushered in a powerful environmental movement in the 1970s. Other factors included (a) increasing press attention to environmental problems (Brand et al. 1997); (b) the protest-oriented counterculture that flourished in university towns and some urban milieus in the late 1960s and 1970s (Koopmans 1995); (c) a series of high-visibility 'events' in the early 1970s, including the Club of Rome Report, the first Earth Day, and the first UN environmental conference (Dominick 1992); (d) growing criticism of Germany's pro-growth ideology (Mayer-Tasch 1985); and (e) maturation of a new generation of economically secure Germans with 'post-materialist' values (Inglehart 1990).

The movement's primary emphasis was what Germans came to call *Umweltschutz* (environmental protection). *Umweltschutz* included nature protection (*Naturschutz*) but also emphasized new issues, such as population, consumption, and pollution's impact on human health and ecosystems. The movement's primary organizational vehicle was not the traditional nature protection associations, with their limited goals and rather conservative memberships, but the BIs and their umbrella organizations (Rat von Sachverständigen 1996; Oswald von Nell-Breuning-Institut 1996).

Initially the movement worked mainly within the system; however, things changed in the mid-1970s, when the government, concerned about oil prices and the economy, slowed environmental legislation and enforcement and initiated a major expansion of Germany's nuclear power programme. New BIs were founded to resist nuclear power plants, and many environmental BIs allied themselves with the anti-nuclear movement. When the government failed to change course, the overlapping anti-nuclear and environmental movements turned to massive protests and site occupations conducted by an uneasy alliance of BIs from affected areas, other environmental BIs and their networks, countercultural protesters, and far left groups. The government viewed the protests as a threat to national security and moved forcefully against them. A series of confrontations – some violent – ensued, radicalizing some participants and polarizing the population (Joppke 1993; Oswald von Nell-Breuning-Institut 1996).

Polarization was reinforced by many environmentalists' involvement in networks of anti-nuclear, peace, feminist and other new social movement groups. This milieu nurtured (a) deep concern about the severity of environmental problems, (b) radical critiques of consumerism, capitalism, technology and militarism, (c) interest in self-realization and alternative lifestyles, (d) commitment to grass-roots democracy and protest and a jaundiced view of the political system, and (e) reluctance to compromise (Koopmans 1995; Oswald von Nell-Breuning-Institut 1996).

Together with other new social movements, the environmental movement gave birth to the Green Party, which coalesced out of slates of Green candidates for local office at the beginning of the 1980s. The Greens placed nature protection higher on the agenda than the other parties, and their efforts increased the visibility of environmental and nature protection; however, nature protection was only one of the many issues the Greens pursued (Mez 1987).

The rise of a powerful movement with a confrontational approach and concerns far broader than nature protection posed difficult choices for Germany's nature protection organizations, with their limited missions, propensity for working within the system, and relatively conservative memberships. Involvement in the movement might bring them new members and influence, but movement involvement risked subordination of nature protection to other goals, offending existing members, and disrupting longstanding ties to government. The nature protection organizations reacted variously. Some, including the Nature Parks and Forest Protection Associations, retained their traditional goals and strategies, often with stagnant or declining membership (Dominick 1992; Rat von Sachverständigen 1996; Oswald von Nell-Breuning-Institut 1996).

Others, including the DNR and WWF, made only minor adjustments. The DNR played a secondary role in framing new environmental legislation, and it adjusted its public education efforts to emphasize that damage to nature threatened the very basis of human life. Nevertheless, the diversity of its member organizations' agendas, its long history of cooperation with government and dependence on government subsidies, lack of resources to support an expanded mission, and concern that new issues would divert attention from nature protection made the DNR hesitant to embrace the environmental movement. The accession of new organizations, such as Greenpeace, and the movement of some older members towards a broader environmental agenda and more activist stance thus exacerbated longstanding internal conflicts over issues such as hunting and nuclear power, and efforts to steer a middle course often satisfied no one. Several member organizations oriented to confrontational environmentalism threatened to leave, and a number of more conservative groups, including the hunters, did depart. These changes allowed the DNR to broaden its agenda, but its leadership continued to avoid confrontation (Leonard 1986; Hey and Brendle 1994; Chaney 1996).

WWF also passed through the period of confrontation without major alteration of its goals or strategies. During the 1970s, it continued to function mainly as a fundraising arm for WWF International. Under new leadership in the early 1980s, it professionalized, added more German projects, and initiated efforts to influence policy through public education and lobbying. Nevertheless, it remained politically cautious, and its ties to business, refusal to oppose nuclear power and undemocratic governance precipitated considerable criticism. Nevertheless, its strong reputation as a nature protection organization allowed it to benefit from growing environmental consciousness through increased membership and donations (Cornelsen 1991; Bergstedt 1998).

Still other nature protection organizations, including the BN and BfV, undertook major expansions of their goals and strategies (Oswald von Nell-Breuning-Institut 1996; Rat von Sachverständigen 1996). In the late 1960s, some members began questioning the BN's focus on protecting small areas and traditions of cooperation with the government. This faction gained control in 1969. It expanded the BN's agenda to include population, consumerism and pollution, and pushed for a more politically activist stance. The BN also moved gradually from mild support of nuclear power to strong opposition, and by the 1980s, it was participating in anti-nuclear protests. By altering course to adopt the role of social movement organization, the BN was able to grow rapidly and add new local groups; however, older members worried about a takeover by radicals, and there were numerous resignations over nuclear power (Hoplitschek 1984; Wolf 1996).

In 1975, the BN, its smaller counterparts in other regions and prominent environmentalists established a new national organization, the Bund Umwelt und Naturschutz Deutschland (BUND) (League for Environment and Nature Protection in Germany). They envisioned a politically effective organization with a broader agenda and wider appeal than the nature protection organizations or the DNR. Its early leaders covered the entire political spectrum, but, during the late 1970s, many conservative supporters withdrew, as BUND became deeply involved in anti-nuclear power protests and began directing harsh criticism toward the government; however, BUND eschewed violence and involvement with the far left. Moreover, despite its growing involvement with the environmental movement, BUND continued its nature protection efforts, buying nature reserves and participating in local projects.

The internal conflicts initially retarded BUND's growth, but it gradually consolidated its position and grew rapidly in the late 1970s and 1980s.

Combining participation in the movement, lobbying, public education and traditional nature protection, it attracted a constituency comprising mainly the well-educated, professional middle class (Hoplitschek 1984; Leonhard 1986; Wolf 1996; Bergstedt 1998).

The BfV entered the period of activist environmentalism with a core membership that included many conservative birdwatchers and hikers with little sympathy for counterculturally tinged environmentalism and minimal interest in issues such as nuclear energy and traffic. Its leadership overlapped with government and business, and it was rarely confrontational. Nevertheless, the BfV too adapted to changing times. During the second half of the 1970s and early 1980s, it adopted a series of increasingly broad mission statements that gradually expanded its goals to include protection of animals, protection of the landscape, and environmental protection. The reorientation accelerated during the 1980s, as leaders of the BfV's youth group initiated a highly controversial push to emphasize environmental issues – including nuclear power – and a more activist strategy. Elections of officers and new goal statements were hotly disputed, and there were 10 000 resignations when the board voted to oppose nuclear power. Nevertheless, membership gains exceeded the losses. The departure of older members by resignation or ageing resulted in a substantial reorientation, although nature protection remained the BfV's strong point (Cornelsen 1991; May 1999; Bergstedt 1998).

The environmental movement also provided the impetus for the 1980 founding of Greenpeace Germany. Protection of whales, seals and other wildlife was a prominent Greenpeace International goal almost from the beginning, and Greenpeace Germany featured these activities in its publicity; however, its actual programme focused mainly on industrial pollution, not nature protection, prompting some activists to abandon it to found a new organization, Robin Wood, to focus on protecting dying forests. Nevertheless, Greenpeace Germany's professionally planned, spectacular actions, such as climbing smokestacks and hanging banners to protest emissions, attracted much media attention. Greenpeace achieved near exponential growth during the 1980s, and became Germany's largest environmental organization (Hey and Brendle 1994; Blühdorn 1995).

Nature Protection in the German Democratic Republic

The postwar situation in Eastern Germany created even more obstacles to nature protection than in the West. Transformed under Soviet hegemony into a socialist state, the GDR struggled without much outside assistance to industrialize an economy that had been primarily agricultural. Until construction of the Berlin Wall, its problems were compounded by mass emigration. Lacking significant oil or gas reserves or hard currency, the

GDR was forced to rely on lignite, one of the most polluting fuels, which it mined from destructive strip mines. Collectivization of farms and efforts to minimize food imports encouraged reliance on industrialized agriculture, and outdated industrial and chemical plants belched air pollution. The official ideology labelled these problems as temporary, information about them was suppressed, and direct public criticism was risky. By the 1980s, the GDR was one of the world's most polluted countries, with visible, widespread damage to forests, soils and rivers, and clear threats to human health (Würth 1985; Rösler et al. 1990).

Committed nature protection advocates resumed work after the war, but the authorities, sceptical of their class background and ideological orientation, placed them under close supervision. After a difficult transitional period, nature protection groups resumed their traditional tasks, organized first as Friends of Nature and the Homeland and, after 1980, as the Gesellschaft für Natur und Umwelt (GNU) (Society for Nature and Environment). The political context caused them to focus mainly on traditional nature protection. They cared for existing nature protection areas, tried to persuade the state to protect new areas, and worked behind the scenes for new nature protection regulations and against government plans that threatened nature (Würth 1985; Rösler et al. 1990; Behrens et al. 1993).

Despite the obstacles, GNU groups did sometimes achieve results, especially in jurisdictions where government and party leaders were sympathetic. Their efforts, together with the GDR's quest for international acceptance, prompted passage of an ambitious nature protection and regional planning law in 1970 and establishment of an environmental ministry in 1972; however, lack of funds for implementation and the state's commitment to maintaining social stability through maximizing industrial and agricultural output limited their effectiveness (Würth 1985; Rösler et al. 1990; Behrens 2003).

Taking note of the escalating problems, the GDR's Evangelical Church initiated an environmental programme in the late 1970s, and environmental groups sponsored by local churches began to appear in the early 1980s. They held informal discussions, sponsored seminars, gathered information about environmental problems and disseminated it in church-sponsored publications, and sponsored symbolic events, such as tree plantings and bicycle rides. The Church's emphasis on protecting God's creation gave nature protection a prominent place in their efforts, and efforts to develop ecologically sound lifestyles figured prominently; confrontation and direct criticism of the government were not initially on the agenda (Rösler et al. 1990; Gensichen 1994).

As the winds of change began to blow in the late 1980s, the church groups established new networks centred around environmental libraries in Berlin, Leipzig and elsewhere, and undertook riskier activities, such as publishing environmental data and smuggling out films showing environmental damage. They were joined by newly formed Stadtökologie (city ecology) groups within the GNU, which focused on urban environmental problems and were more confrontational (Jordan 1993; Behrens et al. 1993; Neubert 1997).

Environmental protection and nature protection were among the concerns of the movement that swept the old regime from power in 1989, but not its top priority. Church and city ecology groups played a significant role during the transitional period, and the new GDR government introduced important reforms, including designating many large nature protection areas and beginning a cleanup of the worst pollution. However, before these reforms could proceed far, the movement had turned to demanding German reunification (Rink 2001).

Relatively few environmental groups survived reunification. Some assimilated into the Green Party, some merged with West German environmental organizations, and others disbanded, including some that joined the BfV, which then took the new name Naturschutzbund Deutschland (NABU) (German Nature Protection League) (Behrens 2003). In 1990 a number of local environmental groups formed a loose network of local environmental groups, Grüne Liga, which still exists (Bergstedt 1998; Rink 2001).

NATURE PROTECTION IN CONTEMPORARY GERMANY

Recent Trends

Polarization and confrontation over nuclear power and other issues continued into the 1980s; however, the trends that influence nature protection efforts today were already emerging. The first of these was the increasing institutionalization of environmentalism.

During the 1980s, the government responded to the electoral successes of the Greens and to public concerns about nuclear power, chemical accidents and acid rain with a series of new initiatives. These included measures to make chemical production less polluting, reduce air pollution, increase recycling and reduce packaging, and improve water quality in Germany's rivers. It also strengthened environmental education, increased budgets for environmental cleanups and nature protection, and established an environmental ministry, and later a nature protection research office (Müller 1986; Brand et al. 1997).

More recent developments have been more ambiguous, although there has been no overall reversal of the trend toward institutionalization. Several *Länder* dissolved their environmental ministries during the 1990s, and the national government placed some environmental initiatives, including updating the nature protection law, on the back burner. It also 'simplified' permission for projects to rebuild infrastructure in the East, reducing protection of nature. However, after electoral losses in the early 1990s, the Greens rebounded in 1998 and became the junior partner in a new coalition government with the Social Democrats. It pushed through a fuels tax, a phase-out of nuclear power, and a revision of the nature protection law, which included new regulations for agriculture, additional national parks, and a provision allowing nature protection organizations to appeal administrative decisions that might damage nature (Jänicke et al. 1999; Rüdig 2002). The Agriculture Ministry became a Ministry for Consumer Protection and Agriculture, and was assigned to a Green Minister, who vigorously promoted organic farming (Lange 2004). On the other hand, the Greens were unable to attain many of their objectives (Blühdorn 2002), and SPD–Green government was replaced in 2005 with a 'grand coalition' of the two major parties.

Institutionalization has also occurred in the economic sector. During the 1980s, German business began to back away from across-the-board opposition to environmental measures. Many firms developed environmental plans and established ecological communication programmes. Some introduced innovative production processes to make them less damaging; others began to market environmental technologies (Rat von Sachverständigen 1996; Brand et al. 1997). The 1980s and 1990s also saw efforts to build cooperative relationships between environmentalists and unions through consultations, joint conferences, and joint projects in areas such as energy and building materials (Oswald von Nell-Breuning-Institut 1996; Krüger 2000).

A second important trend was diminishing polarization over environmental issues. The growing institutionalization of ecology reduced environmentalists' propensity to see themselves as an embattled minority and encouraged a more cooperative approach. By the late 1980s, the environmental/anti-nuclear alliance was dissolving, as moderate environmentalists realized the limits of confrontation and Germany's nuclear power programme stalled (Koopmans 1995; Rat von Sachverständigen 1996). Environmental protest has not disappeared (Rucht and Roose 2001), but it has clearly weakened (Blühdorn 2002).

A third trend is the rise of competing priorities. Reunification required rebuilding the East's institutions and infrastructure, massive environmental cleanups, and privatization or shutting down of industries, with the resultant high unemployment. Closing polluting industries and cleaning up waste sites were of great benefit to nature and the population, but they were offset by the extension of auto transportation and consumerism to the East and the loss of green space to new construction (Hirche 1998). Germany has also been beset by more than a decade of economic stagnation and high unemployment, which has diverted attention from environmental and nature protection, strengthened business arguments that environmental regulation hinders competitiveness, and undermined post-materialist values (Brand et al. 1997; Blühdorn 2000).

A fourth trend is the changing nature of environmental and nature protection problems. The ongoing transition to a service economy, shutdown of much East German industry, and implementation of pollution controls have replaced problems such as belching smokestacks, dying forests and fish kills with issues such as climate change, biodiversity and loss of open space. These problems are no less threatening to nature, but mobilizing the public around them is more difficult because they are often complex, not immediately visible, and more likely to require personal sacrifice (Hey and Brendle 1994; Brand et al. 1997).

Since the 1980s, the trends described above and diminished media coverage have combined to reduce the relative priority of environmental problems in opinion surveys (for example, INRA (Europe) – ECO 1995; Gruneberg and Kuckartz 2003), and environmental issues have been overshadowed by other issues in recent elections (Blühdorn 2002). While Germans have not lost interest in the environment and nature protection, other issues have taken priority (Gruneberg and Kuckartz 2003). These changes created a new situation for the environmental movement, which has been characterized by scholars (for example, Blühdorn 2002; Brand 1999), the press (for example, *Die Zeit* 1999), and even Germany's Council of Environmental Experts (*Berliner Zeitung* 2004) as becalmed. Organizations that grounded their approach in countercultural ideology and protest have been particularly hard hit. Most informed observers report reductions in the number and strength of BIs (Oswald von Nell-Breuning-Institut 1996; Bergstedt 1998; but see Rucht and Roose 2001), and their national and regional networks experienced steep membership declines (Koopmans 1995; Markham 2005).

PROFILES OF NATURE PROTECTION ORGANIZATIONS

The changed conditions were also a major challenge for organizations focused solely on nature protection and organizations that combined environmental and nature protection goals. By developing successful strategies to cope with changing conditions, organizations of the latter type emerged from the 1980s as the dominant actors in national-level nature protection. The five most important of these are listed in Table 4.1. Three of them,

Table 4.1 Most important national nature protection organizations

	Date founded	Number of supporters 2004 (change since 1999)	Budget receipts 2004 in € (change since 1999)	Legal form and governance	Major goals	Major activities	Nature protection areas
WWF Deutschland	1963	284 000 donors (11.8%)	24 200 000 (21.4%); most revenue from individual donations, but significant support from business and some from government	Foundation with self-perpetuating board; no *Länder* chapters and only a few informally organized local groups; supporters are donors without voting rights	Nature protection at national and, especially, at international level; protection of climate and key ecosystems	Public education via publications, member magazine, press releases and Internet; political action via expert reports and position papers, lobbying, participation in hearings and meetings, and infrequent protests	Yes, but most in less developed countries
Naturschutz-bund Deutschland	1899, as League for Bird Protection	393 912 members; includes Bavarian affiliate	19 400 000 (38.0%); most revenue from member dues,	Registered voluntary association with chapters in every *Land*	General environmental organization with strong emphasis on	Public education via publications, member magazine, press releases, Internet;	Large network of reserves; some also used for

		(11.4% since 2000)	but some support from business and government	except Bavaria and 1400 local groups; local officers directly elected; *Land* and national officers elected by delegates' assembly	nature protection, especially at local level	political action via expert reports and position papers, lobbying, participation in hearings and meetings, and infrequent protests	public education and research
Bund Umwelt und Naturschutz Deutschland	1975 (predecessor organization in Bavaria 1913)	392 525 members and donors (7.7%)	13 687 000 (−12.0%); most revenue from member dues and individual donations, but some support from business and some from government	Registered voluntary association with chapters in every *Land* and 2100 local groups; local officers directly elected; *Land* and national officers elected by delegates' assembly	General environmental organization with nature protection among goals	Public education via publications, member magazine, press releases, Internet; political action via numerous well-researched expert reports and position papers, lobbying, participation in hearings and meetings, and occasional protests	Yes, including some used for public education

Table 4.1 (continued)

	Date founded	Number of supporters 2004 (change since 1999)	Budget receipts 2004 in € (change since 1999)	Legal form and governance	Major goals	Major activities	Nature protection areas
Greenpeace Deutschland	1980	548 000 donors (7.5%)	41 538 000 (24.3%); almost all revenue from individual donations	Registered voluntary association with approximately 40 voting members, including many from paid staff and Greenpeace International; other supporters are donors without voting rights	General environmental and peace organization with nature protection among goals, especially at international level	Public education via publications, member newsletter, magazine for general public, press releases, and Internet; political action via expert reports and position papers, lobbying, and participation in hearings and meetings; frequent spectacular actions to call public attention to problems and exert pressure on business and government	No

Deutscher Naturschutz Ring	1950	95 member organizations (−3% since 2000)	No information	Umbrella organization with other organizations as members; national officers elected at representative assembly	General environmental organization with emphasis on nature protection	Public education via publications, press releases, conferences and Internet; coordination of work of other organizations through newsletter and networking; political action via expert reports and position papers, lobbying, and participation in hearings and meetings	No

WWF, NABU and the DNR, once had nature protection as their only goal. All expanded their missions during the environmental movement, but they continue to emphasize nature protection more than BUND and Greenpeace, which generally give other environmental goals more prominence. As the German affiliate of Friends of the Earth, BUND also has an interest in international development issues. Organizations that pursue solely nature protection goals continue to exist, but they lack the membership and financial resources to be major actors (Oswald von Nell-Bruning-Institut 1996; Rat von Sachverständigen 1996).

Membership

The number of member organizations in the DNR has changed little over the last quarter-century. The other four organizations grew rapidly during the 1980s. WWF, NABU and BUND experienced a slowdown in growth during the early 1990s, and Greenpeace lost many supporters (Hey and Brendle 1994; Rucht and Roose 1999). Since 1999, the pattern for all four has been slow, steady growth, with an average total increase of about 10 per cent. NABU and WWF, which emphasize nature protection, have grown more rapidly than BUND or Greenpeace. The four organizations' total of about 1.6 million supporters undoubtedly includes many overlaps, but it remains an impressive number. All four are underrepresented in eastern Germany, and NABU and BUND are overrepresented in southern Germany.

Finances

WWF, BUND, NABU and Greenpeace have annual receipts ranging from €19 to €41 million. The DNR's revenue is tiny in comparison. All of the organizations with individual members except BUND reported increases of at least 20 per cent over the past five years. Their total annual receipts of just under €100 000 000 are impressive, although small in relation to the funds available to business and labour or the cost of extensive land purchases. All except the DNR are supported mainly by membership dues or individual contributions; however, all but Greenpeace receive some support from government and business, and business donations constitute a noticeable fraction of WWF's budget.

Organizational Goals

The activity repertoires of the five organizations are similar, though not identical. All engage in public education via publications, press releases and

Internet sites. The organizations with individual supporters also publish a member magazine or newsletter, and Greenpeace publishes a general-circulation magazine. All work to influence politics through lobbying and submission of expert reports, position papers and testimony. BUND is the most active in this area. All also engage in at least occasional public protest, and Greenpeace continues to stage spectacular actions. BUND and Greenpeace are generally viewed as more confrontational, but both cooperate at times with government and business. NABU has an especially strong commitment to the purchase and operation of nature reserves, while Greenpeace and the DNR do not have them (Blühdorn 1995; Bergstedt 1998; Bammerlin 1998).

Organizational Structure

The organizations that make up the DNR's membership and individual members of NABU and BUND have the opportunity to influence organizational decisions, although relatively few BUND and NABU members actually participate. WWF and Greenpeace limit policy decisions to an inner circle; their donors have no direct voice. BUND and NABU have regional chapters and local groups with considerable autonomy. Greenpeace's local groups, with a total membership of about 2000, are centred in cities and required to give direct support to the activities of the national organization. WWF's local groups are almost without significance, and DNR has no regional or local substructure (Blühdorn 1995; Bergstedt 1998; Bammerlin 1998).

Other Nature Protection Organizations

In addition to the German Forest Protection and Nature Park Associations, there are numerous other organizations with solely nature protection goals, such as the Deutscher Verband für Landschaftspflege (German Association for Landcare), an umbrella association of organizations working to protect the German landscape (Deutscher Verband für Landschaftspflege 2005). The most prominent organization, however, remains the German Forest Protection Association, which has about 20 000 members and receives significant government subsidies (Bergstedt 1998; Schutzgemeinschaft Deutscher Wald 2003). There are also numerous regional nature protection organizations and independent regional birdwatching or ornithological societies. Organizations whose members use nature for recreation or nature study, such as hunters, hikers and anglers, and the Deutscher Alpenverein (German Alpine Association) frequently have nature protection as a secondary goal. They have impressive memberships and enrol constituencies not easily reached by environmental or nature protection organizations; however, other nature protection organizations sometimes see the uses they make of nature as destructive (Oswald von Nell-Breuning-Institut 1996; Rat von Sachverständigen 1996).

STRATEGIES OF THE MAJOR NATURE PROTECTION ORGANIZATIONS

Although there are variations in detail, BUND, NABU, Greenpeace and WWF have all centred their efforts on adapting to the social context in which they find themselves around four key strategies.

First, all four organizations have become highly professionalized. WWF never depended heavily on volunteers, but its rapid growth and increasing involvement in politics and the management of nature reserves have led to significant increases in staff size and professionalization. Greenpeace Germany initially operated informally but quickly developed into a highly professionalized, centralized organization. NABU and BUND, with their long traditions of reliance on volunteers, professionalized more reluctantly, but both now rely on professionals to accomplish most tasks in their national offices – and increasingly in their regional offices as well. In all four organizations, professionals plan campaigns, produce magazines and educational materials, conduct research and write reports, lobby and raise funds. This trend has resulted from: (a) growing emphasis on activities where professional quality work is expected; (b) the increasing professionalization of their opponents and negotiating partners; and (c) the decreasing availability of volunteers with the time, skills and commitment to accomplish the work required (Oswald von Nell-Breuning-Institut 1996; Rat von Sachverständigen 1996; Bammerlin 1998).

The growing institutionalization of environmentalism, the decline of the confrontational environmental movement, and the decreasing priority of environmental issues have contributed to a second development, the organizations' movement away from protests, demonstrations and confrontation in favour of work within the system. WWF was, of course, never very confrontational, and while Greenpeace continues to stage its trademark spectacular actions, it now touts its role in preparing research reports, developing workable solutions, cooperating with business and lobbying government (Oswald von Nell-Breuning-Institut 1996; Rat von Sachverständigen 1996; Brand et al. 1997).

A third adaptation is a growing emphasis on accumulating the largest possible number of supporters. The German government is plagued by budget shortfalls, and businesses are quite selective about what organizations and projects they support, so the support available is limited, and accepting such funds subjects the organizations to criticism from the press and their own core supporters. Even WWF receives only a relatively small portion of its financial support from business or government, so recruiting individual supporters has emerged as the most promising way to fund the organizations' expensive public education projects, political work and professional staffs. Having an impressive number of supporters also increases their credibility and influence (Hey and Brendle 1994; Oswald von Nell-Breuning-Institut 1996; Felbinger 2005).

In the face of declining press coverage and public interest, the four individual membership organizations have had to innovate and work hard to attract supporters. All have developed highly professionalized fundraising operations based on direct mail and solicitation of supporters door to door or from stands in public places. These techniques have been very successful in keeping funds flowing and the membership totals growing; however, they are often criticized as promoting 'chequebook environmentalism', which encourages the public to see nature and environmental protection as tasks for professionals (Haibach 1998; Felbinger 2005).

Finally, all the organizations continue to stress nature protection and advertise their successes in this area (see for example, NABU 2000; *BUNDMagazin* 2004). There are at least three likely reasons for this. First, nature protection – in particular protection of impressive mammals and birds – commands more attention and is easier to understand than many environmental problems. Second, nature protection has proven appeal across ideological and class lines, and provokes little resistance. Third, the decline of the confrontational movement and the reduced priority of environmental and nature protection in public consciousness have made other goals less attractive to potential supporters.

These four strategies are mutually reinforcing. Supporting large professional staffs requires major infusions of funds, and professionals often prefer working within the system over protest. Building mass membership organizations requires additional professionals to solicit supporters, and efforts to attract mass support today are facilitated by emphasizing nature protection and can be undermined by reliance on countercultural ideologies and confrontation.

SUMMARY AND CONCLUSIONS

Nature protection has proven to be both a highly mutable and a highly resilient theme in Germany. Some organizations have pursued it as their sole objective; others have pursued it in combination with a wide variety of other goals: preserving traditional architecture, anti-urbanism, outdoor recreation, and combating air and water pollution. It has, at various times, been embraced by the anti-modernist right, the socialist left, and the countercultural left – and sometimes simultaneously by more than one of these. In some periods, it has been high on the national agenda; in others, it has remained in the background, but it has never disappeared. Nature protection survived depression and runaway inflation, *Gleichschaltung*, postwar chaos, East German socialism, and the confrontational environmental activism of the 1970s. It shows every sign of surviving contemporary challenges and provides much of the appeal of present-day environmental organizations.

In fact, it is quite misleading to talk about 'the German nature protection movement', for nature protection advocates have rarely mounted an independent social movement. Instead, they have typically sought to advance their cause by attaching it to other social movements. Moreover, nature protection has often been appropriated by movements with broader goals, including movements for homeland protection, socialism, national socialism, and countercultural environmentalism, because it fitted into their world-view or served their purposes.

Some nature protection organizations have benefited from alliances with such movements, but others have thought it better to steer clear of them because participation might detract from nature protection. The experiences of organizations that were placed under state supervision after social movements seized control of the state, and instances where nature protection was eclipsed by other objectives, such as protection of traditional architecture or fighting nuclear energy, show that caution about affiliation with other movements is indeed warranted.

German history also shows that nature protection is anything but the exclusive property of ideologies and movements of the left. Nature protection and environmentalist themes have also resonated with ideologies of the right, and continue to do so (Geden 1999). Overgeneralization from the alliance of nature protection with environmental movements of the left during recent decades is therefore inappropriate and potentially misleading. Indeed, the current strategies of the large organizations with environmental and nature protection goals all show movement toward the political centre.

Why then has nature protection continued to flourish? Social constructionists (e.g. Hannigan 1995) suggest that topics such as nature protection become social issues, not mainly because they are self-evidently problematic, but because scientists, the media, or social movement entrepreneurs frame them in ways that persuade the public that they are indeed problems. In part, the history of nature protection in Germany supports this argument, for nature protection attracted its greatest support when it became part of the agenda of social movements that framed it in ways that made it attractive to mass publics.

This approach, however, fails to explain why concern about nature has been so persistent and why so many diverse movements and organizations have taken up the nature protection banner. Part of the explanation may be the sheer visibility of the impact of industrialization and population growth on nature in densely populated twentieth-century Germany. Animal and plant species disappeared, forests were cut, marshes were drained to become agricultural fields, and fields became suburbs. These facts are not subject to dispute in quite the same way as are the effects of low levels of chemical pollution, and Germans could hardly take comfort in the view that there was still plenty of nature left. A second possible explanation, summarized in Chapter 1, is the growth of an Arcadian tradition of concern for nature that emerges out of social changes accompanying industrialization and urbanization. That is, the effects of these changes may be to produce a concern about nature that manifests itself in different ways in various historical circumstances but survives them all. But whatever the reason for the persistence of nature protection as a key theme in German social history, past experience and current events suggest that scholars can expect nature protection to remain a prominent theme for many years to come.

NOTES

1. This chapter is based on the author's forthcoming book, *Environmental Organizations in Modern Germany: Hardy Survivors in the Twentieth Century and Beyond*, scheduled for publication by Berghahn Books in 2008. To conserve space, only key references are cited here. Readers are invited to consult the book for a more extensive bibliography.
2. *Heimat* is conventionally translated as 'homeland', but it also implies strong emotional attachment based on familiarity, family and tradition.

REFERENCES

Bammerlin, Ralf (1998), *Umweltverbände in Deutschland*, Beiheft 24, *Flora and Fauna in Rheinland-Pfalz*, Landau: Naturschutz und Ornithologie Rheinland Pfalz.

Behrens, Hermann (2003), 'Naturschutz in der Deutschen Demokratischen Republik', in Werner Konold, R. Bäcker and U. Hampicke (eds), *Handbuch Naturschutz und Landschaftspflege*, vol. 9, Landberg: Ecomed, pp. 1–20.

Behrens, Hermann, Ulrike Benkert, Jürgen Hopfmann and Uwe Maechler (1993), *Wurzeln der Umweltbewegung: Die 'Gesellschaft für Natur und Umwelt' (GNU) im Kulturbund der DDR*, Marburg: BdWi Verlag.

Berliner Zeitung (2004), 'Verlorener Schwung', *Berliner Zeitung* (6 May), Politik, 6.

Bergmann, Klaus (1970), *Agrarromantik und Großstadtfeindschaft*, Meisenheim am Glan: Verlag Anton Hair.

Bergstedt, Jörg (1998), *Agenda, Expo, Sponsoring*, Frankfurt: IKO – Verlag für Interkulturelle Kommunikation.
Blühdorn, Ingolfur (1995), 'Campaigning for Nature: Environmental Pressure Groups in Germany and Generational Change in the Ecology Movement', in Ingolfur Blühdorn, Frank Krause and Thomas Scharf (eds), *The Green Agenda*, Keele, UK: Keele University Press, pp. 167–220.
Blühdorn, Ingolflur (2000), *Post-Ecologist Politics*, London: Routledge.
Blühdorn, Ingolfur (2002), 'Green Futures? A Future for the Greens?', in Axel Goodbody (ed.), *The Culture of German Environmentalism*, New York: Berghahn Books, pp. 103–12.
Brand, Karl-Werner (1999), 'Tranformationen der Ökologiebewegung', in Ansager Klein, Hans-Josef Legrand and Thomas Leif (eds), *Neue Soziale Bewegungen*, Opladen: Westdeutscher Verlag, pp. 237–56.
Brand, Karl-Werner, Klaus Eder and Angelika Poferl (1997), *Ökologische Kommunikation in Deutschland*, Opladen: Westdeutscher Verlag.
BUNDMagazin (2004), 'Naturschutz im BUND', *BUNDMagazin* No. 3, 15–17.
Chaney, Sandra (1996), 'Visions and Revisions of Nature', unpublished doctoral dissertation, Department of History, University of North Carolina at Chapel Hill.
Cornelsen, Dirk (1991), *Anwälte der Natur*, Munich: Beck.
Deutscher Verband für Landschaftspflege (2005), 'Wir über Uns', accessed 13 July, http://www.lpv.de.
Die Zeit (1999), 'Umwelt ist Uncool', *Die Zeit*, 11 (3 March), Wirtschaft, 17.
Dominick, Raymond H. (1992), *The Environmental Movement in Germany*, Bloomington, IN: Indiana University Press.
Erdmann, Wulf and Jochen Zimmer (eds) (1991), *Hundert Jahre Kampf um freie Natur*, Essen: Klartext Verlag.
Felbinger, Doris (2005), *Ego oder Öko*, Berlin: Logos Verlag.
Fischer, Helmut (1994), *90 Jahre für Umwelt und Naturschutz*, Bonn: Deutscher Heimatbund.
Geden, Oliver (1999), *Rechte Ökologie*, Berlin: Elefanten Press.
Gensichen, Hans-Peter (1994), 'Das Umweltengagement in den Evangelsichen Kirchen in der DDR', in Hermann Behrens and Horst Pauke (eds), *Umweltgeschichte: Wissenschaft und Praxis*, Marburg: Verlag des Bundes Demokratischer Wissenschaftlerinnen und Wissenschaftler, pp. 65–83.
Gröning, Gert and Jaochim Wolschke-Bulmahn (1987), 'Politics, Planning, and the Protection of Nature', *Planning Perspectives*, **2**, 127–48.
Gröning, Gert and Joachim Wolschke-Bulmahn (1998), 'Landschafts- und Naturschutz', in Diethart Kerbs and Jürgen Reulecke (eds), *Handbuch der Deutschen Reformbewegung 1880–1933*, Wuppertal: Peter Hammer Verlag, pp. 23–34.
Gruneberg, Heiko and Udo Kuckartz (2003), *Umweltbewußtsein im Wandel*, Opladen: Leske + Budrich.
Haag, Dietrich W. (1986), 'Die Umweltstiftung WWF-Deutschland', in Rolf Hauer et al. (eds), *Lebensbilder Deutscher Stiftungen*, vol. 5, Tübingen: I.C.B. Mohr, pp. 471–82.
Haibach, Marita (1998), *Handbuch Fundraising*, Frankfurt: Campus Verlag.
Hannigan, John (1995), *Environmental Sociology*, London: Routledge.
Hey, Christian and Uwe Brendle (1994), *Umweltverbände und EU*, Opladen: Westdeutscher Verlag.

Hirche, Walter (1998), 'Umweltschutz in den Neuen Ländern: Bilanz und Perspektive', in Fritz Brickwedde (ed.), *Umweltschutz in Ostdeutschland und Osteuropa*, Onasbrück: Steinbacher, pp. 13–30.
Hoplitschek, Ernst (1984), 'Der BUND Naturschutz in Bayern', unpublished doctoral dissertation, Berlin: Fachbereich Politische Wissenschaften, Freie Universität.
Inglehart, Ronald (1990), 'Values, Ideology, and Cognitive Mobilization in New Social Movements', in Russell J. Dalton and Manfred Keuchler (eds), *Challenging the Political Order*, New York: Oxford University Press, pp. 43–66.
INRA (Europe) – ECO (1995), 'Europeans and the Environment in 1995', Eurobarometer 43.1 BIS. Brussels: Directorate General Environment, Nuclear Safety and Civil Protestion, European Union.
Jänicke, Martin, Philip Kunig and Michael Stitzel (1999), *Umweltpolitik*, Bonn: Dietz.
Joppke, Christian (1993), *Mobilizing against Nuclear Energy*, Berkeley, CA: University of California Press.
Jordan, Carlo (1993), 'Im Wandel: Ökologie und Grüne im Osten', in Gerda Haufe and Karl Bruckmeier (eds), *Die Bürgerbewegung in der DDR und in den Ostdeutschen Bundesländern*, Opladen: Westdeutscher Verlag, pp. 240–61.
Knaut, Andreas (1993), *Züruck zur Natur!*, Bonn: Arbeitsgemeinschaft Beruflicher und Ehrenamtlicher Naturchutz.
Koopmans, Ruud (1995), *Democracy from Below*, Boulder, CO: Westview.
Krüger, Sabine (2000), 'Arbeit und Umwelt Verbänden', Berlin: Wissenschaftszentrum Berlin für Sozialforschung.
Lange, Hellmuth (2004), 'Rapid Change in Agricultural Policies. The BSE Crisis in Germany (2000–2001)', Bremen: Research Center for Sustainability Studies (Artec), Artec-paper No. 119.
Leonhard, Martin (1986), *Umweltverbände: Zur Organisation von Umweltinteressen in der Bundesrepublik Deutschland*, Opladen: Westdeutscher Verlag.
Markham, William T. (2005), 'Networking Local Environmental Groups in Germany: The Rise and Fall of the Federal Alliance of Citizens' Initiatives for Environmental Protection', *Environmental Politics*, **14** (November), 667–85.
May, Helge (1999), *100 Jahre NABU*, Bonn: NABU.
Mayer-Tasch, Cornelius (1985), *Die Bürgerinitiativbewegung*, Reinbek bei Hamburg: Rowohlt.
Mez, Lutz (1987), 'Von den Bürgerinitiativen zu den Grünen', in Roland Roth and Dieter Rucht (eds), *Neue Soziale Bewegungen in der Bundesrepublik Deutschland*, Bonn: Bundeszentrale für Politische Bildung, pp. 379–91.
Milnik, Albrecht (2003), 'Hugo Conwentz: Zur Geschichte des Staatlichen Stelle für Naturdenkmalpflege in Preußen', in Stiftung Naturschutzgeschichte (ed.), *Naturschutz Hat Geschichte*, Essen: Klartext, pp. 131–43.
Müller, Edda (1986), *Innenwelt der Umweltpolitik*, Opladen: Westdeutscher Verlag.
NABU (2000), 'NABU – Grundsatzprogramm', Bonn: NABU.
Neubert, Erhardt (1997), *Geschichte der Opposition in der DDR, 1949–1989*, Bonn: Bund-zentrale für Politische Bildung.
Oswald von Nell-Breuning-Institut (1996), *Die Rolle der Umweltverbände in den demokratischen und umweltethischen Lernprozessen der Gesellschaft*, Stuttgart: Metzler-Poeschel.
Radkau, Joachim and Frank Uekötter (eds) (2003), *Naturschutz und Nationalsozialismus*, Frankfurt: Campus Verlag.

Rat von Sachverständigen für Umweltfragen (1996), *Umweltgutachten 1996*, Stuttgart: Metzler-Poeschel.
Rink, Dieter (2001), 'Institutionalization instead of Mobilization', in Helena Flamm (ed.), *Pink, Purple, Green*, Boulder, CO: East European Monographs, pp. 120–31.
Rösler, Markus, Elisabeth Schwab and Markus Lambrecht (1990), *Naturschutz in der DDR*, Bonn: Economica Verlag.
Rucht, Dieter and Jochen Roose (1999), 'The German Environmental Movement at the Crossroads', in Christopher Rootes (ed.), *Environmental Movements: Local, National, and Global*, London: Frank Cass, pp. 59–80.
Rucht, Dieter and Jochen Roose (2001), 'Von der Platzbesetzung zum Verhandlungstisch', in Dieter Rucht (ed.), *Protest in der Bundesrepublik*, Frankfurt: Campus Verlag, pp. 173–210.
Rüdig, Wolfgang (2002), 'Germany', *Environmental Politics*, **11** (1), 78–111.
Schutzgemeinschaft Deutscher Wald (2003), 'Ziele und Aufgaben', accessed 12 July, http://www.sdw.de/.
Speitkamp, Winifried (1988), 'Denkmalpflege und Heimatschutz in Deutschland zwischen Kulturkritik und Nationalsozialismus', *Archiv für Kulturegeschichte*, **70**, 149–93.
Wey, Klaus-Georg (1982), *Umweltpolitik in Deutschland*, Opladen: Westdeutscher Verlag.
Wöbse, Anna-Katharina (2003), 'Lina Hähnle: Eine Galionsfigur der Frühen Naturschutzbewegung', in Stiftung Naturschutzgeschichte (ed.), *Naturschutz Hat Geschichte*, Essen: Klartext, pp. 113–30.
Wolf, Angelika (1996), 'Die Analyse der Reformfähigkeit eine Umweltverbandes am Beispiel des Bund für Umwelt und Naturschutz Deutschland e.V.: Aufgaben und Struktur', Doctoral Dissertation, Fachbereich Umwelt und Gesellschaft, Technische Universität Berlin.
Wunderer, Hartmann (1991), *Arbeitervereine und Arbeiterparteien*, Frankfurt: Campus Verlag.
Würth, Gerhard (1985), *Umweltschutz und Umweltzerstörung in der DDR*, Frankfurt: Peter Lang.
Zimmer, Jochem (ed.) (1984), *Mit Uns Zieht die Neue Zeit*, Cologne: Pahl-Rugenstein.

5. Nature protection organizations in Italy: from elitist fervour to confluence with environmentalism

Giorgio Osti

INTRODUCTION

Nature protection organizations in Italy have a long history, albeit one that is often overlooked in recent accounts of the Green movement. A number of quasi-national organizations that focused on protecting nature for recreational and scientific purposes were founded during the last decades of the nineteenth century, and their legacy is important for understanding the strengths and weaknesses of the present-day Italian environmental movement. In the course of their history, the strong and innovative nature protection motivations of these organizations faded away, leaving the environmental organizations founded in the 1970s without a wide base of public support. They are, nevertheless, a part of Italian social history that deserves renewed attention. Clarifying this segment of social history and examining the place of nature protection within the environmental movement today is the aim of this chapter.

The first step toward realizing this aim is to clarify the specific profile of nature protection organizations within the galaxy of Italian environmentalism. Looking at the list of associations recognized by the Ministry of Environment, it is quite easy to identify four types of organization: animal protection, environmental, recreational and scientific.[1] All have an interest in the protection of nature, but few have nature protection as their primary goal. If we apply the following criteria: (a) the number and size of nature reserves directly managed by the association; (b) involvement in policy making about national parks; (c) being active in the debate over biodiversity; and (d) campaigning to protect specific plants and animals, the list of Italian nature protection organizations would be limited to one or two cases. Limiting the analysis to such a small number of organizations would keep us from examining the rich and little-known history of the nature protection movement. A more inclusive approach, which takes into account the evolution of all aspects of the environmental movement, is necessary.

My hypothesis is that, in the course of the recent development of the broad set of organizations concerned with environmental and nature protection, distinctions among them in terms of ideologies, repertoires of action and the staff arrangement have become blurred. In other words, the historical evolution of Italian nature protection organizations has brought them – after two crucial turning points – to a period of convergence on a common model. The argument of this chapter will be developed in two steps: first, a description of the history of the Italian nature protection movement; and second, a comparison of the main organizations today, including some that have nature protection as only a secondary concern, in order to demonstrate the tendency toward convergence.

ORIGINS

It is curious that there is little awareness in Italy today of the existence of a movement for the protection of nature rooted in the last decades of nineteenth century. Even the environmental scholars (for example, Giuliano 1991; Poggio 1996; Della Seta 2000) have failed to examine the organizations founded in that period for the protection of natural areas. The reason for this neglect is probably linked to two 'discontinuities' during the historical development of these organizations. These were moments when their previous customary ways of thinking and acting were interrupted by shocking external events.

Examining the founding dates of Italian organizations concerned with nature protection shows that they appeared in the same period as in other countries, the end of the nineteenth century, when the damages of industrialization to the environment first became visible to Europeans. The first two organizations to be founded, the Italian Alpine Club and the Italian Society of Botanists, set the future course of the movement (see Table 5.1). The former was dedicated to excursions in and explorations of remote areas. The latter was a classical 'natural history organization'. Both were well aware of the harm to nature inflicted by modernization. However, their main areas of interest lay elsewhere: the pleasure of hiking, on the one hand, and the pleasure of research in the field, on the other. The first organization directly engaged in the protection of natural areas appeared later, at the end of the nineteenth century. It was Pro Montibus and Silvis (literally, 'In favour of Mountains and Forests'). In a period when membership of many organizations was restricted to elites, the association was open to all citizens willing to pay the dues.

Table 5.1 Chronology of founding of nature protection organizations

1863	Italian Alpine Club
1888	Italian Botanical Society
1894	Italian (Bicycle) Touring Club
1897	Pro Montibus and Silvis Association
1913	National League for the Protection of Natural Monuments
1948	Italian Movement for the Protection of Nature
1955	Our Italy
1965	League for the Protection of Birds
1966	Italian section of WWF

According to the historian Piccioni (1999), Italian nature protection activities at the turn of the nineteenth century constituted a movement in the full sense of the word. The movement was composed of persons who wanted to act in the public arena to introduce laws to protect nature. They were, in other words, militants for a cause, who organized themselves for achieving their objectives and tried, without success, to create a broad consensus for their goals. There were different motivations within the movement, but they were able to converge on the common target of preserving 'natural monuments', precisely in the meaning nowadays given to protected areas category III by IUCN (see Chapter 1). They attained their highest level of success before the First World War, creating a federation of groups, the National League, and obtaining recognition in international circles. By 1914, there were five 'quasi-national' organizations, which covered most of Italy, with support concentrated in the northern and central parts of the country.

The Discontinuity Caused by Fascism

The First World War interrupted the line of development the nature protection organizations had been following, particularly regarding their international contacts; however, the major discontinuity began later with fascism. The fascist regime, which governed in the *ventennio* period of 1922 to the Second World War, laid bare the weaknesses of Italian civil society, including those of the nature protection organizations. This chapter is not the place to elaborate on the numerous and complex reasons for the rise of fascism. It is enough to point out two conditions that facilitated its ascent: (a) class conflict was not mediated by any superordinate national or civic interest, and (b) the organizations of civil society were very weak due to ideological radicalism, widespread illiteracy and mass poverty. In such a situation – according to Alexander (1995) – it is very difficult for a robust civil society to form.

The nature protection movement fitted this pattern well. It was notoriously elitist, and almost all its members came from the radical movement of the period, a sort of left wing of the Liberal Party. The movement was very open to some social issues, as for example universal suffrage, but it was also imbued with the ideology of defence of private property (Sievert 2000, p. 149). The protection of nature implied a defence of the commons, often contradicting the interests and the rights of private landowners. This put the movement in the embarrassing position of having to promote two often antagonistic values. There was no superordinate national or communitarian interest that could bring together the divergent tensions in an Italian society which had attained national unity only a few years before.

There were several signals of this weakness: (a) the failure of a fundraising campaign among citizens for the creation of the Alta Val di Sangro National park, following a Swiss example; (b) the organizations' small memberships; (c) the absence of movement activity in southern Italy; and (d) the ambiguous position of the 'tourist' organizations with regard to the nature protection cause. The last point must be explained. In its early days, the movement suffered from tensions between the motives that inspired it. The most important tension was probably that between aesthetic motives – represented by the Italian Touring Club – and the motives of the natural history groups. The former organization had a large membership, even during the fascist period, but it was generally committed to *instrumental* nature protection issues – using nature for visitors' enjoyment, using nature for economic development, protecting nature for patriotic reasons and so on (Sievert 2000, p. 136). The protection of nature as a common good was not so strongly represented within the tourist component of movement. That created conflicts that continued even after the Second World War, when the movement sought to begin again using a more science-based rationale.

The fact that the so-called aesthetic wing largely dominated the Italian nature protection movement at the beginning had extremely important implications (Silvestri 2004) and probably constitutes a difference with other countries, where a more science-based environmentalism prevailed from the beginning (Frank 2001). The aesthetic wing has two key features: first, it focused primarily on protecting single places and species, and lacked a vision of nature as an ecosystem; second, it saw a strong continuity between nature and the man-made elements of environment. Both are included in a cultural view that is well summarized in the Italian phrase '*bellezze naturali*' (beauties of nature). The historical sources of this view extend far back in time (Strassoldo 2000–2001) and probably represent a plausible perspective on the natural environment in a country such as Italy. This predominant view, however, was poorly integrated with other themes in the early nature protection movement.

In sum, all the weaknesses of a movement with a promising beginning peaked during the fascist period. The dictatorial regime, for its part, abolished all the nature protection associations and terminated any free activity in civil society. Although two national parks continued to function during the *ventennio*, the regime's control over them, through the forest militia, was strong and highly centralized. Individual advocates of nature protection survived the period, but their influence on government and society was marginal. In a very confused historical period, they were able to push successfully only for the government to approve a law for the 'protection of landscape beauties' (National Law No. 1497, 29 June 1939). We can consider this phase as the first discontinuity in the Italian nature protection movement.

The Postwar Period

Nature protection during the post-Second World War period was dominated by the figure of Renzo Videsott, a veterinarian from the province of Trento, who worked first in Turin and later as Director of the Gran Paradiso National Park. He was probably the only leading figure who fully understood the link between the movement of the first decades of the twentieth century and what was taking place in the nature protection field in this period (Pedrotti 1998). In 1948, he founded the Movimento Italiano per la protezione della Natura (Italian Movement for Nature Protection). He was also able to make Italy one of the most important members of IUPN (later IUCN – International Union for the Conservation of Nature) by attending the founding conference in Fontainebleau in the same year.

Despite Videsott's great personal commitment, the Italian Movement for the Protection of Nature failed to achieve its goals. In particular, it failed in its efforts to transform itself into a federation of groups spread throughout the country with a strong headquarters organization and large membership. It changed its name many times and passed through frequent internal crises. Most importantly, it was not able to become a mass organization. This assessment must be qualified, however (Giuliano 1989), as its successor organization, the Federation Pro Natura, still exists and has a unique profile in the Italian environmentalist landscape (see below).

It is crucial to understand why, in this phase, this movement was unable to accommodate new trends in environmentalism coming from America. Videsott's movement belonged to the conservative–scientific wing of nature protection. In the 1950s, when reconstruction and the 'economic miracle' in Italy began, the nation's crucial problems were located in cities (Nebbia 2002, p. 86). The cities were absorbing a great number of migrants from the countryside and from southern Italy, they were polluted by new factories, and they were victims of land speculation. In particular, damage to cultural monuments, caused by urban development, triggered a strong reaction in one segment of Italian public opinion. It is no coincidence, then, that Italia Nostra (Our Italy) was founded in Rome in 1955 to protect historical monuments and buildings from devastation.

The social backgrounds of this movement's supporters – nobility and professionals in major cities – were similar to those of the prewar nature protection advocates, but their target was only incidentally the protection of nature. The old bias of Italian culture towards the manufactured beauties rose once again and found fertile ground. Our Italy established itself quite well, at least in terms of number of members and local groups. According to Sievert (2000, p. 240), its main goal was not establishing protected areas as 'enclaves of wilderness', but urban planning and building regulations. Moreover, its underlying paradigm came not from the natural sciences, but from architecture and town planning. The 'tourist' wing was also of no great help to the nature protection movement in the strict sense. The Touring Club and Alpine Club actually opposed national parks, which they saw as obstacles to tourism.

The organization best able to address nature protection was the Italian section of WWF, which was founded in 1966. Its founders included some former members of Our Italy, who were not satisfied with its urban-oriented perspective and took the initiative to create an Italian section of WWF. Lacking a broad popular support base, WWF focused its attention mainly on lobbying; however, it also introduced some innovations in organizational strategy, not only by using aggressive and modern public education, but also by choosing new objectives. For example, WWF was successful in creating several small nature reserves and in campaigns to protect endangered species (Meyer 1995). This was a useful way to display a practical and efficient approach towards nature protection (Canu 2003). Instead of insisting on promoting big national parks, which were invariably blocked by opposing interests, they began managing small and symbolic pieces of land to keep them out of speculators' hands. With regard to public education, WWF undertook a widely known campaign on behalf of endangered species, which had a great emotional impact, involved children and schools, and was easily communicated by mass media. Moreover, its international emphasis was attractive to the public.

WWF is also involved in national parks policy, but without putting it at the top of its agenda, as other, less successful Italian organizations had done (Cattini and Lanzara 2001). The decision not to concentrate on parks was a good choice. The relevant framework law for creating them was not passed until 1991, so any results would have come too late to help sustain the weak nature protection organizations.

The Italian League for the Protection of Birds (LIPU) was founded in the same period (1965). This organization had none of the elite character of earlier nature protection organizations. It was composed of lovers of animals, a strand of environmentalism not well represented in the classical contraposition between the aesthetic and scientific wings. Nevertheless, it is worth mentioning that the founding date was much later than the dates for similar organizations elsewhere.

With their commitment to the protection of animals, the League for the Protection of Birds and WWF added a new 'moral' component to nature protection, bringing the Italian case nearer to the British one. This moral component had its roots in sentimentalized anthropomorphic ideas about kindness to animals (John Ranlett, quoted in Piccioni 1999, p. 142). It represents a new viewpoint in the Italian nature protection spectrum. It finds its most interesting and extreme development in animal protection groups. It differs from the old nature protection movement in that it focuses on protecting specific interesting or spectacular species, or even individual animals. Empathy for large, symbolic animals, such as bears and eagles, is surely key to understanding the successes in membership and public attention organizations such as the WWF and LIPU have enjoyed.

The Environmental Wave

The 1960s were not only marked by the expansion of nature protection efforts through the establishment of WWF and LIPU, but also by the beginnings of the environmental movement, signalled by the publication of Rachel Carson's *Silent Spring*. This new environmental wave constituted another turning point in the history of nature protection in Italy.

The new environmental wave had several new features. It represented, first, a definitive relegation of the 'scientific' wing of nature protection to the margin, symbolized by the small success of Videsott's efforts. His approach was successful in achieving results – creating protected areas – only when it accepted the political dimension of creating national parks. This occurred notably when the above-mentioned frame law clearly included the development of the local population among the protected areas principles (Ceruti 1993). The scientific wing had to abandon the idea of keeping wilderness as the exclusive aim of parks. That was a compromise which significantly weakened its identity.

Another feature of this period was the failure to create or maintain a solid link between the traditional aesthetic wing of the nature protection movement and the passionate new protectors of spectacular species. Our

Italy and WWF did engage, side by side, in many campaigns. Nevertheless, during the 1960s and 1970s, they remained small and separate worlds cocooned in their own ideological assumptions.

Perhaps the most decisive feature of the new environmental wave, however, was the rise of political ecology. The politicized environmental movement changed the focus completely: from protection of animals or natural areas to safeguarding humans and society, especially in the towns. Pollution, and later nuclear energy, became the main targets of movement rhetoric. According to Diani (1988), nature protection in Italy became one specific current within the ecological movement, which he calls conservationism; it is concerned with assaults on places of unique natural beauty and acts mainly through lobbying.

Besides this traditional nature protection focus, the movement had two other currents: 'political ecology' and 'environmentalism'. The former emerged from social conflicts in the factories and universities prompted by the '68 movement, which in Italy was strongly linked to a Marxist analysis of society. The latter came from the Radical Party, a libertarian group committed to civil rights and individual freedoms. However, Diani insists that the distinction was not primarily ideological but attributable to each wing's distinctive forms of action: lobbying for the conservationists, conflict for political ecology, and 'single-issue' campaigns for environmentalists.

In the last two decades of the twentieth century, when environmentalism flourished throughout the industrial world, the Italian movement retained its characteristic feature of being deeply involved in political parties and struggles. It was mainly a left-wing movement, a fact symbolized by the 1979 founding of the League for the Environment (Legambiente), an association that arose out of the Communist Party milieu (Della Seta 2000, p. 45). Like similar movements in other countries, the Italian environmental movement was tempted to become a political party and strive for seats in lawmaking bodies. While such political involvement was initially regarded as an obvious consequence of militancy, later it tended to be considered, in particular among members of the conservationist wing, as a sort of betrayal of environmentalist ideals, which were thought to stand above political struggles.

After the discontinuity resulting from the emergence of a new wave of environmentalism, nature protection efforts in Italy could be classified as follows:

- traditional protection of nature and man-made monuments, referred to as cultural landscape protection in the typology of Chapter 1, persists as a small niche, with Our Italy as its chief exemplar;

- a branch more able to address the needs of nature protection, embodied by WWF and the League for the Protection of Birds; this branch emphasizes both the protection of wilderness and the protection of wild animals and plants, but pays less attention to protection of cultural landscapes;
- the 'compassion' wing of the nature protection movement, which had been quite latent in Italy, has now finally developed. It is represented by animal protection organizations such as the League against Vivisection. Although these organizations dedicate most of their efforts to protection of animals in laboratories or in agriculture, they are also concerned with the protection of wild animals;
- the political ecology wing did not initially focus on nature protection but later 'discovered' nature and parks as places in which to invest their energies. Thus they are properly included in the category of 'environmental organizations' described in Chapter 1.

This, then, is the static classification. The dynamic dimension is quite different; it shows a great deal of contact among organizations, especially during the periods of broad mobilization. The most salient of such moments in Italy have been abrogation referenda. The first one, a vote against nuclear energy plants, took place in 1987; the second, against hunting, occurred in 1990. The former was won by the environmental front; the second did not attain the 50 per cent of voter turnout required to make the referendum binding.

The differing outcomes of these two referenda reveal something about the nature protection organizations in Italy. The vote more closely linked to nature protection was the one on hunting. It was a partial defeat for the movement. In northern Italy, the referendum achieved the so-called 'quorum'; the great majority of people voted against hunting. In southern Italy indifference prevailed, revealing an old weakness of the nature protection movement. The referendum against nuclear energy, on the other hand, was a crucial point in the history of environmentalism in Italy. It unified all the environmental and nature protection organizations, including Our Italy and WWF (Neri Serneri 2003, p. 378). Since these results, it has become clear to organizations focused on nature protection that the best approach is systemic (Giacomini and Romani 1991), that is, an approach limited not just to single locales, animals or monuments or to lobbying and technical argumentation. In my view, this also initiated a process of homogenization among most environmental and nature protection organizations in terms of internal structure and action strategies.

THE CONVERGENCE OF NATURE PROTECTION ORGANIZATIONS TO A COMMON ENVIRONMENTALISM

Organizations Engaged in Nature Protection Today

The brief history recounted in the previous section shows the rather tortuous path Italian nature protection organizations have followed. Although they were the first to raise the environmental issue, they became a minority in the environmental movement, and in passing their heritage to other groups, they lost their uniqueness. The nature protection legacy seems at present to be involved in a dual process of convergence: the older, nature protection-oriented organizations are becoming more and more committed to the broader aspects of environmentalism, while the more politicized groups from the 1970s have adopted nature protection as an issue to increase their visibility. As will be shown below, nature protection organizations have combined their methods and goals with environmental ones, and are creating a new institutional field where the old classifications lose their capacity to discriminate.

In order to understand the recent evolution of nature protection groups in Italy, seven organizations have been chosen for closer examination. The main criterion for selection was the variety of types, because the aim is to verify how the original goals of the main nature protection organizations spread to groups born later.

Three of the four organizations analysed by Della Porta and Andretta (2001) as representing 'ideal-type' organizations of the Italian environmental movement were included. These are the League for the Environment, the League against Vivisection (Lega Antivivisezione) (LAV) and Friends of the Earth (Amici della Terra–Italia). Greenpeace was excluded. Because its structure and style of intervention is quite similar in every country, the Italian case would not have added much information. Two other organizations, which have an explicit nature protection character, were added: the World Wide Fund for Nature (WWF Italia) and the League for the Protection of Birds (LIPU). Finally, the Federation Pro Natura and Our Italy were included. As we have seen, both are prestigious organizations, born before the social movements of the 1970s. They represent the historic Italian approach; that is, they combine attention to natural and cultural values.

Typically the League for the Environment, WWF and Our Italy have been considered the most important environmental organizations at the national level. The first two also have the largest number of members (see Table 5.2), although in both cases, a great number of young student

Table 5.2 Selected Italian organizations engaged in nature protection

Organization	No. of members	Annual budget (€000s)	Year of founding	Main goals (protection object)
Our Italy (Italia Nostra)	12 000	4600	1955	Cultural landscape
Pro Nature Federation (Federazione Pro Natura)	12 000*	150**	1959	Cultural landscape
League for Bird Protection (LIPU)	40 000	3800	1965	Wild animals
World Wide Fund for Nature (WWF-Italia)	200 000	16 000	1966	Wilderness, wild animals
Antivivisection League (LAV)	30 000	1600	1977	Animals
Friends of the Earth Amici della Terra–Italia)	20 000	400	1977	Environmental organization
League for the Environment (Legambiente)	110 000	5500	1979	Environmental organization

Notes:
* Estimated number of members of all the associated groups.
** Budget of only the Federation central office.
The number of members and the budgets refer to 2003 and are approximate.

members are included by virtue of activities with schools. LIPU and LAV rank next in membership and number of local groups. Our Italy remains a more elite organization, with not more than 12 000 members. Friends of the Earth claims about 20 000 supporters, but this is not to be confused with the number of people paying the annual association fee, who number only 4000. Pro Natura is organized as a federation, an umbrella organization of almost 100 independent local associations; they calculate that they have about 12 000 members, including the members of associated groups.

The law (Legge Nazionale 349/1986) that established the conditions for recognition as a national environmental organization requires an organization to be represented in at least 15 of the 20 Italian regions, and all seven organizations have a national-level presence.

It should be noticed that the League against Vivisection, probably the most important animal protection organization in Italy, has not been included in the Ministry of Environment list, on the grounds that it does not defend the 'environment' but only the rights of animals. Despite that, it is useful to include an animal protection organization in this analysis because 'compassion' for animals represents a latent component of the Italian nature protection movement (see above).

According to LAV leader comments collected by Della Porta and Andretta (2001, p. 12), LAV has a 'deep ecology' inclination because it considers animals as individuals with their own rights; 'there is a great difference between ecologism and environmentalism' – one interviewee said – 'and we are surely more ecologist than environmentalist'.

It appears that, despite the diversity of their histories, ideologies and structures, the seven organizations are converging under the pressure of the institutional milieu toward a common model in the manner suggested by DiMaggio and Powell (1991). This can be seen in terms of three key developments: (1) professionalization; (2) inclusion into the market; and (3) strategies for dealing with uncertainty. After describing these processes, we will analyse their consequences for the forms of action used by the organizations.[2]

Professionalization

There is a common trend among the organizations towards the development of a central paid staff engaged in managing the organization. Among the seven organizations, only one (Pro Natura) does not have at least one paid staff member for the coordination of the activities. Most of the employees, however, lack permanent contracts, and the absolute numbers are very low, ranging from 10 to 30 persons. This confirms the findings of other studies, which show that, in comparison to other European countries, Italian environmental organizations have a weaker structure: fewer members, fewer professional skills, and less political influence (Osti 1998; Della Porta and Diani 2002). Nevertheless, the presence of paid staff, even in relatively small numbers, is a turning point in the organization, and professional staff is a common feature of almost all the organizations.

The organizations also emphasize that they base their work on scientific premises. All of them stress in one way or another on their Internet sites the importance of a scientific approach to the environmental issue, and all have a scientific committee. One might expect a smaller emphasis on scientific discourse in the animal protection group and the League for the Protection of Birds because these groups justify their actions in moral and affective terms, but this is not the case. The general orientation seems clear: most Italian environmental organizations base their identity on the large-scale use of scientific research and evidence. In some cases, they even speak of 'scientific environmentalism' as a basis for avoiding factionalism and as a solid foundation for their actions (Della Seta 2000, p. 89). The recourse to science to legitimate their actions has several implications: (a) distancing the organization from irrational and mystical approaches to environmental issues; (b) an effort to find common ground in a matter as controversial as the environmental crisis; (c) faith in modernity, or at least the belief on the irreversibility of processes triggered by it.

Professionalization reflects more than the fact that some activists – under the pressure of the institutional milieu – have transformed their activism into a permanent job. It represents the attempt to build a specific professional profile on the solid base which is supposed to be found in science. In this sense, scientific ecology plays a major role as 'the science' of environmentalists. Its emphasis on the interdependence and systems rather than on single species, and its use of the concepts such as habitat and ecosystem, provide the framing for the legitimation of the work of an entire generation of activists. They find a normal professional position either in the research institutes or the environmental organizations. The former are more theoretical, the latter more practical, but the source of legitimation is the same: ecology as a science.

Needless to say, the organizations analysed are not completely identical in this respect. Their recourse to science changes in accordance with the key features of each organization. Thus the League for the Environment, Our Italy and Pro Natura Federation, which focus more on the interconnections between nature and society, look to such disciplines as architecture, agronomy and economy. Friends of the Earth, which emphasizes the management of energy and transportation, makes more use of engineering and chemistry. Still, in general, the emphasis on the scientific method has diffused into all the organizations. In short, the environmental organizations have sought to build a distinct community of experts, based mainly on ecology, a science already well rooted in the nature protection milieu.

Market Inclusion

The second process affecting the organizations is their growing reliance on sale of goods and services to finance their operations. Historically, nature protection and environmental organizations depended on member fees and donations for revenue. Some also encouraged their local groups to register themselves on regional administration lists in accordance with the National Law on Volunteer Organizations, which allows them to receive financial and practical support from the authorities. They also declared themselves to be 'non-profits' in order to obtain a tax reduction (Legambiente 2003).

In recent years, however, the organizations have also been forced to look for funding from market activity. One reason for this is the need for increased financial resources to pay the staff and support their activities. Reliance on public funding (Osti 1998) could not continue due to the crisis of public finance and the instability of local governments, which increased the organizations' desire for more independence and the competition for funds. The environmental organizations, therefore, turned to two kinds of company sponsorship: (a) donations given by business leaders or companies seeking prestige and a favourable image; and (b) partnerships for innovation, typically involving a company that is looking for help in producing environmental-friendly goods. The money given in the first way was very constraining, limiting the organizations to activities that would not harm the image of the company. Sponsorship thus helped the organization to survive at the price of weakening its ability to criticize environmental threats from industry. The money given in the second way was less constraining, but it did link the organization to a specific technological path.

Almost all of the seven organizations now have relationships with private firms. However, the strength of the ties varies. Some, such as WWF and the League for the Environment, deal permanently with multinational companies; others, such as Pro Natura Federation or Our Italy, have only sporadic agreements with small local entrepreneurs. Cooperation with industrial firms is quite rare because it requires a great deal of expertise. Only Friends of the Earth reports this kind of involvement. As a result, the cooperation more often occurs at superficial level: either the company or the environmental organization simply wants to *show* that it is committed to saving the planet. Overall, the most frequent relationship is a traditional firm's advertising in the environmental organizations press.

The market inclusion process has also prompted environmental organizations to become 'retailers' of products and services. They have been pushed to enter into the market in two ways. The first way is selling 'gadgets' (shirts, watches, *peluches* and so on) and eco-tourist services (trips, birdwatching and accommodation). Usually, the organizations sell products made or services provided according to more strict environmental norms; sometimes they come from alternative channels, such as 'fair trade'. In this way, environmental organizations get some money and transmit a message about their identity. The products typically have a logo showing the name and the identity of the association. Almost all the Italian organizations, despite their different histories, now have a well-advertised eco-commerce programme.

Another form of inclusion in the market involves selling expertise and consulting services to the authorities. Plans, schemes and projects on environmental matters are developed in the organizations' offices and 'sold' to the government. The most frequent approach is the simple exchange 'money for scheme'; long-term partnerships with a public body in managing a long-term project are more difficult, but they do occur. The European Union's LIFE projects are a typical example of such partnerships. WWF and LIPU are widely involved in such projects. However, it is probably the League for the Environment, the organization most linked to public administration, that obtains the most such contracts. That does not, however, keep it and the other organizations from engaging in conflict with government, because the conflict is usually limited to a specific issue and locality and does not cut across the entire spectrum of environmental issues.

Cooperation with government creates a common culture in which the partners come to share a method of working and a view of the situation. Otherwise, it would be difficult to have a well-managed project or a chance for long-run collaboration. This common culture inevitably pushes environmental organizations, despite their ideology and tradition, to adopt the same language, the language of public administration. It is far less likely that the public administration will modify its style in order to accommodate to any one environmental association. The tendency toward convergence among the environmental organizations is thus driven by the long-term relationship with a stronger actor, the government. Agreements with government are very common among the seven organizations. Their content varies, but – as said – what really matter are the standard protocols for cooperation, and the procedures involved are quite similar whether the cooperation is with a municipality or the European Union.[3]

Comparisons between the amount of money derived from participation in eco-commerce versus the amount from sponsorship and public-funded projects are difficult because the budget categories used by the organizations differ. Some hints can be found, however, by looking at two major nature protection organizations: WWF and the League for the Environment. The former has four main sources of income: member fees, donations, projects and nature reserve management. The distribution among the categories has varied in recent years (2001–3); thus it is difficult to arrive as a definitive picture. The only heading that has remained relatively constant is member dues, which provides about 30 per cent of the budget (WWF 2003). The League for the Environment classifies its receipts under three headings: membership fees and public grants, commercial activities and non-profit activities. In 2001–3 each heading provided approximately one-third of the budget (Legambiente 2004).

It is not possible to make a comparison between the two organizations, but in neither case is member dues more than one-third of total revenue. Thus two-thirds of the budget comes from providing goods and services to government, companies and consumers. It is impossible to calculate the precise share of revenues from each source, but the ranking is quite clear: first, receipts from a wide range of services for the government; then the business sponsorship; and, finally, selling items and services to the public.

In conclusion, the organizations' involvement in the marketplace implies not only changes in the source of funds, but also modification of their style of operation. The environmental organizations are more and more like competing businesses providing services for public administration and private companies.

Dealing with Uncertainty

According to the neo-institutional approach described in Chapter 1, there is also a third mechanism – facing increasing uncertainty – that could lead the organizations to imitate each other and become more similar. The increasing importance of uncertainty in the modern world was highlighted effectively by the work of Ulrich Beck (1986). The primary source of uncertainty is environmental issues themselves. The scientific community is not able to cope with these issues; that is, it is unable to apply its categories and methodology to forecast the consequences for humanity of some decisions. For science a new phase of 'epistemological uncertainty' has thus begun (Funtowicz and Ravetz 1993; Pellizzoni and Osti 2003). GMOs and 'electronic smog' are good examples of issues for which the scientific community is unable to predict the severity and extensiveness of the danger.

It might sound strange that environmental organizations find themselves uncertain in their own area of expertise. In the view of the public, they are the professionals. Why then would one suppose they would imitate one another in order to overcome uncertainty? The answer is not hard to find: today they are on the front line, dealing with the most complex issues. They are committed to identifying environmental problems and to offering solutions. Yet, due to the great uncertainty that surrounds them, these are difficult tasks indeed. In the past, a ready solution was simply to choose a conservative position: defending without compromise the last parts of undisturbed nature, saying 'no' to any modification of remaining natural habitats, and fighting for endangered species.

This remains the aim of the relatively pure 'nature protection organizations'. Nevertheless, at least in Italy, the pursuit of that goal has been undermined by several factors: (a) Italy is a country of very old settlements; nature and culture have been inextricably intertwined for many years, so defending 'pure nature' seems unrealistic; (b) mainstream Italian environmentalism has been marked since its origins by a strong social and political orientation; that is, it originated in the context of a left-wing movement that was very attentive to equity issues. The idea of defending just nature without paying attention to the social issues was seen as a commitment of 'countesses' (Nebbia 2002, p. 91); (c) the deconstructionist approach in social sciences and philosophy has probably affected the environmental movement by arguing that truly 'natural objects' do not exist but are socially constructed (Hannigan 1995), and postmodern trends have helped to undermine the idea, already contested, that nature has a precise and normative order. Nature, whatever that means, cannot be a source of moral order for society, as earlier theorists such as Lombroso (Acot 1988) had supposed. All these forces weaken organizations that attempt to represent themselves as 'paladins' of pure nature. Thus the great uncertainty surrounding environmental issues has channelled the nature protection organizations towards a model of action in which the sociopolitical and ecological dimensions were united. The mix has produced a common set of activities, easily noticed in the seven organizations studied: education in schools, involvement in social issues (e.g. peace and starvation), activities involving conflict mediation and dialogue with specific communities (e.g. Local Agenda 21), and scientific research.

Forms of Action

Facing uncertainty, it seems that all the organizations choose to address a wide variety of themes. Their claim is not that they have the solutions, but that they know the right methods to arrive at them. These methods centre around four principles: education, commitment, mediation and dialogue, and research. Even for the organizations with a strong nature protection orientation, such as WWF and LIPU, how to safeguard nature is not self-evident; it needs a peculiar cultural translation, following the just-mentioned four principles.

National parks are a good example. In the 1990s, when many new parks were established, environmental organizations shared the idea of finding a compromise between nature conservation and the local population's use of natural resources. They were so committed to this idea that, in many cases, they acted as consultants in the process of finding a feasible compromise through education, mediation and research. The desire of LIPU to protect some species of endangered birds, for example, pushed it into research and action concerning the larger socioeconomic environment where these animals live. Specifically, it initiated research on agriculture in order to understand the policies and rules of this sector, which is crucial for the welfare of birds.

It appears that the LAV is the only organization resisting this trend. Its radical goal of defending animal rights pushes it in most circumstances towards protest, which hinders its search for a common ground with government, business and the public. This is a matter of degree, however. LAV has also made some attempts to cooperate with bodies external to its world, for example with local government.

The Italian environmental organizations' common tendency to rely on non-confrontational means is summed up in the word 'campaign'. A campaign is a complex strategy, which includes delimitation of a theme, a multi-level public education effort, and a set of symbolic actions (petitions, sit-ins, marches and so on). The result should be more public awareness of a specific issue and more resources devoted to it. Campaigns also aim to pressure public authorities to provide new tools or legal measures for solving the problem. In such actions, which are very common among the seven organizations,[4] there is a synthesis of the classical dilemma 'protest versus lobby' – captured so effectively by Rootes (1997) with the terms 'the piazza or the palace' – for the two strategies are combined into a single effort, the 'campaign'. Indeed, the environmental organizations show great skill in combining the right amount of protest with the right amount of lobbying. In this sense, the contraposition of the two strategies is less meaningful than it once was, further supporting the convergence hypothesis.

A few possible strategies are practicable only for larger organizations. One example is volunteers' involvement through the participation in summer camps and the promotion of a 'day' for cleaning, for instance, some woods or a beach. Another example is the creation of a special surveillance corps, ecological guards, to protect natural areas. Only the League for the Environment, WWF and LIPU were able to organize camps or to form surveillance corps, as doing so requires great professional skill. In other words, what diversity does exist among the organizations is in the ability to deploy specific strategies, not in the overall style of action.

It might be argued that the convergence described above is occurring only at the national level. The seven cases investigated are national organizations. Less is known about small, local environmental groups; however, many are linked to national groups. Even those involved in a very specific field – often the protection of a natural site – and having an autonomous legal status, frequently have connections with national organizations. Small, local groups that are active over long periods form a dense network, which is interlinked with the larger organizations (Diani 1995).

Such links allow us to clarify another important element: the relationship between centre and periphery in the national organizations. The degree of centralization has often been chosen as a criterion for creating typologies of environmental organizations. Della Porta and Andretta (2001) report, for example, that Friends of the Earth and LAV are considered quite decentralized organizations, while the League for the Environment and Greenpeace lean in the opposite direction. The classification of Greenpeace as centralized is unambiguous, although, as already mentioned, it is an exception. But for the other organizations, the distinction is blurred. Most have three levels of administration: local, regional and national. The local groups generally comprise volunteers who do not want to accept orders from the top, only suggestions and technical advice. The central staff is typically determined to implement a uniform strategy, but it is aware that it has little chance of imposing anything at grass-roots level. The regional level is an attempt to overcome the contrasting problems of too much centralization versus too much decentralization, but, in practice, the regional level tends to be rather weak. Thus, with the exception of Pro Natura, which is the only real federative organization, all the other cases exhibit a precarious and delicate balance between centre and periphery. The image of centralized organizations able to impose the same standard on all the local groups is misleading; instead a dialectic between the two poles is the normal situation.

CONCLUSIONS

Our Italy and Pro Natura are, in many respects, the heirs of the old Italian nature protection movement that began at the end of nineteenth century. They symbolize, for different reasons, the main features of that movement: the former represents the strong emphasis on the man-made environment – the so-called aesthetic wing – the latter represents the fragmentation of associations that are unable to stimulate a mass commitment for the commons. In spite of their important legacy, they are nowadays quite weak and diverge from the dominant model of environmental organizations.

Unlike them, the most central nature protection organizations today, such as WWF and LIPU, are much more vital and much better integrated into the mainstream of Italian environmentalism. Indeed, in some respects, such as staff profile and fundraising strategies, they are models for the other organizations, and it appears that a trend of convergence – or, in the wording of Powell and DiMaggio, isomorphism – has become quite pronounced both within and outside the subgroup of organizations most oriented to the protection of nature. Three mechanisms encouraging convergence have been described.

1. The environmental and nature protection organizations have become more professionalized and more oriented to scientific ecology. Their professionalization is based on employing staff with high levels of formal education (often with university degrees) and significant experience in the field.
2. The environmental and nature protection organizations have responded to consumer demand by making available opportunities that combine commitment to the environment and enjoyable activities, including

volunteer camps and ecotourism. They have reacted to public concern for the environment by providing government with many services, including projects, research and advice. The styles imposed by working with government create a common code of planning; companies, by contrast, usually remain only sources of financial sponsorship.
3. The environmental and nature protection organizations have dealt with the uncertainty that surrounds environmental issues, by diversifying their activities and by relying more on 'methods' such as education, mediation and dialogue than on political activism.

As a result, although the organizations vary in their origins and identities, they have become very similar in structure, action strategies and role in Italian society. In this sense, the distinction between nature protection organizations and other environmental organizations today tends to be more nominal than real, and the contraposition between conservationism (an emphasis mainly on nature protection) and political ecologism, so frequently used in the literature (Dalton 1994; Rootes 1997; Diani and Donati 1998; Diani and Forno 2003), is losing its significance.

If these traditional distinctions are disappearing, what are the reasons? Powell and DiMaggio argued that a strain towards isomorphism is induced by a need for legitimation, the need to be recognized as an appropriate and useful organization in the organization's social milieu. The Italian organizations operate in an environment almost totally transformed by humankind over generations. Their legitimation could come from the capacity to unite the task of preserving the cultural heritage of the past with the new task of protecting nature. Moreover, as time passed, it has become clearer that nobody had 'the' technical solution for the environmental crisis. In such a situation, non-profit organizations have sought legitimation in non-confrontational actions, symbolized by their campaigns – planned mobilizations to promote understanding, discussion and public awareness of specific issues. On the websites the most common strategy of the Italian environmental organizations is the 'campaign'. It is a military word; it means organizing an expedition in order to conquer a new territory. In Italy today it is a reasonable way of keeping open environmental issues in a period of contrasting demands and uncertain solutions.

In the end, is it possible to find a common thread in the history of nature protection organizations in Italy? Since the beginning, the will to organize a nature protection movement has been clear and strong, but powerful external factors, including wars and fascism, have sometimes undermined the project. Later, the imbalance among the movement's core values contributed to the tensions between the sociopolitical and aesthetic wings. In the nature protection movement's recent phase the integration with government and the market has pushed the nature protection organizations to become more similar to other environmental organizations. The call for nature protection has been subordinated in pursuit of a more systemic approach that favours the inclusion of social issues. Thus Italian nature protection organizations' destiny is to lose their distinctiveness and dissolve into a broader field of environmental organizations, unless they find new cultural meanings of nature. The old call of 'beauties of nature' is always charming, but not enough.

NOTES

1. In 2006 there were 64 registered national organizations; the most numerous subgroup was environmental organizations in the sense described in Chapter 1. Recreational and scientific organizations applied later for the registration, and not all the animal protection organizations are registered. The full list is in Ministero dell'Ambiente e della tutela del Territorio (2006).
2. These categories are taken by the literature on neoinstitutionalism (Hoffman and Ventresca 2001). Specifically, they refer to the DiMaggio and Powell (1991) mechanisms creating isomorphism.
3. The growing importance of global issues and European integration push the organizations towards participation in international projects (Nocenzi 2004, p. 80). The pressure for international links is especially strong for organizations founded in other countries, such as WWF and Friends of the Earth and for organizations that seek international legitimation. The latter group includes Legambiente, LIPU (member of BirdLife International) and LAV (member of Eurogroup for Animal Welfare, European Coalition for Animals, and Europe for Animal Rights). It is less important for Our Italy and Pro Natura, which are purely domestic organizations.
4. The exception is the monitoring of pollutants. Only Legambiente engages in this type of campaign (Treno Verde, Mal'aria, Goletta Verde). The reason of the difference could be explained by the capacity of Legambiente to attract a large number of public and private sponsors (see Donati 1995).

REFERENCES

Acot, P. (1988), *Histoire de l'Écologie*, Paris: Presses Universitaires de France.

Alexander, J.C. (1995), 'I paradossi della società civile', *Rassegna Italiana di Sociologia*, **3**, 319–39.

Beck, U. (1986), *Risikogesellschaft*, Frankfurt am Main: Suhrkamp.

Canu, A. (2003), 'Le oasi del WWF', *Equilibri*, **VII** (1), 123–30.

Cattini, G. and G.F. Lanzara (2001), 'La strategia del Panda. Come il WWF crea il proprio ambiente', *Scheda 2001-Ecologia Antropica*, Nuova serie, I (2), 141–74.

Ceruti, L. (ed.) (1993), *Aree Naturali Protette*, Milan: Domus.

Dalton, R.J. (1994), *The Green Rainbow. Environmental Groups in Western Europe*, New Haven and London: Yale University Press.

Della Porta, D. and M. Andretta (2001), *National Environmental Organizations and the Public Policy in Italy*, Siena: Convegno annuale della Società Italiana di Scienza Politica, settembre.

Della Porta, D. and M. Diani (2002), 'Italy', in C.A. Rootes (ed.), *The Transformation of Environmental Activism*, Brussels: EC Environment and Climate Research Programme, Contract no. ENV4-CT97-0514 (Final Report).

Della Seta, R. (2000), *La Difesa dell'Ambiente in Italia. Storia e Cultura del Movimento Ecologista*, Milan: Angeli.

Diani, M. (1988), *Isole nell'Arcipelago. Il Movimento Ecologista in Italia*, Bologna: Il Mulino.

Diani, M. (1995), *Green Networks: A Structural Analysis of the Italian Environmental Movement*, Edinburgh: Edinburgh University Press.

Diani, M. and P.R. Donati (1998), 'Mutamenti organizzativi nei movimenti ambientalisti europei: un modello di analisi', *Quaderni di Scienza Politica*, **3**, 377–406.

Diani, M. and F. Forno (2003), 'Italy', in C. Rootes (ed.), *Environmental Protest in Western Europe*, Oxford: Oxford University Press, pp. 135–65.

DiMaggio, P.J. and W.W. Powell (1991), 'The iron cage revisited: institutional isomorphism and collective rationality', in W.W. Powell and P.J. DiMaggio (eds), *The New Institutionalism in Organizational Analysis*, Chicago and London: The University of Chicago Press, pp. 63–82.

Donati, P.R. (1995), 'Mobilitazione delle risorse e trasformazione organizzativa: il caso dell'ecologia politica', *Quaderni di Scienza Politica*, **2** (2), 167–99.

Frank, D.J. (2001), 'The origins question: building global institutions to protect nature', in A.J. Hoffman and M.J. Ventresca (eds), *Organizations, Policy and the Natural Environment: Institutional and Strategic Perspectives*, Stanford, CA: Stanford University Press, pp. 41–56.

Funtowicz, S. and J. Ravetz (1993), 'Science for the post-normal age', *Futures*, **25** (7), 739–55.

Giacomini, V. and V. Romani (1981), *Uomini e Parchi*, Milan: Angeli.

Giuliano, W. (1989), *La Prima Isola dell'Arcipelago. Pro Natura Quarant'Anni di Ambientalismo*, Turin: Pro Natura.

Giuliano, W. (1991), *Le Radici dei Verdi. Per una Storia del Movimento Ambientalista in Italia*, Pisa: Ipem Edizioni.

Hannigan, J. (1995), *Environmental Sociology*, London: Routledge.

Hoffman, A.J. and M.J. Ventresca (2001), 'Introduction', in idem (eds), *Organizations, Policy and the Natural Environment: Institutional and Strategic Perspectives*, Stanford, CA: Stanford University Press, pp. 1–38.

Legambiente (2003), *Rappresentazione Socio-economica delle Attività*, Rome: Legambiente.

Legambiente (2004), 'Verso un Bilancio Sociale', Rome, www.legambiente.com/documenti/2004/.

Meyer, E.H. (1995), *I Pionieri dell'Ambiente*, Milan: Carabà.

Ministero dell'Ambiente e della tutela del Territorio (2006), Associazioni di Protezione Ambientale, www2.minambiente.it/sito/link/associazioni.asp, 29 September.

Nebbia, G. (2002), *Le Merci e i Valori. Per una Critica Ecologica al Capitalismo*, Milan: Jaca Book.

Neri Serneri, S. (2003), 'Culture e politiche del movimento ambientalista', in F. Lussana and G. Marramao (eds), *Culture, Nuovi Soggetti, Identità*, Soveria Mannelli: Rubbettino.

Nocenzi, M. (2004), 'I movimenti ambientalisti: ieri, oggi, domani', *Sociologia e Politiche Sociali*, **7** (1), 63–106.

Osti, G. (1998), *La Natura, gli Altri, la Società. Il Terzo Settore per l'Ambiente in Italia*, Milan: Angeli.
Pedrotti, F. (1998), *Il Fervore dei Pochi. Il Movimento Protezionistico Italiano dal 1943 al 1971*, Trento: Temi.
Pellizzoni, L. and G. Osti (2003), *Sociologia dell'Ambiente*, Bologna: Il Mulino.
Piccioni, L. (1999), *Il Volto Amato della Patria. Il Primo Movimento per la Protezione della Natura in Italia 1880–1934*, L'uomo e l'ambiente-32, Università di Camerino.
Poggio, A. (1996), *Ambientalismo*, Milan: Editrice Bibliografica.
Rootes, C.A. (1997), 'Environmental movements and green parties in western and eastern Europe', in M. Redclift and G. Woodgate (eds), *The International Handbook of Environmental Sociology*, Cheltenham, UK and Northampton, MA, USA: Edward Elgar, pp. 319–48.
Sievert, J. (2000), *The Origins of Nature Conservation in Italy*, Bern: Peter Lang.
Silvestri, F. (2004), 'Una breve storia della conservazione del paesaggio in Italia (con particolare attenzione ai parchi naturali)', *Storia e Futuro*, **4**, 1–9.
Strassoldo, R. (2000–2001), 'Il sentimento della natura in Italia e in Germania: spunti di storia culturale', *Annali di Sociologia-Soziologisches Jahrbuch*, **15**, 83–108.
WWF (2003), 'Prospetto economico', www.wwf.it/ambiente/dossier/Bilancio/.

6. Dutch nature protection between policy and public

C.S.A. (Kris) van Koppen

INTRODUCTION

Measured by sheer number of supporters, civil society action for nature protection has developed amazing strength in the Netherlands, expanding from a small, rather elite group in the first half of the twentieth century into an extensive network of organizations with a broad support base. Although its membership decreased somewhat in the early years of the twenty-first century, the Society for the Preservation of Nature (Vereniging tot Behoud van Natuurmonumenten) still boasts a membership of nearly 900 000, more than 5 per cent of the total Dutch population, and WWF and Greenpeace have some 740 000 and 590 000 members respectively. This does not mean, however, that optimism about nature protection prevails among Dutch nature protection advocates. A recent special nature issue of a leading Dutch newspaper (*Volkskrant*, 9 April 2004) exemplified their mixed feelings. 'Nature is losing', the editorial states. Despite the successful institutionalization of nature protection policy and management in the Netherlands, the gradual deterioration of nature remains hard to halt in a country so urbanized and industrialized. Moreover, this degradation does not seem to evoke as much public protest as it did in the 1970s. Other articles in the special issue point to the gap between ecologists and policy makers, on the one hand, and the public, on the other, and suggest that public concern about nature protection is declining.

Against this backdrop, this chapter explores the development of nature protection in the Netherlands from its origins at the turn of the twentieth century up to the present. It distinguishes four historical periods and examines the motives and arguments of nature protection advocates during each. It also describes the activities of the nature protection organizations that put these ideas to work and the governmental policies developed in close relationship with nature protection organizations. The historical overview is followed by an analysis of the historical development from the standpoint of ecological modernization theory and from the perspective of the Arcadian tradition (see also Chapter 1).[1]

NATURE MONUMENTS AND NATURAL BEAUTY, 1900–1940

The early development of nature conservation in the Netherlands went hand in hand with the flowering of Romantic nature appreciation. Growing sensibility towards nature was manifested not only in the arts, but also in the institutionalization of animal protection. The Hague Society for Protection of Animals (Gravenhaagsche Vereeniging tot Bescherming van Dieren), later renamed the Dutch Society for Protection of Animals (Nederlandse Vereniging tot Bescherming van Dieren), was founded in 1864. Animal protection obtained legal status in 1880, when the Act for the Protection of Animal Species Useful to Agriculture and Forestry was implemented. Through the efforts of nature lovers and animal protectors this Act was extended to the protection of rare and 'remarkable' animal species. Terns, which were threatened by the extensive use of their feathers in women's hats, thus became a protected species in 1906 (Van Zanden and Verstegen 1993, pp. 182–6; Van der Windt 1995, pp. 41–4).

Other examples of early nature protection organizations include the Netherlands Society for the Protection of Birds (Nederlandse Vereniging tot Bescherming van Vogels, now Vogelbescherming Nederland), founded in 1899, and the Royal Dutch Society for the Study of Wildlife (KNNV: Koninklijke Nederlandse Natuurhistorische Vereniging) (1901). The most important, however, was the Society for the Preservation of Nature (Vereniging tot Behoud van Natuurmonumenten), which was founded in 1905 (Van der Windt 1995). Especially in the first half of the twentieth century, nature protection activities in the Netherlands were centred in this organization. Hence the aims and strategies of 'Natuurmonumenten' – as the society is commonly known – are an appropriate basis for examining the arguments and practices during the early days of Dutch nature protection.

Aims and Motives

Natuurmonumenten's founders – a small group of nature-loving scientists, business people and teachers – including Jac. P. Thijsse, whose name would become a household word – set out to protect 'nature monuments'. What they considered to be nature monuments was described in the bylaws of the new society: 'All remarkable parts of the Dutch soil, all remarkable animals, plants, and communities present in the Netherlands, as well as important remains of prehistoric human activity, endangered by the expansion of culture or other causes'. The society did not oppose modernization or development in general. On the contrary, land reclamation and drainage were valued, provided that 'a few of these areas' remain unspoilt (Van der Windt 1995, p. 57).

In selecting nature monuments worth preserving, protecting living nature played a much more important role than the other two elements mentioned in the definition of nature monuments – soil formations and prehistory. The pre-eminent role of living nature was also visible in prominent representation of biologists among the early conservationists. The primary rationale for preservation of nature monuments was their aesthetic and scientific value. Aesthetic value meant having scenic beauty and harbouring valued species, such as the spoonbill in the Naardermeer area. When assessing scientific value, biological significance was ranked above geological or archaeological significance. 'Scientific value', in this context, referred primarily to science as a contribution to human knowledge and culture, rather than science as a tool for economic progress.

Aesthetic and scientific motives for nature protection were not considered to be in conflict. Artists were involved in nature protection – though not as intensive as in Belgium and France (Van der Windt 1995) – and nature protection pioneers, such as Thijsse and Heimans, also pursued literature and the visual arts (Coesèl 1996). The importance of aesthetics was also clearly expressed in the term most frequently used in referring to valuable areas and species during this period: 'natural beauty'.

Motivations for nature protection also included an element of nationalism. The nature monuments seen as deserving protection were monuments of importance to the *nation*. The Dutch viewpoint here was consistent with, and probably influenced by, nationalist elements in nature protection abroad, as in Germany (where the similar concept 'Naturdenkmal' was used) and in the USA.

Although the Dutch protected areas could hardly be characterized as 'wilderness', most nature protection advocates preferred that nature monuments not be disturbed by human intervention. Thijsse, for instance, repeatedly argued that nature monuments should not be 'violated', although he recognized that this principle had to be abandoned occasionally in practice. The value of this 'freely developing nature' was justified by more than the need for undisturbed areas for scientific study or the argument that untouched nature had more aesthetic appeal. Spiritual and moral motives played a part too. While it would be possible to live without free nature, 'it would be life of a lesser quality, without flights of fancy, without the intimacy of contemplation, and with only little chance of a reawakening of spiritual life' (Thijsse 1932, p. 154). Arguments for nature's right to exist for its own sake, however, were hardly present in nature conservation debates (Coesèl 1993; Van der Windt 1995). Only societies for animal or bird protection were explicitly motivated by the moral rights of animals.

Practical Activities

The most important activities of Natuurmonumenten were aptly summarized in the invitation to its founding meeting, which listed the following key activities:

1. to set up a fund, mainly to acquire and take over the management of nature monuments;
2. to make a complete inventory of all nature monuments that still exist in our country;
3. to lobby government, corporations and individuals on this matter;
4. to reinforce a sound public opinion on this (Gorter 1986, p. 16, my translation).

Acquisition of nature areas was by far the most important activity. Indeed, the immediate reason for establishing Natuurmonumenten was to purchase the Naardermeer – a lake to the east of Amsterdam which had been designated by the city as landfill site even though it provided a nesting site for the rare spoonbills. Its purchase in 1906 was funded by a bond, with interest paid by the revenues from reed cutting and leases for hunting, fishing and farming in the area. Many other nature reserves were subsequently purchased this way. They included both country estates and 'scientific' nature monuments, such as heathlands, marshlands and breeding grounds. The acquisition of country estates and recreational forest areas served a double purpose. On the one hand, their financial exploitation – for example, by logging – generated funds. On the other hand, a wide circle of people took walks within them; therefore, they were important for spreading nature protection interest among the population (Gorter 1986).

The success of Natuurmonumenten was based largely upon what Gorter characterized as 'the happy unity of nature-loving financiers, manufacturers, and business people with people moving in scientific circles and many nature lovers who are not blessed with earthly means' (Gorter 1986, p. 21). Nevertheless, from the outset, Natuurmonumenten considered the diffusion of concern for nature protection of paramount importance. This diffusion did begin to take place during the 1920s, as exemplified by the increasing membership of Natuurmonumenten and the establishment of the Provincial Landscape Foundations (Provinciale Landschappen), which were initiated by Natuurmonumenten (1927–36). These organizations focused on the protection and management of valuable landscapes, often cultural landscapes, in their specific part of the country. Additional signs of the diffusion process included the founding of a Dutch Youth Organization for Nature Studies (NJN: Nederlandse Jeugdbond for Natuurstudie) by the KNNV and Natuurmonumenten and the establishment of the Liaison Committee for the Protection of Nature (Contact-Commissie inzake Natuurbescherming) by Natuurmonumenten and other organizations – including the Royal Dutch Touring Club (ANWB), the Royal Institute of Dutch Architects, and even two large land reclamation companies, Heidemij and Grontmij. The key aim of the Liaison Committee, which defined itself as the 'central organ of private nature protection in the Netherlands', was to influence government policy (Gorter 1986).

Government Policy

Natuurmonumenten's lobbying was quite successful from the beginning, not least because of personal connections between it and the National Forest Service (the director of the National Forest Service served on Natuurmonumenten's board). Beginning in 1908, many state-owned nature monuments were established, and conservation of natural beauty became an official assignment of the National Forest Service in the 1920s. Nature protection advocates obtained official standing in the National Forest Service in 1934 in the form of an Advisory Committee on the Nature Reserves. The Committee advised, among other matters, about reclamation projects set up during this period as part of relief work (Gorter 1986).

The first law aimed explicitly at nature protection was the Bird Act of 1912, which focused on protection of all wild bird species. It was followed by the Natural Beauty Act of 1928, which provided tax benefits to owners of country estates deemed important for the conservation of natural beauty – and additional tax relief if estates were opened to the public.

These modest policy efforts to protect nature were the result of informal lobbying, rather than the outcome of explicit policy debate. There was, however, an area of active policy debate about urban development and public health, which related to nature protection. This debate was rooted in typical nineteenth-century concerns about social housing and hygiene and spurred on by the social-democratic movement (Van Schendelen 1997). Many architects and urban developers argued that parks and public gardens in cities and green belts around them were indispensable for public health (Van Zanden and Verstegen 1993). For example, a committee including the well-known architect Berlage and the conservationist Thijsse recommended that Amsterdam should buy available heathland, country estates and dune areas. 'Everything should be done to stimulate city dwellers on Sunday to escape the stuffy city into free nature, where birds are still singing and wild flowers grow' (Report from 1909, quoted in Van Schendelen 1997, pp. 197–9). Before the Second World War, however, the practical impact of this policy discourse remained restricted largely to the layout of green spaces in urban areas and did not extend to the countryside (Van Schendelen 1997).

NATURE AND LANDSCAPE PLANNED, 1940–70

Although the Second World War and the German Occupation of 1940–45 posed specific problems for Natuurmonumenten – including a ban on Jewish members and heavy logging in parts of the forests – the organization was allowed to continue most of its activities. Other nature protection organizations, such as the Liaison Committee, also continued their work, adapting to the Occupation (Gorter 1986).

The postwar period brought new problems. The first postwar decades saw expansive economic growth, accelerated development of industry, and a radical modernization of agriculture. Also, governmental efforts in the area of spatial planning and state intervention in rural areas, which had started modestly before the war, were expanded. These trends came together in the form of land consolidations, which rapidly changed the appearance of the countryside. The main nature protection organizations at the time – Natuurmonumenten, the Provincial Landscape Foundations, and the Liaison Committee – faced the difficult task of safeguarding nature against the negative impacts of agricultural modernization and land consolidation. They tried to cope by utilizing new planning and consultation instruments that were introduced in Dutch spatial policy at the time. An important tool in nature protection planning was inventories of valuable areas. Conducting such an inventory had been mentioned at the founding of Natuurmonumenten, but it was 1939 before the first complete list was compiled. This report entitled 'The Most Important Areas of Natural Beauty in the Netherlands' identified 747 areas of first and second choice (Gorter 1986).

Aims and Motives

In some respects, 'The Most Important Areas of Natural Beauty in the Netherlands' manifested the characteristics of nature protection during the preceding period; that is, both scientific value and recreational potential and scenic beauty were emphasized in selecting the areas, having almost equal weight in the selection for the 'First Choice List' (Van der Windt

1995). Another feature carried over from the past was the use of 'natural beauty' as an umbrella term.

At the same time, however, the report marked a shift in perspective. The need to survey and prioritize areas implied making selection criteria more explicit. Increasingly, a distinction was made between 'nature' and 'landscape', with nature referring to nature reserves, and landscape to cultural landscapes. Recreation and scenic beauty were considered to be the priority issues in landscape protection, while arguments for the protection of nature reserves concentrated on scientific value, but nature protection experts acknowledged that the boundary between areas of scientific interest and recreational use could not be sharply defined in practice (Dekker 1993; Van der Windt 1995).

Before long, 'natural beauty' came to be viewed as too 'subjective' an argument for justifying protection of nature, even of cultural landscapes. Nature protection advocates now searched instead for arguments based on cultural–historical and scientific elements as 'scientifically established values' (Gorter 1986). Nature protection organizations still referred to natural beauty, but the term rarely figured prominently and was never used as an umbrella term. Similar developments took place in other European countries (for Germany and England, see Ditt 1996).

Practical Activities

Major shifts also occurred in the activities of nature protection organizations, both in their own nature management and protection efforts, and in their relations to government.

Before the Second World War, management of nature protection areas had focused on preserving the situation at the time of purchase. Usually, this implied the continuation of existing uses of nature: fishing, reed cutting, forestry, grazing and hunting. In some areas, new forms of management were introduced to facilitate recreation or protect particular species. Deliberate 'non-intervention' existed in only a few small areas (Van der Windt 1995). Nature protection organizations thus tried to steer a course between promoting the undisturbed development of nature, obtaining revenue from exploitation, and preserving natural beauty, cultural history and species diversity.

Tensions nevertheless increased, in part because the old types of nature use were losing their economic viability. Some groups – especially the youth organization NJN – used romantic and biological–scientific rationales to argue for a firm policy of non-intervention in nature. Yet it was clear that such a policy would endanger a substantial part of the existing nature reserves; heathlands, dunes and drift sands would become overgrown with vegetation, and open waters would turn into land. A heated debate ensued during the mid-1940s. It led to the conclusion that some nature reserves should be characterized as 'semi-natural ecosystems', which required continuing management to remain in their current state (Gorter 1986; Van der Windt 1995). An important corollary was that, even though traditional uses of nature remained an important element of management, their consequences should be analysed and monitored by the biological sciences, especially plant ecology. Van der Goes van Naters, a prominent politician, nature protection activist and long-time chairman of the Liaison Committee, characterized this episode as the birth of 'scientific nature conservation' (Van der Goes van Naters 1956).

The increasing costs of land purchase and management in the decades following the Second World War resulted in a radical change in the financial practices of nature protection organizations: they had to appeal increasingly for government funding. The Dutch government responded by allocating substantial budgets to support private organizations in their acquisition of land, often on the condition that the areas be open to the public and to 'scholars and artists' for making studies. In 1970, the subsidies for acquisition provided by the national and provincial governments had grown to a total sum of NLG 20 million (about €9 million), alongside NLG 10 million for acquisitions by these governments themselves. In addition, subsidies became available for management of these areas. As a result of these financial ties, the activities of those nature protection organizations involved in area management became closely interwoven with government (Gorter 1986).

Government Policy

Along with increases in financial resources for nature acquisition and management came extensions of government regulations and administrative bodies in the area of nature protection. The Provisional Council for the Protection of Nature was set up in 1946, together with a scientific advisory committee. The committee provided an important avenue for scientists oriented to nature protection to influence government. Policy tasks for nature protection were assigned first to the Ministry of Education, Arts, and Sciences and, after 1965, to the Ministry of Culture, Recreation, and Social Work. After long and difficult consultations between various Ministries and Parliament, the Nature Protection Act was adopted in 1967, marking an important step in the formal protection of nature areas (Gorter 1986).

The most important framework for designation and protection of nature areas, however, was the spatial (or physical) planning policy, which assumed concrete form in the Spatial Planning Act in 1965 and a series of

National and Provincial Spatial Plans. Agricultural policy, too, became a major influence on nature protection. Partly due to the influence of European unification, rationalization of agriculture received high priority in postwar politics. Agricultural interests – often referred to in Dutch politics as the 'Green Front' – tended to have greater influence on government policy than protests by nature protection organizations. Resistance from nature protection advocates in spatial planning and land consolidation procedures could not prevent many of the cultural landscapes they cherished from being drastically transformed by the land consolidations, which were aimed at reallotment and drainage improvements to facilitate further rationalization.

Reclamations, land consolidations and other rationalization measures in agriculture during the first 70 years of the twentieth century led to decline in flora and fauna. The estimated total hectares of forest and nature areas fell between 1900 and 1950 from almost 900 000 to about 500 000 (RIVM et al. 1997). The nature protection organizations' efforts to counter this process required them to become increasingly intertwined with government. They depended on government for funding of land acquisition and saw influencing government policy as the most promising way to realize their objectives. Changes in the arguments of the nature protection movement described above were doubtless coloured by this situation. To make their arguments more acceptable to relevant government agencies, they emphasized scientific values rather than stressing the more 'subjective' enjoyment of natural beauty. Scientific value was, however, still understood in terms of culture rather than in terms of technological know-how contributing to economic development, public health or environmental control. This was illustrated by the assignment of nature policy to the Ministry of Culture, Recreation, and Social Work. In the words of Van der Goes van Naters: 'In most civilized countries, including the Netherlands, with regard to government, nature protection is part of the cultural ministry, of arts and sciences. Nature protection politics is cultural politics' (quoted in Gorter 1986, p. 107). As part of cultural politics, nature protection secured its recognized but modest position within government policy in the period 1940–70.

ON THE WINGS OF THE ENVIRONMENTAL MOVEMENT, 1970–90

The rise of the environmental movement beginning in the early 1960s implied a decisive change in the situation of nature protection. New environmental organizations, such as Friends of the Earth Netherlands

(Vereniging Milieudefensie), emerged, provoking a broad debate about issues such as exposure to dangerous substances, acidification, nuclear energy, and depletion of natural resources. Soon, environmental protection occupied a much stronger political position in industrialized countries than nature protection had ever achieved.

Several environmental laws were passed, and an environmental ministry was established in 1971 – initially as the Ministry of Public Health and the Environment, and later as the Ministry of Housing, Physical Planning and Environment. The Green wave also strengthened the nature protection organizations. New ones, such as the Dutch chapter of WWF (WNF: Wereld Natuur Fonds) emerged, and existing organizations, such as Natuurmonumenten and the Society for Bird Protection, experienced sharp membership increases (see Figure 6.1 and Table 6.1 on p. 155).

Relations between the older nature protection organizations and the new environmental organizations were not free from friction, and there were clear differences in objectives and strategies. The old nature protection organizations were mostly oriented towards lobbying and reaching consensus, whereas environmental organizations, such as Friends of the Earth Netherlands, were geared towards direct action and political confrontation. Yet overall, a spirit of cooperation prevailed. The Netherlands Society for Nature and Environment (Stichting Natuur en Milieu) was founded in 1972 as a central node in the network of provincial environmental federations set

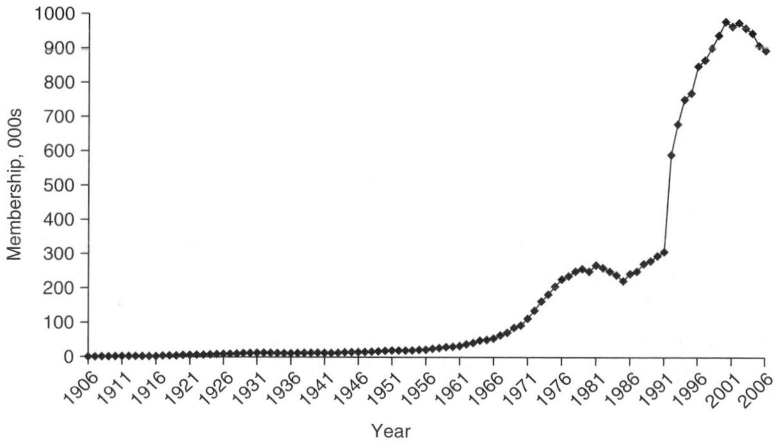

Sources: Gorter (1956), pp. 16, 53; Van Zanden and Verstegen (1993), p. 196; VARA Vroege Vogels Parade 1999–2005; approximate membership numbers at the start of the year.

Figure 6.1 Membership of Natuurmonumenten 1906–2006

up at the time. It also served as a coordinating platform for the national organizations, including the Society for the Preservation of Nature, Friends of the Earth Netherlands, and WNF. Finally, it took over the lobbying role of the Liaison Committee, with which it later merged.

Aims and Motives

Under influence of the environmental movement, the aims and motives of nature protection shifted. In 1970, a working group of nature protection organization representatives formulated their common goals as follows:

> The aim of nature protection organizations is to preserve and manage the collective environment of organisms living on earth, including the natural environment of humans, as a precondition for the preservation of different landscapes and of nature elements in optimal diversity. This is done both to the benefit of the mental and physical well-being of human beings and for the sake of nature itself. Therefore, their efforts are directed to:
>
> a. promoting preservation and restoration of nature and landscape;
> b. improving the purity of water, soil, and air, and protecting silence;
> c. enhancing the awareness that humankind bears responsibility for this.
>
> (Quoted in Gorter 1986, p. 372, my translation)

Two key changes of emphasis command attention here. First, 'the sake of nature itself' is listed as a motive for nature protection. Second, preservation of nature and protecting soil, water and air are linked together, framing nature protection in terms of ecosystems and revealing the influence of ecological science. These changes deserve further discussion.

'For the sake of nature itself' represents a remarkable addition to the rationale for nature protection. Dutch nature protection organizations had previously argued for nature protection – at least in statements intended for the general public – on the basis of benefits for humankind, such as academic research, aesthetic enjoyment, education, recreation, and the preservation of nature monuments and natural resources for future generations. Moral obligations towards protecting nature for its own sake had previously been formulated only in relation to animals as individual beings (as in the case of protest against, for example, mistreatment of dogs or horses) or as a basis for protest against 'massacres' of certain bird populations (as in the case of terns, described above). These arguments were now extended to nature protection in general, arguing that society has a moral responsibility towards endangered species and ecosystems.

This shift was closely related to the rise of environmental ethics as a field of philosophy (see, among others, Hargrove 1989; Nash 1989; and for the

Netherlands: Verhoog 1982; Achterberg and Zweers 1984, 1986). Many writers in this field criticized the dominant anthropocentric ethic of Western society and advocated a 'biocentric' or 'ecocentric' ethic, which included non-human species. Shifting moral views of nature in this period were also expressed in attitudes toward hunting. Hunting had traditionally been considered an acceptable form of exploitation of nature, and sometimes even a hobby of nature protection advocates, but strong anti-hunting sentiments were now voiced both within and outside nature protection organizations, for instance as objections to Natuurmonumenten leasing hunts on their own lands (Dahles 1990).

Somewhat ironically, this moralization of nature was accompanied by the scientification of nature protection. Alongside botanical and zoological characteristics, the abiotic features of nature protection (such as soil condition, water management, and concentrations of nutrients and pollutions) received increasing attention in the monitoring and management of nature. While botany and ornithology had been key disciplines in the early decades of nature protection, and plant ecology had come to the fore in the 1940s and 1950s, systems ecology became the prominent approach in the 1970s and 1980s (Worster 1985). In systems ecology, ecological relationships came to be analysed in terms of materials and energy flows (for examples, see Odum 1971; Werger and Westhoff 1985). This approach provided new, technological–scientific guidelines for directing ecosystems into a preferred course (Van der Windt 1995) and connected species-oriented nature management with environmental management oriented to physical and chemical factors (Stortenbeker and Berendse 1985). In this way, it linked nature preservation arguments to environmental arguments. Nature was viewed as having more than cultural significance; it became valued as a set of resources and regulating processes that constituted the life support systems of humanity. Perhaps the most important motto of nature protection organizations in this period – and, tellingly, the statement concluding Gorter's history of Dutch nature protection – was 'Nature preservation is self-preservation' (Gorter 1986).

Two quite different developments were thus visible in the viewpoints and framings of nature protection organizations and networks: a new emphasis on the moral value of nature 'in itself' and a new emphasis on nature as a vital material resource for humankind. While the contrast between these two views generated fierce disputes within environmental philosophy, especially in terms of the anthropocentrism–ecocentrism debate, it did not raise much controversy within nature protection organizations or society at large. Instead, against the background of growing public interest in nature and environment, both environmental ethics and ecological science contributed to what Nash (1989) called 'the new, ecological morality'. Here, the concept of ecology performed a bridging function. For large parts of the environmental movement, ecology was not just a scientific discipline, but also a new perspective on human beings, society and nature. This was demonstrated by terms such as the 'ecological movement', the 'ecological society' and 'ecological politics' (Van Koppen 1985). In this double meaning, ecology became the dominant framing of nature protection in this period.

Practical Activities

Propelled by the 'Green wave', the activities of the nature protection organizations expanded rapidly. Whereas some 50 000 hectares, more or less evenly divided between Natuurmonumenten and the provincial Landscape Foundations, were managed by nature protection organizations in 1970, by 1990 this had more than doubled, to approximately 120 000 hectares. There was a division of labour among the organizations: Natuurmonumenten and the Landscape Foundations devoted most of their attention to managing protected areas, while WNF and Greenpeace (founded in the Netherlands in 1979) focused mainly on public opinion, and the Netherlands Society for Nature and Environment was oriented largely to lobbying. The Dutch Society for Bird Protection, which was less influential than these organizations but also benefited from the trend toward increasing membership, gradually shifted its emphasis from protection of birds to protection of habitats, moving it closer to the concerns of the other nature protection organizations.

The activities of environmental organizations on nature protection issues and changes in the activities of nature protection organizations during this period produced a shift in focus from acquisition and management of nature areas to public persuasion and education. Environmental education had been of interest to nature protection organizations from the beginning, and a special organization, the Association for Environmental Education (IVN, Instituut voor Natuurbeschermingseducatie), had existed for this purpose since 1960. From 1970 on, this organization extended its activities to a wider audience, including especially the primary schools. Other organizations too became actively involved in environmental education. Natuurmonumenten, for example, initiated an information service and a magazine, and, around 1970, established the first visitor centres (Cramer 1989).

Public protest was, however, the most typical activity in this period. Mobilization for these actions was carried out mainly by new environmental organizations, such as Friends of the Earth Netherlands. Protests often focused on environmental issues, such as pollution by firms and cars, shipments of dangerous substances, and nuclear energy, but there were also protests oriented to nature protection. One well-known action of the early

1970s opposed construction of a motorway through Nieuw Amelisweerd, a country estate near Utrecht. The 'classic' nature protection organizations maintained some distance from such activism, although many of their members sympathized with it.

Government Policy

Changes in this period also accorded nature protection a higher profile in policy debates. Nature policy was developed primarily as part of spatial planning, via various policy documents and spatial plans. As a result of both economic developments in agriculture (such as overproduction leading to a reduction of the number of farms) and their own increasing power, nature protection organizations gained more influence in discussions with the agricultural sector. Consequently, preserving the natural and cultural values of rural areas gained an increasingly significant place in land use planning in comparison to agricultural uses.

None the less, the institutionalization of nature policy was slow in comparison with environmental policy. Not until the second half of the 1980s, when – after several years of economic recession and declining public interest – nature and environment regained prominence on the political agenda, did nature protection receive its own policy structure. One signpost was the 1989 renaming of the Ministry of Agriculture and Fisheries, which had taken over responsibility for nature management in 1982, as the Ministry of Agriculture, *Nature Management* and Fisheries. The growing importance of nature protection was also reflected in expansion of protected areas. The pioneers of nature protection had sought to reserve 'a few' areas for the preservation of natural beauty, and nature protection organizations in the 1940s had requested about 50 000 hectares as strict nature reserves. But by the end of the 1980s, over 250 000 hectares were under strict protection, including nature reserves, forests managed with a focus on nature protection, and strictly protected cultural landscapes (RIVM et al. 1997). Moreover, the Ministry aimed to bring other areas – including country estates, forest areas and cultural landscapes – within the compass of nature policy. The Ministry's plans were laid out in the first Nature Policy Plan of 1990, a milestone in the institutionalization of nature protection policy in the Netherlands (Ministerie L.N.V. 1990).

NEW NATURES, NEW ALLIANCES, 1990–PRESENT

With the publication of the Nature Policy Plan, a full-fledged policy planning structure had been established. Like the previously adopted environmental policy, it provided for planning, monitoring and evaluation in the form of strategic national plans, and annual 'Nature Balances' and 'Nature Outlooks'. The latter focused on evaluation of existing policies and exploration of future scenarios (RIVM et al. 1997, 2002). The key framework for protecting nature, described in the Nature Policy Plan, was the National Ecological Network (NEN). It included not only the previously mentioned nature areas under strict protection, but also other forests, agricultural areas, rivers, lakes, and marine areas with important nature values. The NEN was projected to grow from some 500 000 hectares in 1990 to 700 000 hectares in 2018 by acquisition of cultural landscapes and development of new nature reserves (RIVM et al. 1997). Especially the latter was a major innovation in Dutch nature policy.

A spectacular increase in support for Natuurmonumenten and other nature protection organizations accompanied the increasing institutionalization of nature protection. As Figure 6.1 shows, the increase was even larger than in the 1970s. Moreover, the orientation of public support shifted. During the 1970s and 1980s, the growth rates of general environmental protection organizations and more narrowly focused nature protection organizations were comparable (including a dip in the mid-1980s). Growth – both in number of organizations and in total membership – after 1990 occurred mainly in nature protection and animal protection organizations (Van der Heijden 2002), although some environmental organizations, such as Friends of the Earth Netherlands, also experienced membership growth. Two noteworthy newcomers among the large organizations are AAP and IFAW-Netherlands. The first organization shelters exotic animals coming from pet owners, animal testing, circuses and the like; since 2005 it has also engaged in lobbying against abuse of exotic animals (Stichting AAP 2006). IFAW-Netherlands works to improve the welfare of pets and wild animals through lobbying and public information (IFAW 2006). By focusing on wild animals and pets rather than the more polarizing issue of meat production and consumption, both organizations appeal to a broad public.

Table 6.1 shows membership change for the eight largest national environmental organizations in the Netherlands. The Provincial Landscape Foundations are not included because they are not national organizations. They totalled 292 000 members in 2005 (Netherlands Environmental Assessment Agency 2006).

Aims and Motives

The dramatic increase in support for nature protection has been reflected in the nature protection organizations' taking of more self-confident and proactive positions in the political arena. This trend has been clearly

*Table 6.1 The largest national environmental organizations in the Netherlands, with membership and income**

Organizations with Dutch and English names	Year founded	Membership (end-of-year numbers)				Total income (million €)
		1991	1995	2002	2005	2004–2005
Natuurmonumenten (Dutch Society for the Preservation of Nature)	1905	500	826	960	895	114.5
Wereld Natuur Fonds (WWF Netherlands)	1962	350	724	825	737	49.7
Greenpeace Nederland (Greenpeace Netherlands)	1979	830	608	699	580	22.0
Nederlandse Vereniging tot Bescherming van Dieren (Dutch Society for Animal Protection)	1877	119	196	201	202	26.8
Stichting IFAW Nederland (International Fund for Animal Welfare Netherlands)	1981	n.a.	142	325	186	4.8
Vogelbescherming Nederland (Netherlands Society for the Protection of Birds; or: BirdLife International in the Netherlands)	1899	68	83	125	123	8.6
Stichting AAP (AAP, Sanctuary for Exotic Animals)	1972	2	28	91	87	4.4
Vereniging Milieudefensie (Friends of the Earth Netherlands)	1971	28	35	71	85	6.9

Notes: *Membership figures are derived from Dekker and de Hart (2003) and the Netherlands Environmental Assessment Agency (2006). Total income is based on annual reports from 2005, except for WWF and IFAW (2004/2005 annual report) and Dutch Society for Animal Protection (2004 annual report). Total income includes fundraising costs.

expressed in the emergence of the concept 'nature development'. At the root of this concept, which has significant implications for nature protection, lies the idea that nature can be not only preserved, but also redeveloped or developed anew by creating the right conditions. Internationally, this idea is often referred to as 'nature restoration' (Light and Higgs 1996), but in the Netherlands the usual term is development (*ontwikkeling*). (Many of the areas involved are polders reclaimed from lakes or the sea, or flood plains that for centuries have been used as meadow lands, making it hard to speak of restoration.) This idea of 'new nature', introduced by some more radical advocates of nature protection in the 1980s (Baerselman and Vera 1989), took off in the early 1990s (Van der Windt 1995, pp. 203–10). Until then, the guiding principle of Dutch nature protection had been preservation of the species diversity of natural and semi-natural landscapes as they existed in about 1900. For 'new nature' developers, however, the guiding image was 'rough', self-regulating nature, as free from human intervention as possible. To develop this 'rough' nature, rigorous intervention was often required, including redirecting streams, digging watercourses and lakes, and removing soil layers. Large herbivores, such as Highland cattle (long-haired cows of Scottish origin) and Konik horses, were introduced to maintain an open landscape. After such measures were taken, however, nature was to be allowed to take its own course. Not surprisingly, the emergence of nature development projects has sparked hot debates between advocates of existing cultural landscapes and advocates of 'new nature' about the goals of nature protection (Van der Heijden 2005).

The strong position of nature protection was also reflected in how nature protection was framed. The right of species and ecosystems to exist independent of any human preference, first introduced into public discourse during the 1960s, was increasingly presented as self-evident. These 'intrinsic' or 'ecological' values, as they were called, gained a prominent place even in official policy documents. The second Nature Policy Plan, published in 2000, for example, assigned a central role to these intrinsic values. It acknowledged the amenity and the commodity values of nature, but these were regarded as secondary. 'In a crowded country such as ours these values should be recognised and developed without doing damage to nature's intrinsic value' (Ministry of Agriculture, Nature Management and Fisheries 2000, p. 11). In a similar vein, a recent national advisory council for countryside policy document stated that intrinsic value constituted a more than sufficient motive for species protection (Raad voor het Landelijk Gebied 2002).

The strengthened position of nature protection was also manifest in demands to designate additional areas, not only for developing new nature, but also for surrounding protected areas with buffer zones and connecting them with corridors. Such buffer zones and corridors were to be included in the NEN (RIVM et al. 1997).

Practical Activities

The rise of new concepts of nature protection resulted in diversification of the activities of nature protection organizations. Natuurmonumenten continued and expanded its activities in its existing areas of emphasis, while WNF profiled itself as a strong proponent of nature development. Indeed, the nature development 'boom' is to a fair extent the result of initiatives taken by nature developers from outside official circles; these initiatives were supported strongly by the WNF, both financially and through publicity. For example, the Living Rivers project, drawn up by WNF on the basis of the ideas from nature development advocates (Helmer et al. 1992), provided the impulse for numerous nature development projects along the main Dutch rivers.

There is also differentiation in scope. Some nature protection organizations, such as Natuurmonumenten, retain a largely national focus; others, such as WNF, devote most of their resources to projects abroad. Overall, however, there is a tendency towards more internationally oriented activities. A case in point is the Netherlands Society for the Protection of Birds, which now devotes a significant part of its resources (10 per cent in 2005) to international activities and presents itself as the Dutch chapter of BirdLife International (see Chapter 1) (Vogelbescherming Nederland 2006). One of the major international targets of Dutch nature protection organizations is EU policy, which exerts ever more influence on the Dutch nature policy. WWF and BirdLife International have their own lobbying offices in Brussels. Other nature protection organizations and environmental organizations are represented by the EEB (see Chapter 1).

Increasing professionalization in raising funds and recruiting supporters is another feature of the current period. Natuurmonumenten and WNF, among others, have stimulated membership by intensive media campaigns, including major television productions, where celebrities and prominent politicians appealed to citizens to support them. In addition to government funding and membership fees, a national lottery provides significant continuing funding for several nature protection organizations. Natuurmonumenten, for example, received €19 million in 2005, 16 per cent of its total income and more than its receipts from membership fees. Nevertheless, government subsidies remain the most important funding source for Natuurmonumenten and many other nature protection organizations. Somewhat problematically, the dramatic growth in public financial support in this period has not been matched by growth in visits to nature reserves or volunteer work for nature protection (Bervaes et al. 1997; Volker et al. 1998; RIVM et al. 2003).

New alliances in which non-governmental actors attempt to circumvent the limitations of national policy are perhaps the most striking characteristic of the years since 1990. WNF, in particular, is actively engaged in partnerships, not only with local communities and local authorities, but also with business organizations, such as its cooperation with the multinational firm Unilever to promote the Marine Stewardship Council ecolabel and with timber companies to promote the Forest Stewardship Council ecolabel. In such partnerships, WNF has also broadened its scope beyond nature protection, to include, for instance, energy-saving projects (WNF 2005). The involvement of business in nature protection fits in with the international trend for companies, particularly large industries and banks, to undertake initiatives for promoting nature and biodiversity conservation as an aspect of sustainable production and corporate social responsibility (Abbott et al. 2002).

Government Policy

Although realization of the NEN has been slowed by local resistance, 'red tape', and lack of funds for land acquisition, implementation of the first and second Nature Policy Plans has generally proceeded successfully. Within the NEN, areas designated under the EU Bird and Habitat Directives are considered the most strictly protected. Most other nature parks and reserves, and most of the new nature development areas, are also securely protected through state or nature protection organization ownership and management. The now semi-autonomous State Forest Agency (Staatsbosbeheer), Natuurmonumenten and the Provincial Landscape Foundations are the largest owner–managers.

As described above, the arguments of nature protection organizations and the government's conservation biologists for strict nature protection invoke mainly ecological values and international obligations, thus seeking to wall off compromises with other societal claims on nature. The increased emphasis on international obligations corresponds to the growing importance of international nature policy since the 1970s. The Netherlands is a party to various international treaties, such as the Ramsar Convention on Wetlands and the Convention on International Trade in Endangered Species of Wild Fauna and Flora (CITES). Most influential in the last decade, however, have been EU regulations, in particular the aforementioned Birds and Habitat Directives (Council Directive 79/409/EEC and Council Directive 92/43/EEC) (see Chapter 1). The European Commission has even forced the Netherlands to modify its nature policy, as the Dutch spatial planning framework was considered inadequate to provide legal protection to Habitat and Birds Directive areas.

At the same time, policy makers have become more concerned about lack of public support for nature protection. They were alarmed, for example, by several conflicts with local communities over the designation of areas in the NEN (Keulartz et al. 2000). To retain public support for nature protection policy and enhance the level of nature protection outside the NEN, policy makers believe that more attention should be paid to citizens' perceptions of nature, including those elements of nature that are part of their everyday world. This attention to *vermaatschappelijking van natuur* (societal embedding of nature) was reflected in the first part of the title of the second Nature Policy Plan: 'Nature for People, People for Nature'. The plan's opening statements interpret nature in a broad sense, as including the birds and wild plants on people's doorsteps (Ministry of Agriculture, Nature Management and Fisheries 2000). The report also advocates more active involvement of the public in nature management and planning. Obviously, there is a continuing tension between such a participatory approach, which implies taking into account the aesthetic, cultural, historical and utilitarian motives that prevail among citizens, and current policy approaches based on 'ecological' values and international obligations.

The biodiversity concept, which has become prominent in Dutch policy since the 1992 UN Rio Conference, plays a role in this dilemma. On the one hand, 'biodiversity' is promoted as a new, more science-based concept for internationally and ecologically valuable nature. Yet it has also stimulated concern for combining species preservation with sustainable use of resources, for instance through projects aimed at enhancing biodiversity on farm land (Van Koppen 2002).

DISCUSSION AND CONCLUSIONS

Ecological Modernization, Arcadian Tradition

Ecological modernization is an especially interesting framework for analysing Dutch nature protection because, in many respects, it accounts for the development of environmental policy in the Netherlands well (Spaargaren and Mol 1992; Hajer 1995; Mol 1995). Ecological modernization has rarely been applied to nature protection, but several features of the recent development of nature protection in the Netherlands fit well with this perspective (Van Koppen 2003). First, similar and interrelated frameworks for environmental nature policy and management have been successfully institutionalized. These rational frameworks for planning, monitoring and evaluation can easily be classified as manifestations of a new sphere of ecological rationality that is gaining an independent and influential role in society. Second, the establishment of these policy frameworks has been paralleled by a shift in the stance of the environmental and nature protection movement from radical opposition to constructive cooperation. Indeed, for Natuurmonumenten and WNF this orientation predominated from the very start. Third, paralleling similar developments in environmental management, market mechanisms and economic actors have become increasingly implicated in nature protection efforts. Farmers, private landowners and companies are more and more often invited and allowed to take part in nature protection activities, and there are efforts to introduce market mechanisms into nature protection. Examples include efforts to involve consumers in nature protection and preserving cultural landscapes through promotion of ecolabelling, buying regional products, and shopping at farmers' markets.

Other features of nature protection in the Netherlands, however, are much harder to fit into the ecological modernization perspective. To understand this, we should consider the special position of nature protection within environmentalism. Although some nature protection organizations, such as WNF and the Society for Nature and Environment, have taken up environmental issues, and many environmental organizations, for example, Friends of the Earth Netherlands, are also active in nature protection, nature protection in the Netherlands remains a specific domain of civil action. Nature protection organizations such as Natuurmonumenten and the Netherlands Society for the Protection of Birds have maintained their exclusive focus on nature protection, and recent growth in number of organizations and supporters has occurred mainly in nature protection organizations.

This suggests that while close ties between environmental protection and nature protection exist, these two domains are, at least to some extent, driven by different aims and motives. The unique aims and motives of nature protection supporters are found in the aesthetic and moral orientations that already fuelled nature protection efforts at the beginning of the nineteenth century. Here I understand the aesthetics of nature in a broad sense, including such considerations as rarity and uniqueness, connections to cultural and natural history, and appeal to fantasy and imagination. Also crucial are moral and spiritual values regarding nature, including the moral rights of nature itself and beliefs that humankind is a part of nature.

Central to the ecological rationality envisioned by ecological modernization theory, however, is the conservation of humankind's material sustenance base as a precondition for sustainable production and consumption. Aesthetic and moral concerns are considered secondary, or 'cosmetic' (Spaargaren and Mol 1992, after Schnaiberg 1980). It appears, however, that these motives are central to nature protection advocates and to a substantial part of environmentalism as well. Samuel Hays's statement on US environmental history would apply to the Netherlands equally well: 'The first and most lasting environmental value to develop involves an aesthetic and intellectual interest in the natural world' (Hays 2000, p. 26).

In earlier publications, I have suggested the concept of Arcadian tradition to account for the emergence of this set of moral and aesthetic values and its persistence at the heart of Western nature protection and environmentalism (Van Koppen 2000, 2002; see also Chapter 1). This tradition is characterized by a combination of symbolic nature images and values (wilderness, intrinsic values) and concrete practices of nature enjoyment and care (gardening, voluntary nature management, recreation in nature). Both aspects are reflected in Dutch nature protection. Rather abstract and symbolic arguments dominate in national policy documents, but concerns that are more pragmatic, aesthetic, and related to cultural history emerge as central in the actual designation and management of natural areas (Keulartz et al. 2000). They are also apparent in the discourse of nature protection organizations, which tend to stress 'ecological' or intrinsic values in the national policy debates, but emphasize recreation in nature and natural beauty in information for the public.

Outlook

Nature protection organizations in the Netherlands have been successful in recent years in increasing their public support base and lobbying for the institutionalization of nature protection in government policy. In the process, several of them have developed into well-organized, professional organizations with increasingly strong links to government, both in terms of funding and exchange of information and expertise. The large memberships of the major nature protection organizations provide them with income from membership dues and individual contributions, but, more importantly, they are a major source of legitimation with government and corporate sponsors. The recent shift towards involvement of new economic actors and a larger role of market mechanisms appears to be not so much replacing the key role of government and nature protection organizations, but rather adding new mechanisms of protection.

Similar developments can be witnessed in many other countries in Northwestern Europe and the USA. The enormous memberships of nature protection organizations, however, appear to be a unique feature of the Netherlands. If the Arcadian tradition is indeed an important motivation for nature protection, one might hypothesize that 'Arcadian', moral and aesthetic sentiments towards nature have found particularly strong resonance among Dutch citizens. Among the plausible causes for this broad resonance are included: relative affluence, implying leisure and recreation opportunities for many; a high level of industrialization and urbanization, reducing direct dependence on nature, and the high density of population within a constructed landscape, making nature a scarce and desirable good. Deeply rooted sensibilities to nature are also exemplified by strong anti-hunting sentiment and efforts to create new wilderness through nature development. (Another telling example is the recent success of the 'Party for the Animals', which in the November 2006 elections won two seats in the Dutch Parliament, and thereby is the first political party with an exclusive focus on animal welfare to be represented in a national parliament.)

Nevertheless, the concern voiced in the introduction to this chapter is not unfounded. Nature in the Netherlands is under serious pressure, and measures to safeguard it are costly in several respects. The question is whether the broadly shared nature appreciation of Dutch citizens provides a sufficient support base for such measures. When public appreciation of nature is mainly articulated in idealized images and symbolic moral values, and not sufficiently rooted in citizens' actual practices of enjoying and caring for nature, it may fail to effectively change people's attitudes and behaviours. Dutch national nature policy, with its mix of top-down, technocratic policy making and an abstract ethic of intrinsic values, is strongly biased to the symbolic side. Many of the efforts of nature protection organizations to raise membership, too, appeal to symbolic emotional sentiments rather than actual practices of dealing with nature. This is exemplified by the new animal protection organizations that campaign to protect wild, exotic animals, but avoid discussing meat production and consumption. More attention to nature in the day-to-day lifeworld of citizens and policy efforts towards 'societal embedding' of nature are needed to cultivate a public support base prepared to do more than write cheques.

NOTE

1. The chapter is partly based on a more elaborate chapter on the history of Dutch nature protection in Van Koppen (2002).

REFERENCES

Abbott, C. et al. (2002), *Business & Biodiversity. The Handbook for Corporate Action*, Geneva: WBCSD.

Achterberg, W. and W. Zweers (eds) (1984), *Milieucrisis en filosofie. Westers bewustzijn en vervreemde natuur*, Amsterdam: Ekologische Uitgeverij.

Achterberg, W. and W. Zweers (eds) (1986), *Milieufilosofie tussen theorie en praktijk*, Utrecht: Van Arkel.

Baerselman, F. and F.W.M. Vera (1989), *Natuurontwikkeling*, Den Haag: Ministerie L&V.

Bervaes, J.C.A.M. et al. (1997), *Draagvlak voor natuur? Een peiling bij het publiek en bij maatschappelijke organisaties*, Wageningen: Instituut voor Bos- en Natuuronderzoek.

Coesèl, M. (1993), *Zinkviooltjes en zoetwaterwieren. J. Heimans (1889–1978) Natuurstudie en natuurbescherming in Nederland*, Hilversum: Verloren.

Coesèl, M. (1996), 'Opkomst van natuurstudie en natuurbescherming in Nederland: feiten en achtergronden', in A. van Loon et al., *De eeuw van Thijsse*, Amsterdam: Heimans en Thijsse Stichting, pp. 17–28.

Cramer, J. (1989), *De groene golf. Geschiedenis en toekomst van de Nederlandse milieubeweging*, Utrecht: Van Arkel.

Dahles, H. (1990), *Mannen in het groen. De wereld van de jacht in Nederland*, Nijmegen: SUN.

Dekker, J. (1993), *De ontdekking van het cultuurlandschap*, Utrecht: Vakgroep Natuurwetenschap en samenleving, Rijksuniversiteit Utrecht.

Dekker, P. and J. de Hart (2003), 'Participatie', in T. Roes (ed.), *De sociale staat van Nederland*, Den Haag: Sociaal en Cultureel Planbureau, pp. 151–72.

Ditt, K. (1996), 'Nature conversation in England and Germany 1900–70: Fore-runner of environmental protection?', *Contemporary European History*, **5** (1), 1–28.

Gorter, H.P. et al. (1956), *Vijftig jaar natuurbescherming in Nederland*, Amsterdam: Vereeniging tot Behoud van Natuurmonumenten in Nederland.

Gorter, H.P. (1986), *Ruimte voor natuur*, 's-Graveland: Natuurmonumenten.

Hajer, M.A. (1995), *The Politics of Environmental Discourse. Ecological Modernization and the Policy Process*, Oxford: Clarendon Press.

Hargrove, E.C. (1989), *Foundations of Environmental Ethics*, Englewood Cliffs, NJ: Prentice-Hall.

Hays, S.P. (2000), *A History of Environmental Politics since 1945*, Pittsburgh, PA: University of Pittsburgh Press.

Helmer, W. et al. (1992), *Levende rivieren*, Zeist: Wereld Natuur Fonds.

IFAW (2006), *Financieel verslag per 30 juni 2005*, Den Haag: Stichting IFAW.

Keulartz, J., S. Swart and H. van der Windt (2000), *Natuurbeelden en natuurbeleid. Theoretische en empirische verkenningen*, Den Haag: NWO.

Light, A. and E.S. Higgs (1996), 'The politics of ecological restoration', *Environmental Ethics*, **18**, 227–47.

Ministerie, L.N.V. (1990), *Natuurbeleidsplan, regeringsbeslissing*, Den Haag: SDU Uitgeverij.

Ministry of Agriculture, Nature Management and Fisheries (2000), *Nature for People, People for Nature*, Den Haag: Ministry of Agriculture, Nature Management and Fisheries.

Mol, A.P.J. (1995), *The Refinement of Production. Ecological Modernization Theory and the Chemical Industry*, Utrecht: Van Arkel.

Nash, R.F. (1989), *The Rights of Nature. A History of Environmental Ethics*, Madison, WI: University of Wisconsin Press.

Netherlands Environmental Assessment Agency (2006), 'Environmental data compendium', www.mnp.nl/mnc/index-en.html, 17 October.

Odum, E.P. (1971), *Fundamentals of Ecology*, Philadelphia: Saunders.

RIVM et al. (1997), *Natuurverkenning 97*, Alphen a.d. Rijn: Samsom H.D. Tjeenk Willink.

RIVM et al. (2002), *Natuurverkenning 2: 2000–2030*, Alphen a.d. Rijn: Kluwer.

RIVM et al. (2003), *Natuurbalans 2003*, Alphen a.d. Rijn: Kluwer.
Raad voor het Landelijk Gebied (2002), *Voorkomen is beter. Advies over soortenbescherming en economische ontwikkeling*, Amersfoort: Raad voor het Landelijk Gebied.
Schnaiberg, A. (1980), *The Environment. From Surplus to Scarcity*, New York: Oxford University Press.
Spaargaren, G. and A.P.J. Mol (1992), 'Sociology, environment, and modernity: ecological modernization as a theory of social change', *Society and Natural Resources*, **5**, 323–44.
Stichting AAP (2006), *AAP Opvang voor üitheemse dieren. Jaarverslag 2005*, Almere: Stichting AAP.
Stortenbeker, C.W. and F. Berendse (1985), 'Het beheer van natuur en milieu', in K. Bakker et al. (eds), *Inleiding tot de oecologie*, Utrecht: Bohn, Scheltema & Holkema, pp. 521–56.
Thijsse, J.P. (1932), 'Natuurbescherming en Natuurmonumenten', *Tijdschrift der Nederlandsche Heidemaatschappij*, **44** (5), 150–65.
Van der Goes van Naters, M. (1956), 'Natuurbescherming en natuurbeheersing', in H.P. Gorter et al., *Vijftig jaar natuurbescherming in Nederland*, Amsterdam: Vereeniging tot Behoud van Natuurmonumenten in Nederland, pp. 223–6.
Van der Heijden, H.A. (2002), 'Dutch environmentalism at the turn of the century', *Environmental Politics*, **11** (4), 120–30.
Van der Heijden, H.A. (2005), 'Ecological restoration, environmentalism and the Dutch politics of "new nature" ', *Environmental Values*, **14**, 427–46.
Van der Windt, H. (1995), *En dan: wat is natuur nog in dit land? Natuurbescherming in Nederland 1880–1990*, Meppel: Boom.
Van Koppen, C.S.A. (1985), 'De milieubeweging tussen Verlichting en Romantiek', in C.S.A. van Koppen et al. (eds), *Natuur en Mens*, Wageningen: Pudoc, pp. 119–31.
Van Koppen, C.S.A. (2000), 'Resource, Arcadia, Lifeworld. Nature concepts in environmental sociology', *Sociologia Ruralis*, **40** (3), 300–18.
Van Koppen, C.S.A. (2002), *Echte natuur. Een sociaatheoretisch onderzoek naar natuurwaardering en natuurbescherming in de moderne samenleving*, Wageningen: Dissertation, Wageningen University.
Van Koppen, C.S.A. (2003), 'Ecological modernisation and nature conservation', *International Journal of Environment and Sustainable Development*, **2** (3), 305–23.
Van Schendelen, M. (1997), *Natuur en ruimtelijke ordening in Nederland. Een symbiotische relatie*, Rotterdam: NAi Uitgevers.
Van Zanden, J.L. and S.W. Verstegen (1993), *Groene geschiedenis van Nederland*, Utrecht: Het Spectrum.
Verhoog, H. (1982), 'Ethiek en milieuproblematiek', *Filosofie en Praktijk*, March, 14–30.
Vogelbescherming Nederland (2006), *Jaarverslag 2005 Vogelbescherming Nederland*, Zeist: Vogelbescherming Nederland.
Volker, C.M., A.E. Buijs and M. Pleijte (1998), *Vrijwilligerswerk voor natuur en landschap – Eindrapport*, Wageningen: Staring Centrum.
Werger, M.J.A. and V. Westhoff (1985), 'Systeemecologie, structureel', in K. Bakker et al. (eds), *Inleiding tot de oecologie*, Utrecht: Bohn, Scheltema & Holkema, pp. 283–322.
WNF (2005), *Jaarverslag Wereld Natuur Fonds 2004/2005*, Zeist: WNF.
Worster, D. (1985), *Nature's Economy: A History of Ecological Ideas*, Cambridge: Cambridge University Press.

7. Trees, ecology and biological diversity: Norwegian nature protection and environmentalism

Ørnulf Seippel

INTRODUCTION

As of 2005, about 12 per cent of Norway was protected under the Nature Conservation Act. Behind this accomplishment stands a long, cumbersome process in which individuals, voluntary organizations and public actors all played decisive roles. Indeed, even though the environmental protection of today's late modern era is quite different from early twentieth-century efforts to mobilize on behalf of nature or the political ecology of the 1970s, one common theme runs through them all: nature protection. In the early years, nature protection was mainly articulated as concern for small areas, specific species, or even single trees; later it manifested itself as efforts to protect ecosystems and more recently as maintaining biological diversity.

There is a large body of literature about Norwegian organizations that have concerned themselves with nature protection and environmentalism, and some research about nature protection policies; however, surprisingly little research focuses specifically on the intersection of the two: that is, on the part voluntary organizations and networks have played in the development of nature protection efforts. This chapter helps to fill this gap by addressing the development of nature protection and environmental organizations, their role in the development of nature protection policies, and, more briefly, their contribution to the general political modernization of Norwegian society.

Norwegian organizations concerned with nature and environmental protection can be succinctly described as having developed from petty bourgeois and scientific concerns (1850–1962), via a period of political radicalization (1962–85), to a situation where both environmental issues and environmental and nature protection organizations are thoroughly institutionalized and differentiated (1985–present). This chapter is organized around these three historical periods. For each period I focus on three main topics: (1) the characteristics of organizations concerned with nature protection, including size, constituency, issues addressed, ideologies, resources, organizational structures and action strategies; (2) nature protection as a social and political issue, i.e. shifts in nature protection policies in the context of overall societal developments, including developments in politics, economic structure, science, culture and ideology; and (3) the relationship between nature protection and wider environmental concerns and movements. Nature protection organizations have also played an important role in the more general political modernization of Norwegian politics. In a fourth section of this chapter, I look at the extent to which nature protection organizations in particular and environmental organizations in general have had democratic effects. A final section sums up the findings and draws conclusions.

WHAT TO STUDY?

In the introduction to this book, the core of nature protection is conceptualized as protection of cultural landscapes, wild animals and plants, and wilderness, and the book's focus is identified as organizations and networks that emphasize nature protection and are national, large and influential. Yet, even with these relatively clear guidelines, it is not always obvious which organizations and networks to include. I begin, therefore, with a recent, large study of 'Power and Democracy' in Norway, which devoted one book to environmental organizations (Bortne et al. 2002). This study focused mainly on relations between environmental organizations and the state, but it also categorized organizations according to the thematic fields in which they are active. Specifically it distinguished among organizations that focus on classic nature protection, environmentalism (*miljøvern*), consumption, local issues (e.g. traffic), preservation of cultural heritage, outdoor recreation (*friluftsliv*), biological diversity, and what the authors call interest organizations (including the Norwegian Water Organization and the Norwegian Organization for Biology).

The study lists four organizations in the nature protection category: the Norwegian Society for the Conservation of Nature (Norges Naturvernforening – NSC/FoEN[1]), 'The Future in Our Hands' (Framtiden i våre hender – FIOH), WWF and Our Predators (Våre rovdyr). A coordinating network – the 'Cooperation Council for Biological Diversity' (Samarbeidsrådet for biologisk mangfold) – is also mentioned. In terms of size and influence, two of these organizations are central for a study of nature protection organizations and networks: NSC/FoEN and WWF. In addition, there are other organizations, such as FIOH and Nature and

Youth (Natur og ungdom – NY) (not included as such above), for which nature protection goals are always present but only sometimes central, depending upon how nature protection is prioritized relative to a larger set of environmental issues. The other organization mentioned in the Power and Democracy study, Our Predators (Våre rovdyr), is relatively small and new and mainly operates in one region.

A few organizations that have emerged more recently and are not mentioned in the Power and Democracy study are also relevant to present-day nature protection. Bellona is actually a foundation, but it has turned out to be one of the most visible and outspoken environmental organizations of the last decade. Greenpeace has had a Norwegian branch for almost 20 years, but is probably less central to environmentalism and nature protection than Greenpeace in some other countries. Other organizations have played important yet more historical roles in the evolution of nature protection in Norway. The organization most central to nature protection in the early history of Norwegian nature protection was the Norwegian Mountain Touring Association (Den norske turistforening – NMT). Finally, according to NOU (1980, p. 23) (Official Norwegian Reports), the Norwegian Association of Hunters and Anglers (Norges jeger- og fiskerforbund – NJFF) has at times played a role in nature protection, as have organizations such as the scouts and 4H.

In summary, the story of voluntary organizations concerned with nature protection in Norway includes four major actors. First, NSC/FoEN has played a key role throughout almost the whole history of nature protection. NMT played a key role in initiating nature protection efforts in the early years, but later became less important. Third, during the last decade, WWF has emerged as the most visible nature protection organization. Fourth, organizations such as FIOH, NY and Bellona have played important roles in nature protection in recent decades, even though nature protection is mostly of indirect concern to them. Organizations in this last category will be included in the present study to the extent they are relevant. Table 7.1 gives an overview of the whole field of Norwegian nature protection organizations and environmental organizations with nature protection goals.

NATURE PROTECTION ORGANIZATIONS IN NORWAY

The next three sections summarize the history of Norwegian organizations that have played an important part in nature protection during the historical periods identified above. I describe the various organizations in terms of membership, constituencies, goals, ideology, resources, organizational

Table 7.1 Norwegian environmental organizations, 2005

Name of organization (abbreviation)	Year of foundation	Number of 'members'[1]	Revenues[2]
The Norwegian Mountain Touring Association (NMT)	1868	207 000	45.4[4]
The Norwegian Society for the Conservation of Nature (NSC/FoEN)	1914/63[3]	17 000	20
World Wild Fund for Nature (WWF) Norway	1970	6 000	37
Nature and Youth (NU)	1967	4 800	6.5
The Future in our Hands (FIOH)	1974	20 850	11
Bellona	1986	1 700	24
Greenpeace Norway	1988	3 100	1.3
NOAH – animal rights	1989	2 000	1
Green Everyday Life (GEL)	1991	44 000	14

Notes:

1 Not all organizations have members in the traditional meaning of the term: Greenpeace and Bellona have 'supporters' or 'donors'; Green Everyday Life has 'participants'.

2 Figures in Norwegian Kroner (8 NOK = 1 EUR).

3 Change of name in 1963.

4 This figure excludes local branches.

structures and repertoires of action, i.e. how the organizations have adapted their goals and strategies to the political, economic, cutural and scientific context.

1850–1962: Classical Nature Protection[2]

Historians have long claimed that traditional societies were aware of the need to preserve certain aspects of nature in order to secure future harvests, even if their efforts sometimes failed dramatically (McNeill 1980; Ponting 1991). In the introduction to the most comprehensive study of the history of Norwegian environmentalism, Berntsen (1994) shows that awareness of the precariousness of nature also existed in medieval Norway. Indeed, the need to protect game and fish was recognized and even legislated prior to the Black Death.[3] The easing of population pressures following the Black Death made this legislation superfluous, but the problems and people's awareness of the need to protect nature returned in the following centuries. For example, the introduction of saws powered by water wheels around 1500 resulted in rules against the felling of trees (Berntsen 1994; Hågvar and Huse 1996).

The nineteenth century saw the emergence of several social processes that played a central role in the growth of more widespread and intense concern for nature. The first factor was industrialization and the resulting need for energy, which, in the Norwegian context, created pressure to develop hydroelectric power. A second factor was the emergence of a Romantic ideology concerned with Norwegian traditions, history and nature. In combination with a third factor, growing nationalism, this increased interest in things seen as distinctively Norwegian. This linkage also made it possible to articulate nature protection concerns in a way that tied concerns about nature to other ideological trends and to create a degree of public resonance for nature protection. A fourth important factor was the growth of science, which opened the door to new knowledge and insights about nature and increased interest in nature.

Taken together, these developments provided a discursive field in which concern for nature could be articulated. During the same period, the emergence of a more open and responsive polity provided a political opportunity structure which made it possible and worthwhile to establish voluntary organizations to work for nature protection. In short, these shifts – which constituted the basic modernization of Norwegian society – provided (1) the basis for addressing a specific set of political questions regarding nature protection and (2) the opportunity, within relative narrow social class constraints, to mobilize organizations around these issues.

According to Berntsen (1994), the first efforts to organize around nature protection questions during this period focused primarily on cultural issues – first and foremost preservation of old buildings like the stave churches (churches built of wood, a tradition stretching back to the beginning of the last millennium (1100)). The most important nature protection issues in this era, however, involved protection of populations of specific plants (DN 1995, p. 17). These concerns were mostly articulated by scientists. The first organization to work in this field was the Association for Preservation of Norwegian Ancient Monuments (Foreningen til Norske Fortidsminnesmerkers Bevaring), founded in 1844. The association exists today as the Society for the Preservation of Norwegian Ancient Monuments (Fortidsminneforeningen).

The next step towards organized nature protection was a side effect of emerging interest in outdoor recreation, which was partly promoted by foreign (mainly British) tourists. The result was the founding of the Norwegian Mountain Touring Association (NMT) (Den norske turistforening) in 1868, which functioned as an important voice for nature protection during the last part of the nineteenth century. NMT was deeply involved in several conflicts over dams for hydroelectric power: it even purchased the legal rights to some waterfalls to save them. When industrialization increased the pressure for hydropower projects, there were serious discussions about whether NMT should try to obstruct them, but in most cases, NMT did not oppose the projects too strongly, and industrialists' interests triumphed. These conflicts gave a strong foretaste of what later became a main line of conflict for Norwegian environmentalists: hydroelectric power and economic growth versus nature protection.

The first government initiative to preserve nature came in 1884 when a small beech forest was set aside as state property (Berntsen 1994; DN 1995). The focus on a small site of botanical interest was typical of early efforts to preserve land. Nature in general was not considered threatened, only specific areas or species. As in many other nations, scientists were pioneers in this area. Through seminars and discussions, they paved the way for the first set of protection laws, which took effect in 1910. Nevertheless, the tools needed to actually execute an ambitious nature protection policy were not yet in place, there were few opportunities for funding land purchases, and a public agency equipped to implement the new policies did not exist. The steps taken in this period were mostly the result of close links between individual initiatives, organizations and politicians. There was as yet no broad public opinion concerning nature protection (Hågvar and Huse 1996).

With continued industrialization and more interest in nature – both for scientific study and for recreation – the same groups and persons that had promoted the first protection laws took the initiative in establishing an organization solely for nature protection. This was the National Association for Nature Preservation in Norway (Landsforeningen for naturfredning i Norge), founded in 1914. It later became the NSC/FoEN. The early leaders of the association were mainly scientists and government officials. This elite constituency was reflected in the ideological orientation and action repertoire of the association. During its early years, the NSC/FoEN focused almost all of its attention on preserving specific botanical entities or geological formations, such as ancient trees, small populations of plants, small nature reserves, or particular waterfalls. In subsequent decades, the picture remained much the same. Even though more and more nature protection areas were gradually set aside, they remained small.

For a good many years the organization had only 200 to 300 members, but this had increased to approximately 1000 by the beginning of the Second World War. The leader of the Association – Adolf Holm – collaborated actively with the Nazis during the war, which resulted in a serious setback for the organization and the whole issue of nature protection. Almost no activity took place during the war, and the organization was close to collapse at the war's end. It did not really become operational again until the early 1950s.

The immediate postwar period brought no major changes in Norwegian nature protection. Norwegian society's orientation during these years is nicely captured by the phrase 'growth and prosperity' (Bergh 1977); the nation was geared towards economic growth and, with the emergence of the social democratic welfare state, social distribution of the fruits of the nation's prosperity. The overall goal of economic growth was far from an optimal situation for nature protection. The ambiguous relation between labour organizations and the environment is indicative of this situation. On the one hand, labour unions and environmentalists are characterized by a common radicalism based on a critique of capitalism. On the other hand, labour organizations are very much in favour of industrialization, whereas environmentalists are to a large extent sceptical towards industrialization. These contradictory perspectives made this a difficult issue for social democrats and other leftists to handle.

On the other hand, the successful economic modernization of the postwar period revealed that industrialization had its costs. It became increasingly apparent to some segments of the population that there were inherent conflicts between economic growth and nature protection, and that growth was producing significant environmental problems. Part of the explanation for the intensified concern for nature was the increased scale of industrial facilities and the growing understanding that many of the consequences of industrialization were irreversible. By the late 1950s, there was growing public awareness of and impatience about questions of nature protection. There were initiatives for new and extended laws concerning nature protection (1949), and these were put in place in 1953. What was qualitatively new was that these new laws were backed by a new nature protection administration, and, after 1960, also by a specific position, 'Inspector' for nature protection (DN 1995, p. 17). This implied a more activist preservation politics.

In summary, during this first period, what some people today retrospectively call environmentalism was actually strongly focused on nature protection; that is, on preserving specific trees or plants, landscapes, rivers and waterfalls. During this period, a combination of state actions and efforts by nature protection organizations prepared the ground for nature protection policies. Voluntary organizations played a role in creating an emerging awareness about these issues, but they did not operate as part of what we now consider social movements. Instead the organizations that pursued nature protection during this period functioned as relatively small and weak interest groups, attempting to influence government to protect specific segments of nature. They represented mainly elite, establishment constituencies and were very dependent upon specific nature protection pioneers for their success. NMT was the most important organization in the early years of this period, whereas NSC/FoEN played the leading role later in the first part of twentieth century. The first nature protection law was passed in 1910, even before NSC/FoEN was established, but strong government agencies to implement the new nature protection regulations were absent. Finally, at the beginning of the 1960s, there was a change. Organizations promoting nature protection went on the offensive, and the state – and the rest of the establishment – came under pressure from increasing public impatience to get nature protection off the ground in a more serious way. Yet, as Hågvar and Huse (1996) point out, Norway's political priorities remained directed towards industrial growth, the time was still not ripe for putting into place the right tools.

1962–85: Political Ecology

The next 20 years gave us what we today understand as environmentalism, a new framing of problems that included a broader set of goals than traditional nature protection. This period clearly brought nature protection to the centre of the new environmental movement, and Berntsen (1994, pp. 114–32) has even termed the developments of this period a 'breakthrough of nature protection'! On the other hand, the growth of an environmental movement also reduced nature protection to just one part of a broader environmental agenda. Important also, in this period, were the terminological shifts taking place: 'nature' became 'environment', and 'ecology' emerged as an important concept in the environmental discourse of the period.

Several postwar developments set the stage for this change. They included intensified industrialization, which further increased the demand for energy and increased air, water and soil pollution. Many people became convinced, drawing in part on ideas first developed abroad, that industrialization – and for many modernization in general – had undesirable side effects for nature and, according to some, for society as well. One famous proponent of combining concern for nature and society, the deep ecologist Næss (1991, ch. 7), encouraged people to live 'simpler yet richer lives'.

Science played a double – if not a triple – role in these developments: on the one hand, it was a strong force promoting environmentally destructive industrialization. On the other hand, it was also producing research findings that highlighted the problems. Finally, science was seen as part of the solution by those promoting technological fixes for environmental destruction.

This period also saw changes in views of nature. First, more people came to support taking care of nature, and, as shown below, nature protection was at the core of the main conflicts of this period. Second, nature protection was incorporated by some into an increasingly complex ideological landscape. The growing popularity of more radical ideas based on ecological perspectives contributed to a more politicized discourse about nature protection: Marxists questioned the beneficence of the market, whereas liberals and anarchists attacked the power and dominance of the state. These critiques expressed more than a deeply felt concern for nature; the underlying problems were seen as inherent in modernization, capitalism, statism, or anthropocentric human culture. According to these new views, nature needed to be preserved not only for its natural resources and economic value, its beauty or its scientific interest, but also for 'wider' social and existential reasons; i.e. modernization was viewed as leading to a superficial, one-dimensional and/or alienated life. Another aspect of the ideological shift during this period was a demand for a broader understanding of politics, both with respect to what issues should be debated and a more widespread acceptance of forms of political participation situated outside the established political system. Important as they were, these new ideological orientations were represented mainly by left–liberal groups. The view of the general public during this period, as for example found in the election studies, is probably better described as favouring 'growth with protection' [*vekst med vern*] (Jansen 1989; Aardal 1993).

The terms 'environment' and 'ecology' grew in prominence during this period at the expense of 'nature protection'. Environmentalism included more issues, reducing nature protection to being merely one issue among others. Moreover, environmental ideas were linked to an even wider set of new social movement themes, including traffic, general lifestyle questions, feminism, peace and international solidarity. Although nature protection was now typically pursued as a component of environmentalism, environmental organizations retained nature protection as an important concern, and nature protection was central to disputes that represented the peak of contentious environmentalism in Norway.

The most significant sign of increasingly widespread acceptance of the value of nature protection was the establishment of national parks beginning in 1962. This period also saw an extensive institutionalization of environmentalism within the state apparatus, including updating and expansion of nature protection laws. One key innovation was that projects threatening landscapes with irreversible degradation now had to be presented to public authorities previous to any decision (Hågvar and Huse 1996). Two very important offices relevant to nature protection were also established in 1973, the Norwegian Pollution Control Authority and the Ministry of the Environment. Moreover, both nature protection and environmental concerns were gradually integrated in law and politics. Good examples of this trend were passage of a new nature protection law in 1970 and a series of three 'protection plans'. Whereas the fights for protection of waterways were all lost during the 1960s, the new protection plans focused especially on waterways. In the first plan, passed in 1973, 95 waterways were protected, the 1980 plan saved 51, and the last plan (1986) protected seven larger waterways. The last plan also aimed to integrate more environmental issues than hitherto.

At the beginning of this period, in 1962, NSC (the National Association for Nature Preservation in Norway) changed its name to 'The Norwegian Society for Nature Preservation' (Norges naturvernforbund). Although the change appears minor, it reflected both an extension to new issues along the lines indicated above and a more activist stance; the organization thus sought to become more visible in the public sphere and to increase its membership (Hågvar and Huse 1996). During this period, NSC/FoEN also moved toward functioning as a social movement organization, i.e. it became part of a mass movement in which the number of supporters (members and participants in demonstrations) was seen as among the most important bases for its influence. But at the same time, NSC/FoEN remained an organization which took care not to be too involved in conflictual issues and actions; the challenge facing the organization was – and remains – to balance the many conflicting issues related to environmental questions: to retain a large membership it has to be a credible watchdog without becoming too controversial.

No additional significant organizations with nature protection goals were founded until 1970, when WWF established a Norwegian section. Its focus on nature might seem to imply increased attention to nature protection, but the Norwegian branch initially played a rather marginal role.

In 1967, 'Nature and Youth' (NY – Natur og ungdom), the young people's section of NSC/FoEN, was set up. It adopted a more activist and radical stance than NSC/FoEN. In 1974 'The Future in Our Hands' (FIOH) was established to emphasize a wider set of issues – environment and international solidarity – and to integrate these issues into a wider concern for alternative lifestyles. The FIOH and NY were typical representatives of the more radical environmentalism of the second period in that they covered a wider spectrum of environmental issues, were more political, manifested alternative values, and used more direct action strategies.

This period also saw the two most spectacular protest events in the history of Norwegian environmentalism, both related to the construction of hydropower plants that required damming of rivers and waterfalls. The first protest was not organized by any of the established organizations, but by an *ad hoc* organization, SNM (the Cooperation Groups for Nature- and Environmental Protection – Samarbeidsgruppene for natur- og miljøvern) in 1970. In this case, a confrontation over destruction of a famous waterfall turned into a large non-violent sit-in from which protesters were carried away by the police. The second conflict, which took place in the north of Norway (Alta), continued for a decade, but it came to a climax in a spectacular demonstration in 1979, in which several participants in a large non-violent demonstration were removed by the police (Andersen and Midttun 1985).

Both these confrontations revealed the ambivalent approach to environmental issues typical of Norwegian politics and environmentalism during this period. In other countries, growing demand for energy led to controversy over whether to use nuclear energy. In Norway the question was adding new hydropower facilities, and the best argument against more of these was nature protection, not pollution or threats to human health. Both the battles described above brought much attention and good will to the environmental cause, yet in the end, both battles were lost to proponents of growth. Nevertheless, the fact that these hydropower dam projects – inevitably involving questions of preserving landscapes and wilderness – became the central environmental conflicts of the period showed that nature protection remained central to Norwegian environmentalism.

This period was not only the peak of social movement mobilization for nature protection, but also the period during which the relationship between nature protection and environmentalism was transformed. At the beginning of the period, nature preservation was *the issue*, and, in the middle of the period, it was the focus of the most spectacular environmental protest events in Norwegian history. This focus on nature preservation in these protests, however, combined genuine concern for nature with anti-modernization sentiments less directly concerned with specific nature preservation. Also in this period, nature protection, along with environmental protection, was successfully politically institutionalized. At the end of this period, public concern for nature was increasingly widespread, even though most of the key battles were lost, and there were more environmental organizations working with a broader range of environmental issues in a society that had become more structurally and ideologically complex. The results of this extension and institutionalization also point towards the next phase where there seems to be a displacement of nature protection as the central environmental issue and of voluntary organizations as the most important actors for articulating nature protection issues.

1985–Today: Differentiated Environmentalism

According to Jamison (2001, p. 6), 'The 1980s were not kind to environmentalism. Rather than moving forward and gaining new members and enthusiasts, the environmental movement tended to decompose and split apart, for reasons that were not so much internal as external. . . . a counter-revolution was under way'. Whereas proponents of this view claim that strong forces against radical environmental changes had become dominant and accounted for environmentalism's difficulties, proponents of ecological modernization theory offer a different diagnosis (Hajer 1995; Mol 2001). They argue that, for the most part, environmentalism has become integrated into the institutions of late modern society, creating a new situation for nature protection and environmentalism. There is considerable evidence for this claim. The previous period was already characterized by the political institutionalization of the environment; now environmental issues came to be taken seriously by business, law, education, science, religion and consumers. Ecological modernization was thus clearly an important explanatory factor in the weakening of environmentalism, which even if not experiencing a counter-revolution, had at least to adjust to this new situation.

This should not be taken to mean that environmental problems or environmental conflicts had disappeared. The new situation had simply made it difficult to argue that an environmental revolution was needed or that there was much possibility that one would occur. Environmentalists today find it difficult to argue that the environment is being ignored or that it is impossible to address environmental issues within existing institutions – even though one could obviously hope for a higher priority for environmental concern. In other words, this period saw the decline of the grand environmental narrative that spawned the environmental movements and its replacement by many small Green stories. Environmental organizations did not so much encounter strong resistance against environmental concerns as find themselves forced to adjust to this new situation.

To understand the development of environmentalism during the last 20 years one must consider not only changes related to economics or conventional politics, but also changes in political ideologies and a higher acceptance of unconventional politics, such as social movement organizations. By the beginning of this last period, environmental concerns were institutionalized, there was a wide acceptance of the importance of environmental issues, and environmental organizations were generally seen as legitimate political actors. A study of political parties' commitment to environmental concerns also revealed a widespread acceptance of the importance of the issue (Aardal 1993).

One important part of the continuing political institutionalization of environmental issues was the attempt to integrate ideas about environment with ideas about development through the concept of sustainable development. This process was particularly important, at least for a while, since the

Norwegian prime minister was central in acting as midwife to the concept and had a central role at the Rio conference. While the earlier discourse had been based on traditional nature protection vocabulary, science was now providing new concepts for the environmental discourse. The concept of biodiversity, in particular, offered a new way to frame nature preservation issues. Technology also played an important role. Some contributors, including both establishment actors and some environmental organizations, emphasized technological solutions, while others argued that developments in technology, such as biotechnology, spawned new environmental problems.

Despite the institutionalization of environmentalism, specific events continued to trigger heightened interest in environmental and nature protection issues from time to time. Among the most important were the disaster at Chernobyl, a sudden flourishing of algae in the Norwegian fjords, and an invasion of seals. This last case was probably caused by a lack of food in the north, which made seals invade fjords further south, thereby threatening species, such as cod, in these areas. These were significant and qualitatively new issues, and they functioned as reminders of the continued existence of environmental problems and threats to nature. Periodic confrontations over nature protection also continued, most involving hydropower projects, but they were smaller than those of the previous period. Media attention was also drawn by conflicts related to whaling and protection of wild animals, especially wolves. Both of these controversies mobilized supporters and opponents along urban versus rural lines. Also related to nature protection were protests against designating areas for military training. Among the qualitatively new issues were the greenhouse gas effect and ozone layer degradation. Because they are not directly observable, their acceptance by the public depended on the credibility of scientific discourses. A major challenge for Norway as both an oil- and gas-producing country and a country with ambitious environmental goals was increased CO_2 emissions that would result from planned gas-fired power plants. Yet these issues did not turn out as the kind of issues conducive to larger mobilization. Opponents could not mobilize great numbers of people except for short periods at construction sites.

Ideologically the 1980s was a period of deradicalization or apoliticization, and this generalization applied equally well to environmentalism. There was concern about concrete environmental issues, but these were generally not linked to the ideologies, whether Marxist, anarchist, or ecocentrist, of the past. Environmental issues were no longer perceived as part of larger radical ideological packages, but as problems to be solved here and now, within the context of existing institutions. With the environment thoroughly institutionalized and every citizen an environmentalist, environmental concerns and worries, as well as the felt need for environmentalism, lost their urgency. Successful ecological modernization had apparently eliminated the basic need for environmentalism as a watchdog. What appeared to be needed, and what was available, was organizations addressing more concrete questions.

These developments left Norwegian environmentalism in a rather ambiguous position. On the one hand, Norway is a self-proclaimed member of the ecological avant garde, and Prime Minister Brundtland is celebrated (at least at home) as the environmental minister of the world. On the other hand, it has proved quite difficult to truly integrate environmental concerns into the policies of a major oil-producing country.

It has also proved difficult to sustain a viable environmental movement or strong social movement organizations under these new conditions. According to Tilly (2002), the political influence of social movements and social movement organizations depends on the attention they receive in the public sphere. However, influence requires more than attention. It also requires worthiness, unity, numbers and commitment. At the end of the 1980s, and continuing well into the 1990s, neither environmental issues in general, nor nature protection issues in particular, were providing very much of any of these mobilizing resources. The routinization of environmental and nature protection meant that organizations promoting environmentalism came to be seen as rather ordinary and not especially worthy. There was a lack of strong public commitment to the issue, which was fragmented (both in the public sphere and among organizations) and did not provide the basis for a unitary movement. Finally, the number of supporters was smaller. The result was both to reduce the potential of nature protection and environmental issues to generate movements and a loss of interest in environmental protection as a political issue (Aardal 2003).

Given this lack of public attention as a resource for influence, nature protection organizations and environmental organizations had to look elsewhere for resources and support.[4] The result was a focus on specific, smaller problems and on acquiring resources from specific political and commercial actors. Bellona's work with the nuclear threat represented by Russia – especially outdated military equipment – close to the far northern Norwegian border, for example, has been partly funded by the Ministry of Foreign Affairs. What organizations could use to obtain for influence was not large demonstrations or events to communicate the importance of environmental disaster, but rather the specific knowledge they provided as consultants and experts on the many small facets of environmental problems.

Several important new environmental organizations, most with nature protection as one among other goals, appeared in this period. It is difficult to generalize about them because they were highly differentiated in goals and strategies and differed from both older nature protection organizations and the radical environmental organizations in a number of ways, including topics addressed, political profile, allies and enemies, strategies of action, ideology and, not least, organizational form.

Among the new organizations, Bellona (established in 1986) has turned out, according to news media, to be the most important because of its clear and distinct voice in the public sphere. Bellona is an offshoot of Nature and Youth (NY), which in turn was an offshoot of NSC. It has been described as having developed from a group of 'rebels to consultants' (Søgård 1997). Initially, Bellona and NY both had a relatively radical, rebellious action repertoire, but over time, Bellona has become more directed towards cooperation with the establishment, especially private business corporations. Today Bellona informs and educates the public through reports and its website, it has a clear voice in public environmental discourses, and it cooperates with volunteers and various business and political actors in finding solutions to environmental problems – often through technological and scientific means. The organization today has an explicitly apolitical ideology and draws its financial support from 'supporting members' rather than traditional members. For Bellona, which focuses mainly on various energy questions, nature preservation is a secondary issue.

Greenpeace, established in Norway in 1988, emerged at about the same time as Bellona. The Danish and Swedish branches were already operating, so a decision was made to coordinate the three branches from a Nordic main office in Sweden. Later, a Finnish branch was added. Greenpeace relies on financing from supporting donors and uses rather dramatic forms of action to attract media coverage. Greenpeace Norway includes nature protection goals among its main goals, but it also pursues a broad range of environmental issues. Partly because of its opposition to Norwegian whaling policies, Greenpeace has been met with some scepticism in Norway and has never achieved a strong position.

Among the older organizations, WWF has strengthened its position in Norway during the last decade. It is mainly concerned with rather classic nature protection. From the beginning, WWF Norway, like WWF chapters elsewhere, was without ordinary members, but it later established a section within the organization with a more democratic organizational structure as a prerequisite for receiving state funding (Bortne et al. 2002). Today the issues given priority by WWF Norway are clearly preservationist: biodiversity and endangered species, saving and preserving forests, lakes, waterways and coastal areas, toxic pollution, climate change and nature protection in developing countries. WWF Norway also has a clear political aim: to be present at the arenas where weighty environmental decisions are taken.

Three organizations of marginal significance for the preservation but important for an understanding of the field of environmental organizations are NOAH, Green Everyday Life, and Attac. Although there is a lack of good data, it appears that, as for other national cases (Rootes 2003), Norwegian animal rights organizations operate in relative isolation from other environmental organizations. 'NOAH – For Animal Rights' (NOAH – for dyrs rettigheter, established 1989), for example, works for animal rights in general and is at present perhaps the most radical and activist organization in the field. Green Everyday Life (GEL – Grønt hverdagsliv), which was established in 1991, is probably the least politically contentious environmental organization in Norway. Its 'members' are not true members but 'participants'. Their focus is on members' green consumption in everyday life, not running the organization. Interestingly, in terms of numbers, GEL is the success story of current Norwegian environmentalism. At the moment it has about 100 000 participants. An interesting development late in this period has been the emergence of a Norwegian branch of Attac, which received a lot of attention for a short period before fading away. Its success was partly due to its ability to frame existing environmental problems in original ways by linking them to 'new' neoliberal discourses and questions of globalization (Sandberg 2005).

As the brief descriptions above suggest, the result of the new constellations of issues, actors and ideologies that have emerged since the mid-1980s has been a differentiation of environmental organizations in terms of ideological orientations, strategies, action repertoires and constituencies. For nature protection, the result was that there was not just *one* 'classic' democratically organized organization working for nature protection as its only goal. FoEN and several other organizations from the 1970s now treat nature protection as one important issue among others. Moreover, many organizations with more specific goals have appeared. It would be misleading to say they were not concerned with nature protection, but this was not their main focus. Nevertheless, responding to the pressure for differentiation, one organization, WWF, has emerged as an organization thoroughly focused on classic nature protection.

This period thus presented a new picture in which a host of different – both general and more specialist – environmental organizations emerged. What these organizations had in common was that they operated against a background of diffuse consensus about the importance of environmental and nature protection. Yet the existence of a large number of organizations working in similar ways, oriented to the same publics, and aiming for the same resources triggered a search for new ways to work for the environment. The result was an evolution towards a set of organizations that addressed various themes, were structured differently, gained their resources from various sources in different ways and applied diverse modes to influence various kinds of societal actors.

For nature protection, the result of this change was mixed. On the one hand, nature protection was widely embraced as one issue among many by nearly all environmental organizations. In this sense, nature protection occupies a relatively strong position in today's environmental discourse. In particular, nature protection has a central position within WWF. Consequently, nature protection remains at the core of environmental discourses.

NATURE PROTECTION, ENVIRONMENTALISM AND DEMOCRATIC EFFECTS

The narrative above illustrates the historicity and diversity of nature protection organizations and of nature protection policies in both content and form, but it is also clear that these organizations have played important roles when it comes to the political functioning of civil society in general. It is therefore appropriate to ask what democratic effects organizations with nature protection goals have had and have today. This is also a question often discussed in recent studies of social movements and voluntary organizations (Giugni et al. 1998; Warren 2001).

What exactly the term 'democratic effects' signifies in this context is obviously not without controversy. Here I rely on Warren (2001), who, working within the context of theories of civil society, has developed a theoretical framework suitable for this purpose. He distinguishes three kinds of democratic effects. First, 'development effects' concern how taking part in political action might further various social competencies of the participants. Participation in voluntary organizations might develop political skills, civic virtues (reciprocity, trust and recognition) and skills in critical thinking and analysis. Participation also has the potential to develop feelings of efficacy: a conviction that one's participation in political processes matters. Voluntary organizations also might function as carriers of information. Second, voluntary organizations might have 'public sphere effects'. According to Warren, 'The democratic significance of public spheres is that they provide the means for forming opinions and developing agendas outside the state, as well as outside the structures of economic markets' (Warren 2001, p. 77). Finally, Warren identifies 'institutional effects', implying that voluntary organizations influence institutions – parliament, government and state administration – that make and implement collective political decisions.

Historically, the first organizations working for nature protection in Norway played a pivotal role in establishing voluntary organizations as a way to influence public policies. For the organizations working for nature protection in the first two periods described in this chapter, it also seems warranted to assume that each of the relevant organizations, at least to a certain extent, fulfilled all the three democratic effects: they gave individuals the chance to develop, they played a role in the public sphere, and they influenced formal institutions; that is, they linked the interests and values of at least a certain segment of the population to political decision makers.

Along with the diversification of nature protection and environmental organizations, there has been a shift in how these organizations play their roles in civil society. For example, in terms of the 'developmental effect', there is an important difference between organizations with active members versus only donors. With respect to nature protection organizations, this means that NSC/FoEN, a traditional voluntary organization with (relatively) active members has such 'developmental effects', whereas WWF, with mostly donors, has problems producing them. In terms of 'public sphere effects', some organizations are more geared towards and better at operating in the mass media. The distinction between organizations with active members and donors is again important here, but this time the pattern is in the opposite direction. WWF is able to have a clear public voice partly because it does not have to take the opinions of its donors into consideration in the same way as an organization with members. NSC/FoEN, by contrast, has to consult its members – or at least, be accountable to them – before voicing strong opinions. Finally, the diversification of the organizations has led to more varied ways to achieve 'influential effects': some organizations still work for public attention, some work more directly with commercial actors, others have closer links to political actors, and still others aim to change the citizens' consumption patterns. It is interesting to note in this context that, even though both NSC/FoEN and WWF probably have a degree of political influence, the source of legitimation of this influence is very different. NSC/FoEN is a legitimate political actor because it is a democratic organization representing a certain segment of the population. WWF does not have members who are actively involved as volunteers. Its legitimacy depends instead on the quality and kind of knowledge and insight it provides.

SUMMARY AND CONCLUSION

Summing up the history of nature protection up to 1980, the NOU (Official Norwegian Report) stated, 'The voluntary organizations' work with nature protection has long traditions in Norway. Their focus upon the problems of nature protection has also been a direct reason for the public engagement with nature and environment as we see it today' (NOU 1980, p. 129). There is no doubt that nature protection and environmental organizations have played a pivotal role in the process of nature protection and continue to do so.

Yet their role has changed significantly over time. Historically nature protection developed far in advance of the other concerns that are now part of environmentalism, even though it took some time to establish voluntary organizations (NMT, NSC) working with this issue. Nature protection was later joined by other environmental issues, but it remained at the core of Norwegian environmentalism during its period of peak social movement mobilization during the 1970s and 1980s. Although the movement lost many important battles, the environmentalists and nature protection advocates of this era paved the way for a thorough institutionalization of nature protection and other environmental concerns.

As one issue among many for the environmental organizations of the 1970s, nature protection was absorbed into a larger environmental narrative and lost its exclusive place. This change was also reflected in the growing diversity of organizational structures, ideological orientations, alliances and action repertoires that occurred as nature protection and environmentalism lost their strong public appeal in the 1980s and 1990s. As the potential for influence through public attention and social movement mobilization decreased, organizations had to approach other actors, including political and commercial actors, to gain resources and influence.

Yet through all these changes, nature protection has never lost its key role. In the most recent Norwegian White Paper on environmental policy issued by the Norwegian government, nature protection is viewed as part of a wide and complex environmental agenda (St.meld. 2004–2005). In its list of ten 'main priorities and main challenges' for the future, priority number one is 'stopping the loss of biological diversity', and the discussion of how to achieve this aim lists nature protection as the most important step. The specific policy tools suggested to achieve this aim include establishment of 'national parks' and 'protection areas'. Along the same lines, the newest work programme of the dominant Norwegian environmental organization NSC/FoEN identifies three priorities, the first of which is 'protecting biodiversity and habitats'. The central task for both main actors in the environmental field is still – nearly 100 years after the first nature protection laws and the establishment of NSC/FOEN – nature protection.

NOTES

1. I will apply the abbreviation NSC/FoEN throughout the chapter to indicate that this is one organization even though (1) there was a change of name (1962) that makes the abbreviation technically incorrect for the first period and (2) the link to Friends of the Earth (FoEN) is of more recent date.

2. The most important source for the following sections on the history of Norwegian environmentalism is Berntsen (1994). On a more general historical level, Furre (1992) and Benum (1998) provide interesting insights regarding environmentalism as part of general Norwegian history. NOU (1980, p. 23) (Official Norwegian Report) includes an overview of the history of nature preservation. Reports from the Directorate for Nature Protection also provide useful information on areas protected (DN 1995). Gundersen (1991) also contains important information on the earlier period of Norwegian environmentalism. Seippel (1998, 1999a, 1999b, 2000, 2001, 2002) and Bortne et al. (2001, 2002) present more up-to-date analyses of various aspects of Norwegian environmentalism. Witoszek (1998) gives an overview of the ideological and historical understanding of nature in Norwegian culture, whereas Arne Næss (1991) addresses most kinds of ecological and societal questions from a more philosophical standpoint. For a comparative analysis of Norwegian environmentalism, see Dryzek et al. (2003).
3. The Black Death was the worst European plague. It spread through the continent in the middle of the fourteenth century. Estimates indicate that only one-third of the Norwegian population survived it.
4. This development is similar to those described in demographic or ecological approaches to organization theory see; e.g., Carroll and Hannan (2000); Barman (2002).

REFERENCES

Aardal, Bernt (1993), *Energi og miljø [Energy and Environment]*, Report 93:15, Oslo: Institute for Social Research.

Aardal, Bernt (2003), *Velgere i villrede. En analyse av Stortingsvalget 2001 [Unsure Citizens. An analysis of the Parliament Election 2001]*, Oslo: Damm.

Andersen, Svein S. and Atle Midttun (1985), 'Conflict and local mobilization: The Alta hydropower project', *Acta Sociologica*, **28**(4), 317–35.

Barman, Emily A. (2002), 'Asserting difference: The strategic response of non-profit organizations to competition', *Social Forces*, **80**(4), 1191–222.

Benum, Edgeir (1998), *Overflod og fremtidsfrykt. 1970–1997 [Surplus and Fear of the Future 1970–1997]*, Oslo: Aschehoug.

Bergh, Trond (1977), *Vekst og velstand: Norsk politisk historie 1945–1965 [Growth and Prosperity: Norwegian Political History 1945–1965]*, Oslo: Universitetsforlaget.

Berntsen, Bredo (1994), *Grønne linjer. Natur- og miljøvernets historie i Norge [Green Lines. The History of Norwegian Nature and Environmental Protection]*, Oslo: Grøndahl Dreyer.

Bortne, Øystein, Gunnar Grendstad, Per Selle and Kristin Strømsnes (2001), *Norsk miljøvernorganisering mellom stat og lokalsamfunn [Norwegian Environmental Organization between State and Local Communities]*, Oslo: Samlaget.

Bortne, Øystein, Per Selle and Kristin Strømsnes (2002), *Miljøvern uten grenser? [Environmentalism without Borders?]*, Oslo: Gyldendal.

Carroll, Glenn R. and Michael T. Hannan (2000), *The Demography of Corporations and Industries*, Princeton, NJ: Princeton University Press.

DN (1995), *Naturvernområder I Norge 1911–1994 [Nature Protection Areas in Norway 1911–1994]*, Trondheim: Direktoratet for naturforvaltning (Directorate for Nature Management).

Dryzek, John S. et. al. (2003), *Green States and Social Movements. Environmentalism in the United States, United Kingdom, Germany, & Norway*, Oxford: Oxford University Press.

Furre, Berge (1992), *Norsk historie 1905–1990 [Norwegian History 1905–1990]*, Oslo: Samlaget.
Giugni, Marco, Doug McAdam and Charles Tilly (eds) (1998), *From Contention to Democracy*, Lanham, MD: Rowman & Littlefield.
Gundersen, Frode (1991), 'Utviklingstrekk ved miljøbevegelsen i Norge' [The development of the Norwegian environmental movement], *Sosiologi i dag* **21**(2), 13–23.
Hajer, Maarten A. (1995), *The Politics of Environmental Discourse. Ecological Modernization and the Policy Process*, Oxford: Clarendon Press.
Hågvar, Sigmund and Sigmund Huse (1996), *Naturvernets verdigrunnlag og dagens utfordringer [The Value Foundation of Nature Protection and Today's Challenges]*, Ås: NLH.
Jamison, Andrew (2001), *The Making of Green Knowledge: Environmental Politics and Cultural Transformation*, Cambridge: Cambridge University Press.
Jansen, Alf-Inge (1989), *Makt og miljø [Power and Environment]*, Oslo: Universitetsforlaget.
McNeill, William H. (1980), *The Human Condition. An Ecological and Historical View*, Princeton, NJ: Princeton University Press.
Mol, Arthur P.J. (2001), *Globalization and Environmental Reform: The Ecological Modernization of the Global Economy*, Cambridge, MA: MIT Press.
NOU (1980), *Naturvern i Norge [Nature Protection in Norway]*, Oslo: Official Norwegian Documents.
Næss, Arne (1991), *Ecology, Community and Lifestyle*, Cambridge: Cambridge University Press.
Ponting, Clive (1991), *A Green History of the World*, London: Penguin Books.
Rootes, Chris (ed.) (2003), *Environmental Protest in Western Europe*, Oxford: Oxford University Press.
Sandberg, Sveinung (2005), 'Attac – oppgjøret som forsvant?' [Attac – The revolt that disappeared], *Nytt Norsk Tidsskrift*, **22**(1), 60–71.
Seippel, Ørnulf (1998), 'Natur, politikk og mangfold – Miljøbevegelsens ideologi i et moderne samfunn' [Nature, politics and diversity – Environmental ideology in a modern society], *Sosiologisk tidsskrift*, **6**(4), 315–40.
Seippel, Ørnulf (1999a), 'Environmentalism, democracy and political opportunity structures: The case of Norwegian environmental movements', *Environmental Politics*, **8**(3), 49–76.
Seippel, Ørnulf (1999b), 'Political environmentalism: Class interests, modern values or postmodern feelings', *Innovation*, **12**(2), 129–53.
Seippel, Ørnulf (2000), 'Ecological modernization as a theoretical device: Strengths and weaknesses', *Journal of Environmental Policy and Planning*, **2**(4), 287–302.
Seippel, Ørnulf (2001), 'From mobilization to institutionalization? The case of Norwegian environmentalism', *Acta Sociologica*, **44**(2), 123–37.
Seippel, Ørnulf (2002), 'The differentiation of environmental organization and their democratic functioning in a late-modern society: The case of Norway', paper for International Sociological Association, Brisbane.
St.meld 21 (2004–2005), *Regjeringens miljøvernpolitikk og rikets miljøtilstand [The Governmental Environmental Policy and the Environmental State of Art]*, Oslo: Det kongelig miljøverndepartement.
Søgård, Christina (1997), 'Fra rebeller til konsulenter. En casestudie av miljøorganisasjonen Bellona' [From Rebels to Consultants. A Case Study of Bellona], in Ann Nilsen (ed.), *Miljøsosiologi [Environmental Sociology]*, Oslo: Pax.

Tilly, Charles (2002), *Stories, Identities, and Political Change*, Lanham, MD: Rowman & Littlefield.

Warren, Mark E. (2001), *Democracy and Association*, Princeton, NJ: Princeton University Press.

Witoszek, Nina (1998), *Norske naturmytologier. Fra Edda til økofilosofi [Norwegian Nature Mythologies. From Edda to Ecophilosophy]*, Oslo: Pax.

8. Nature protection NGOs in Poland: between tradition, professionalism and radicalism

Piotr Gliński and Małgorzata Koziarek

THE HISTORICAL BACKGROUND OF NATURE PROTECTION IN POLAND

Early Origins (Thirteenth to Nineteenth Centuries)

The tradition of nature protection in Poland goes back at least to the thirteenth century, when a royal edict on the protection and winter feeding of the aurochs (*Bos primigenius*) in the Jaktorowska Forest was issued. It was one example of so called *regalia*, legal acts granting the privilege to members of royal and aristocratic courts to hunt specific animals. At the turn of the sixteenth century, King Władysław Jagiełło placed the yew tree under protection for military and economic reasons, as its wood was used for the production of bows. In 1529, the Lithuanian Statute provided for protection of beaver lodges. These legal regulations, although motivated by reasons other than nature protection, indirectly provided a degree of protection to specific animal and plant species (Karaczun and Indeka 1999, p. 392).

The modern nature protection movement in Poland, however, appeared much later – in the mid-nineteenth century. At that time, ideas about nature protection were tightly linked to ideas about the development of the Polish culture and national independence. (Since the late eighteenth century, Polish territory had been divided among Russia, Prussia and Austria.) Nature motifs also played an important role in nineteenth-century Polish poetry and prose, and were dominant factors in shaping public awareness of Polish identity. All three of the most important cultural and literary currents of the nineteenth century: Romanticism, positivism and modernism (the Polish variety of the last is referred to as Young Poland) made references to nature and its protection (Kolbuszewski 1992).

Changes in public awareness of nature protection led to concrete initiatives and actions. Due to the political situation of the time, civic nature protection activity found the most fertile ground for development in Galicia, the part of Poland under relatively moderate Austrian rule. The first concrete steps were protection of the Tatra Mountains from devastation. In 1866, on the initiative of Polish naturalists, a special volunteer-based guard was established to protect the chamois and the alpine marmot there. In 1873 the first modern nature protection organization on Polish soil was established – the Tatra Society (Towarzystwo Tatrzańskie). It pushed for many important nature protection initiatives, including the 1888 proposal to create a national park in the Tatra Mountains on the model of Yellowstone National Park in North America (Kolbuszewski 1992, pp. 96–7). (The park was not, however, finally established until 1954.)

Similar initiatives began later in the Prussian sector of partitioned Poland, where, for instance, the magazine *Nature and Industry* (*Przyroda i Przemysł*) was published. In the territory that remained under Russian rule, nature protection organizations were all but non-existent, and nature protection was promoted primarily in the arts. There were also nature-oriented periodicals, including *Physiographic Diary* (*Pamiętnik Fizjograficzny*) and *Universe* (*Wszechświat*). These brought together nature protection supporters who did not have other opportunities to organize themselves and act due to the restrictions imposed by the occupying authorities. Not until after the revolution of 1905, which brought freedom of association, did circumstances become favourable for launching the Commission for the Protection of Natural Monuments within the structure of the Polish Country-Lovers Society (Polskie Towarzystwo Krajoznawcze). It promoted the beauty of the Polish homeland and its monuments of nature and culture through education, publications and excursions.

Nature protection activity in Poland during the early twentieth century had various motivations: (1) utilitarian and pragmatic, including the growing realization of threats to man; (2) philosophical, as nature began to be perceived as a value in itself; (3) aesthetic; (4) religious; (5) patriotic, which is understandable, given the historical and political context; and (6) economic, viewing nature as a national resource. Yet all these motives were overshadowed by the scientific–academic viewpoint of biologists. That is, nature protection came into existence, above all, as a branch of scientific knowledge. The developing movement was dominated by biologists, botanists and geologists, and making inventories of natural monuments was the predominant activity. This narrow perspective was to determine the activities of the nature protection movement for many years to come (Gliński et al. 1990, pp. 9–11).

Independence and State Protection (1918–Second World War)

In 1919, one year after Poland became independent, a Temporary State Commission of Nature Protection was established, with prominent naturalist, Władysław Szafer, as its first chairman. The Commission set four key tasks for itself: (1) making an inventory of nature monuments in Poland; (2) proposing and establishing national parks and nature reserves; (3) passing nature protection legislation; and (4) promotion of nature protection ideals, mainly among youth, through cooperation with the schools. In 1925, the Commission was transformed into the State Council for Nature Protection. Its structure included local Nature Protection Committees consisting of representatives of local government and local associations. Besides its core activities, the Council issued various publications, including the nationally distributed periodical *Nature Protection* (*Ochrona Przyrody*) and 47 regional titles. The year 1934 saw the adoption of a long-awaited nature protection law; however, its provisions were criticized by nature protection activists as too bureaucratic because the law established positions of nature protection administrators but lacked provisions for NGO participation in decision making.

In order to provide a framework for wider civic action in the protection of particularly valuable natural sites, the League for the Conservation of Nature (Liga Ochrony Przyrody – LOP) was set up in 1928, following a Swiss model. Its founders counted on raising funds from the public to purchase the most valuable natural sites from private owners. It was assumed that funding would be provided by membership fees, private donations and *ad hoc* public fundraising actions with well-defined objectives. These would be linked to promotional and educational campaigns organized under such slogans as: 'Save the Beauty of the Tatra Nature' or 'Protect the Remains of Our Steppes'. Unfortunately, despite the organization's truly dedicated leadership, its 6000 members, and its active role in the nature education of the younger generation in newly independent Poland, LOP's hopes for wide support and generous donations from society at large were not met.

Nature protection activities during the pre-Second World War period were dominated by the preservation of both natural and cultural heritage. Six national parks and about 200 nature reserves and landscape parks were established, representing a great success for the nature protection movement and a testimony to its influence. On the other hand, the movement also had its limitations, and there were some spectacular failures. It limited its efforts to scientific circles and promoters of the 'know-your-country' idea (originated by the Polish Country-Lovers' Society). Poland's numerous and diverse local cultural traditions were not successfully protected from transformation, and – despite numerous protests – a project to build a cable railway to Kasprowy Wierch, which opened the interior of the Polish Tatra Mountains to mass tourism, was not stopped (Gliński et al. 1990, pp. 11–14; Hrynkiewicz 1990, p. 7).

Communist Rule (Second World War–1980s)

In communist Poland, the totalitarian state assumed control over the State Council for Nature Protection, which was allowed to continue only those among its activities that were least incompatible with the new industrialization policy. In effect, this limited it to the narrow conservation aspects of nature protection. Mass tourism and the timber industry now intruded into national parks, and the expansion of heavy industry led the country towards ecological disaster. 'Poland's post-World War II industrialization and urbanization campaign resulted in a rapid and extensive deterioration of the nature environment', writes Barbara Hicks, an American researcher studying Polish environmental policy. 'Almost all environmental indicators show the state of Poland's natural environment declining and pollution rising steadily throughout the communist era' (1996, pp. 30–31). 'In 1983 Poland's Communist government listed 27 official "ecological danger zones", encompassing eleven per cent of the nation's territory and 35 per cent of its citizens' (Cole 1998, p. 13). Prominent experts dealing with Polish environmental problems, Daniel H. Cole and John Clark, put it bluntly: 'Communism may have been the dirtiest social order ever constructed, and People's Poland was perhaps the dirtiest of communist countries' (1998, p. 1).

Yet despite serious environmental damage, Poland retained substantial areas of high biodiversity and largely unspoiled landscape, mainly due to: (1) low levels of mechanization and chemical use in agriculture; (2) lack of investment funds for industrial development; and (3) the general ineffectiveness of the centrally planned economy. For example, contrary to the goals of communist planners, the Vistula River escaped construction of a series of dams, and north-eastern Poland was not developed as an iron-mining region.

Until at least 1980, there were no truly independent environmental organizations in socialist Poland. A few 'official' nature protection associations existed, but they had to submit to control by the Party, and the rules set by the authorities. The League for the Conservation of Nature (LOP), which resumed its operation soon after the end of the Second World War, was by far the largest. In 1956, its charter was revised to shift its focus mainly to education. Promotion of respect for and love of nature among youth became the organization's top priority, and its activities were targeted toward schools. In 1967 the proportion of adult members was only 8.5 per cent.

LOP enjoyed support from the authorities and benefited from a constant flow of state subsidies. These enabled it to maintain a sizeable structure of chapters with full-time employees in each province, coordinate the activities of numerous school clubs, and produce a large volume of educational publications, including posters, leaflets, stickers and the continuation of *Przyroda Polska*, a monthly magazine. According to official data, in the communist era LOP's membership exceeded one million, and as late as the early 1990s, LOP still claimed 800 000 members (Gliński 1996, p. 241); however, this total included 'passive masses' automatically enrolled in the organization (for instance a biology teacher could easily enrol all of his or her pupils). Other nature protection organizations of the communist era, such as professional associations of naturalists, on the other hand, had rather small, narrow memberships. Like LOP's, their operations were fully under government control.

Informal groups of naturalists and amateurs existed outside official structures, but their operations were necessarily limited to hobby activities. The best-known circles of that type set up so-called 'ornithological regions' (regional groupings). They later evolved into the numerous regional ornithological associations of post-communist Poland (Gliński 1996, p. 274).

Beginning in the late 1960s, independent nature protection oriented activity was also manifested in the activities of scientific and journalist circles, which included appeals and protests to save sites of high natural value that were endangered by industrialization and development schemes. An informal press club, 'Landscapes' (Krajobrazy), emerged from this milieu. It later became one root of the environmental movement in Poland (Hrynkiewicz 1990, p. 8).

The dramatic political developments of the 1980s, centred on the rise of Solidarność (Solidarity), resulted in a weakening of totalitarian control and provided more opportunities for citizen self-expression. It is no surprise, then, that LOP published its first 'Report on the State of Natural Environment in Poland and Threats to Human Health' in 1981. Also in the early 1980s, LOP formally requested to be consulted on bills and other policy drafts before their adoption, a step that would have been unthinkable in previous decades. This period also saw the establishment of new independent organizations with both naturalist and environmental foci, that is, the birth of the environmental movement in Poland.

Nature Protection Organizations as Part of Re-emerging Civil Society

Since its emergence in 1980, the Polish environmental movement has gone through three stages of development: resistance, professionalization and politicization. These stages provide a useful framework for discussing the position of nature protection and nature protection organizations in Poland. It is important to note that, in the Polish circumstances, which were characterized by both the spontaneous development of a network of nature protection organizations and the continued impact of the communist organizational and cultural legacy, nature protection has been dealt with not only by nature protection organizations but many other types of environmental organizations, which differ in their action strategies, commitment to nature protection and radicalism (see below). Hence the status and development of the environmental movement remains a necessary reference point for any discussion on nature protection and nature protection organizations in Poland.

Cracks in the Communist System: Rise of Independent Initiatives (1980–89)

The independent environmental movement emerged in Poland alongside the Solidarność revolution of 1980/1981. During the 1980s it was primarily a movement of protest and self-defence involving people directly affected by environmental damage. It was spearheaded by informal groups, as well as by the intelligentsia and countercultural milieus. The movement had two goals: the struggle against the anti-environmental policy of the authorities and the formation of state-independent pro-environmental public opinion.

The first nationwide, independent environmental organization, the Polish Ecological Club (Polski Klub Ekologiczny), was founded in 1981. Nature protection was addressed, in particular, by its National Parks Section. In the later 1980s, several important youth movements appeared, including the Freedom and Peace movement (Wolność i Pokój), which was strongly involved in politics, the countercultural Green Federation (Federacja Zielonych), and the environmental/peace movement, 'I Prefer to Be' (Wolę być). Numerous local pro-environmental circles also organized protest actions against threats to health and nature. In particular, they mobilized against nuclear risks, especially after the Chernobyl disaster of 1986, and against environmental destruction caused by heavy industry.

The first grass-roots organizations with a focus on nature protection were set up in different regions of Poland during the 1980s. These included the Lubusian Naturalists' Club (Lubuski Klub Przyrodników), the North Podlasian Bird Protection Society (Północnopodlaskie Towarzystwo Ochrony Ptaków – PTOP), as well as groups of expert and amateur naturalists involved in spontaneous informal activities, such as bird counting. The activities of those organizations were rather scattered and limited, compared to the relatively well-publicized resistance-oriented actions of the new mainstream environmental organizations described above.

The emerging environmental movement constituted a small (about 135 autonomous groups and organizations) yet significant enclave within the civil opposition that was emerging in Poland during the late 1980s. For this reason, in the Round Table negotiations that preceded the first quasi-free elections of June 1989, a separate environmental table, which included several representatives of the independent environmental movement, was set up (Gliński 1996, 1998, 2001). The movement, including its nature protection organization constituents, was only one part of what Western literature called the rebirth of civil society in Central and Eastern Europe (Pełczyński 1988); however, it could also be seen as the practical embodiment of the idea of 'new evolutionism'. This idea, formulated by Polish dissidents as far back as the 1970s, called for the grass-roots, independent creation of institutions for organizing public life to replace inefficient state structures and/or the non-existent market (Michnik 1985).

Opportunities for Democratic Change: Growth, Integration and Professionalization (1989–97)

The changes of 1989 enabled the environmental movement to grow rapidly. The first stage of development (1980–89) had been marked by its oppositional character. The next period was marked by its maturation and professionalization. Beginning in the early 1990s, protests and demonstrations were increasingly supplemented by alternative proposals for 'civic' solutions and forms of action, that is, by participation in cooperative decision-making processes with government, advising on legal solutions or lobbying, and independent management of non-governmental environmental projects (for example, installation of nesting platforms for the white stork). This phase was also characterized by increasing integration of the movement and the growing visibility of nature protection organizations.

The movement's maturation and professionalization were driven largely by two factors: (1) processes of self-education and self-development, which are well known from theories of civil society and of social movements (Eder 1993); and (2) assistance, both financial and non-financial, from Western partners. A very large, and often underestimated, factor in the growth of the non-governmental sector in Poland was the cultural influence of both private and governmental Western organizations and aid agencies. This included assistance with: (1) developing professional organizational skills; (2) building a positive image of volunteerism; and (3) pressuring Polish government elites and agencies to accept and enlarge the role of the local third sector as a necessary condition for promoting environmental protection and a stronger civil society in Poland (Poland had to comply with relevant EU laws and World Bank standards in this respect). The Polish NGOs soon discovered that, in many cases, it was very effective to pressure the Polish government via Western agencies, such as the European Commission – the so-called 'boomerang effect'.

In the 1990s, newly established nature protection organizations oriented primarily to direct nature protection assumed an important and visible place in the Polish environmental movement. Their goals made them quite distinct from nature protection organizations such as the League for the Conservation of Nature (LOP) carried over from the Polish People's Republic. The older groups' activities had been largely limited to education and had little in common with the more professional activities undertaken by nature protection organizations in democratic countries. A few forerunner nature protection organizations, such as the Lubusian Naturalist Club and PTOP, had been set up during the 1980s, and others, such as the Committee for Eagle Protection (Komitet Ochrony Orłów – KOO), evolved from informal groups that had existed under communism. However, the majority of nature protection organizations appeared as part of the boom in civil society activity after 1989.

The trail for the new nature protection organizations was blazed by PTOP, which had proved especially resilient during the liberalization and transformation of the system during the late 1980s and was strongly involved in conflicts with the local authorities and the agricultural drainage lobby. Even after 1989, PTOP experienced government persecution on account of its struggle to protect the Biebrza wetlands. Indeed, the government even sought to dissolve it. With assistance from German and Swiss NGOs, PTOP became the first Polish organization since the Second World War to purchase valuable natural sites from private owners to establish nature reserves.

By the beginning of the 1990s, there were at least a dozen new modern nature protection organizations, including four national organizations and several regional ones. Their expert naturalist background distinguished them from many other environmental groups and circles in Poland, in which there were also naturalists, but primarily professionals from related fields. Their founding and development were facilitated by the fact that they were often based in already integrated communities of researchers, students, amateur ornithologists and the like.

In addition, a major role was played by the patronage of Western nature protection organizations. They provided funding for start-up, land purchases and projects, as well as models of organization and professional operations and assistance through direct contacts. German and Swiss organizations aided in the development of PTOP, while the Royal Society for the Protection of Birds (UK) played the major role in the establishment of the National Bird Protection Society (Ogólnopolskie Towarzystwo Ochrony Ptaków – OTOP), the largest Polish ornithological organization. RSPB offered inspiration and funding, which helped OTOP to acquire its own office space. Other major supporters of OTOP were BirdLife International and the Danish Ornithological Society.

OTOP and, to some extent, another nature protection organization, Salamander ('Salamandra'), provide typical examples of imitation of proven Western professional organization models and patterns of operation. OTOP is a professional organization in two senses of the word: first, it is led by natural science experts; second, it is professionally organized and managed. Furthermore, it has become a relatively large organization by Polish standards – already boasting 1600 members in the 1990s – and it runs a permanent and flexible member recruitment campaign, a rarity among Polish NGOs. Salamander is another one of the very few Polish environmental organizations that raise funds from membership dues and private donations. It deliberately copied the Nature Conservancy, an American-based organization with international operations, in developing its organization structure and defining its purposes and mode of operation.

By the mid-1990s both organizations had permanent managerial and administrative staffs. Salamander had five half-time employees, while OTOP had a professional office with a staff of six. The new nature protection organizations were also characterized by a professional approach to raising funds from domestic sources and foreign donors operating in Poland. These included the Polish Office of the Hungarian-based Regional Environmental Centre for Central and Eastern Europe, the Eco-Fund Foundation, which administered funds from the swap of the Polish foreign debt for environmental projects, the Global Environmental Facility programme (located at the UNDP Office), and the National and Regional Funds for Environmental Protection and Water Management, which allocates governmental funds from environmental fees and fines to environmental projects.

The range of achievements and scale of operation of the nature protection organizations were very wide, involving enormous effort on the part of thousands of volunteers. OTOP, for instance, carried out a programme of protecting 118 bird sanctuaries; another nature protection organization, Pro Natura, succeeded in obtaining protection measures for the biggest breeding population of mud turtle (*Emys orbicularis*) in Poland and contributed to the reintroduction of the beaver in Silesia. KOO carried out monitoring of rare birds of prey nesting areas and constructed artificial nests. Salamander received the prestigious Ford Conservation Award for its project to save the Morasko Meteorite Reserve. Other nature protection organization activities included scientific research, expert analyses, and interventions in the field in response to emergencies, such as illegal tree cutting.

Nature protection organization successes like these provided incentives and models for other environmental organizations and groups and stimulated the self-education and growth of the movement. Increased contacts among the modern nature protection organizations and the other participants in the environmental movement encouraged exchanges of experience and views, not only about environmental issues, but also regarding the value-related foundations of the operation of the movement, its identity, the external factors affecting its operation, and the like. This helped to forge a shared self-awareness in the movement and reduce its fragmentation.

The integration of the movement was also promoted by the annual All-Polish Meetings of the Environmental Movement and various intra-sectoral media, including periodicals such as *Green Brigades* (*Zielone Brygady*), or *The Wildlife* (*Dzikie Życie*), and the Internet network *Bridge* (*Most*). Increasingly formalized movement structures, along with specialized information, service and financial institutions, undergirded this development. The members of the movement trained themselves in nature protection law, mediation and negotiation skills, and NGO management and fundraising. Environmental organizations increasingly worked out rational action strategies and coordinated their actions and campaigns nationwide.

Throughout this period, numerous joint actions were organized, many of them with important nature protection goals. In 1990–93, protest against the construction of a dam in Czorsztyn in the Pieniński National Park gained a great deal of publicity. It involved both the Polish Ecological Club, which prepared an expert analysis of the impact of the project on the unique local nature, and leaders of the Freedom and Peace movement and the Green Federation, which organized protest actions. Later on, with the growing involvement of the new nature protection organizations and other actors, dozens of different, nationwide pro-environmental campaigns were launched, many of which have continued to the present. Campaigns in defence of 'wildlife' led to expanding species protection in the cases of wolf and lynx, as well as to the enlargement of the Białowieski National Park to cover more – although still not the whole – of the unique Białowieża Forest. The Coalition for the Protection of the Tatra Mountains, composed of dozens of groups closely cooperating with the Tatra National Park, was able to enlist the support of prominent Polish intellectuals, including Nobel Prize winner poets Czesław Miłosz and Wisława Szymborska, in its struggle to dissuade the government from nominating Zakopane (located on the border of the Park) as a candidate site for the 2006 Olympic Games. The above-quoted examples well illustrate the network approach (see Chapter 1) in pursuing nature protection goals, which has remained a distinctive feature of the nature protection motivated collective action in Poland.

The numerous conflicts and difficulties that nature protection activities encountered contributed strongly to the integration processes within the environmental movement as a whole. Nature protection advocates sought allies among other environmental groups; they needed support for their efforts from the entire environmental movement, and they usually got it. Sometimes nature protection organizations joined various environmental campaigns or supported the activities of other environmental groups, especially deep ecology groups such as the Workshop for All Beings (Pracownia na rzecz Wszystkich Istot) or the Gaia Club ('Klub Gaja'). The shared identity of the environmental movement was forged through conflicts. Examples include the PTOP's struggle against the devastation of the Biebrza River Valley and the involvement of OTOP – and later also of WWF – in protests against the series of dams on the Lower Vistula River and the East–West Waterway (the former was led by the Gaia Club) and in the critique of a purely technocratic water bill (Gliński 1996).

In spite of the strong trends toward integration after 1989, the environmental movement remained internally differentiated. This turned out to be the key factor in the crisis that marked the beginning of the next phase and revealed the limits to movement-wide cooperation.

Limits to Joint Action: Radicalism and Political Involvement (1997–)

As the environmental movement became increasingly professional, its leaders discovered that environmental problems could not be effectively addressed without policy changes at national level, but these had proved almost impossible for NGOs to achieve. Hence, in 1997, several environmental leaders decided to stand for parliament in coalition with a well-known political party, The Union of Freedom (*Unia Wolności*). The party was known for its liberal programme, but at the same time it hosted the only significant environmental political group in Poland – the Ecological Forum of the Union of Freedom. This decision sparked a crisis within the environmental movement, revealing deep internal divisions.

Even though this political initiative did not involve leaders from the nature protection organizations or deep ecology groups, the resulting break-up of the movement did bring cooperation among them to a halt. This was symbolized by the nature protection organizations' failure to support radical environmentalists trying to stop the construction of a highway via the St Ann's Mountain Landscape Park in 1998. The protest on St Ann's Mountain, which was publicized nationwide by the media, turned out to be a spectacular failure and the last major radical action in defence of wildlife in Poland to date. Although it did not mark the complete cessation of cooperative initiatives within the environmental movement, it did demonstrate the limits of joint action and the inability of the movement to speak with one voice. In the absence of a single united environmental forum (the All-Polish Meetings of the Environmental Movement ended), cooperative efforts now involved developing smaller networks and project initiatives with differing casts of supporters, often including nature protection organizations.

At the end of the 1990s, European integration naturally commanded the attention of environmental and nature protection organizations with diverse expertise. The Institute for Sustainable Development (Instytut na rzecz Ekorozwoju – InE), a Polish environmental think-tank, thus organized a broad-based capacity-building and consultation process to this end. Within this framework, Polish environmental NGOs formulated their positions on the environmental effects of Poland's accession to the European Union in various policy domains in a report (InE 1999). The working version of the chapter on nature protection was written by experts from Pro Natura, and some other nature protection organizations contributed comments. The following year a leader of the Workshop of All Beings contributed a chapter on the implementation of Natura 2000 and the related problems to another InE publication (Korbel 2001). In this way, several nature protection organizations, including supporters of deep ecology, entered the field of environmental policy making.

The possible positive effects of the European integration, such as the promotion of the Natura 2000 ecological network approach to nature protection (see Chapter 1), were not considered as likely to counterbalance the expected negative effects of other EU policies, especially the Common Agricultural Policy. However, the environmental impacts of developments such as the industrialization of agriculture, increasing consumption, and recreational use of wild nature areas were seen as inevitable 'as long as it [Poland] follows the economic model of developed countries', irrespective of its future membership in the EU (InE 1999, p. 30).

At the same time, the preservation of democracy during the transition to EU membership proved problematic. NGOs openly complained that their participation in planning, decision making and monitoring was 'far too limited' (InE 1999, p. 28), especially with regard to their complementing or replacing the work of the often inefficient authorities. 'Very often officials divide organisations into better and worse depending on the degree of their submissiveness rather than the actions they undertake or their expertise' (ibid.). This approach was seen by the NGOs as posing the risk that they would become marginalized either as expert organizations with no public appeal or as organizations with broad membership but no influence on important nature protection issues (Korbel 2001, p. 54).

The years 2001 and 2002 marked the beginning of the third stage in the post-communist development of the environmental movement in Poland – the phase of more direct participation in politics. This involved the construction of strictly political structures (Gliński 2001), which led in 2003 to the establishment of an autonomous environmental party, 'The Greens 2004'. However, nature protection leaders were not actively involved in this initiative, and the party won only negligible public support (0.28 per cent of votes) in the European Parliament elections.

So far we have outlined the historic background of nature protection activities in Poland, as well as the growth of the nature protection organization community against the wider background of political change and stages in the development of the environmental movement. This historical analysis leads inevitably to questions about the present and future.

NATURE PROTECTION ORGANIZATIONS ON THE EVE OF POLAND'S ACCESSION TO THE EU

Types of Nature Protection Organizations

The organizations involved in nature protection in Poland during the last decade can be roughly classified into seven types: (1) modern nature protection and ornithological organizations set up in the 1980s and later; (2) the League for the Conservation of Nature (LOP), which emphasizes youth education; (3) organizations focusing on nature education; (4) organizations representing deep ecology and radical environmentalism, which mainly organize protest actions and campaigns to raise awareness about threats to ecologically valuable areas; (5) Polish chapters of international nature protection organizations, including WWF, IUCN and Greenpeace; (6) environmental organizations that undertake nature protection projects along with work on other environmental issues; and (7) Polish and foreign organizations providing funds for nature protection projects.

In recent years, nature protection efforts have been characterized by the persistence of very weak public and political support, fragmentation of effort, the deficiencies of Poland's fledgling democracy, and the growing impact of the EU integration and membership, as well as by the remarkable increase in the visibility and involvement of international environmental and nature protection organizations, particularly WWF, on the Polish scene and the transformation of some regional nature protection organizations into national organizations.

Table 8.1 Nature protection organizations in Poland (exemplary selection)

Organization name (Polish)	Year founded	Number of members (geographic scope)	Budget (expenditure) in 2004 (€)[1]	Goal reference categories Keywords
Type (1): modern nature protection and ornithological organizations set up in the 1980s and later				
The National Society of Bird Protection (Ogólnopolskie Towarzystwo Ochrony Ptaków – OTOP)	1991	About 2000 (website estimate) (national)	309 463	Protection of wild animals (wilderness/landscapes) Birds, habitats, education, data collection, nature protection plans, legal action
The Committee for Eagle Protection (Komitet Ochrony Orłów – KOO)	1981 (established as an informal group); registered in 1991	About 400 (website estimate) (national)	Not available	Protection of wild animals Birds of prey, monitoring, active protection, education, law drafting
The Polish Society of Nature Protection 'Salamander' (Polskie Towarzystwo Ochrony Przyrody 'Salamandra')	1993	2263 (national)	218 923	Protection of wild animals and plants, wilderness, cultural landscapes Fauna, flora, ecosystems, landscapes, education
The Naturalists' Club (Klub Przyrodników)	1983; Under current name in 2002	300 (national)	Not available	Protection of wild animals and plants, wilderness, cultural landscapes Nature protection, education

Table 8.1 (continued)

Organization name (Polish)	Year founded	Number of members (geographic scope)	Budget (expenditure) in 2004 (€)[1]	Goal reference categories Keywords
Type (1): modern nature protection and ornithological organizations set up in the 1980s and later				
The Polish Society of Nature Friends, 'Pro Natura' (Polskie Towarzystwo Przyjaciół Przyrody 'Pro Natura')	1990	Not available (national)	Not available	Protection of wild animals and plants, wilderness, cultural landscapes Nature protection, education
Naturalist Society 'The White Stork' (Towarzystwo Przyrodnicze 'Bocian')	Early 1980s as an informal group, registered in 1994; under current name in 2003	350 (national)	122 690	Protection of wild animals and plants, wilderness, cultural landscapes Education, data collection, nature protection plans, legal action
The North Podlasian Bird Protection Society (Północnopodl-askie Towarzystwo Ochrony Ptaków – PTOP)	1985	260 (regional)	Not available	Protection of wild animals (wilderness/ cultural landscapes) Birds, habitats, data collection, monitoring, education

Notes: All the data quoted come from nature protection organization websites (February 2006), except for membership figures, which come from the survey, unless stated otherwise. Non-availability of budget data, indicated below, means only that such information was absent from particular nature protection organization websites.

[1] Annual average PLN/EUR exchange rate of the National Bank of Poland was applied.

In sketching a portrait of nature protection organizations in Poland today, we focus on the most relevant types listed above (1, 4 and 5, and to some extent 2 and 6). We omit purely educational organizations and funds-providing organizations. This section draws heavily on the results of a qualitative study carried out by Małgorzata Koziarek in December 2004–January 2005.[1] The analysis also takes into account subsequent developments, as well as Koziarek's observations in the course of her professional experience with the environmental movement in Poland.

Main Fields of Activity

In general, the activities of nature protection organizations in Poland are focused on the preservation and restoration of Poland's natural heritage, which could be generally characterized as biodiversity protection. A few organizations define nature protection in very general terms, that is, as encompassing protection of wild animals and plants, wilderness and cultural landscapes; however, even nature protection organizations that are mainly interested in the protection of wild species are necessarily also interested in preserving their habitats – both wilderness and valuable ecosystems that are dependent on particular land use practices, such as meadow maintenance and traditional farming practices. What more visibly differentiates nature protection organizations from one another is the scope of their objectives, that is, whether they focus on nature protection in general or protecting a limited set of species, particular types of ecosystems, or particular sites.

The specific activities of the nature protection organizations include practical nature protection work in the field, field research, site-oriented nature management, promotion of good practices in selected fields of action, influencing policy making and legislation, education of the public and community involvement, *ad hoc* interventions to prevent environmentally damaging activities, and land purchases. As a rule, several of the above-listed activities are combined in a single programme or project, although there are differences in their relative emphasis among the different types of nature protection organizations.

It is commonly understood that effective nature protection requires a comprehensive approach which also addresses the impact of other non-environmental sectors and community development needs. In this context, a number of factors have encouraged the nature protection organizations to broaden their agendas beyond nature protection. First, agenda broadening is part of an international process favouring the integration of environmental targets into specific sectoral policies. This is how IUCN Poland became interested in agricultural policy and rural development. Second, entering new areas is sometimes necessary because of the nature of specific projects. For example, flood protection is connected to management of nature in river valleys, and the need to dispose of biomass is a by-product of peatland maintenance. Third, agendas expand as new problems arise and new needs are identified, such as the threat to agricultural biodiversity posed by industrial farming practices and the controversial routing of the Via Baltica express road. Fourth, nature protection organizations often try to combine nature protection with the socioeconomic development of local communities to win the support of local people and to combat their passivity.

Among the goals most frequently added to nature protection have been agricultural biodiversity (protection of breeding species and varieties) and local community development goals, such as preserving cultural heritage and promotion of ecotourism or sustainable development. There are also instances of agenda broadening due to institutional considerations, such as efforts to build the capabilities of the organization or to meet the requirements of donors. In a country where almost all funding of environmental NGOs comes from institutional donors, the agendas of the organizations are inevitably sensitive to the priorities of funders. This seems to have encouraged some environmental NGOs (type 6) to include or emphasize nature protection projects within their otherwise rather broad agendas and deep-ecology groups to become involved, for instance, with climate change.

Because of its relatively strong impact, the donor market may also be seen as promoting isomorphism among potential applicants. Indeed, a number of national-level nature protection organizations have goals that can hardly be distinguished from one another (see Table 8.1, type 1). Each was established in a different region and originally targeted that region. Later, however, these nature protection organizations expanded their scope to the national level, making themselves eligible for funding that would otherwise have remained unavailable. The potential overlap among these groups is addressed to some extent by an informal division of labour. It is based on a combination of criteria, including differences in geographical focus, in goals (protection of specific species or types of ecosystems), in types of activities, in audiences targeted, and in areas of expertise.

Organizational Structure and Membership

The nationwide nature protection organizations that cover the whole country relatively well with their field networks include: LOP (type 2), the National Bird Protection Society (OTOP) and the Committee for Eagle Protection (KOO) (type 1). LOP has the best-developed field structure, with three levels. (In 2003 it comprised 41 chapters, 248 divisions and over 4000 local clubs.) OTOP has 18 local groups, while KOO is a national network of individuals directly involved in the protection of the nesting sites of birds of prey throughout Poland. Most of other national-level organizations of types 1 and 6 remain strongly rooted in the regions where they were founded and have their headquarters. At the regional level, there are regionally oriented nature protection organizations, including several ornithological societies, the North Podlasian Bird Protection Society (PTOP) being the leader in terms of achievements, expertise and impact.

Compared to their Western counterparts, the membership of Polish nature protection organizations is modest, but it is nevertheless higher than the average for the Polish environmental movement. Most nature protection organizations (types 1 and 4) have between 100 and 400 members. Organizations with a broader environmental orientation (type 6) typically do not exceed 100. The largest are LOP, which has retained much of its nationwide network, infrastructure, and official recognition from communist times (see section on communist rule), with nearly 211 000 members, and the two modern nature protection organizations described above as pioneers in membership-building programmes: Salamander, with 2300 members, and OTOP, which has about 2000. Organizations such as IUCN Poland or WWF Poland, whose members are other organizations (ten and 15 respectively) constitute a separate category. WWF in Poland has not yet started to develop a base of individual donors.

As a rule, nature protection organizations do not consider attaining a large membership to be a priority. Member dues, if collected at all, are nominal, so unless membership is very large, they contribute little to a nature protection organization's financial survival. Winning support of large number of members would require large-scale efforts, while raising funds from other sources, such as grant programmes, is much more cost-effective. Organizations are therefore more interested in recruiting members who will be actively involved than passive supporters. Hence they typically leave the initiative to potential members who seek them out after having come across relevant information (printed materials, websites, or press coverage) or after direct contact with nature protection organization activities, such as training workshops, seminars, conferences, events and campaigns. The handful of organizations that do take a more purposeful approach to member recruitment have seen larger membership increases. For instance, Salamander experienced a 50 per cent increase (1000 new members) over five years (1999–2004), and 'The White Stork' grew from 50 to 70 to 350 members, while membership levels of the majority of nature protection organizations surveyed have remained stable. Some reported slight increases, but in three cases, including LOP, membership has dropped. Typical measures to help maintain membership levels include free subscriptions to nature protection organization periodicals and providing other informational materials. Members of some nature protection organizations have the opportunity to participate in nature excursions and camps at a reduced rate or take part in interesting nature research and fieldwork as volunteers.

Youth and undergraduate students dominate the membership of many nature protection organizations, especially those with the largest memberships. In LOP, for example, they make up 80 per cent and in Salamander, 75 per cent. In general, members with higher education prevail, and persons who are professionally involved in environmental and nature protection clearly outnumber those from other walks of life. Almost all age groups are represented, though to differing extents and not in every organization. Nature protection organizations, as a rule, do not maintain membership data in a way that would enable tracking membership composition, but responses from the nature protection organizations surveyed suggest that between 1999 and 2004 it did not change significantly.

Cooperation Within and Outside the Movement

Involvement in wider cooperative efforts within the movement is typical of – though not limited to – organizations that operate at the regional or national levels. The dominant focus of cooperation is nature protection. The major forms of cooperation include: (1) coalitions such as the Alliance for Wetland Protection and the Coalition for the Protection of the Białowieża Forest (the latter is *de facto* also a campaign); (2) campaigns, such as the Natura 2000 'Shadow List' (a list of sites that, according to NGOs, should be included in the EU Natura 2000 network) and the Campaign to Save the Rospuda River; (3) joint projects to protect particular species coordinated by one nature protection organization but involving many others, such as Pro Natura's White Stork programme; and (4) joint activities that are not projects, such as involvement in law drafting. Only a few nature protection organizations participate in networks that extend beyond pure nature protection. Examples include the coalitions Time for the Odra River and Save the Carpathians, the Via Baltica Campaign, and the Polish Green Network. Involvement in ventures with a broader ideological scope is unusual. It is quite common for the same organization to have different roles in different networks: initiator, coordinator, equal partner, participant, adviser, or member of the governing board.

In addition to joint activities among nature protection organizations, *all* the nature protection organizations cooperate with partners from other sectors, including local government, schools, research institutes, regional nature protection administrators, national and landscape parks, the State

Forests, and non-environmental NGOs. Most frequently, such cooperation involves implementation of concrete projects. One recent innovative and unique cooperative venture is Pro Natura's Black Sheep Project, which involves cooperation with prison administration.[2] Another common practice is participation in advisory bodies and working teams set up by various governmental authorities. Examples include the agri-environmental programme team of the Ministry of Agriculture, the Forest Forum of the State Forests, advisory councils for various landscape parks, etc. Cooperation is undertaken for the sake of greater efficiency, successful goal implementation and wider impact.

In spite of the obvious benefits of cooperation, there are many obstacles, resulting especially from lack of financial and human resources. Since Polish nature protection organizations are almost entirely project-funded, they typically concentrate on projects at the cost of building their own institutional capacity. Undesirable side effects of this include insufficient information flow, weak coordination of activities, lack of ties among organizations, and, more importantly, absence of coherent objectives. All these problems hinder the development of a coherent approach within the movement. Elaboration of clearly formulated goals that could be shared across the movement is hindered not only by differences in organizational goals and priorities, but also by differences in institutional capacities, modes of action, and attitudes towards controversial issues such as undertaking radical actions. In more general terms, personal ambitions, competition among leaders and organizations, the strong sense of autonomy and unwillingness to compromise are among the obstacles most frequently mentioned by the survey respondents.

Nature Protection Organizations and Policy Making

Limited public support – and in some cases even lack of public acceptance – of nature protection goals and the insufficient cooperation described above weaken the nature protection organizations' impact on policy making and the agendas of parties or politicians. None the less, the organizations do undertake at least a few relevant activities, including: (1) participation in policy making; (2) participation in drafting laws; (3) enforcement and monitoring of regulations; (4) lobbying; (5) media campaigns; and (6) radical actions. Radical actions, however, are rather exceptional. As the survey has shown, they are more likely to be mentioned by type 4 organizations (see Table 8.1), and, albeit in their moderate version, by WWF or Greenpeace. Overall, however, professionalized approaches dominate over ideology.

Professionalization may explain the occasional aversion towards politics; however, there are other reasons for the organizations' relatively weak involvement in policy making. The most frequently mentioned externally imposed barrier is the politicians' and authorities' dislike for public consultations. Often government leaders do not see the need for such consultations, and Poland lacks an appropriate political tradition and well-developed mechanisms for consultation. The authorities usually undertake efforts to establish structures for dialogue only when they are forced to do so by international obligations. Even then, consultations are often organized *pro forma*, with too little time allowed for submitting comments and no real intention to take the comments seriously. The nature protection organizations' ability to exert influence on the authorities is also limited by the deficiencies of the political scene, such as lack of transparency and politicians' invulnerability (a recent illustration of the latter phenomenon is the nomination of a politician with court convictions to the position of Deputy Prime Minister). Nature protection organizations complain that decision makers are too dependent on their political affiliations, informal networks and corruption, creating contradictions between the interests of the political class and those of nature protection organizations. On the other hand, the internationally driven demand for public participation apparently gives the NGOs more influence than their meagre memberships might suggest.

Another set of barriers to effective political participation is the previously discussed limited capacity of the nature protection organizations, which lack staff time, funds and volunteers with the skills or motivation to work on policy issues. These deficiencies are sometimes accompanied by missing skills in using democratic procedures and lack of confidence in their effectiveness. This naturally puts nature protection organizations with more such resources in a better position to be involved in policy making. Hence it is not surprising that it is WWF that represents the nature protection perspective in the coalition of Polish environmental NGOs set up in early 2004 to monitor EU funds expenditure in Poland and their environmental impact. Three of the five nature protection organization representatives in the Steering and Monitoring Committees come from WWF, one from IUCN and one from a nature protection organization with a wider environmental focus. The same organizations, plus OTOP and the Naturalists' Club, have been actively involved in commenting on drafts of the National Development Plan for 2007–13. Finally, OTOP, the Naturalists' Club and Salamander prepared the above-mentioned Natura 2000 Shadow List that was officially submitted to the European Commission and the Polish Government as part of a WWF project. Due to their limited resources, nature protection organizations often resort to international organizations, most often to EU agencies, to influence decision makers in Poland, and they participate in the activities of EU level NGOs and in international networks.

International Relationships

In our survey, the national chapters of international organizations predictably reported international contacts; however, nearly half the other organizations operating on the national level also reported such contacts. In addition to IUCN (three mentions) and Eurosite, a nature conservation management network (two mentions), single references were made to contacts with several other organizations (for example BirdLife International). Isolated cases of involvement in cross-border projects were also reported by organizations operating at various geographical levels. A remarkable proportion of surveyed organizations (nine) participate in international projects (for example the programme for white stork protection), while six are involved in international campaigns.

International cooperation has an important educational dimension, as it helps to widen the organizations' horizons and increase their potential (see above). The survey revealed many examples of the successful transfer of ideas and solutions. The dominating direction was from the old EU countries to Poland, as illustrated by implementation of nature management plans for the Natura 2000 network. Poland was also an exporter of solutions and ideas, such as a method for reintroducing salmon, applied in Lithuania, and the educational programme 'The White Stork', transferred to Germany, Slovakia and Ukraine.

As mentioned earlier, international cooperation can also strengthen the nature protection organizations' position *vis-à-vis* the authorities at home. It provides better access to European institutions and the opportunity to influence the Polish authorities from the European level, which has often proved more effective than direct influence attempts. A good example was the controversial routing of the Via Baltica, part of a major trans-European route connecting Helsinki with Southern and Western Europe, which endangered four Natura 2000 sites. As a result of actions by nature protection organizations and other NGOs at EU level, the Bern Convention Standing Committee in Strasbourg recommended to the Polish authorities that they carry out a strategic environmental assessment of the Via Baltica before the final decision on routing as a condition for eligiblity for EU funding. Finally, international cooperation provides access to funds and supports integration into the international environmental movement.

Despite these benefits, international cooperation also poses many challenges. First, there may be mismatch of interests and priorities among the countries involved. For example, the Bialowieza Forest, the last piece of primeval forest in the European lowland, did not fit into European priorities, which did not take into account the need for saving natural forests, as the latter are not found in EU outside Poland. Second, discrepancies between the resources, capacities and public support of the partners may be an obstacle. Polish nature protection organizations are usually much weaker than their Western partners in these respects. Third, differences in legal and sociopolitical environments may be consequential. Finally, working on an international scale requires more resources. Lack of funds is frequently an obstacle to participation in various international fora and events, which restrains Polish nature protection organizations' international involvement. Their lack of resources appears to condemn them to the role of participating in the initiatives of stronger Western organizations rather than initiating or coordinating international projects.

CONCLUDING REMARKS: NATURE PROTECTION ORGANIZATIONS AS AN ELEMENT OF CIVIL SOCIETY

Nature protection organizations constitute a relatively viable and distinct grouping within the Polish environmental movement. They lack broad public support, which weakens their political position, but in a movement where NGOs with fewer than 30 members prevail, they are much larger than the average environmental organization. In addition, the majority of their work is scientifically grounded, and even those with a more spiritual reference framework (for example, deep-ecology groups) display a respectable level of nature protection knowledge. Therefore they play an important role as a reservoir of expertise for institutions involved in preservation of threatened natural heritage.

The nature protection organizations also cooperate better with one another than do organizations in the environmental movement as a whole, although their reliance on project-oriented funding aggravates the competition among them and leads to fragmentation of effort and of goals. Dependence on project funding also leaves little room for building their capacities and resources, and diminishes their independence in setting their agendas. The competition and dependence on project-related funding explains the prevalence of isolated initiatives and absence of a national nature protection coalition capable of speaking with one voice and of broad, sustained cooperative efforts that could consolidate the movement. Instead, cooperative efforts appear to be largely limited to *ad hoc* situational responses such as the campaign against the controversial routing of the Via Baltica.

Polish nature protection organizations appear similar to their Western counterparts today in their tendency to avoid politics and rely on non-confrontational approaches. Under the conditions of deficient democracy and lack of respect for the rule of law, they seem to be doomed to occupy a marginal position. Their situation could be improved if they could win wider public support, which would also reduce their dependence on institutional donors and their policies.

The weak public support base, which clearly distinguishes Polish nature protection organizations from their Western counterparts, is largely a legacy of the communist period. The communist regime engendered atomization and demobilization of society, reserving legal status for top-down, regime-controlled forms of collective action and eradicating spontaneous citizen initiatives. Membership in various regime organizations and participation in 'voluntary' community work were often imposed. The political changes of 1989 provided the opportunity and ideological framework for the liberation of long-suppressed individualism, which then found a fertile ground in atomized society.

The communist economic system also left Poland far behind the West. Poland thus entered the period of political and economic transformation with vast and relatively undisturbed natural areas, which the communist economy had not managed to transform, but also with an impoverished population, which was fed up with ideology and different types of controls and yearning to improve its economic status and consumption levels. Hence it is not surprising that nature protection has lost out to other priorities. In this regard, Poland fits Inglehart's postmodernization theory (Inglehart 1997), which suggests that post-material values do not gain importance until a society's economic growth reaches the stage of diminishing returns, whereupon quality of life gains increasing importance.

With the end of the communist era, Poland experienced a remarkable growth of civil society, but the resulting civil society had an enclave character (Glinski 2001a, p. 41). That is, civil structures operate only in specific, partially isolated areas of societal life. Nature protection organizations are clearly one such enclave. They are an important manifestation of the self-organization of civic life, that is, of the bottom-up articulation of values, government power control, and defence of the public interest embodied by nature protection. Hence, they perform all the fundamental functions of civil society structures. In the context of the environmental movement crisis described above, nature protection organizations have become fairly independent actors and more an element of civil society than part of a social movement[3].

NOTES

1. The population of the research was defined as the nature protection organizations and networks, including the major national organizations, national branches of international

organizations and major regional organizations and networks within the country. The sample consisted of the grantees of the Global Environmental Facility Small Grants Programme (the most popular source of funding biodiversity projects in Poland) that met the population criteria, and IUCN Poland. Of the sample of 31 organizations, 20 responded, including all national ones except one, and all the international ones. The research was carried out by means of an electronically circulated questionnaire consisting of mainly close-ended and some open-ended questions.

2. The project combines protection of valuable meadows through grazing and cutting; setting up a reproductive herd of the endangered indigenous sheep variety *wrzosówka*; training of prisoners in sheep breeding, grazing and cutting, and nature protection. The project targets prisoners coming from a rural environment and aims at preparing them for independent sheep breeding and farm work.
3. Referring to the theory of social movements, it may be said that bonds between NaPOs and other environmental organizations are weak, while the whole movement has only a weakly developed collective identity (Melucci 1995) and a low level of consensus mobilization (Klandermans 1988). The lack of collective cultural identity and mobilization consensus follows from the immaturity of the movement, its short gestation period, great internal diversity and the failure of integration processes in the movement.

REFERENCES

Cole, D.H. (1998), *Instituting Environmental Protection: From Red to Green in Poland*, London and New York: Macmillan and St Martin's Press.

Cole, D.H. and J. Clark (1998), 'Poland's Environmental Transformation: An Introduction', in J. Clark and D.H. Cole (eds), *Environmental Protection in Transition: Economic, Legal and Socio-Political Perspectives on Poland*, Aldershot, UK, Brookfield, USA, Singapore and Sydney: Ashgate, pp. 1–18.

Eder, K. (1993), *The New Politics of Class: Social Movement and Cultural Dynamics in Advanced Societies*, London: Sage Publications.

Gliński, P. (1996), *Polscy Zieloni. Ruch społeczny w okresie przemian*, Warsaw: Wydawnictwo IFiS PAN.

Gliński, P. (1998), 'Polish Greens and Politics: A Social Movement in a Time of Transformation', in J. Clark and D.H. Cole (eds), *Environmental Protection in Transition. Economic, Legal and Socio-Political Perspectives on Poland*, Aldershot, UK, Brookfield, USA, Singapore and Sydney: Ashgate, pp. 129–53.

Gliński, P. (2001), 'The Ecological Movement as the Element of the Civil Society', in H. Flam (ed.), *Pink. Purple, Green: Women's, Religious, Environmental and Gay/Lesbian Movements in Central Europe Today*, Boulder, CO: East European Monographs (distributed by Columbia University Press, New York), pp. 112–19.

Gliński, P. (2001a), 'The Civil Society in Poland', in Piotr Salustowicz (ed.), *Civil Society and Social Development*, Bern and Vienna: Peter Lang, pp. 21–49.

Gliński, P., A. Siciński and A. Wyka (1990), *społeczny aspekty ochrony i kształetowania środowiska w Polsce*, Warsaw: Wydawnictwo SGGW-AR.

Hicks, B. (1996), *Environmental Politics in Poland: A Social Movement. Between Regime and Opposition*, New York: Columbia University Press.

Hrynkiewicz, J. (1990), *Zieloni: Studia nad ruchem ekologicznym w Polsce 1980–1989*, Warsaw: Uniwersytet Warszawski.

InE (1999), *The Position Papers of the Polish Environmental Non-Governmental Organizations on the Environmental Effects of Poland's Accession to the European*

Union Concerning the Selected Fields of: Transport, Nature Conservation, Energy Management, Waste Management, Agriculture and Rural Development, Warsaw: Institute for Sustainable Development.
Inglehart, R. (1997), *Modernization and Postmodernization: Cultural, Economic, and Political Change in 43 Societies*, Princeton, NJ: Princeton University Press.
Karaczun, Z.M. and L.G. Indeka (1999), *Ochrona środowiska*, Warsaw: Agencja Wydawnicza ARIES.
Klandermans, B. (1988), 'The Formation and Mobilization of Consensus', in B. Klandermans, H. Kriesi and S. Tarrow (eds), *International Social Movement Research. Volume 1. From Structure to Action: Comparing Social Movement Research Across Cultures*, Greenwich, CT and London: JAI Press, pp. 173–96.
Kolbuszewski, J. (1992), *Ochrona przyrody a kultura*, Wrocław: Towarzystwo Przyjaciół Polonistyki Wrocławskiej.
Korbel, A.J. (2001), 'Natura 2000 w aspekcie działalności organizacji pozarządowych', in *Wdrażanie Europejskiej sieci ekologicznej Natura 2000 w Polsce i związane z tym problemy*, Warsaw: Instytut na rzecz Ekorozwoju, pp. 50–54.
Melucci, A. (1995), 'The Process of Collective Identity', in H. Johnston and B. Klandermans (eds), *Social Movements and Culture. Social Movements, Protest, and Contention. Volume 4,* Minneapolis, MN: University of Minnesota Press, pp. 41–63.
Michnik, A. (1985), *Letters from Prison and other Essays*, Berkeley, CA: University of California Press.
Pełczyński, Z.A. (1988), 'Solidarity and "The Rebirth of Civil Society" in Poland, 1976–81', in J. Keane (ed.), *Civil Society and the State: New European Perspectives*, London and New York: Verso, pp. 361–80.

9. The historical and contemporary roles of nature protection organizations in Sweden

Magnus Boström

INTRODUCTION

The Swedish environmental movement today is dominated by three major environmental organizations, the Swedish Society for Nature Conservation (SSNC), the World Wide Fund for Nature (WWF) and Greenpeace Nordic. The fact that SSNC and WWF, the two largest, have their origins in the nature protection movement suggests that nature protection is not only significant for the historical origin of the Swedish environmental movement, but remains an important part of if. Nevertheless, over their histories, the roles, strategies, identities and framings of nature protection organizations have been repeatedly transformed as a result of changing social context. This chapter describes and analyses the development of the Swedish nature protection movement in relation to such changes, including the growth of a state administration for nature protection, the rise of the environmental movement, and, more recently, the 'greening of business'.

Sweden is an especially interesting case for three reasons. First, it has much nature and wilderness to save. As in the USA, Swedish citizens have long sought out experiences, adventures, silence and recreation in rivers, forests and mountains distant from urban areas, and the Swedish right of legal access to private land for everyone (*allemansrätten*) is very unusual. Second, Sweden has been viewed as a frontrunner in environmental protection. For example, the Swedish Environmental Protection Agency (SEPA), established in 1967, was the first agency of its kind (Lundqvist 1971; Jamison et al. 1990, p. 14). A third reason is Sweden's characteristic political culture, with its cooperative ideals, preference for pragmatic problem solving, reformist orientation, traditional state centrism and corporatist pattern of policy making, which provides a different context for nature protection organizations than most of the other nations included in this book (cf. Jamison et al. 1990; Micheletti 1995; Lundqvist 1996).

I organize the historical description into five time periods. Although there is some overlap between them, the periodization reflects important shifts in both movement practices and the social context. In the description of each phase, I present information about major nature protection organizations, as well as their resources, strategies, and framings of nature protection and their external relations. I also describe changes in the role of the state and general societal developments that have influenced interest in nature protection. Although I pay considerable attention to history, I emphasize the most recent period, which begins with the 1980s.

1870s–1930s: THE EMERGENCE OF A NATURE PROTECTION MOVEMENT[1]

The First Mobilization: a Scientific–Aesthetic Elite

In Sweden, industrialization and urbanization came into full swing in the latter part of the nineteenth century. A general optimism accompanied these changes; however, some upper-class members of scientific, tourist, artist and hunting circles began to express worries about negative consequences for nature. In the 1870s, mobilization began around animal and bird protection. Natural scientists cooperated with hunters, who due to their profession or personal interest, were observing ongoing decimation of game as a result of exploitation of natural areas by industry and increased recreational hunting. Some small local bird protection groups set up bird protection areas through acquisition of land, but this proved to be an expensive strategy.

In the 1890s, growing national romanticism spawned new patriotic feelings about Sweden and Swedishness, including genuine 'Swedish' nature and wilderness. Painters, writers and poets played a key role in promoting a new picture of Swedish nature as an aesthetic, emotional and national resource – that is, as something that ought to be protected. The same period also saw an increased interest in local folklore, and its connections to local natural landscapes.

The leaders of the early nature protection movement were not critical of industrialization or economic progress as such. They simply wished to protect specific parts of the Swedish natural and cultural landscapes. Natural scientists wanted to protect certain areas to study how untouched nature develops in the absence of human intervention. The Swedish Tourist Club (Svenska Turistföreningen, STF), on the other hand, emphasized tourism. It was founded in 1885 as a vehicle for a small clique of rich citizens to travel to beautiful mountain areas in the north of Sweden and similar areas (Abrahamsson et al. 1996). It became one of the main organizations that spoke for the establishment of national parks such as Yellowstone in the USA.

The early movement was founded by a 'scientific–aesthetic' patriotic elite with many personal linkages among its adherents (Lundqvist 1971), most of whom lived in the large university cities. The movement was therefore unknown to most citizens, so it was unable to mobilize a broad constituency. In the context of the rather harsh economic conditions characteristic of Sweden at the time, ordinary people saw little intrinsic value in nature unless it could be used to improve social and economic conditions.

The First Law

The year 1904 saw a breakthrough for the emergent national nature protection movement. In several lectures held in Sweden, the German professor, Hugo Conwentz, presented a model he was developing in Germany for systemizing and administering nature protection and for establishing 'natural monuments'. In response, the liberal politician, Karl Starbäck, persuaded the Swedish parliament to commission the Royal Swedish Academy of Sciences (KVA) and its committee for nature conservation (KVAN) to investigate the need for nature protection. KVAN developed draft legislation, which led to the introduction of the 1909 Nature Protection Act.

The 1909 legislation made it possible to protect nature as national parks or natural monuments, providing an important legal mechanism for the movement. Nine of Sweden's current 28 national parks were established immediately following passage of this legislation. Movement leaders suggested that scientific and aesthetic (tourism) criteria should be the basis for selection of areas and objects for protection. The protected areas should also symbolize Swedishness; that is, they should illustrate native landscapes and prehistoric nature. The original inhabitants of northern Sweden, the Laplanders, were also viewed as 'part of nature'. Animal and bird protection were not covered by the new law, but treated as hunting issues, which were to be handled in subsequent policy making.

The new law clearly subordinated nature protection to economic progress. Politicians were generally positive toward nature protection, but only in so far as the protected areas remained few and uncontroversial. The office responsible for administration of the law received few resources; KVAN's staff consisted of just three peoples. Only state (crown) land areas could be incorporated into national parks, and natural monuments could only be protected if the private landowner agreed. In other words, areas could only be protected if they were commercially irrelevant and did not encroach on private property rights. The first major test of the legislation occurred in less than a decade. Vattenfall, a state-owned hydroelectric power enterprise, argued that it needed to build a plant in an area within a legally protected national park (Stora Sjöfallet). Despite protests from some – but not all – nature protection activists, the parliament decided to reduce the protected area so that the project could proceed.

The Swedish Society for Nature Conservation

As a result of these developments, KVA (and KVAN) emerged as an important, semi-official organizational platform for the early nature protection movement. KVA, established in 1739, with Carl von Linné (Linnaeus), among its first members, represented various branches of the natural sciences. It had great symbolic status and a leading role in the scientific community. 'The ombudsmen of nature within KVA belonged to the cream of science; men with authority, esteem and influence, the foremost representatives of a scientific elite at key positions in the society' (Hillmo and Lohm 1990, p. 92, my translation).

Through KVAN, the leaders of the early nature protection movement were involved both in constructing the new law and in the administration of nature protection. However, KVAN did not remain the only major group representing nature protection interests. In the same year the first nature protection law was enacted, the 'scientific–aesthetic elite' also established another nature protection organization – the Swedish Society for Nature Conservation (SSNC). Its leaders hoped the SSNC would grow to a large popular movement (*folkrörelse*), but that goal proved difficult to achieve. SSNC soon mobilized around 500 members, and by 1919, it had 3400, but for decades thereafter it did not grow significantly. SSNC also set out to establish local and regional affiliates. By the 1930s, approximately a dozen local and regional nature protection associations had been established, but they were not connected to SSNC because it was seen as too elitist and centralized.

During its early years, SSNC was a small, expert-driven organization; however, it was nevertheless relatively influential (Lundqvist 1971; Haraldsson 1987; Rothstein 1992; SNF 1999), and it enjoyed an important, semi-official status in nature protection politics. It was charged with making inventories of areas that could be considered for protection measures (A KVAN participant also sat on the SSNC's board), and it received state funding for its information campaigns, supplied information to schools, and issued the book *Sveriges Natur* (*Sweden's Nature*) annually. Another important SSNC role was to lobby the government to protect more nature. Several natural parks and monuments (and later nature reserves), and bird and animal protection projects clearly bear the stamp of SSNC (see SNF 1999).

Natural scientists, including biologists, zoologists and geologists, dominated the SSNC leadership in the early years, although it also had representatives from STF, forestry and artists' circles. A rational, scientific-oriented approach to protection dominated. Some leaders from the scientific wing even argued that tourists should be prevented from visiting national parks, precipitating tensions within SSNC during its first two decades. These tensions were mainly between a preservation orientation, which held that nature protection should be an issue for experts and nature protection areas should be protected *from* man, and a conservation orientation, which saw nature protection as relevant to all types of people and believed that nature areas should be protected *for* man. The historian Désirée Haraldsson (1987) thus argues that the dominance of the preservation orientation in the SSNC board hindered a mass mobilization of supporters for nature protection.

1930s–50s: A BROADENING AGENDA

After the mid-1930s, the scientific orientation lost ground to cultural, social and economic factors in both framing nature protection issues and policy making (Lundqvist 1971, pp. 26ff.; Haraldsson 1987; Hillmo and Lohm 1990, pp. 98–101). SSNC, in particular, functioned as an important venue for discussions, development and dissemination of three new views on nature protection.

The first new argument in the debates was that 'untouched' nature areas, especially in southern Sweden, were actually 'cultural landscapes' affected by earlier husbandry. The human being was increasingly seen as an important factor that interacts with nature to develop such landscapes. Scientific research within biology was a basis for this new view, which caused some leading preservationists within SSNC to begin to revise their previous views. Nature was now seen as more dynamic, a view that challenged traditional, preservation-oriented conceptions of nature protection. Experiences from an overgrown national park (Ängsö) and the deterioration of some other protected areas in southern Sweden gave support to this new view. Once these areas had been legally protected, there had been no human intervention, and the results were accordingly unfortunate.

A second new theme can be traced to the ongoing urbanization and industrialization that resulted in a more wealthy population with legally assured leisure time (two weeks in 1938, three in 1951, four in 1963 and five in 1977). Most of the population lived in southern Sweden, and the national parks in the far north were too distant. The result was increasing demand for new protected nature areas near the cities for outdoor activities such as hunting, fishing, bird watching and excursions. SSNC leaders also noted that earlier protection measures had often been biased towards fascinating and extraordinary objects. An interest in the typical, rather than the unique, now became more prominent.

A third theme was that nature protection was relevant for economic reasons. Protecting nature was increasingly seen as compatible with economically rational management of natural resources. Moreover, investments in new hotels, hostels and other spaces and arrangements for people's growing demand for outdoor life were a promising growing business.

SSNC was affected by these developments. Indeed, the historical literature on nature protection suggests that it played a proactive role in developing concepts and strategies of nature protection in line with the new views. After the 1930s SSNC thus purposefully developed an orientation that stressed nature protection as relevant for large segments of the population (Haraldsson 1987; Hillmo and Lohm 1990). For example, in the late 1930s a committee for 'social nature protection' was established in SSNC. It was charged with addressing questions concerning landscape, land and outdoor life. Other committees were for science, public education, bird protection and juridical issues (Haraldsson 1987, pp. 148–51). Moreover, in opposition to KVA(N), SSNC began to back away from according science the dominant role in nature protection (Hillmo and Lohm 1990, p. 103).

The SSNC's reorientation attracted new members only gradually (Jamison et al. 1990, p. 17; Lundgren 1991, p. 146). Perhaps the Second World War impinged on its growth potential. However, Sweden's neutral status saved the country and its economy from the destruction that affected most European countries. Surprisingly, to my knowledge, available literature contains basically no information on how the Second World War may have affected nature protection. The economy thrived after the Second World War, but in 1955 SSNC still had only 5000 members.

Beginning in the late 1930s, SSNC also developed more cooperative relations with other types of civil society organizations (Haraldsson 1987), such as the Swedish Homestead Society (Samfundet för Hembygdsvård, SfH), an organization for the protection of cultural landscapes, and the Swedish association for ornithologists (Sveriges Ornitologiska Förening, SOF). SOF, established in 1945, grew out of the Committee for Bird Protection within SSNC. SSNC also managed to recruit several independent local nature protection organizations as local affiliates. In 1948, SSNC, following a Dutch model, established its youth organization, the Field Biologists (Fältbiologerna) (SNF 1999).

Pressures for a Stronger State

As more groups articulated nature protection interests during the 1940s to 1960s, many debates arose about the proper roles of nature protection organizations and the state. A common opinion, expressed especially by the SSNC, was that the 1909 law was old-fashioned and its administration too weak. The law was therefore a poor tool for controlling industries that were destroying nature. SSNC argued that the state should take a more active role in balancing the diverging demands of various interest groups. Policy makers responded to the increasing pressures. The revised Nature Protection Law of 1952 included an important new provision allowing for expropriation of land to establish natural monuments. The same year saw passage of a law aimed at protecting public access to shores in seas, lakes and rivers. Another implication of the revised law was strengthening the roles of the SSNC and SfH as official advisory organs. They were now empowered as adequate bodies for setting up commissions of inquiry.

SSNC welcomed this development and made internal organizational changes to enable it to carry out state-related tasks (Lundqvist 1971). It even allowed representatives of state agencies to sit on its board. The borderline between the state and this civil society organization thus became blurred – a typical corporatist pattern (Rothstein 1992). In the 1950s, about two-thirds of SSNC's personnel had tasks related to the state administration (e.g. advising, investigations), as did the major part of the organization's volunteer corps (Lundqvist 1971, p. 44).

During the same period, SSNC pressed for its positions on hydroelectric power interests, in particular against the state-owned enterprise, Vattenfall (Lundqvist 1971, pp. 44–6; Rothstein 1992, pp. 257–8; SNF 1999, pp. 27, 62–6). The early nature protection movement had not made the ongoing exploitation of rivers a major issue, and several key figures actually favoured investment in hydroelectric power plants, as they were seen as necessary for economic progress and welfare. However, a push to protect the remaining untouched rivers grew in the 1950s, with SSNC and SfH taking the lead. New investment plans led to conflicts, and a state committee, consisting of representatives of nature protection interests (SSNC, SfH, KVAN) and exploiting interests (Vattenfall), was set up in the early 1950s to investigate and negotiate about which rivers should be protected from exploitation. Several years later, in 1961, the negotiations led to an important agreement called *Freden i Sarek* (Peace in Sarek). (Sarek is the name of a mountain area in Sweden's far north.) This agreement was a compromise that stated which rivers could be exploited and which should be protected or decided on later (Lundqvist 1971, pp. 45–7). Many activists were disappointed by the compromise, and the status of several rivers remained unclear. Nevertheless, the process helped to set a new agenda and triggered many protest activities in the 1960s and 1970s. The issue of river protection has since been one of the most central in Swedish nature protection mobilization.

1950s–60s: THE STATE 'TAKES OVER'

Nature protection organizations had occupied a key position in nature protection politics and administration. At the same time, they considered the existing state administration weak and ineffective. They carried on official tasks with voluntary labour and received, in their view, inadequate economic compensation in return (Hillmo and Lohm 1990, p. 111). Existing legislation and its implementation had not prevented far-reaching exploitation of nature (Lundqvist 1971, pp. 47ff.). By the end of the 1950s, damage to nature areas due to roads, airports, urban areas and hydroelectric power was increasing, and exploiters and protectors of nature increasingly collided (Lundgren 1991, p. 146; Hillmo and Lohm 1990, pp. 107ff.). Politicians became concerned that voluntary organizations with scarce resources had been given too much responsibility for dealing with nature protection (Hillmo and Lohm 1990, p. 111).

These concerns led in 1963 – just seven years after passage of the revised nature protection law – to appointment of a new general commission for nature protection, the State Nature Protection Council (Lundqvist 1971). For the first time, nature protection had its own state agency, albeit still a temporary one. A revised nature protection law was passed in 1964. It established a new and important institution, nature reserves. 'Nature reserve', in Swedish vocabulary, is a rather broad concept including not only strict reserves and wilderness areas, but also areas protected for their landscape and recreation value (IUCN category V – see Chapter 1). Nature reserves could be used to protect both state and privately owned lands that were considered valuable for scientific, cultural and social (recreation or outdoor life) reasons. They were to be set up by the regional county administrations.

Further development of the state administration soon strengthened its capacity even more. A broadened interest base for nature protection, new scientific knowledge and increasing public concerns about environmental degradation (described in the next section) led in 1967 to establishment of the Swedish Environmental Protection Agency (SEPA) (Lundqvist 1971, pp. 102ff.), to replace the State Nature Protection Council. SEPA was the first agency of this kind in the world. It had responsibility for handling both traditional 'green' (nature protection) and 'blue' (air and water pollution, sewage etc.) issues (Lundqvist 1971; Lundgren 1991). Sweden was also the first country to pass a comprehensive environmental protection law (1969), and it became one of the most active in supporting research programmes in environmental science and technology (Jamison et al. 1990, p. 14).

The establishment of SEPA was in some respects a success for the nature protection organizations, but, ironically, it reduced their influence over and access to the state administration. Like other corporativist political systems, the Swedish system effectively and systematically includes some interest groups, such as labour unions, in policy making, while at the same time excluding others. Nature protection organizations, in this case, were suddenly moved from among the included to the excluded ones. The policy makers wanted a composition for SEPA that would enable it to act in an authoritative and resolute way against competing interests (Lundqvist 1971; Rothstein 1992). This required a governing board of limited size, which could not reflect all possible interests. In the process of planning SEPA, no one except the nature protection organizations themselves spoke explicitly for representation of the nature protection movement. (Earlier, the nature protection organizations had been more successful in finding allies within Parliament.) Hence SEPA's board included representatives of the Federation of Swedish Industries, the Swedish Association of Local Authorities, the Cooperative Union and Wholesale Society (KF), the Swedish Trade Union Confederation (LO), the Centre Party, the director-general of SEPA and one jurist from SEPA. Nature protection organizations were not represented. Nature protection interests were to be represented by the agency itself despite the fact that its governing board was composed of other interests. When SEPA began to make and implement policy, it developed close contacts with industry, but it saw no reason to orient itself to the nature protection organizations (Lundqvist 1971, 1996). The designers of the agency believed that the most important task for nature protection organizations was providing information and education at the grass-roots level.

As a result, the state largely took over from civil society the role of protecting nature. Several Swedish studies have noted and criticized SEPA's closeness to nature-exploiting interests (e.g. Lundqvist 1971; Lundgren 1991; Rothstein 1992; Christiansen and Lundqvist 1996), and Rothstein (1992) maintains that the relative impact of nature protection organizations decreased significantly to the advantage of industry after the establishment of the SEPA.

1960s–80s: THE NEW ENVIRONMENTAL MOVEMENT AT THE FOREFRONT

Although the SSNC lost its formal access to the state administration, the period of the 1960s to 1980s was none the less a period of expansion for the society. Between 1955 and 1970, its membership grew from 5000 to 50 000 (Jamison et al. 1990, p. 22). Its growth occurred in step with (1) the rise of a newly urbanized ' "leisure class", or at least the extension of vacationing and tourism into broader segments of the population' (Jamison et al. 1990, p. 17) and (2) new problem definitions and understandings of environmental conditions. The growth that occurred as a result of these new framings might be denoted 'the Rachel Carson effect', but long before Rachel Carson's famous *Silent Spring*, a small number of Swedish writers and critics, including Elin Wägner, Harry Martinsson and Georg Borgström, were publishing books and articles that employed what could be termed an environmental perspective. While they were not particularly influential in the Swedish discourse at the time, they prepared the way for the reception of the new ideas in the 1960s (Jamison et al. 1990, pp. 18–21; cf. Abrahamsson et al. 1996, pp. 414–20).

As in earlier periods, SSNC played an important role in the reframing of environmental problems. SSNC leaders began as early as the 1960s to talk not only about nature protection, but also about environmental problems, such as mercury pollution and acidification, that are less visible in the natural landscape and more widespread (Lundgren 1991). A healthy physical environment was no longer just a question of 'standard of living', but a question of 'the survival of humankind'. Nature protection was thus becoming 'only' one part of the broader environmental agenda, and this was reflected within SSNC.

Concerns about diffuse, abstract and trans-boundary risks like these gradually became cornerstones of the emerging environmental discourse (cf. Beck 1992), yet concrete and visible damage to nature continued to be the object of contention. The 1960s and 1970s were thus marked not only by sharp disputes over issues such as pesticides and mercury pollution, but also continued contention over hydroelectric power (Jamison et al. 1990), and several demonstrations were directed against new hydroelectric dam projects on northern rivers.

However, new organizations, such as Friends of the Earth Sweden (established in 1971), the Environmental Union (established in 1976 and united with Friends of the Earth in 1995), and the Field Biologists (SSNC's youth organization) developed a more radical and activist approach to environmentalism using more confrontational strategies (Jamison et al. 1990). They complained that the SSNC was too passive, not sufficiently radical and too much a part of the establishment (Sjöberg 1988; Jamison et al. 1990, p. 27; Klöfver 1992; SNF 1999, pp. 60–61). The Field Biologists grew rapidly from fewer than 4000 members in the early 1970s to about 12 000 members in the mid-1970s (Klöfver 1992, p. 36). The Environmental Union had about 10000 members in the 1970s and FoE about 3000. All of these organizations were non-partisan, but the Environmental Union had a leftist orientation.

Despite the criticism, SSNC continued to grow, reaching 66 000 members in the 1970s (SNF 1999, p. 30). It continued to work for protection of rivers in conjunction with new issues, such as acidification and pollution (ibid., p. 29). During this period, SSNC also started new well-known species protection projects, such as 'Project Peregrine' and 'Project Sea-eagle'. Accordingly, although SSNC played an active role in reframing issues, traditional nature protection did not vanish from its agenda.

Nature protection also received attention because of the founding of WWF Sweden in 1971, ten years after WWF International. WWF Sweden had quite a spectacular opening, attended by many distinguished persons from the Swedish elite, including the crown prince (now king of Sweden) Carl Gustaf (Wahlstedt 1996). Key figures from other civil society organizations (including SSNC, SOF, STF, LO and KF), government authorities (e.g. SEPA) and the Swedish Church, as well as natural scientists and representatives from the business sector, participated in WWF's Council and committees. Sweden's king Carl Gustaf was an honorary member: today he is President of the Council.

Despite its auspicious beginning, during the 1970s WWF remained a small organization with only a few thousand supporting members. It was almost totally ignored by the more radical environmental movement and seen as an elite organization with no power to oppose established interests. Practical nature protection projects were the trademark of WWF Sweden. A major part of its work was raising and distributing funds for research-related nature protection projects, mostly regarding endangered species. Indeed, the activities of WWF were largely dependent on the applications for funding submitted to it. Practice-oriented researchers from universities, other organizations such as SOF, and even state agencies, all received funding from WWF.

1980s–2000s: REVITALIZATION OF NATURE PROTECTION[2]

During the 1980s, environmentalism became firmly institutionalized in Sweden. This was embodied in the dramatic growth of the environmental movement, both in terms of popular support and representation in party politics. Polls documented that the general public was deeply concerned over environmental issues, viewing them as among the most important political issues. Greenpeace Sweden was established in 1983; by 1988, it had reached 210 000 supporters. The Green Party of Sweden (Miljöpartiet de Gröna), which was established in 1981, became the first new party in more than 70 years to enter the Swedish parliament in 1988. In 1987, the Ministry of the Environment (originally called the Ministry of Environment and Energy) was established, providing environmental politics with a solid and legitimate position. The Natural Step, a new environmental organization with an aim to improve the environmental practices of large corporations, was started in 1989 – indicating a new openness toward green issues in the business sector. The Natural Step was set up as a foundation. Its main aim is integration of a holistic and systemic view of environmental reform based on natural science (thermodynamics) into all kinds of practices. It has mainly used a cooperative strategy of assisting corporations with education and consultation.

There were thus many signs that environmental politics had gained momentum, but this did not by any means imply that traditional nature protection vanished. In fact, the membership of nature protection organizations, especially SSNC and WWF, rose dramatically at the same time that the environmental movement was flowering. Between 1985 and 1991, SSNC grew from 85 000 members to more than 206 000, and between 1982 and 1995, WWF's membership grew from 2000 to 170 000.

As described above, the rise of a prosperous, vacationing 'leisure class' was one of the most important explanations for the growth of SSNC between 1955 and 1970, but other factors appear to have been more important during the period of the environmental movement. These included greater media attention to environmental problems, intensive campaigning by environmental movement actors, and new framings and awareness of a global crisis fuelled by catastrophes such as the Chernobyl accident (which indeed had great consequences for outdoor activities such as hunting and mushroom picking in parts of Sweden) and the widespread death of seals in the North Sea.

These successes did not, however, continue through the 1990s, when all three of the largest organizations within the environmental movement lost members. By 2000, SSNC had shrunk to 128 000 members, although it has since resumed growth and reached 168 000 members in 2004 (SSNC 2005). WWF was able to stabilize the number of sustaining members at around 150 000.[3] Today these older nature protection organizations constitute a large part of the environmental movement. Indeed, they have been able to retain more support than Greenpeace. By 2004, Greenpeace appears to have stabilized with about 100 000 members, but this includes supporters from other Nordic countries, since the Nordic Greenpeace sections merged in the late 1990s. In Sweden, Greenpeace mobilizes 65 000 members (Greenpeace 2005), less than one-third of its support in 1988.

To my knowledge, there is no research about the social origins of members in Swedish environmental organizations; however, the leaders of the major organizations generally assume that the core of their support comes from the middle class, with political opinions ranging across the right–left spectrum (cf. Boström 2001, pp. 151ff.).

New Orientations and Stronger Organizational Platforms

The nature protection organizations were transformed by their encounter with the environmental movement. Radical groups in the environmental movement made an impact on SSNC, which became willing to formulate tougher political demands during the late 1970s and early 1980s (Sjöberg 1988) and gradually changed its identity, framings and priorities. Although it has retained its focus on nature protection issues, it also absorbed basically every new environmental issue: energy, traffic, chemical risks, pollution, acidification, green consumerism, Local Agenda 21 and several others. Its current activities are divided into forest, climate (including traffic and energy), chemicals and waste, agriculture, sea/fishing, species protection, and green consumerism and consumer power. It also has departments for international work and information. SSNC uses various strategies, including political lobbying, information campaigns, promoting ecolabelling, boycotts and nature protection activities. It communicates with all kinds of actors: the public, state agencies, political parties, the government, business actors and other civil society organizations. Although it sometimes engages in protest activities, it more often employs cooperative strategies.

During the 1980s, SSNC became highly professionalized, financing its growing staff with the huge inflow of funds from new paying members. It also upgraded its magazine *Sveriges Natur* (*Sweden's Nature*) with a professional staff. Today it is probably the best-known nature protection magazine in Sweden. SSNC is democratically organized, with 24 regional and 273 local units. The local groups are formally independent. The national assembly is the highest organ for decision making. All regional and local units have at least one representative with a vote in the assembly. In 2004, SSNC's income was 99.8 million Swedish crowns (approximately (€11 million), which enables it to employ 66 people (SSNC 2005). SSNC's income sources and expenditures are presented in Tables 9.1 and 9.2.

Although the agenda of the SSNC has broadened significantly in recent years, concrete nature protection remains one of its central activities and an important motive for local activists. Local circles of activists have long been engaged, for example, in protecting rivers and forest areas from exploitation and clear-cutting. Their knowledge about valuable nature areas and objects has often been instrumental for SSNC's campaigning and is acknowledged by state authorities.

Table 9.1 SSNC's income sources, 2004

The state	34%
Members	30%
Private donors and corporations (gifts, wills)	19%
Licence fees from the SSNC ecolabel, Good Environmental Choice	9%
Sales (e.g. its yearbook)	8%

Source: SSNC annual report for 2004 downloaded 3 February 2006 from http://www.snf.se/pdf/internt/dok-vb-2004.pdf.

Table 9.2 SSNC's expenditures, 2004

International projects	29%
Administration, fundraising, member issues	28%
Information and PR material	17%
Swedish nature and environmental protection projects	16%
Supporting the regional units and local groups	10%

Source: SSNC annual report for 2004 downloaded 2 March 2006 from http://www.snf.se/pdf/internt/dok-vb-2004.pdf.

Due to its organizational form, which incorporates established interests groups (see above), WWF cannot be as confrontational, conflict-oriented or uncompromising as FoE, Greenpeace or SSNC. Nevertheless, unlike the situation before the 1990s, when it rarely involved itself in controversy, it has become more politically progressive and active. WWF today continues to fund nature protection projects, but has chosen to take more control of its own agenda and the direction of its activities, as opposed to just selecting among projects submitted to it to fund. Informants say that its 20 years of experience with funding research have provided it with a knowledge base that now enables it to operate more independently.

In contrast to SSNC, WWF supporters have no voting rights or influence in the organization; they simply support WWF with their donations and receive its magazine, *WWF Eko*. Nevertheless, they have helped WWF to increase its resource base, which in turn enables it to mount more effective campaigns. WWF's income in 2004 was 118.6 million Swedish crowns (approximately €13 million), which enables it to employ 44 people permanently (WWF 2005). In 2003, 24 per cent of its expenditures went to Swedish projects, 18 per cent to projects in the Baltic region, and 58 per cent to international projects. Income sources and budget allocation are presented in Tables 9.3 and 9.4.

Table 9.3 WWF's income sources, 2004

Supporters and the public (gifts etc.)	50%
The state	30%
Corporations	14%
Foundations	6%

Source: WWF's annual report of 2004, downloaded 3 February 2006 from http://www.wwf.se/source.php/1015163/WWF%20Årsredovisning%202004.pdf.

Table 9.4 WWF's budget allocation, 2003

Programme areas	
Forest	36%
Sea and coast	13%
Wetlands and freshwater	8%
Education and youth	24%
Information, etc.	19%

Source: WWF's annual financial report for 2003.

Both SSNC and WWF have a great deal of symbolic capital; that is, they are well known and recognized among the Swedish public, and they tend to be recognized and appreciated by established interest groups, political actors and state agencies – even if they sometimes are opponents of these groups. This symbolic capital is a collective resource, alongside material resources and labour, which organizations can mobilize, accumulate, control and use (cf. Ahrne 1994; Boström 2001, pp. 165–70). The symbolic capital of an organization could be its name or logo, which can be known, recognized and associated with particular meanings and identities. Symbolic capital is thus an essential asset that affects action capacities and power positions in interactions with other actors. Several informants from WWF, FoE and Greenpeace maintained that it brings great symbolic strength to be part of a global organization. Many informants also maintained that the global organizations were good sources for personal contacts, ideas, concepts, expertise, and sometimes joint strategies. Having symbolic capital means that targeted actors (politicians, companies, etc.) take a risk if they ignore demands from these organizations. It also means that surrounding actors seek out cooperation with these organizations because this can be good public relations.

During the 1990s, both SSNC and WWF developed closer contacts with business actors through various cooperative projects, including concrete nature protection projects and ecolabelling (see discussion on forest certification below). Their cooperative image – in contrast to Greenpeace's confrontational identity – suited them well for work in the more receptive political context and the 'greening of the industry trend' that began in the early 1990s.

As described above, SSNC lost its close working relationship with the state administration when the SEPA was established. However, more recently, SSNC and WWF have developed numerous informal contacts with SEPA officials, and informants from both nature protection organizations now say they have no problems obtaining access to political bodies and central state agencies, especially SEPA (Boström 2001, pp. 208–20). Indeed, they are invited to take part in many more commissions and advising groups than what they have resources for. They also cooperate frequently with SEPA on nature protection issues and generally share its agenda, even if they sometimes express more radical political goals.

SSNC and WWF also often develop cooperative projects with a wide variety of other civil society organizations in Sweden and abroad. Other organizations that are often engaged in nature protection in different ways include (1) Greenpeace, which has engaged in protest activities for forest and marine protection, (2) Friluftsfrämjandet, an association for outdoor life, (3) SOF, the Swedish association for ornithologists and, (4) the Swedish Anglers' Association (Sportfiskarna), an association for sport fishing. SOF has 22 000 members, many of whom are involved in bird protection (Castillo 2004). SOF and the Swedish Anglers' Association often cooperate with SSNC and WWF. Friluftsfrämjandet, which has about 100 000 members, has been taking an active part in urban planning since the 1960s. It has struggled to protect nature in urban areas for outdoor life, often with the perspective that children should have natural playing environments (Friluftsfrämjandet 2006). Friluftsfrämjandet, as well as a number of scouting associations, offers a rich repertoire of outdoor activities for youth and children in Sweden. Some basic facts about major interest organizations for nature protection in Sweden are presented in Table 9.5.

Reframing

In recent years, a fundamental reframing of concerns about nature and environment around the concept of sustainable development has helped to bring various interest groups, including especially business interests and environmental interests, significantly closer to each other (see Chapter 1 and Boström 2004 on the concept of framing). This new framing has facilitated a more cooperative orientation, including new strategies, such as the certification and labelling programmes described below.

Table 9.5 Main organizations concerned with nature protection in Sweden

Organization	Members/ supporters	Year established	Goals	Budget
Swedish Society for Nature Conservation[1]	168 000	1909	Protection of wilderness and animals. Energy, climate, consumption, traffic, chemicals, etc.	100 million SEK (€11 million)
WWF Sweden[2]	150 000	1971	Protection of wilderness and animals	119 million SEK (€13 million)
Greenpeace Nordic[3]	100 000 Sweden: (66 000)	1983 (Sweden)	Protection of forests, marine environment. GMO, chemicals, climate, energy, etc.	57 million SEK (€6 million)
Friends of the Earth[4] Sweden	2 000[5]	1972	Global justice, climate, GM, forest protection, etc.	3 million SEK (€300 000[6])
Swedish Association for Ornithologists[7]	22 000	1945	Birdwatching, bird protection, habitat protection	Not available
The Field Biologists[8]	3 500	1948	SSNC's youth organization. Nature protection, courses, exhibitions, etc.	3 million SEK (€300 000)
Friluftsfrämjandet[9]	100 000	1892	Outdoor life (especially youth and children).	30 million SEK (€3 million)

Table 9.5 (continued)

Organization	Members/ supporters	Year established	Goals	Budget
			Protection of nature locales in urban areas	
Swedish Tourist Club[10]	327 000	1885	Tourism. Awareness, concern and protection of wilderness and cultural landscapes important sub-goals. Ecotourism	229 million SEK (€25 million)

Notes:
1 See http://www.snf.se/ 14 February 2006.
2 See http://www.wwf.se/ 14 February 2006.
3 See http://www.greenpeace.org/sweden/ 14 February 2006.
4 See http://www.mjv.se/ 14 February 2006.
5 Figures from Boström (2001, 1999), not available on their website.
6 Figures from Boström (2001, 1999), not available on their website.
7 See http://www.sofnet.org/ 14 February 2006.
8 See http://faltbiologerna.se 14 February 2006.
9 See http://www2.frilufts.se/flf/flf.Index 14 February 2006.
10 See http://www.stfturist.se/ 14 February 2006.

It is also important to emphasize another new frame with strong connections to the traditional identities of nature protection organizations: biodiversity. A focus on endangered species is a key component in the identities and framings of WWF in particular, but also of SSNC and Greenpeace. WWF's early international activity focused exclusively on saving endangered species, especially large and striking fauna. In Sweden too, WWF and SSNC have invested a great deal of effort in protecting highly visible species such as sea-eagles, eagle owls, peregrines, seals and 'the Swedish four large predators', wolf, bear, wolverine and lynx. However, both organizations' agendas have gradually shifted from protecting specific species to protecting ecosystems, and the frame and goal of biodiversity has been particularly compatible with this shift. Informants from WWF, for example, maintain they have been reflecting upon their earlier 'biases' toward protecting certain species and now find it more appropriate to define a rich biodiversity as WWF's top goal.

Swedish nature protection organizations frequently refer to biodiversity because they see it as a powerful frame that appeals to scientific audiences and other policy actors (Rientjes 2002; Hannigan 2006), while at the same time having the potential to resonate with traditional nature protection interests. Moreover, emphasizing biodiversity helps to widen the nature protection agenda in that it encompasses both agrarian and urban nature – not just the distant, 'untouched' areas emphasized by the early framings – and the day-to-day management of nature and natural resources.

Despite its advantages as a frame, preserving biodiversity can sound a bit abstract and technical in contrast to traditional, more easily visualized narratives about species protection. Consequently, even as they shift their conceptual focus and resources to a more abstract and holistic level, Swedish nature protection organizations continue to feature pictures of endangered animals in their communications to the public. WWF informants point out that pictures of threatened animals are a very powerful mobilizing tool because they help the public visualize what might otherwise seem diffuse environmental problems. They also believe that engagement on behalf of certain species is what motivates many individuals to support WWF. It would therefore be risky to completely drop the focus on species. Finally, they give both methodological (it is important to study species that are indicators of the conditions for ecosystems) and substantive (protecting species requires protecting ecosystems) reasons for continuing to provide resources for protecting specific species.

New Strategies

During the last 15 years, SSNC and WWF have never abandoned their traditional roles in Sweden, including allocating resources to concrete nature protection projects, participating in state commissions and advising groups, and lobbying for nature protection – especially in the form of nature reserves; however, they have complemented these roles with strategies beyond the national level.

Sweden's entry into the EU in 1995, for example, provided Swedish nature protection organizations with a potential new ally in their efforts to lobby for more nature protection in accordance with Natura 2000 (see Chapter 1 in this book). WWF, SSNC and SOF, like nature protection organizations in other European countries (Christophersen and Weber 2002), have been active in monitoring how well government and state agencies work with Natura 2000. Moreover, they constructed a list of 2700 areas proposed for inclusion in the Natura 2000 network, and they provided the Commission with information about the situation in Sweden. Comparing Sweden with other nations, the nature protection organizations and the Commission have labelled the Swedish government a straggler and pressured it to comply with the EU rules more completely and rapidly, and provide adequate resources for completing Natura 2000 (e.g. SSNC 2001). This intense pressure led the government to include additional areas from the nature protection organizations' list, resulting in a better standing for Sweden in the EU Natura 2000 Barometer (see European Commission 2006).

The nature protection organizations have also been quite successful in promoting market-based approaches to nature protection, including forest certification and ecolabelling. By the early 1990s, the nature protection organizations had already come to understand that administrative measures, such as creating additional nature reserves and additional concrete nature protection projects, were not sufficient to secure biodiversity in forests and other ecosystems. WWF thus took the initiative in 1993 to introduce a system for private certification of sustainable forests in Sweden. With the help of SSNC, it built alliances and promoted introduction of the Forest Stewardship Council (FSC), a global voluntary certification for sustainable forestry. Sweden was the first country to adopt a nationally based FSC standard (Boström 2003b; Cashore et al. 2004).

FSC certification has been uniquely successful in Sweden. Almost half of Swedish forestland is certified, and there is a major agreement between a large part of the business sector, the environmental movement and social interests (e.g. labour unions, representatives of indigenous people). While all big Swedish forest companies adopted FSC, the association for non-industrial private forest landowners developed an alternative standard within the framework of the Programme for the Endorsement of Forest Certification schemes (PEFC) with looser, more flexible criteria. However, in contrast to developments in other countries and regions (Cashore et al. 2004), this countermove did not marginalize the FSC standard. To be certified according to the FSC standard, forests must meet several criteria with important implications for nature protection. These include a ban on clear-cutting large areas; saving trees with 'high biodiversity value'; permanently protecting 5 per cent of each landowner's forests (the area with greatest nature protection value) from harvesting, and saving forests near watercourses.

Although the FSC campaign is viewed as a success by WWF and SSNC, it did not lead to a perfect result. The FSC standard is based on a general compromise. It allows some intensive forest use practices, which Greenpeace, for example, refused to accept. In addition, SSNC and SOF sometimes accuse forest companies of poor compliance of specific standard criteria. Another drawback inherent in this choice of strategy is its reliance on market dynamics. If the demand for certified wood and paper should suddenly decrease, the forest companies can simply drop FSC. On the other hand, the significant symbolic capital and influence of the nature protection organizations may make it a risk for forest companies previously committed to FSC to abandon it. While a certified forest area certainly does not have the same robust protection as national parks and nature reserves, the extent of forest certification's implementation in Sweden makes it a significant contribution to nature protection. Some data about the certification and other traditional nature protection measures are presented in Box 9.1.

BOX 9.1 DATA ON NATURE PROTECTION IN SWEDEN

Some Figures on Nature Protection in Sweden

National parks and nature reserves: By 2004, slightly more than eight per cent of Swedish land is protected in the form of national parks and nature reserves, of which 80 per cent by nature reserves. There are 28 national parks in Sweden, which are set up mainly in mountain areas. There are 2600 nature reserves in Sweden, distributed more equally in the country. Other legal forms of protections are natural monument and culture reserves.

Natura 2000: A major part of Swedish Natura 2000 areas are already legally protected as national parks or nature reserves. By 2004, the government had suggested about 3900 areas, about 14 per cent of the national territory).

Certification: In Sweden, a bit more than ten million hectares of forest land have been certified according to the FSC standard. All large Swedish forest companies (including the state-owned Sveaskog) have certified their forests according to the FSC standard, along with about 70 municipalities and some of the Swedish church's dioceses. Nearly half of the Swedish productive forestland is certified according to the FSC standard. Beyond that, about 6.6 million hectares of Swedish forestland are certified according to the competing PEFC-standard (mainly by private forest landowners and the rest of the Swedish church's dioceses).

Sources: http://www.naturvardsverket.se/ downloaded 27 January 2006; http://www.fsc.org/en/about downloaded 27 January 2006; http://www.pefc.se/ downloaded 27 January 2006.

SUMMARY AND CONCLUSIONS

Sweden, a country with much natural beauty and wilderness, including rivers, forests and mountain areas, has sustained organizations and networks for nature protection for over a century. Using various strategies and framings in different time periods, nature protection organizations have argued that nature should be protected and have suggested methods for doing so.

Views of nature have not remained static over the years, and conceptions of nature protection have broadened, often as a result of internal debates within the movement. An important trend throughout the 1900s, for example, was the growing interest of various political constituencies in nature protection – for scientific, aesthetic, cultural, environmental, recreational, outdoor, economic and ethical reasons. This development was facilitated especially by increasing welfare and leisure time. Paralleling these developments, the state nature protection administration grew steadily stronger, although it was not until the 1960s, and especially the 1980s, that nature protection organizations were able to permanently mobilize a mass membership base.

Swedish nature protection organizations throughout the twentieth century have shown tendencies towards expert orientation, pragmatist problem solving and cooperative ideals, reflecting a specific Swedish political culture. While this corporativist structure and the associated political culture can be a barrier to expressing radical political positions, it may help to explain why Swedish nature protection organizations have been comparatively effective in pushing for such new market-based strategies as ecolabelling and certification, as the spirit of cooperation and pragmatism brings a certain readiness among interest groups to negotiate about standard principles and criteria (e.g. Boström 2003b).

The contemporary Swedish movement, with its assumption that it is possible to operate in a sustainable way through use of new efficient methods and without radically altering old institutions, also displays an affinity to an eco-modernist discourse (cf. Hajer 1995; Boström 2001, 2003a). Although the large-scale institutionalization of nature protection in a state-centred administration for nature and environmental protection in the 1960s marginalized the nature protection movement – or at least deprived it of some of its former roles – for a period, the largest nature protection organizations perceive the state administration today as relatively open and responsive. They have also found potential allies from other quarters (e.g. in their campaigns for certification and labelling) and authorities superior to the nation-state (e.g. the EU's Natura 2000).

The Swedish nature protection organizations have been significantly affected by the Swedish political culture and the state administration. But it would be a mistake to conclude that the movement therefore lacks an autonomous identity or that it has been unable to grow and thrive, as Jamison with colleagues claimed in their well-known analysis of the Swedish environmental movement (Jamison et al. 1990; see Boström 2004 for more discussion).

The rise of the environmental movement in the 1970s also threatened to marginalize nature protection, as some new environmental groups criticized the traditional nature protection organizations for being too integrated with established society. This chapter demonstrates, however, that the nature protection movement in Sweden is much more than simply the antiquated predecessor of today's environmental movement. Since the 1980s, the institutionalization of environmental politics and the environmental movement have instead provided the basis for a revitalization of nature protection through organizational growth and transformations, new framings, such as sustainability and biodiversity, and new strategies, such as certification and labelling.

There is also more continuity than is sometimes recognized between the old 'conservationism' and the 'new environmentalism'. First, by addressing new environmental themes and generalizing and radicalizing the nature protection agenda early on, the SSNC and its youth organization, the Field Biologists, provided the organizational platform for parts of the new movement. The appearance of new groups stimulated the older ones to modify their goals and strategies, and vice versa, so it can be misleading to divide environmental organizations into two categories with distinct ideological orientations: conservative versus ecological orientation (Dalton 1994). The identities of contemporary environmental organizations are, in fact, more complex and composite, reflecting a palimpsest of roles, framings, priorities and values that have been integrated successively through history (Boström 2001). It is thus no accident that the oldest nature protection organization (SSNC) has the most complex identity.

Second, the fact that older nature protection organizations (SSNC and WWF) constitute a major part of the contemporary environmental movement indicates the continuing mobilizing potential of nature protection issues, including species protection. Even though diffuse, abstract and trans-boundary risks have become cornerstones of environmental discourse, visible threats to concrete nature areas (mountains, forests, rivers) and objects, including specific species, have never ceased to be bones of contention and have never ceased to be relevant for the mobilization of broad constituencies of supporters and protesters.

Third, traditional nature protection organizations have been influential and active in reframing environmental problems. By embracing the concept of biodiversity, for example, nature protection organizations have had an impact both in terms of strengthening protection of specific nature areas and features and by reforming the day-to-day management of nature and natural resources. Nature protection is increasingly viewed as involving entire areas, both in Sweden and abroad, the diversity of habitats within these areas, and the links between them. Forest certification and Natura 2000 are concrete policy expressions of this view. None the less, phrases and metaphors such as 'national heritage', 'unbroken wilderness', 'virgin nature' etc. are still frequently used in the framings of nature policies (cf. Mels 2002). This indicates that traditional concepts of nature protection have not yet lost their public appeal.

As the forest certification case shows, nature protection organizations today are, in a way similar to 100 years ago, playing central roles in pushing for regulatory innovations. History suggests, however, that the roles, strategies and relations change constantly as a result of interplay with changing contexts. In the case of the establishment of the SEPA, the roles of nature protection SMOs were marginalized in parallel to the institutionalization of protection policies. Today there is a parallel risk that nature protection organizations might lose ground relative to other groups after accomplishing the building of new institutions such as certification. What will then be their next major task?

NOTES

1. This section is primarily based on the historian Désirée Haraldsson's dissertation (1987) about the early development of the nature protection movement and the SSNC. Details are taken from this dissertation except when I explicitly refer to others' work.
2. This section is primarily based on my dissertation about the recent Swedish environmental movement (Boström 2001) and on an empirical report prepared for the dissertation (Boström 1999). Details are taken from this work except when I explicitly refer to others' work.
3. The figures are taken from Boström (2001). In its recent annual financial reports WWF does not report how many members it has – as it did earlier – perhaps because of the increasing variety of categories of subscribers. However, WWF reports a positive financial trend, so there is good reason to believe that it currently has at least 150 000 of what could be termed as members.

REFERENCES

Abrahamsson, K.-V., J.-E. Hällgren, T. Sundström and S. Sörlin (1996), *Humanekologi. Naturens Resurser och Människans Försörjning*, Stockholm: Carlsson bokförlag.

Ahrne, G. (1994), *Social Organizations. Interaction Inside, Outside and between Organizations*, London: Sage.

Beck, U. (1992), *Risk Society. Towards a New Modernity*, London: Sage Publications.
Boström, M. (1999), 'Den Organiserade Miljörörelsen. Fallstudier av Svenska Naturskyddsföreningen, Världsnaturfonden WWF, Miljöförbundet Jordens Vänner, Greenpeace och Det Naturliga Steget', in *Score Working Report Series 9*, Stockholm: Score.
Boström, M. (2001), *Miljörörelsens Mångfald*, Lund: Arkiv förlag.
Boström M. (2003a), 'Environmental organisations in new forms of political participation. Ecological modernisation and the making of voluntary rules', *Environmental Values*, **12**,175–93.
Boström, M. (2003b), 'How state-dependent is a non-state-driven rule-making project? The case of forest certification in Sweden', *Journal of Environmental Policy & Planning*, **5**, 165–80.
Boström, M. (2004), 'Cognitive practices and collective identities within a heterogeneous social movement: the Swedish environmental movement', *Social Movement Studies*, **3**, 73–88.
Cashore, B., G. Auld; and D. Newsom (2004), *Governing through Markets: Forest Certification and the Emergence of Non-state Authority*, New Haven, CT: Yale University Press.
Castillo, D. (2004), 'BirdLife International och Sveriges Ornitologiska Förening', unpublished manuscript, Stockholm: Score.
Christiansen, P.M. and L. Lundqvist (1996), 'Conclusions: A Nordic environmental policy model?', in P.M. Christiansen (ed.), *Governing the Environment. Politics, Policy, and Organisation in the Nordic 'Countries'*, Copenhagen: Nordic Council of Ministers, pp. 259–338.
Christophersen, T. and N. Weber (2002), 'The influence of non-governmental organisations on the creation of Natura 2000 during the European policy process', *Forest Policy and Economics*, **4**, 1–12.
Dalton, R. (1994), *The Green Rainbow. Environmental Groups in Western Europe*, London: Yale University Press.
European Commission (2006), http://europa.eu.int/comm/environment/nature/nature_conservation/useful_info/barometer/barometer.htm, downloaded 14 February.
Greenpeace (2005), Annual report for 2004, downloaded 3 February 2006 from www.greenpeace.org/raw/content/sweden/rapporter-och-dokument/arsrapport-2004.pdf.
Friluftsfrämjandet (2006), www2.frilufts.se/flf/flf.Index, 14 February.
Hajer, M. (1995), *The Politics of Environmental Discourse. Ecological Modernisation and the Policy Process*, Oxford: Clarendon Press.
Hannigan, J. (2006), *Environmental Sociology*, 2nd edn, London: Routledge.
Haraldsson, D. (1987), *Skydda Vår Natur! Svenska Naturskyddsföreningens Framväxt och Tidiga Utveckling*, Lund: Lund University Press.
Hillmo, T. and U. Lohm (1990), 'Naturens ombudsmän', in S. Westerlund (ed.), *Miljö Media Makt*, Stockholm: Carlssons bokförlag, pp. 86–122.
Jamison, A., R. Eyerman and J. Cramer (1990), *The Making of the New Environmental Consciousness. A Comparative Study of the Environmental Movements in Sweden, Denmark, and the Netherlands*, Edinburgh: Edinburgh University Press.
Klöfver, H. (1992), *Håll Stövlarna Leriga och för Bofinkens Talan. En Studie av Naturintresse, Miljömedvetenhet och Livsstil inom Organisationen Fältbiologerna*, Linköping University: Department of Water and Environmental Studies.

Lundgren, L.J. (1991), 'Miljöpolitik på längden och tvären. Några synpunkter på svensk miljövård under 1900-talet', in *Människan och Miljön XX! Nordiska Historikermötet*, Umeå University: Department of history, pp. 143–62.

Lundqvist, L.J. (1971), *Miljövårdsförvaltning och Politisk Struktur*, Lund: Bokförlaget Prisma/Nämnden för Verdandi.

Lundqvist, L.J. (1996), 'Sweden', in P.M. Christiansen (ed.), *Governing the Environment. Politics, Policy, and Organisation in the Nordic 'Countries'*, Copenhagen: Nordic Council of Ministers.

Mels, T. (2002), 'Geokodifiering: produktionen av de svenska nationalparkernas natur', in J. Hedrén (ed.), *Naturen som Brytpunkt. Om Miljöfrågans Mystifieringar, Konflikter och Motsägelser*, Stockholm: Symposion, pp. 243–74.

Micheletti, M. (1995), *Civil Society and State Relations in Sweden*, Aldershot, UK: Avebury.

Rientjes, S. (2002), 'Making nature conservation modern: an analysis of developments in nature conservation policy in relation to macro-social changes – The Netherlands as a Case Study', *Journal of Environmental Policy & Planning*, **4**, 1–21.

Rothstein, B. (1992), *Den Korporativa Staten. Intresseorganisationer och Statsförvaltning i Svensk Politik*, Stockholm: Norstedts.

Sjöberg, F. (1988), *På Maktens Tröskel. Miljörörelsen i det Sena 80-talet*, Stockholm: Carlssons bokförlag.

SNF (1999), *Naturskyddsföreningen – 90 år ung!*, Stockholm: SSNC.

SSNC (2001), 'Natura 2000 skyddar redan idag', downloaded 3 February 2006 from www.snf.se/snf/hallbart/2001/hallbart401/natura-2000.htm.

SSNC (2005), Annual report for 2004, downloaded 03 February 2006 from www.snf.se/pdf/internt/dok-vb-2004.pdf.

Wahlstedt, J. (1996), *I Pandans Tecken. Boken om Världsnaturfonden WWF*, Västerås: Ica Förlaget.

WWF (2005), Annual report of 2004, downloaded 3 February 2006 from www.wwf.se/source.php/1015163/WWF%20Årsredovisning%202004.pdf.

10. The 'nature' of environmentalism: nature protection in the USA

Angela G. Mertig

INTRODUCTION

The US environmental movement has been one of the most successful and enduring social movements of the twentieth century. Like most other social movements, the US environmental movement has arguably fallen short of achieving many of its stated goals (Brulle 2000); however, it has succeeded in building and maintaining a substantial organizational and public support base, and it has had a documented and significant effect on the legal, political, educational and cultural milieu of the USA (Mertig et al. 2002; Bosso 2005).

Like environmental movements elsewhere, US environmentalism encompasses several distinguishable yet overlapping ideologies, each with characteristic goals. These 'frames' or 'discourses' (see, for example, Snow et al. 1986) represent the ideological glue which binds various sets of organizations, activists and public supporters together. One key frame within US environmentalism is that of 'nature protection', more commonly known in the USA as 'preservation'. Preservationist-oriented organizations and activists focus much, if not all, of their time on setting aside protected areas (e.g. parks, forests, wilderness areas) and protecting wildlife and their habitats from human use. From the preservationist perspective, it is vital to protect wilderness and wildlife because nature is 'an important component in supporting both the physical and spiritual life of humans' (Brulle 2000, p. 98). Preservationism represents one of the earliest sources of collective action on behalf of the environment in US history, and it remains a vital component of the contemporary US environmental movement.

Another important frame[1] relevant to nature protection has coexisted with preservationism within US environmentalism from the beginning. 'Conservationism', which emphasizes the stewardship of natural resources and their continued use for 'the greatest good to the greatest number' of people (Pinchot 1910), arose at roughly the same time as preservationism (Brulle 2000). These two frames formed the crux of the US nature protection movement at the turn of the twentieth century (Hays 1959; Nash 1982). For this chapter, both preservationism and conservationism are considered part of the larger frame of nature protection. While preservationism represents a stricter or 'purer' approach to nature protection, conservationism is also an important element of nature protection due to its emphasis on the wise stewardship and protection of natural resources.

Over time, US environmentalism has undergone a substantial broadening and deepening of its discourse (Mertig et al. 2002), and several additional frames have developed within the movement (see, e.g., Brulle 2000). Nevertheless nature protection remains a key discourse (Johnson 2006). The frame associated with many contemporary environmental organizations and activists in the USA has been referred to as 'reform' environmentalism. This frame includes a greater interest in addressing issues of pollution, environmental quality and human health, and in mitigating human impacts on the natural environment; however, it also advocates nature protection. An even more recently developed frame is that of deep ecology. Also referred to as 'radical' environmentalism, deep ecologism espouses ecocentrism, the protection of nature for nature's sake. In this sense, deep ecologists represent a reshaping of the preservationist frame by advocating a purely non-anthropocentric basis for nature protection (Norton 1986).

In this chapter, I focus specifically on the nature protection elements of the US environmental movement. Nature protection was the earliest source of collective action on behalf of the environment, has sustained the movement through hard times, consistently garners substantial public support, remains a core element of environmentalist thought and action, and has evolved to incorporate both institutionalized and radical elements. In the next part of the chapter I delve into the historical background of nature protection as part of the larger environmental movement; this is followed by a discussion of what the nature protection movement currently looks like, structurally and socially. I then turn to the role that the nature protection frame has played in the environmental movement as a whole and end the chapter by speculating on the future of nature protection as a component of the environmental movement.

HISTORICAL BACKGROUND

The history of the environmental movement in the USA can be characterized as consisting of at least four eras: (1) the pre-movement era up to the late 1800s; (2) the conservation and preservation movement era of the late 1800s to early 1900s; (3) the world war era of the early to mid-1900s; and

(4) the modern environmental movement era from the mid-1900s to present. The frame of nature protection has persisted throughout each of these eras.

Like the history of many other countries, US history is marked by a profound ambivalence with regard to nature. The dominant worldview in the USA holds that nature is to be used in order to perpetuate growth and progress (Catton and Dunlap 1980); yet nature has also been seen as a source of inspiration and an object of reverence (Huth 1957; Nash 1982). Much of US history, particularly in the nation's early years, has been characterized by a *laissez-faire* approach to the use of natural resources in which people, as the sole authors of their destinies, are viewed as unregulated controllers of their own property and of nature. Enlightenment ideas of progress and scientific rationality, which ultimately fed into the conservationist impulse at the turn of the twentieth century, modified these notions only in that natural resources were now to be used in a more carefully considered way; people were still expected to use them rather than to protect them from use (Petulla 1977).

Yet, throughout US history, nature has also been seen as a vital component of the national landscape and character, and as a representation of the divine. This view, vividly espoused by the Romantic movement of the 1800s, has frequently clashed with both the *laissez-faire* and the Enlightenment/conservationist approaches to nature and natural resources. The conflict between these larger social forces led to the development of an environmental consciousness in the USA; the first public stirrings of this consciousness began to coalesce in the decades before the turn of the twentieth century.

The Pre-movement Era

Early European settlement of the American continent was marked by noticeable contempt for the natural world and its original inhabitants. The natural resources of the continent were used more quickly and wastefully than many had probably anticipated (Petulla 1977). Early voices against this profligate use of natural resources generally went unheeded, but they increased in intensity and frequency as America became increasingly urbanized, industrialized and settled (Petulla 1977; Nash 1982). The earliest advocates of nature protection tended to be intellectuals, who couched their concerns in religious terms that were beginning to appeal to a general public that was afraid of losing its morals in the onrush of urbanization.

The Romantic movement of the early 1800s, which started in Europe primarily as a reaction to the Enlightenment (Petulla 1977) and manifested itself largely through literature, was an important impetus for concern about nature, as it cherished the natural world as a source of inspiration, imagination, creativity, freedom and beauty. Romantics, along with their heirs, the Transcendentalists, including, most famously, Ralph Waldo Emerson and Henry David Thoreau, extolled a life of communion with nature away from the squalor of the city (Nash 1982). Transcendentalists, in particular, believed that people achieved union with God through nature. Reform movements in the early 1800s likewise blamed many social evils on rapid changes, particularly the growth of cities; the solution for many of these ills (e.g. delinquency, crime, poverty, alcohol abuse) was to put people back in nature. Nature, therefore, needed to be protected as a refuge for humanity.

Several prominent figures openly espoused the protection of nature in the 1800s, including John James Audubon, George Catlin and Frederick Law Olmstead (Nash 1982). Appreciation for nature also received impetus from the scientific world via such works as that of Charles Darwin in *The Origin of Species* in 1859 and George Perkins Marsh's *Man and Nature* in 1864. The protection of nature was not only becoming more readily accepted; its implementation, at a national level, was also beginning: in 1872, the first national park, Yellowstone National Park, was established in north-western Wyoming.

The Conservation and Preservation Movement Era

The 1890 US Census declared that the US frontier was closed – that is, a boundary line between the settled and unsettled portions of the continent could no longer be distinguished. As the frontier era came to a close, so too did the age of apparently limitless resources, rugged individualism, and personal and economic freedom (Nash 1982). In its quest to prove itself as a fledgling nation, particularly in comparison to Europe, America had viewed its frontier and the presence of wild nature as the foundation of its unique democratic tradition. As the frontier disappeared, so too, it was feared, would the source of America's uniqueness and greatness.

The closing of the frontier, coupled with high rates of industrialization and urbanization and rapid depletion of initially vast resources, such as the extinction of the passenger pigeon and the near extinction of the bison, led to widespread efforts to preserve and protect the very nature that previously was to be conquered via 'manifest destiny', the notion that God mandated people of European descent to spread democratic civilization by taking possession of and exploiting the continent (Nash 1982). General social unease and dismay over profligate use of resources led to growing pressure for the regulated and efficient (non-wasteful) use of remaining resources and the preservation of tracts of Western land as a means of keeping a perpetual frontier as a lasting source of US democracy and purity. Similar concerns were echoed in the progressive movement at the turn of the twentieth century, which advocated reforming people's living conditions; protecting nature was again viewed as a central aspect of improving the condition of humanity (Petulla 1977).

Even though the period is usually referred to simply as the period of the conservation movement, ideas regarding the protection of natural resources at this time were divided into conservationist and preservationist approaches. Although organized activities on behalf of preservationism began somewhat earlier than organization on behalf of conservationism (Brulle 2000), the latter had greater success in having its frame associated closely with the larger movement. Early preservationist interests were led by naturalist John Muir, who was instrumental in the establishment of the second US national park, Yosemite National Park in California, in 1890. In 1892, Muir organized the first national nature protection organization, the Sierra Club, which focused on preserving wild lands. Initially limited to the San Francisco area, the Club has since become one of the foremost environmental organizations in the nation. Several other prominent organizations dedicated to nature protection, including forerunners of the National Audubon Society, which is devoted primarily to bird protection, also formed during this time. Preservationist goals became institutionalized in the National Park Service (1916), whose purpose has been to preserve natural beauty and facilitate recreation in the national parks.

Conservationist interests, led by Gifford Pinchot, the nation's first professional forester, had less organized support from the public; however, they were very successful at getting their agenda incorporated into new government agencies – largely due to the close relationship between Pinchot and President Theodore Roosevelt (Hays 1959). Conservationist ideas were institutionalized in the form of the Forest Service and the Bureau of Reclamation, both of which focus on the 'multiple use' of resources, as opposed to the National Park Service, which preserves land purely for recreational or aesthetic purposes.

Despite obvious affinities between preservation and conservation, they represent distinct ideologies and desired outcomes that have led to conflicts throughout the history of nature protection in the USA. Preservationists and conservationists came into direct opposition, for example, in the struggle over damming the Hetch Hetchy river valley inside the Yosemite National Park, a battle that lasted from 1908 to 1913. Conservationists and developers led by Gifford Pinchot urged that the dam be created to provide water to a thirsty San Francisco, which had been ravaged by a catastrophic earthquake in 1906, while John Muir and other preservationists decried the despoliation of a beautiful valley inside a national park (Nash 1982).

President Roosevelt, a great believer in conservation and a friend to both Muir and Pinchot, ultimately sided with Pinchot, and the valley eventually was dammed. While this was a momentous defeat for preservationists, it did not stop them from pressing their cause in the ensuing decades.

The World War Era

Although two world wars and the Great Depression of the 1930s dominated the nation's attention for almost three decades, the conservationist and preservationist causes persisted (Nash 1974). President Franklin Delano Roosevelt initiated several 'New Deal' conservation programs, such as the Civilian Conservation Corps and the Tennessee Valley Authority, which dealt simultaneously with the social devastation of the Great Depression and several contemporaneous environmental disasters, including massive flooding and the devastating loss of topsoil in Oklahoma and adjacent states during the 'Dust Bowl'. Two important conservationist oriented organizations also began at this time: the Izaak Walton League (1922) and the National Wildlife Federation (1936); the latter has since become one of the country's largest environmental groups, dedicated to issues that go beyond purely conservationist causes and garnering substantial clout. Both of these organizations were founded by sportsmen eager to protect natural resources for recreational uses (Mitchell 1989).

Preservationist causes were also advanced. Aldo Leopold, a forester, initiated the idea of granting wilderness status to undeveloped portions of the National Forests. In 1924, 500 000 acres in the Gila National Forest in New Mexico were designated as the first Forest Service wilderness area (Nash 1974). Later in his career, Leopold became America's first professional wildlife manager, and in the 1930s he developed a philosophy termed 'the land ethic', which is often cited as a basic tenet of modern US environmentalism (Nash 1974). The land ethic promoted the idea that humankind was to be seen as a part of nature rather than a master of it. In 1935, Leopold and another forester, Robert Marshall, organized the Wilderness Society, a national organization which continues to be a strong advocate for the preservation of wilderness (Nash 1982). Other preservationist organizations that developed during this time were the Defenders of Wildlife (1947) and the Nature Conservancy (1951; initially named the Ecologists' Union).

In the 1950s, preservationists scored a significant victory in another controversy over the building of a dam. Hydropower and irrigation interests proposed the development of Echo Park Dam on the Colorado–Utah border in the Dinosaur National Monument, a protected area. Opposition to the dam was spearheaded by the Wilderness Society and the Sierra Club.

Their eventual success prompted the Wilderness Society to urge the development of a national wilderness preservation system (Nash 1974). Through their efforts and those of other activists, the Wilderness Act of 1964 was passed, immediately protecting nine million acres of federally owned wilderness (Nash 1974). In the mid-1960s economic interests eyed water project proposals in the Grand Canyon (Arizona), but preservationists, led by the Sierra Club, again unleashed heavy public protest (Nash 1974).

The Environmental Movement Era

Despite important continuities with the earlier conservation movement, the contemporary environmental movement is typically considered, both popularly and academically, as a distinct movement. While no specific date or event marks a clear break, at least three events have typically been used to demarcate the beginning of the modern environmental movement in the USA. The first event was the publication of Rachel Carson's *Silent Spring* in 1962. Her book played a key role in the development of a new 'environmental' frame, since she persuasively articulated to an educated lay audience the burgeoning research concerning the detrimental effects of the array of new chemicals and pesticides unleashed by postwar industry and agriculture. The second event was the founding of the Environmental Defense Fund (1967; renamed Environmental Defense in 2000) and the Natural Resources Defense Council (1970). Their development reflected substantial shifts in environmental organizing. They focused on a qualitatively different set of issues (also known as 'reform' environmentalism), were founded with corporate and foundation sponsorship (e.g. the Ford Foundation), and specialized in scientific and legal aspects of environmental issues (Mitchell 1989). The final event was the first Earth Day in 1970, which mobilized massive and highly visible public support on behalf of environmental causes.

The shift from nature protection to a broader environmental movement marked an important ideological shift in US environmental consciousness. Reform environmentalism encompassed a much broader set of concerns than either conservationism or preservationism (Mertig et al. 2002). Even so, the concerns of the earlier era did not disappear. If anything, the new frame of reform environmentalism was grafted onto the older agenda, augmenting rather than displacing it (Brulle 2000; Johnson 2006), and the older nature protection organizations gradually evolved to incorporate both the older and newer concerns. While numerous 'reformist' environmental organizations sprouted during this time, they also eventually added the more traditional focus of nature protection to their repertoires. The older organizations were also immensely helpful to the newer environmental organizations, providing an important source of encouragement, strategies, activists and material resources (see, e.g. Mitchell 1989; Mitchell et al. 1992).

Nature protection concerns continued to resonate strongly with the general public even though other environmental issues, especially those more reformist in nature, appeared to take centre stage at this time. For instance, a large oil spill off the California coast in 1969 (the Santa Barbara oil spill) generated concerns not only about the pollution of waters and beaches, but also about the damage to wildlife, as the media presented pictures of oil-soaked birds and dying animals. Due in part to increases in education, affluence and leisure time after the Second World War, people were also spending more time outdoors, prompting many to revere and then fight for landscapes that were threatened by development (Gale 1972). In fact, nature protection organizations such as the Sierra Club had been sponsoring nature field trips since their beginning as a means to recruit members and enlist supporters for protecting natural areas (Faich and Gale 1971). Concern about wildlife and nature protection has thus remained important in mobilization efforts during the contemporary environmental movement.

The contemporary environmental movement was also ushered in with important legislative and governmental policy changes. Before 1970, the federal government's role in environmental issues and policy had been mostly that of public lands manager (Kraft and Vig 2003). This role aided both the conservationist and preservationist causes, as the government set aside some public land for full protection from human uses and other land for multiple use, including government-regulated extractive activities such as logging and mining. In the 1970s, however, the federal government began to take on a greater role by passing a plethora of legislation and developing environmental policy that was in line with the agenda of reform environmentalism. The National Environmental Policy Act (1969), the Clean Air Act (1970) and the Clean Water Act (1972), the best-publicized initiatives, were aimed directly at mitigating environmental damage, but nature protection issues were also important in the policy and legislative initiatives at this time. Among the best-known examples are the Endangered Species Act (1973) and the Alaska National Interest Lands Conservation Act (1980), which promoted the protection of wildlife and set aside a vast portion of Alaska for protection (Vig and Kraft 2003).

The environmental movement's apparent success in the early 1970s led to the development of a countermovement known as the 'Sagebrush Rebellion'. Political and business leaders from several western US states pushed strongly to turn federally owned public lands over to private or state control. Their agenda was strengthened by the election of Ronald Reagan to the presidency in 1980. In addition to appointing one of the Sagebrush leaders as Secretary of the Interior, the department which oversees federal land management issues, the Reagan administration operated under the assumption that environmental regulation was inherently bad for economic growth and should be opposed (Vig 2003). Strong public support for environmental protection, however, caused the Reagan administration to tone down its anti-environmental policies (Vig 2003). Ironically, Reagan's anti-environmental agenda actually aided the environmental movement by stimulating dramatic growth in organizational memberships, particularly for those organizations focused heavily on nature protection (Dunlap 1992; Mitchell et al. 1992).

Despite relatively consistent and strong public support for environmental and nature protection, the countermovement, more recently calling itself the 'Wise Use Movement', continued to grow throughout the 1980s and 1990s (Brick 1995). Despite efforts on both sides of the environmental debate during the George H.W. Bush (1989–93) and Bill Clinton (1993–2001) administrations, neither side seemed to gain the upper hand. In spite of strongly positive environmental policy statements by President Clinton, his ability to promote environmental protection was limited by other governmental forces; he did, however, at the end of his tenure, provide for the immediate protection of millions of acres of forested land and the creation of several national monuments, which are protected natural or historic areas similar to but typically not as extensive as national parks (Vig 2003).

Reminiscent of Ronald Reagan, however, the G.W. Bush administration has been marked by extreme hostility toward environmental protections and regulations (Vig and Kraft 2003; Bosso 2005). Ironically, public backlash against recent efforts to dismantle environmental protections has been relatively subdued, probably due to America's preoccupation with the events and ramifications of the terrorist attack of 11 September 2001 (Dunlap 2003; Brechin and Freeman 2004; Dunlap 2006). Because of this passive response, some have been quick to conclude that the era of environmental legislation and reform is over; some have even proclaimed the 'death of environmentalism' (Shellenberger and Nordhaus 2004). Others, however, have noted the tenacity of the environmental movement and the continuing support of environmental causes among the US public (Brechin and Freeman 2004; Bosso 2005; Dunlap 2006). While membership in several core environmental organizations has apparently declined somewhat, probably due to harder economic times (see, e.g. McLaughlin and Khawaja 2000), other organizations have continued to grow in terms of both membership and budgetary means, including at least two of the more prominent nature protection organizations, the Sierra Club and Defenders of Wildlife.

Despite its problems and challenges, the environmental movement remains a key component of contemporary US society, and nature protection organizations continue to be prominent players within the movement. In the following section, I discuss important characteristics of nature protection organizations in the USA, beginning with the large, national organizations and ending with the newer radical groups which have developed in large part due to perceived weaknesses of the large national organizations in responding to threats to the natural world.

NATURE PROTECTION ORGANIZATIONS IN THE USA[2]

The environmental movement is probably one of the largest social movements in the USA in terms of organizations, memberships and monetary means (Brulle 2000). Literally thousands of groups and organizations in the USA work for environmental causes (Kempton et al. 2001; National Wildlife Federation 2005). Many of them are relatively short-lived, small, of only local or regional scope, or focused on specific topics. Such groups provide critical support to environmental and nature protection efforts in the USA and even internationally. Brulle (2000) estimates there are at least 10 000 environmental organizations in the USA that are registered with the Internal Revenue Service as tax-exempt organizations with receipts of $25 000 or more. Total membership in these organizations is estimated at somewhere between 19 and 41 million (Brulle 2000). Among all the organizations involved in the US environmental movement, preservationist organizations generally have the highest net worth and the largest annual incomes, and are among those groups with the largest memberships and staffs. This is a testament to the continuing importance of nature protection in the environmental movement.

The Large, National Organizations

Brulle (2000) estimates that over 1000 environmental organizations in the USA are fairly large and command budgets in excess of $100 000, but a relatively small set of organizations comprises what is commonly known as the mainstream environmental movement (Bosso 2005). These organizations are typically national or international in scope and have relatively large memberships; they garner substantial resources, including membership revenues and grants from government, foundations and corporations, and they often wield considerable name recognition and political power. Despite occasional dips in memberships and resources, the number of these mainstream organizations and the number of members they attract has generally remained strong (Mitchell et al. 1992; Sale 1993; Shabecoff 1993; Bosso 2005).

The mainstream environmental movement includes several organizations that are primarily preservationist or conservationist in orientation, but such organizations typically focus on several types of issues and reflect varying discourses. Several primarily preservationist and conservationist organizations, for instance, expend considerable resources on issues directly associated with reform environmentalism, such as air and water pollution or toxic waste, since protecting nature and wildlife often requires fighting such threats as well. Even organizations considered more reform environmentalist in orientation devote some (and in some cases substantial) resources to nature protection as defined above. Indeed, many of the major national environmental organizations in the USA can be considered 'hybrids' in that they address a host of issues that span the gamut from traditional to more contemporary environmental concerns (see, e.g. Johnson 2006).

While some organizations are more narrowly focused and others are more blended in terms of issues and philosophy, environmental organizations in the USA can still be usefully distinguished in terms of their primary philosophy and program focus (Brulle 2000). Table 10.1 lists the large, national environmental organizations most commonly considered to be preservationist or conservationist in orientation (Brulle 2000; Mertig et al. 2002; National Wildlife Federation 2005). Most of these organizations were set up before the advent of contemporary environmentalism and are direct or slightly delayed products of the conservation movement at the turn of the twentieth century.

Geographical and Topical Focus

Before 1960, nature protection organizations tended to be heavily focused on particular geographic regions or on fairly specific wildlife species or issues. For instance, the Sierra Club concentrated its efforts on the Sierra Mountains of California and drew the bulk of its members from the West Coast region; in 1951, however, it established an Atlantic chapter and began to spread out geographically (Mitchell 1989). The National Audubon Society, named after John James Audubon, initially focused solely on the preservation of birds and their habitats, but by the end of the 1960s, it had begun to widen its agenda (Mitchell 1989). Interestingly, in response to an increasing dependence on 'local politics' in environmental decision making in the USA, the Society has more recently chosen to return to its preservationist roots, placing emphasis once again on birds and wildlife habitat (Welsh 2004). Defenders of Wildlife was initially named Defenders of Furbearers, as its founders were concerned about the effect of steel-jawed traps and poisons on fur bearing animals; however, the organization's interests have since widened to include broader issues of nature protection

Table 10.1 Major nature protection organizations in the USA

Organization	Year founded	Estimated membership, 1960–2004, in thousands										2003/2004 revenue (thousands $US)
		1960	1969	1972	1979	1983	1989	1990	1995	2000	2004	
Sierra Club	1892	15	83	136	181	346	493	560	550	550	782	82170
Wildlife Conservation Society	1895	4	8	7	13	26	34	34	68	107	87	144988
National Audubon Society	1905	32	120	232	300	498	497	600	600	550	525	74150
National Parks Cons. Assoc.	1919	15	43	50	31	38	83	100	450	500	285	21094
Izaak Walton League	1922	51	52	56	52	47	47	50	40	50	50	3534
The Wilderness Society	1935	(10)	(44)	(51)	48	100	333	370	310	300	205	27003
National Wildlife Federation	1936	n.a.	(465)	(525)	(784)	(758)	(925)	975	(975)	945	4200*	117836
Defenders of Wildlife	1947	21	(12)	(15)	(48)	63	68	80	80	250	460	30919
Nature Conservancy	1951	2	19	23	72	194	365	600	705	(1000)	872	865831
World Wildlife Fund	1961	–	n.a.	n.a.	44	94	312	940	1200	1200	1200	126350
Rainforest Alliance	1986	–	–	–	–	–	n.a.	18	4	14	31	8880
Conservation International	1987	–	–	–	–	–	1	55	40	4	70	92213

Notes:
Numbers in parentheses are estimates; n.a. = not available.
* National Wildlife Federation changed its definition of membership, which now includes all those enrolled in its school programmes (Bosso 2005). Bosso (2005) estimates the Federation's 'actual' membership in 2003 to be 650000.

Sources: Tober (1989); Mitchell et al. (1992); Mertig et al. (2002); annual editions of the National Wildlife Federation's *Conservation Directory*; Gale Research Group's annual *Encyclopedia of Associations*; organization websites, annual reports, most recently available IRS 990 forms available either on organization websites or through guidestar.org, and directly from organization personnel.

(Mitchell 1989; Mitchell et al. 1992). The National Parks and Conservation Association (which no longer has an 'and' in its name) was founded in order to promote expansion of the National Park System. Early on its leader was the first Director of the National Park Service, Stephen Mather. While the organization is still focused on the protection and expansion of national parks and monuments (including historical parks, as opposed to purely 'natural' parks), its interests have necessarily expanded to other issues that also affect the parks more indirectly.

Although the Izaak Walton League and National Wildlife Federation have traditionally focused on promoting conservation for the recreational interests of sportsmen's groups, both have also increasingly pursued broader concerns. The Izaak Walton League, for example, works on several wilderness and national parks issues, as well as water pollution, energy efficiency and clean air (Izaak Walton League 2003). In fact, the League was the first of the early environmental organizations to add water pollution to its agenda, undoubtedly due to the concern its fishermen had with the degradation of sportfish-bearing streams and lakes (Mitchell 1989). Likewise, the National Wildlife Federation has broadened its scope. According to its website (www.nwf.org), the Federation focuses today on three goals: (1) to 'connect people with nature'; (2) to 'protect and restore wildlife'; and (3) to 'confront global warming'. The National Wildlife Federation, like most of the preservationist organizations, has taken a strong role in attempting to thwart the opening of the Arctic National Wildlife Refuge in Alaska for oil production.

Several of the organizations in Table 10.1, particularly the newer ones, are heavily focused on international nature protection. Conservation International, for example, started when some members of the Nature Conservancy concluded that it was not international enough in its focus (Mitchell et al. 1992). Likewise, the Rainforest Alliance's mission is to 'protect ecosystems and the people and wildlife that depend on them' around the world (Rainforest Alliance 2005). Several of the older preservationist organizations have also added strong international components. The Wildlife Conservation Society (renamed in 1993) was initially formed as the New York Zoological Society in order to develop and manage the Bronx and other zoos in New York City. It began conducting international programmes as early as the 1940s and currently works in 53 nations around the globe (Wildlife Conservation Society 2005). Finally, several of the other organizations, including the Sierra Club and Defenders of Wildlife, are affiliated with counterpart groups in other countries, and several also address international issues. For instance, the Sierra Club's motto is to 'explore, enjoy and protect the wild places of the *earth*' (emphasis added) (Sierra Club 2005) and the Nature Conservancy proclaims itself as 'a leading *international*, nonprofit organization dedicated to preserving the diversity of life on *Earth*' (emphasis added) (Nature Conservancy 2005).

Headquarters

All the organizations listed in Table 10.1 are headquartered on the East Coast of the USA (in or near New York City or Washington, DC), except for the Sierra Club, which is currently headquartered in San Francisco but also has a legislative office in Washington, DC. In the decades immediately following Earth Day in 1970, most large environmental organizations moved their headquarters close to Washington, DC, due to their growing participation in political lobbying and litigation, which required greater proximity to the centres of political power. However, recent trends toward the 'devolution' of environmental decision making in the USA have prompted several organizations, such as the Wilderness Society, Defenders of Wildlife and the National Audubon Society, to increasingly emphasize regional projects and offices (Welsh 2004).

Monetary Resources

All the large, national organizations report multi-million-dollar revenues for fiscal year 2003, from a low of \$3.5 million for the Izaak Walton League to a high of over \$865 million for the Nature Conservancy. Brulle (2000) notes that the Nature Conservancy, in particular, can actually distort statistical analyses of environmental movement resources, as it commands a substantial portion of the income received by all environmental organizations (roughly 30 per cent) and an even larger portion of their assets (66 per cent). All the organizations except the Rainforest Alliance engage in some degree of lobbying, either to sway political leaders (US tax authorities refer to this as 'direct' lobbying) or to influence public opinion ('grass-roots' lobbying). Lobbying expenses for the fiscal year 2003 ranged from a low of just over \$5000 for Conservation International to over \$3 million for the Nature Conservancy; most of these funds went for direct lobbying (as opposed to grass-roots lobbying). Lobbying is a vital activity for any social movement, but the US government limits the amount of lobbying – relative to an organization's total funds and programme activities – it can engage in and still remain entitled to receive contributions that donors can deduct from their taxable income (Mitchell et al. 1992). The Sierra Club lost its tax-exempt status in the 1960s due to its aggressive efforts under the leadership of David Brower to sway (i.e. 'lobby') public opinion (Mitchell 1989); a companion organization, the Sierra Club Foundation (founded in 1960), accepts tax-deductible contributions in support of Sierra Club programmes that do not involve lobbying. Because of the complexity of tax laws, many movement organizations have developed similar structures.

Membership

In 1960, the membership of the nature protection organizations was quite small, probably fewer than 100 000 members combined; today most of these organizations individually have substantially more than 100 000 members. While there is probably some overlap in membership across the organizations, their total membership is nevertheless considerable. Some of the organizations (e.g. Sierra Club, National Audubon Society, National Wildlife Federation) also have hundreds of chapters or affiliates nationwide, which adds to their influence at the local, regional and national levels. Since the 1970s, membership growth of the preservationist groups has been more pronounced, on average, than that of other prominent national environmental groups. While some of the preservationist organizations (e.g. National Parks Conservation Association and the Wilderness Society) have experienced small membership losses in recent years, others, such as the Nature Conservancy and the World Wildlife Fund, have grown substantially.

As is the case for many social movement organizations, members of nature protection organizations tend to be highly educated and are typically above average in income and occupational prestige (Milbrath 1984; Morrison and Dunlap 1986). Members tend to work primarily in relatively well-paying, but non-extractive occupations such as professional, service and creative art careers (Morrison and Dunlap 1986; Mertig and Dunlap 2001). Mainstream organization members tend to be younger on average than their counterparts in the general public, although this age differential has not been consistent across all studies (Manzo and Weinstein 1987). Members of these organizations have been primarily white and leaders have tended to be male (Dowie 1995).

Action Strategies

Like other environmental organizations, those focused on nature protection rely heavily on research, education, litigation and lobbying to achieve their desired goals. Several engage in relatively unique tactics, especially when compared to many reformist environmental organizations in the USA. The Wildlife Conservation Society, for instance, manages numerous urban wildlife parks and nature centres to aid in scientific research and promote environmental awareness (Wildlife Conservation Society 2005); the World Wildlife Fund is likewise involved in setting aside and managing wildlife preserves (World Wildlife Fund 2005). Rainforest Alliance runs programmes of certification for forestry, agriculture and tourism to ensure that companies comply with important environmental and social standards (Rainforest Alliance 2005). The Nature Conservancy, which was formed by a small group of scientists from the Ecological Society of America who wanted to take 'direct action' to protect natural areas, is well known for purchasing land to ensure its protection (Nature Conservancy 2005). Purchased lands are then either protected by one of the Conservancy's numerous affiliates or passed on to other groups, such as local agencies or educational institutions, for protection or maintenance for educational purposes.

Professionalization

As has been noted in numerous social movements (McCarthy and Zald 1987), nature protection organizations, as well as other environmental organizations, have undergone a transition in organizational structure. These organizations typically began as fairly small, volunteer-based and charismatically led groups, which made only limited forays into the policy arena. They have since evolved into relatively large, staff-based and professionally led organizations which mount extensive efforts to sway public policy (Bosso 2005). Because environmental organizations have generally been growing in size, membership and influence since the beginning of the contemporary environmental movement, they have necessarily come to rely increasingly on professional staff and professionalized, bureaucratic strategies for generating resources and memberships and for influencing specific targets (Mitchell et al. 1992).

The professionalization of the mainstream environmental movement has disheartened many observers. They claim that it has dampened concern about environmental outcomes because bureaucrats and professionals care more about organizational stability and career success than about movement principles (Snow 1992; Dowie 1995; Bosso 2005). Others believe the movement has been co-opted by the *status quo* and has accommodated itself to economic and industrial interests, embracing the very interests it originally sought to overcome (Devall 1992; Austin 2002). In short, the institutionalization of the large, national organizations has been heralded, on the one hand, as a sign of their strength and capacity to deal with a changing political and bureaucratic environment; on the other hand, it has drawn extensive criticism from other environmentalists, many of whom have joined or formed alternative types of groups in response. I now turn to a brief review of one type of alternative organization with particular import for the issue of nature protection: radical or deep-ecology-based environmental groups.

DEEP ECOLOGY AND THE RADICAL GROUPS

The term 'radical' is usually used to distinguish those environmental groups that have at least two elements in common: (1) their use of highly confrontational, 'direct action' techniques, and (2) an ecocentric worldview referred to as 'deep ecology' (Manes 1990; Scarce 1990; Devall 1992). While the radical groups employ some of the same strategies that mainstream groups use, they often add direct-action tactics that are considered too extreme by the mainstream movement. While Greenpeace (usually classified as a reformist organization) is typically considered the pioneer of direct-action techniques, such as plugging effluent pipes and steering inflatable rubber boats between whalers and whales, groups such as Earth First! (founded in 1980), Sea Shepherd Conservation Society (1977) and the Earth Liberation Front (1992) have gone even further, condoning property damage and sabotage, sometimes referred to as 'monkey wrenching', meaning to interfere with the orderly completion of a production process. They have contaminated the fuel for bulldozers used at logging operations, nailed spikes into trees in order to hinder potential timber harvesting, rammed drift-net ships on the high seas, and committed arson at a ski resort (Foreman and Haywood 1987; Manes 1990; Scarce 1990). In fact, Paul Watson, the founder of the Sea Shepherd Conservation Society, was ousted from Greenpeace, a group he had helped to co-found, for being too radical. The radical groups' actions target property, taking pains to ensure that people are not physically harmed by their activities. Because of their direct challenge to property rights, all of these groups have come under the watchful eye of the Federal Bureau of Investigation. In fact, the Earth Liberation Front reports that it is considered the number 1 domestic terrorist group within the USA (Earth Liberation Front 2005).

Radical groups justify their actions through the ideology of 'deep ecology'. In contrast to what radicals label the 'shallow' ecology and anthropocentric worldview of reformist, mainstream organizations – even preservationist ones – deep ecology revolves around a biocentric ethic and a passionate self-identification with nature (Manes 1990; Scarce 1990; Devall 1992). Rather than protecting the environment for the sake of humans, radicals seek to protect nature for its own sake. In this sense, they take the idea of nature protection even further than most of the earlier preservationists; rather than protecting nature for the aesthetic, recreational or even ecological interests of humans, these activists aim to protect nature for nature's sake. They believe that nature has a right to exist in and of itself, apart from human values. Activists' identification with nature – solidified through frequent contact with wilderness and rituals such as the 'Council of All Beings' – is thought to transform them from activists working to protect nature to that of nature working to protect itself (Devall 1992).

Organizationally, radical groups attempt to avoid the professionalization and bureaucratization that they despise in the mainstream organizations (Scarce 1990; Lee 1995). Likewise, they operate on significantly smaller budgets and have substantially lower membership numbers than the mainstream nature protection organizations. Membership size is often difficult to determine for these groups, especially for the Earth Liberation Front, which operates almost entirely in a covert manner. Earth First! may have as many as ten to 15 thousand members nationally and worldwide (Mitchell et al. 1992; Lee 1995), while the Sea Shepherd Conservation Society has around 35 000 members (Hunt 2004; Bosso 2005). In 2004, the Sea Shepherd Conservation Society reported revenue of $350 000, while revenues for Earth First!, which can only be estimated from subscription income received by its journal, were roughly $85 000 (*EF! Journal*, personal communication). While having fewer resources, the radical groups represent an important challenge to the older nature protection organizations and to those interests that conflict with the goal of protecting nature.

CONCLUSION AND A LOOK AHEAD

Nature protection has played and continues to play a vital role within the overall environmental movement in the USA, and it has apparently sustained the environmental movement during difficult times. Preservationism, in particular, has been a potent source of mobilization for the environmental movement, as issues involving wild land and wildlife are typically highly appealing to the US public. This has led preservationist organizations to fare better overall than other kinds of environmental organizations, even during the early decades of the modern environmental movement and, especially, during the political backlash during the Reagan administration. It is also likely that these organizations will survive the current anti-environmental onslaught.

Nevertheless, it is ironically often the issues of reformist environmentalism that arouse greater concern among the US public at large, even though preservationist organizations, in general, have enjoyed more success in recruiting and sustaining a mass membership base. This is undoubtedly related to the notion that members and supporters of organizations often represent those portions of the public that are relatively well off, whereas public opinion polls are more representative of the general public, whose concerns are more broadly representative of the full range of issues within the wider environmental movement. Although there is evidence to suggest that the US public makes little distinction between nature protection and other environmental issues (Mertig and Dunlap 2001), public opinion polls often find that reformist environmentalist issues, such as water or air pollution, top the list of environmental concerns, with the nature protection issues of rainforest destruction or loss of biodiversity receiving somewhat or even considerably less support (Belden and Russonello 1996; Roper Survey 1998; *Los Angeles Times* 2001; Pew Research Center 2001; Belden et al. 2002; Gallup Organization 2006). When viewed in comparison to other environmental issues, the US public is clearly concerned about nature protection, but is even more concerned about issues that fall more squarely in the reform environmentalist slate of issues. Issues of pollution may be seen as more directly and immediately related to human health, thus engendering an even greater level of concern for them; or perhaps the public feels that these are the issues that have not been receiving enough attention from government and elites.

Even so, support for protecting nature remains an important element of public concern for the environment, and several recent polls have found substantial support for nature protection. According to a *Los Angeles Times* poll conducted in April 2001, 91 per cent of the US public says that it is important (51 per cent extremely so, 40 per cent somewhat so) to them 'personally that wilderness and open spaces' be preserved (*Los Angeles Times* 2001). A Mellman Group poll in 1999 found that nearly half of the public felt that not enough wilderness was protected, and a NSRE (National Survey on Recreation and the Environment) poll in 2000–2001 found almost half (49.2 per cent) felt that not enough land was designated as wilderness (Campaign for America's Wilderness 2003). An April 2001 *LA Times* poll reported 40 per cent saying there was too little land protected as wilderness in the USA. This poll also found that a majority of the public would choose 'protecting endangered species from extinction even if some people may not be able to develop the land they own' over 'protecting the right of property owners' (*Los Angeles Times* 2001).

What role will nature protection play in the environmental movement and in the USA in the twenty-first century? Given its importance during roughly the past century and a half, it seems highly unlikely that nature protection will decline or disappear. Public support for protecting nature remains high, even when compared to the much more publicly resonant concerns of pollution and toxic waste. Monetary and membership support for nature protection organizations, while declining in some cases, remains strong and appears to be increasing for others.

The 'big' environmental issues looming on the horizon today, such as global warming, may appear to overshadow concerns with protecting natural areas and endangered species. Yet nature protection issues are becoming inextricably intertwined with reformist environmentalist issues, and as environmental issues become even more complex over time, understanding of how everything is interconnected grows. Protecting natural areas and species has become part and parcel of concerns for mitigating environmental problems and preventing risks to human health and communities. Rainforest destruction, a key nature protection concern, is implicated in global warming, and the recent catastrophic flooding of New Orleans, Louisiana in the wake of Hurricane Katrina highlighted the vital role of preserving wetlands and natural river flows as mechanisms not only to protect habitats and wildlife, but also to protect human health and communities. While preserving nature for its own sake has always been a hard sell relative to protecting nature in order to benefit humans, the fact that these can no longer be easily separated means that neither can entirely disappear.

Nevertheless, both recent events and scholarly analyses have suggested that the environmental movement, including both nature protection organizations and other environmental organizations, may be losing effectiveness (Austin 2002; Shellenberger and Nordhaus 2004). Emblematic of the movement's problems, one of the largest nature protection organizations in the USA, the Nature Conservancy, has recently undergone a great deal of criticism from the *Washington Post*, a leading national newspaper, which ran a series of scathing articles in May 2003. The hostile Bush administration, coupled with a growing countermovement (see, e.g. Brick 1995; Austin 2002; Mertig et al. 2002) and seeming public acquiescence to anti-environmental moves (due largely to the events of 9/11), appear to bode ill for the future of the environmental movement in general and nature protection in particular.

On the other hand, it is precisely when government becomes hostile to environmentalism and nature protection that the role of organizations within civil society becomes even more important (Schlosberg and Dryzek 2002). Civil society, the component of society represented by voluntary organizations which exists apart from both the state and the market (Brulle 2000), has thus become key to furthering nature protection, both in the USA and globally. Neither the market nor the state appear able – or at times even willing–to correct, or even to recognize, ecological problems (Brulle 2000). To the extent that the environmental movement, as a key actor in civil society, remains beholden to the government or to market forces, future progress in protecting the environment may be hindered.

The movement for nature protection certainly has the potential to overcome its current challenges, just as it has apparently done so in the past. Nature protection organizations, such as the Nature Conservancy, have been responding to public criticisms of their programmes (Nature

Conservancy 2006). The environmental movement as a whole, and several organizations in particular, have substantial resources, and the issues they espouse have strong public support. The key to utilizing this support is ensuring that the public is aware of what is going on. The USA appears to be at a critical juncture; civil society organizations must take over where the state and the market have failed, often on purpose. Recent public opinion polls further note a substantial decline in public approval of current governmental policies, including the open disregard for environmental issues (Gallup Organization 2006). If the past is any guide, the environmental movement, particularly through its strong base of nature protection organizations and substantial public support for its cause, can provide the impetus for radical change.

NOTES

1. The use of frames in this chapter is purely descriptive in nature. While these frames overlap within the US environmental movement, several scholars have utilized the distinctions presented here as a way to categorize movement ideas and organizations (see, e.g. Brulle 2000; Mertig et al. 2002).
2. Information on the US organizations was collected from several sources: recent and past editions of the National Wildlife Federation's *Conservation Directory*, Gale Research Group's annual *Encyclopedia of Associations*, organization websites, organization annual reports, most recently available IRS 990 forms available either on organization websites or through guidestar.org, and references cited throughout.

REFERENCES

Austin, Andrew (2002), 'Advancing accumulation and managing its discontents: The U.S. antienvironmental countermovement', *Sociological Spectrum*, **22**, 71–105.

Belden and Russonello (1996), 'Current trends in public opinion on the environment: Environmental compendium update', www.biodiversityproject.org/resourcespublicopiniontrends.pdf, accessed 23 September 2005.

Belden Russonello and Stewart (2002), 'Americans and biodiversity: New perspectives in 2002. Questionnaire and Topline Results', www.biodiversityproject.org/02toplines.PDF, accessed 23 September 2005.

Bosso, Christopher J. (2005), *Environment, Inc.: From Grassroots to Beltway*, Lawrence, KA: University Press of Kansas.

Brechin, Steven R. and Daniel A. Freeman (2004), 'Public support for both the environment and an anti-environmental president: Possible explanations for the George W. Bush anomaly', *The Forum*, **2** (1), Article 6; www.bepress.com/forum/vol2/iss1/art6.

Brick, Phil (1995), 'Determined opposition: The wise use movement challenges environmentalism', *Environment*, **37** (8), 17–20, 36–42.

Brulle, Robert J. (2000), *Agency, Democracy, and Nature: The U.S. Environmental Movement from a Critical Theory Perspective*, Cambridge, MA: MIT Press.

Campaign for America's Wilderness (2003), *A Mandate to Protect America's Wilderness: A Comprehensive Review of Recent Public Opinion Research*, Washington, DC: Campaign for America's Wilderness.
Catton, William R. and Riley E. Dunlap (1980), 'A new ecological paradigm for post-exuberant sociology', *American Behavioral Scientist*, **24** (1), 15–47.
Devall, Bill (1992), 'Deep ecology and radical environmentalism', in R.E. Dunlap and A.G. Mertig (eds), *American Environmentalism: The U.S. Environmental Movement, 1970–1990*, Philadelphia, PA: Taylor and Francis, pp. 51–62.
Dowie, Mark (1995), *Losing Ground: American Environmentalism at the Close of the Twentieth Century*, Cambridge, MA: MIT Press.
Dunlap, Riley E. (1992), 'Trends in public opinion toward environmental issues: 1965–1990', in R.E. Dunlap and A.G. Mertig (eds), *American Environmentalism: The U.S. Environmental Movement, 1970–1990*, Philadelphia, PA: Taylor and Francis, pp. 89–116.
Dunlap, Riley (2003), 'No environmental backlash against Bush administration', *Gallup Poll Analyses* (21 April), www.gallup.com/poll/releases/pr030421.asp?Version=p, accessed 17 December.
Dunlap, Riley E. (2006), 'Show us the data: The questionable empirical foundations of "the death of environmentalism" thesis', *Organization and Environment*, **19** (1), 88–102.
Earth Liberation Front (2005), 'Earth Liberation Front' and 'Recent ELF News', www.earthliberationfront.com/, accessed 4 August.
Faich, Ronald G. and Richard P. Gale (1971), 'The environmental movement: From recreation to politics', *Pacific Sociological Review*, **14** (3), 270–87.
Foreman, Dave and Bill Haywood (eds) (1987), *Ecodefense: A Field Guide to Monkeywrenching*, 2nd edn, Tucson, AZ: Ned Ludd.
Gale, Richard P. (1972), 'From sit-in to hike-in: A comparison of the civil rights and environmental movements', in William R. Burch, Neil H. Cheek and Lee Taylor (eds), *Social Behavior, Natural Resources and the Environment*, New York: Harper and Row, pp. 280–305.
Gallup Organization (2006), 'Environment', www.galluppoll.com/content/default.aspx?ci=1615&pg=1, accessed 16 October.
Hays, Samuel (1959), *Conservation and the Gospel of Efficiency*, Cambridge, MA: Harvard University Press.
Hunt, Kimberly N. (2004), *Encyclopedia of Associations*, 41st edn, Detroit, IL: Gale.
Huth, Hans (1957), *Nature and the American: Three Centuries of Changing Attitudes*, Lincoln, NE: University of Nebraska.
Izaak Walton League (2003), 'Annual report', www.iwla.org/reports/annrep03.pdf, accessed 1 August 2005.
Johnson, Erik (2006), 'Changing issue representation among major United States environmental movement organizations', *Rural Sociology*, **71** (1), 132–54.
Kempton, Willett, Dorothy C. Holland, Katerine Bunting-Howarth, Erin Hannan and Christopher Payne (2001), 'Local environmental groups: A systematic enumeration in two geographical areas', *Rural Sociology*, **66** (4), 557–78.
Kraft, Michael E. and Norman J. Vig (2003), 'Environmental policy from the 1970s to the twenty-first century', in N.J. Vig and M.E. Kraft (eds), *Environmental Policy: New Directions for the Twenty-First Century*, Washington, DC: Congressional Quarterly, pp. 1–32.
Lee, Martha F. (1995), *Earth First! Environmental Apocalypse*, Syracuse, NY: Syracuse University Press.

Los Angeles Times (2001), '*Los Angeles Times* poll: Study #458, nation: Environmental issues, April 2001', www.latimesinteractive.com/pdfarchive/stat_sheets/la-timespoll458ss.pdf, accessed 23 September 2005.
Manes, Christopher (1990), *Green Rage: Radical Environmentalism and the Unmaking of Civilization*, Boston, MA: Little, Brown.
Manzo, Lynne C. and Neil D. Weinstein (1987), 'Behavioral commitment to environmental protection: A study of active and nonactive members of the Sierra Club', *Environment and Behavior*, **19** (6), 673–94.
McCarthy, John D. and Mayer N. Zald (1987), 'The trend of social movements in America: Professionalization and resource mobilization', in Mayer N. Zald and John D. McCarthy (eds), *Social Movements in an Organizational Society: Collected Essays*, New Brunswick, NJ: Transaction Books, pp. 337–91.
McLaughlin, Paul and Marwan Khawaja (2000), 'The organizational dynamics of the U.S. environmental movement: Legitimation, resource mobilization, and political opportunity', *Rural Sociology*, **65** (3), 422–39.
Mertig, Angela G. and Riley E. Dunlap (2001), 'Environmentalism, new social movements, and the new class: A cross-national investigation', *Rural Sociology*, **66** (1), 113–36.
Mertig, Angela G., Riley E. Dunlap and Denton E. Morrison (2002), 'The environmental movement in the United States', in R.E. Dunlap and W. Michelson (eds), *Handbook of Environmental Sociology*, Westport, CT: Greenwood Press, pp. 448–81.
Milbrath, Lester W. (1984), *Environmentalists: Vanguard for a New Society*, Albany, NY: State University of New York.
Mitchell, Robert Cameron (1989), 'From conservation to environmental movement: The development of the modern environmental lobbies', in Michael J. Lacey (ed.), *Government and Environmental Politics: Essays on Historical Developments Since World War Two*, Washington, DC: The Wilson Center Press, pp. 81–113.
Mitchell, Robert Cameron, Angela G. Mertig and Riley E. Dunlap (1992), 'Twenty years of environmental mobilization: Trends among national environmental Organizations', in Riley E. Dunlap and Angela G. Mertig (eds), *American Environmentalism: The U.S. Environmental Movement, 1970–1990*, Philadelphia, PA: Taylor and Francis, pp. 11–26.
Morrison, Denton E. and Riley E. Dunlap (1986), 'Environmentalism and elitism: A conceptual and empirical analysis', *Environmental Management*, **10** (5), 581–9.
Nash, Roderick (1974), *The American Conservation Movement*, St Charles, MO: Forum Press.
Nash, Roderick (1982), *Wilderness and the American Mind*, 3rd edn, New Haven, CT: Yale University Press.
National Wildlife Federation (2005), *Conservation Directory, 2005–2006*, Washington, DC: Island Press.
Nature Conservancy (2005), 'About the Nature Conservancy' and 'History and milestones of the Nature Conservancy', www.nature.org/, accessed 3 August.
Nature Conservancy (2006), 'Setting the record straight regarding *The Washington Post* "big green" series', www.nature.org/pressroom/links/art10505.html, accessed 16 October.
Norton, Bryan G. (1986), 'Conservation and preservation: A conceptual rehabilitation', *Environmental Ethics*, **8** (3), 195–220.
Petulla, Joseph M. (1977), *American Environmental History: The Exploitation and Conservation of Natural Resources*, San Francisco, CA: Boyd and Fraser.

Pew Research Center (2001), 'Bush's base backs him to the hilt', people-press.org/reports/print.php 3?ReportID=14, accessed 23 September 2005.
Pinchot, Gifford (1910), *The Fight for Conservation*, Garden City, NY: Harcourt, Brace.
Rainforest Alliance (2005), 'Our mission', www.rainforestalliance.org/about/mission.html, accessed 4 August.
Roper Survey (1998), 'The 1998 National Environmental Education and Training Foundation/Roper survey', www.neetf.org/roper/roper.htm, accessed 25 January 1999.
Sale, Kirkpatrick (1993), *The Green Revolution: The American Environmental Movement 1962–1992*, New York: Hill and Wang.
Scarce, Rik (1990), *Eco-Warriors: Understanding the Radical Environmental Movement*, Chicago, IL: Noble Press.
Schlosberg, David and John S. Dryzek (2002), 'Political strategies of American environmentalism: Inclusion and beyond', *Society and Natural Resources*, **15**, 787–804.
Shabecoff, Philip (1993), *A Fierce Green Fire: The American Environmental Movement*, New York: Hill and Wang.
Shellenberger, Michael and Ted Nordhaus (2004), 'The death of environmentalism', www.thebreakthrough.org/images/Death_of_Environmentalism.pdf, accessed 23 September, 2005.
Sierra Club (2005), 'Our mission statement', www.sierraclub.org/inside/, accessed 1 August.
Snow, Donald (1992), *Inside the Environmental Movement: Meeting the Leadership Challenge*, Washington, DC: Island Press.
Snow, Donald A., E. Burke Rochford, Jr. Steven K. Worden and Robert D. Benford (1986), 'Frame alignment processes, micromobilization, and movement participation', *American Sociological Review*, 51, 464–81.
Tober, James A. (1989), *Wildlife and the Public Interest: Nonprofit Organizations and Federal Wildlife Policy*, New York: Praeger.
Vig, Norman J. (2003), 'Presidential leadership and the environment', in N.J. Vig and M.E. Kraft (eds), *Environmental Policy: New Directions for the Twenty-First Century*, Washington, DC: Congressional Quarterly Press, pp. 103–25.
Vig, Norman J. and Michael E. Kraft (eds) (2003), *Environmental Policy: New Directions for the Twenty-First Century*, Washington, DC: Congressional Quarterly Press.
Welsh, Michael W. (2004), 'Reaction of the national environmental groups to devolution', *Society and Natural Resources*, **17**, 293–304.
Wildlife Conservation Society (2005), 'About the Wildlife Conservation Society' and 'History of the Wildlife Conservation Society', www.wcs.org, accessed 11 August.
World Wildlife Fund (2005), 'About WWF: History', www.worldwildlife.org/about/history.cfm, accessed 4 August.

11. Nature protection in Western environmentalism: a comparative analysis

C.S.A. (Kris) van Koppen and William T. Markham

INTRODUCTION

When we started the project that culminated in this book, we believed that a comparative study of the development of Western nature protection organizations and networks from the past to the present would make a meaningful contribution to the literature. As pointed out in Chapter 1, nature protection organizations and networks have not been the object of much comparative research. Yet they have occupied an important place in the hearts and minds of citizens of virtually every Western nation for over a century. They have a substantial record of achievement, and they are increasingly involved in worldwide efforts to protect nature. They have played influential roles as interest groups, as components of social movements, and in the development of environmentalism and civil society, and there is every reason to expect that they will continue to play these roles in the future.

Our initial assumptions have proven to be well grounded. The foregoing chapters demonstrate the continuing influence of nature protection organizations and networks within the environmental movement and within civil society at large. They illustrate not only striking similarities between countries, but significant differences as well. In this chapter, we endeavour to take stock of the findings in the context of the theoretical considerations presented in the first chapter. When we embarked on this task, we soon came to realize that it is not possible for a single chapter to encompass the rich diversity of the individual stories nor to do justice to all theoretical perspectives that are of interest in analysing nature protection. Thus the analysis presented here should be read not as a set of definitive conclusions that tie together all the material in the book, but rather as a selection of conclusions that we consider to be among the most salient lines of enquiry.

We begin by highlighting several key similarities and differences among the countries studied. In the second section, we explore some more theoretical explanations for the patterns in our findings. We then take another look at the international level, which overarches the different national histories and which is certain to exert increasing influence on national and local developments in the future. Finally, we present some thoughts about the further development of nature protection and its relationship to environmentalism and civil society in the years to come.

NATURE PROTECTION IN NINE NATIONS: PERSISTENT ROLES AND SHARED TRANSFORMATIONS

Green Waves

Despite the numerous differences among countries documented above, the chapters clearly demonstrate that the emergence of nature protection in Western nations was an international phenomenon with many commonalities across nations. All the countries included here experienced two characteristic periods of marked change, sometimes referred to in the literature as the first and second green waves (e.g. Spaargaren and Mol 1992).

The first wave began in the late nineteenth century and continued in the first decades of the twentieth. During this period the first national organizations with a major focus on nature protection were founded. Two kinds of motives were at the heart of the early organizations: on one hand the scientific interests of naturalists, botanists and zoologists; on the other hand aesthetic interests including preservation of valued landscapes and vistas, landmark structures, spectacular and rare species, and simple appreciation of nature's beauty and tranquillity. Although the emphasis differed – scientific interests, for instance, played an important role in early nature protection efforts in Poland, whereas in Italy the 'aesthetic wing' was dominant – both kinds of concerns are found in all countries covered. Closely related to the aesthetic concerns of early nature protection were recreational interests in tourism and outdoor sports. The role of touring and mountaineering clubs was prominent in, for example, Norway, Sweden and France. Outdoor sports were, among others, prominent in the USA, where they typically included hunting, as for instance in the National Wildlife Federation. Also noteworthy are the close links between nature protection organizations and automobile clubs in the Netherlands and the UK. Although less prominent than scientific and aesthetic motives, resource conservation also played a role. Resource conservation was, for instance, a central motive for a substantial part of early nature protection efforts in the USA; as a result, nature conservation and nature preservation have a different connotation in the USA, whereas they are more or less synonymous in Europe.

In every country, membership in early nature protection organizations and networks was small. Generally, it was concentrated in elite groups. The activities of nature protection organizations were directed toward protection of specific species, designation of protected areas, public education on nature protection, and–mainly in Europe – preservation of cultural landscapes. Representing only small numbers of people, the power of the early nature protection groups was very limited. Relative to their size, however, they were rather successful in England, the Netherlands, Sweden and the USA, among others. Even in countries such as Italy and France, where their position was much weaker, they were able to exert some influence on nature protection policies and the designation of reserves. In several European countries and the USA, nature protection pioneers were able to establish nature parks and reserves, either by acquiring land themselves or lobbying governments to do so. In some instances, they also successfully advocated for species protection, as for example in the campaigns against the use of wild bird feathers for hat decoration in England, Germany, the Netherlands and the USA.

Although at times disrupted by depression, the rise of fascism and wars, the general situation described above persisted well into the second half of the twentieth century in Western Europe and the USA. (The situation was different in Poland and the GDR, where nature protection organizations were placed under state supervision after the war.) Most of the established organizations continued their activities, and some new ones emerged. Additional protected areas were designated and new nature protection laws issued, but the general picture remained one of modest successes and limited growth in public support. Even the Second World War represented more of an interruption than a basic shift. In Germany and Norway the main nature protection organizations' images were damaged by their sympathies with the Nazi regime, but nature protection in both nations survived and gradually returned to prewar patterns. In other nations, the USA, the UK, Sweden and the Netherlands, it is even hard to speak of an interruption. Nature protection organizations continued their work, while adapting to the war situation. After the war, rebuilding the economy dominated the public and political agendas, particularly in Europe, and attention to nature protection, though never absent, remained a secondary priority.

Except in Poland and the GDR, the 1960s and 1970s marked the beginning of a second period of dramatic change, propelled this time by the dramatic rise of the environmental movement. The movement brought new issues – air and water pollution, threats to human welfare, population growth and resource depletion – to the fore. It was also associated with spectacular growth in the size and breadth of public interest in environmental and nature protection issues and support for the environmental movement, especially among the well-educated middle class. Under the influence of the environmental movement, framings of nature protection shifted noticeably – not concern for preservation of nature's beauty and wildness, but pollution, resource depletion and threats to human health now assumed centre stage, and nature protection was frequently redefined as protecting the ecosystems on which human life depends. Existing strategies of public education, purchasing land directly, or persuading government to place key areas under protection were supplemented by more confrontational social movement strategies: mass petitions, demonstrations and countercultural ideologies became prominent. In several countries (including the USA, the UK, France, Netherlands and Germany), anti-nuclear campaigns figured among the most confrontational expressions of the new movement. Ecology and environmental science emerged as growing fields of research and came to be considered key disciplines for engineering 'spaceship earth' – an approach far removed from the natural history emphasis of nature protection pioneers at the beginning of the twentieth century. Existing nature protection organizations found themselves challenged to broaden their goals and change their strategies, and new organizations and networks emerged. These changes eventually occurred in all nine countries. In Poland and the GDR, the flowering of the environmental movement was delayed by authoritarian governments, but in both countries it emerged with full force as part of the movements that swept the old regimes out of power.

Institutionalization and New Challenges

While the second 'green wave' brought new themes, new strategies and new impetus to the work of nature protection organizations, nature protection was by no means marginalized or superseded by new environmental concerns. Nature protection issues were instead incorporated into the agenda of many of the new environmental movement organizations such as Greenpeace and Friends of the Earth. At the same time, some of the classic nature protection organizations, such as the US Sierra Club and the German League for Bird Protection, adopted new environmental issues, such as pollution and resource depletion. Equally indicative of the staying power of nature protection was the founding of WWF in 1961 and its rapid spread to most Western nations. Initially concerned almost exclusively with nature protection, the WWF later moved gradually toward assimilating newer environmental concerns. The melding of nature protection concerns with newer environmental ones was, in part, the result of actions by organizations and movements seeking survival and support; however, the new combination of issues also made sense from a physical perspective, for the degradation of nature, pollution and resource depletion were often closely interrelated. Prominent examples include acid rain (the problem of *Waldsterben* in Germany), eutrophication, soil erosion and depletion of water resources.

Nevertheless, nature protection and other environmental issues remained, to some extent, distinct. In some cases they were even pitted against one another. Archetypical examples were the conflicts over hydropower dams in Norway and Sweden, where the 'environmentalist' goal of sustainable energy contradicted the 'preservation' interest of leaving rivers untouched. More recently, similar conflicts have emerged in the form of conflicts over wind turbines in Germany and elsewhere.

How the various organizations and networks have combined environmental and nature protection concerns and responded to conflicts between them differs among the countries studied. However, in general, the case studies document the continuing – and in some cases even growing – importance of nature protection issues. One of the reasons for this importance is continuing media attention and public support for nature protection.

One noteworthy change in public support over recent years is the growth of animal-welfare-related organizations in several nations, including the USA, the Netherlands and Italy. Animal protection organizations, which often combine efforts to protect both wild species and domestic animals, have been among the fastest-growing civil society organizations of the last decades. Indeed, unlike the 1970s when the attention of radical activists was often focused on environmental issues such as nuclear power and chemical spills, today's most radical exponents of environmental concerns – organized in networks such as Earth First! – are often found in groups that combine nature protection and animal rights.

Not least because of pressure from nature protection organizations and networks, significant advances have been made over the past two decades in the institutionalization of nature protection in all of the countries. Institutionalization has occurred via legislation, the establishment of governmental agencies to protect nature and the environment, and the designation of nature areas. This process of institutionalization has also assumed an increasingly international character. Internationalization has been propelled by international treaties and conventions, such as the Convention on Biological Diversity (1992) and by the internationalization of nature protection organizations and networks. In Europe, an important impetus for internationalization has been provided by the EU. Its Natura

2000 network of protected areas constitutes a strong force for homogenizing nature policy and management in the member states, which include all European countries of this book except Norway. Parallel to these processes of institutionalization and internationalization, we can observe an increasing cooperation with business organizations in recent years. WWF is a case in point, although the intensity of cooperation does vary among its national chapters.

DIVERGING CHARACTERISTICS

Wilderness and Cultivation

Notwithstanding the common patterns described above, there are also striking differences in the histories and current functioning of nature protection organizations and networks among the nine countries. In this section, we address four main areas of difference. The first area, which has manifested itself from the early origins of nature protection to the present, concerns perceptions of what nature deserves to be protected.

As ideal types, two opposing views can be distinguished. The first holds that human reshaping of nature, such as in the transformation of forests into cultivated lands and the presence of human artefacts, such as traditional farmhouses or historical buildings, do not necessarily diminish the value or protection-worthiness of nature. Indeed, they may even enhance it. The second view maintains that nature is only worth preserving if it is 'wilderness', that is, if it is free from human use or management.

Nature protection advocates in the countries covered in this book have approached this question differently. At one end of the spectrum lies Italy, where, especially in early nature protection efforts, protection of nature areas and cultural monuments seemed almost inseparable. At the other extreme is the USA, where, until the recent emergence of efforts to protect agricultural lands near cities, nature protection focused almost exclusively on wilderness. Other countries are arrayed between these extremes. The combination of preservation of cultural heritage and nature protection is expressed in the idea of protecting 'nature monuments', which we encounter in France, the Netherlands, Germany, Norway and Sweden. Protection of cultural landscapes was, and continues to be, of importance in Italy, France, Germany, the UK, the Netherlands and Poland. In Scandinavian countries, the view of nature is more similar to that in the USA, but, as was mentioned, the concept of nature monuments also emerged early on in Swedish and Norwegian nature protection, and protected areas in Scandinavia also include cultural landscapes.

Obviously, the prevailing character of cultural landscapes and the sheer availability of large wilderness areas help to explain these differences, but there are other factors as well. The UK, for instance, has a longstanding cultural tradition of appreciating the rural nature of the countryside (Thomas 1993). In France, the institution of Parcs Naturels Regionaux (regional nature parks) involves significant influence of local authorities and communities on the designation and management of such parks. The result is a flexible protection regime, which allows for continuation of agricultural and other forms of exploitation in conjunction with nature protection (Finger-Stich and Ghimire 1997). At the wilderness end of the spectrum, the Netherlands provides a remarkable example. While there are no untouched nature areas left in the Netherlands, efforts are being made to develop 'new wilderness' from previously cultivated land. Clearly, then, not just the physical availability of different types of 'nature', but also cultural and political traditions may be of influence on the diverging preferences concerning nature.

A similar observation can be made with regard to the protection of wild animal and plant species. Where cultural landscapes are regarded as valuable nature, species that live in symbiosis with human cultivation – such as plants that are thriving in heathlands, or meadow birds living in farm lands – are included in protection efforts. Where wilderness is prominent, species in wild habitats become central to nature protection.

Diverging Roles of the State

A second area of difference among countries is related to the role of the state in nature protection efforts. In some nations, as in Norway and Sweden, the state has played a strong and active role in promoting, planning and implementing nature protection. This has undoubtedly contributed to these nations' success in protecting large areas. High levels of state activity are not, however, necessarily all to the good. In some instances, the active role of government has cut the ground from under the feet of nature protection organizations. In Sweden, for instance, the establishment of a first-in-the-world environmental agency went hand in hand with the exclusion of nature protection organizations from direct influence on government policy. Active and supportive roles of the state also prevailed the Netherlands and the UK. Less favourable situations were found in Germany, France and Italy. In these countries, support for nature protection organizations, and involvement in nature protection of the states themselves, were very limited. In Germany and Italy, the emergence of a fascist regime paralysed civil society activities for nature protection in the 1930s and 1940s. A rather similar situation occurred in Poland and the GDR under communist regimes. In

Poland, the state had been actively involved in the first decades of the twentieth century, installing a state council for nature protection and establishing many protected areas. Under communism, however, lack of support and state control hampered the successful development of independent and effective nature protection organizations, a legacy that persists even today. Though not affected by such shifts of regime, the role of the US government has also undergone substantial changes in the last century. While it was actively involved in nature conservation and preservation in the first decades of the twentieth century, it took a much more passive and, to many observers, even anti-environmentalist stance under recent Presidents Ronald Reagan and George W. Bush.

Closely related to the role of the state is the issue of land ownership. In Norway and Sweden, but also in Germany, Poland, France and Italy, the large majority of protected areas are owned by the government. Also in the USA, where significant areas of land are owned by nature protection organizations, government holdings are much more vast. In the UK and the Netherlands, however, substantial parts of the protected areas are acquired and owned by nature protection organizations, often with financial support of government, and in the UK much protected land remains in private hands. Specific legislation, such as the 1907 National Trust Act in UK, has been enacted to facilitate this type of private ownership with public-good aims. Normally, landowning nature protection organizations are also directly involved in management of their holdings. Involvement in nature management tasks of different kinds also exists in many other countries. In France, for instance, nature protection organizations are involved in management of nature areas in cooperation with the state. These forms of involvement, however, are less intensive than for landowning organizations. Major landowning nature protection organizations are the National Trust in the UK, Natuurmonumenten in the Netherlands, and the Nature Conservancy in the USA. Owning and managing nature areas, and opening them to the public, provides these organizations with a high public profile and a relatively strong position in political arenas.

Differences in the influence of the state also exist in the emphasis on central versus decentralized execution of nature policy. Where the central state is dominant, as in Scandinavia and the Netherlands, nature protection organizations also tend to focus on the national level. In federal states, such as the USA and Germany, substantial decision-making power resides in respectively the States and *Länder*. Also in Poland, Italy and the UK, the local and regional levels appear to be relatively important, although in varying forms and degrees. In general, decentralization tends to strengthen regional and local organizations or chapters of national organizations, at the expense of national-level organizations, including national chapters of international organizations. France presents a special and different case in this respect. Here, a highly centralized state has been accompanied by strong feelings of regional identity and autonomy, and this tension affects the position of nature protection organizations, which are relatively loosely organized at the national level, but at regional and local levels play significant roles in policy implementation. At least in some of the countries, for instance France and the Netherlands, there appears to be a tendency of decentralization of nature protection issues in recent years. Historically, strong central state influence existed under fascist and communist rule. In the period following the Second World War, the communist systems of Poland and the GDR not only controlled nature management, but also nature protection organizations, leaving them only state-approved and controlled tasks, such as youth education or small-scale practical nature protection projects. In doing so, the organizations' strategies were more or less reduced to volunteer support of government programmes.

Public Support

A third key area of difference is the strength of public support for nature protection. Public support is manifested in membership size and donations from private persons, in the number of volunteers for work in nature management activities and education, and in the number of citizens willing to engage in public protest and campaigns. In addition to this, public support is a crucial factor in the political legitimacy and influence of nature protection organizations. Public support for nature protection organizations and networks varies widely across our countries, with the Netherlands and the UK at one end of the spectrum and France, Italy and Poland at the other.

Propelled by the green waves mentioned above, public support for nature protection has increased over time in all Western countries, although not without occasional setbacks. None the less, the relative differences in public support among countries, e.g. between the UK and France, seem to have remained comparatively stable, even over the period of interruption caused by the Second World War. Exceptions to this general observation, however, are situations of dramatic changes in governmental regime. Particularly in the case of Poland, the establishment of a communist regime, after a devastating world war, appears to have deeply affected the vitality and public support of nature protection over several decades.

Strategies of Nature Protection Organizations and Networks

A fourth area of difference concerns the strategies followed. In some of the countries, perhaps most prominently the UK, Norway and the Netherlands, the development of nature protection organizations seems to have followed a path of differentiation, in which organizations assume different roles, such as land ownership and management, mobilization of the public, environmental education and lobbying for nature. In other countries, in contrast, a homogenizing tendency is observed. Most explicitly, this process of converging strategies is discussed in the case of Italy, but tendencies in this direction are also evident in, for instance, Germany and Poland.

That strategies of organizations depend on specific national contexts is also evidenced by the diverging roles that national chapters of international organizations assume in different countries. WWF, for illustration, has different profiles in all the countries studied. To give a few examples: in Italy it has been active in the establishment of small reserves and management activities; in the Netherlands it has profiled itself by promoting nature development; in the UK it has been prominent in linking conservation and development; while in Germany it has followed a more traditional path of lobbying, education and land purchase.

Another difference in strategies among countries concerns the relative influence of internationally based organizations on the one hand and nationally, regionally and locally based organizations on the other. Particularly in Norway, France and Poland, international organizations have a gained a much weaker position than in most of the other countries studied. Notwithstanding these differences, it should be stressed that informal international networks played and still play a major role in nature protection, facilitating an intensive international exchange of nature protection views and strategies. As mentioned earlier, the concept of 'nature monuments' dispersed over many countries. Similarly, early models of nature protection in Switzerland were adopted by Italy and Poland.

On a national and local level, networks among nature protection organizations, environmental organizations and other civil society organizations have been influential in all the countries studied. The importance of networking is demonstrated, among others, by the establishment of organizations with the aim of creating permanent networks between nature protection and environmental organizations such as the Wildlife Link in the UK, the Deutscher Naturschutzring in Germany, and the Fédération France Nature Environnement in France. While it is hard to make reliable comparisons of the strength of networks among the different countries, it is obvious that these strengths vary. In the UK and the Netherlands, ties between organizations are relatively intensive and durable; in France and Poland, among others, they appear to be much looser.

IN SEARCH OF EXPLANATION

Strategies, Resources and Adaptation

From the description of similarities and dissimilarities among countries, we now turn to exploring the underlying factors that may help to explain these phenomena. We base our exploration on the theoretical approaches described in the first chapter of this book.

A useful point of departure for this exploration is the insight, derived from the open systems approach in organization theory, that nature protection organizations and networks must adapt their strategies to changing circumstances if they wish to survive and move towards their goals. That is, they must seek out a niche within the nature protection landscape that allows them to mobilize the resources needed for subsistence and growth. Broadly based on the evidence of the preceding chapters, we can distinguish the following strategy types – in varying combinations applied by nature protection organizations and networks. Each type appears to be linked to a particular combination of resources.

- *Ownership and management of land*, as mentioned above, is a powerful strategy, but it is available only to a limited number of nature protection organizations. When pursued on a large scale, it requires government approval and facilitation and significant financial resources. Once achieved, however, land ownership can boost an organization's public profile and its attractiveness to members. Characteristic sources of funding for land acquisition include government grants, funding from sponsors, membership dues, and other types of donations, such as legacies. These may be supplemented by revenues from the protected areas themselves, including admission fees and proceeds from shops and restaurants. Protecting lands and opening them to the public can also be an important source of legitimacy.
- *Lobbying* is a second traditional activity of nature protection organizations, and, in some countries, specific organizations have concentrated their efforts on this strategy. One prominent example of such a specific organizations is the Netherlands Society for Nature and Environment. Significant lobbying efforts on the national, EU and international levels are also undertaken by international organizations such as WWF or Birdlife International. Organizations that emphasize lobbying typically rely on resources such as membership dues, government grants, and sponsors for financial support. Non-financial resources are also of major importance for successful

lobbying. Historically, the personal status and contacts of the representatives of nature protection organizations was often a decisive factor, but more recently, the emphasis has shifted to having a large support base, in terms of direct members or associated organizations, and being able to provide professional expertise to lawmakers or government agencies.

- *Public information and education* also have a long history in the repertoire of nature protection organizations. These activities are less visible than more confrontational actions, and their impact is less direct than lobbying, but they have always been important in the work of nature protection organizations and networks. Public information is often an important element of campaigns, where it is combined with various other activities, such as public protest. To date, environmental education and public information are major concerns for environmental and nature protection organizations. In the UK, for instance, environmental education was the most frequently mentioned concern in a 1999 survey of environmental organizations (see the chapter on England), and the chapter on France describes how environmental education has become a key activity. Government contracts and funding, payments from other organizations for educational activities, membership fees and volunteer work are important resources for public education activities. With regard to legitimacy, trust in the information and education provided is crucial. Professional expertise thus plays an important role in building this legitimacy.
- *Protest and litigation* are confrontational strategies designed to exert pressure on business or government. Protest accomplishes this by means of demonstrations and campaigns; litigation, by applying juridical tools. Protest strategies have been developed mainly by the new organizations established during and after the green wave of the 1960s and 1970s. Often used in combination with public information campaigns, they have become the central strategies of organizations such as Greenpeace and FoE. Protest strategies can aim at directly mobilizing supporters, or they can focus on influencing the opinions of the public and policy makers by arousing media attention. Greenpeace actions provide typical examples of the latter. As a consequence of the establishment of nature protection regulation, litigation has increased as an action strategy, for instance in France during the 1980s and 1990s. Lawsuits before the European Court, as well as other procedures at the European level, have become powerful tools for environmental and nature protection organizations, for example in Poland. Used alone, litigation is a rather technical strategy, which

relies heavily on professionals, but it can also be combined with campaigns and other protest strategies. For organizations emphasizing these confrontational strategies, membership fees, private donations and volunteer work are important resources. Because of their confrontational character, such organizations are less likely to attract business or government funding. Nevertheless, in countries such as Norway, Sweden and the Netherlands, government funding is also a major resource for organizations that use these strategies. Such support is, however, not free of controversy, as it can limit the independence of nature protection organizations and networks, undermining an important source of public trust and legitimacy.

- *Consultancy and mediation* have emerged as increasingly important strategies in recent years. Consultation refers to advice and research provided by organizations, for instance to assist with monitoring the implementation of nature protection legislation and programmes; mediation refers to guidance and support provided by organizations in resolving conflicts and facilitating public participation in policy processes. Consultancy and mediation services are an important strategy of environmental and nature protection organizations in countries such as France and Italy. In Poland, too, many nature protection organizations rely heavily on this activity to obtain funding, often via EU-related programmes. In Germany and the USA, however, these strategies are scarcely used at all. A related strategy is active cooperation with industries and other business actors, for instance by WWF in Sweden, the UK and the Netherlands. Here, payments for services such as expert advice, facilitation of policy implementation, ecolabelling audits and the like, constitute a major source of financial support. In order to provide these services, nature protection organizations must have adequate expertise, which requires either professionalization or a pool of expert and committed volunteers. In cases of mediation, another important requirement is that the organization be trusted by citizens involved.

Over the history of nature protection, the types and amounts of resources available to nature protection organizations and networks have constantly changed. Consequently, they have had to modify their strategies repeatedly. In a few instances, nature protection organizations, such as the state-sponsored nature protection organization in the GDR, were simply outrun by the pace of change and could not adapt fast enough to survive. However, many of the organizations in the nine countries have, as resource dependence models suggest, successfully transformed themselves to adapt to changing circumstances. This was manifest, for example, at the time of the emergence of the environmental movement, when several existing nature protection organizations broadened their range of activities to embrace new environmental issues and adopted new, often more confrontational, strategies. Other nature protection organizations chose to remain focused on their traditional activities. This pattern was typically followed by the major landowning organizations but also, to a considerable extent, by WWF in Germany and the USA, and by the Council for the Protection of Rural England.

Comparing strategies of organizations described in this book, it is apparent that the configuration of available resources and niches varies significantly from country to country, and it appears that the differences in strategies chosen by the organizations are correlated with these variations. The different strategies of WWF chapters, for example, are related to the niches available in the individual countries. If we take the case of the Netherlands for illustration, such a niche was found in supporting the initiatives of ecologists and nature protection activists towards developing 'new nature' in formerly agricultural areas, at a time when most other nature protection organizations were still focused on preserving existing nature areas.

In addition to these variations in specific strategies, there also appear to be differences in tendencies toward differentiation and homogenization. The chapter on Italy explicitly elaborates on a tendency towards isomorphism among the nature protection organizations there. Major reasons for organizations to choose a more or less similar mix of strategies are the limitations in financial support and the uncertainties about the future caused by cuts in state funding. In Poland, it is observed that due to the fact that resources are limited and come mainly from international institutional donors, the competition between nature protection organizations has increased, and strategies converge towards adopting a broad mix of activities, and directing activities on the same, national, level. In other countries, by contrast, differentiation appears to prevail. Particularly in the UK and the Netherlands, the overall trend in the past – it is more difficult to say so about the present – has been one of specialization. Although most organizations are not confined to a single type of strategy, many of them have a clear orientation towards one or two strategies within the spectrum of lobbying, local conservation, environmental concerns, land ownership, preservation of birds, education, consultancy, mobilizing public opinion and others.

These comparisons suggest that isomorphism tends to emerge in situations where resources are limited, uncertain, and mostly available from a small range of sources, through competitive procedures. On the other hand, differentiation is more likely to prevail in situations where the amount of resources is larger, where access is less competitive because of more or less established relationships between fund providers, nature protection organizations and others, and where a variety of relatively stable sources of income is available, including memberships.

Social Dynamics of the State and of Public Support

As the chapters about the individual countries demonstrate, the character and amount of resources available to nature protection organizations and networks depends on wide range of factors. Within this range, however, we can point to two major factors: the structure and role of the state; and the amount of public support for nature protection.

The interest group theories presented in Chapter 1 are especially helpful in understanding the effects of the structure and role of the state. As we pointed out there, nature protection organizations frequently, though not invariably, take on the characteristics of interest groups. How governments deal with interest groups, therefore, strongly affects the resources and opportunities available to them. In typical pluralist political systems, such as the USA, and to some degree also the UK, the political system is relatively open to influence from interest groups. Here nature protection organizations that can obtain adequate support and organize effectively can successfully and legitimately play the role of defenders of nature. Their resources typically come from membership and donations. Government support, however, may be limited, as is the case in the USA.

In neo-corporatist systems, such as Sweden, Norway and the Netherlands, the state plays a stronger role in supporting organizations, thus creating additional resources. In these societies, broad public support is not only a source of income in itself, but also a means to become eligible for government funding. Evidence from the nine countries seems to support the theoretical notion that neo-corporatism tends to soften conflicts between interest groups and government, as relations between government and nature protection organizations in Norway, Sweden and the Netherlands seem to be less confrontational than in, for instance, the USA and Germany.

Another form of state–NGO cooperation is provision of services by nature protection organizations. Provision of consulting services, education and mediation services to international, national and local government-related bodies on a more or less commercial basis has become a major strategy of some nature protection organizations. In Poland, proceeds from such activities represent a major financial resource, and such contracts also play a significant role in France and Italy. Where nature protection organizations are dependent on government in this way, a professionalized, non-confrontational approach tends to prevail.

Next to the state, public support is plausibly the most important factor influencing the strategies and success of nature protection organizations and networks. As noted above, there are major differences in levels of public support among the countries studied. According to social movement theorists, successful framing of nature protection issues is one important means of broadening public support. In line with this insight, we can observe that a majority of organizations indeed invest much effort in influencing public appreciation of nature and concern about nature degradation. None the less, the general picture is that nature protection advocates are able to influence such framings to only a rather limited extent. Substantial changes in public opinion and support depend to a greater extent on broader trends in society at large, including changes in lifestyles, broad waves of social movement mobilization, and changes in media attention, as well as on spectacular events, such as natural disasters or oil spills. The green wave of the 1960s and 1970s is a case in point. Although generally supported by nature protection organizations, it was not primarily a result of efforts by nature protection organizations to frame nature protection in new ways. Indeed, many nature protection organizations struggled to accommodate themselves to the new definition of nature protection as just one environmental issue among many. None the less, the shift provoked by this green wave proved decisive in elevating nature protection, together with environment issues, on public and political agendas.

The country studies also suggest several observations about the motivational bases that have generated and sustained public support for nature protection in the populations of Western nations. Since the 1960s, the environmental movement, interpreted broadly, has invoked a range of motives – ranging from concerns about human health, pollution and depletion of resources, through concerns over degradation of the scenic and cultural–historical aspects of landscapes, to moral concerns about species extinction and the welfare of wild and domestic animals. Clearly, this a heterogeneous set of motives. They attract support under different constituencies, and may even be in conflict. None the less, there appears to be a degree of coherence and continuity in the underlying values. Were it not so, it would be hard to explain why so many organizations are successful in appealing to combinations of these motives, why there is so much overlap among members and supporters of the various organizations, and why firm networks are built between organizations that appeal to motives from different parts of the spectrum. A relationship between nature-oriented aesthetic and moral motives, and environment-oriented motives such as public health and resource conservation, is also manifest in the historical development of support bases for nature protection and environmentalism.

In countries with traditionally strong nature protection organizations, we see a stronger environmental movement emerging. The converse is equally true. Countries such as Italy and France, where nature protection organizations have historically been weak, also showed less public support for both environmentalism and animal protection.

It is beyond the scope of this chapter to investigate in detail the commonalities in the value base of nature protection and environmental activism. We can observe, however, that these values, at least to some extent, reflect what new social movement theorists term 'post-material' values; that is, they focus not just on political and economic power, but also involve 'environmentally friendly' or 'ecological' lifestyles and identities (see Chapter 1).

Another observation, explicitly made in the US chapter, but probably applying to other countries as well, concerns what might be called the skewed translation of public concern into organizational support. For many people, environmental pollution, with its threats to health and human welfare, is of greater concern than degradation of natural areas, disappearance rare species, or mistreatment of animals. Yet memberships are, in general, higher for organizations that emphasize animal and nature protection than for those engaged solely in fighting pollution. Apparently, it is easier to make a successful appeal to the public for supporting protection of nature areas and animals than for engaging in environmental protection. One obvious reason for that is the less controversial character of nature protection. Many nature protection and animal protection activities threaten neither economic development nor jobs and do not require radical changes in lifestyles.

This factor alone, however, cannot account for the fact that nature protection has persisted for over a century in all nine countries, at times under very unfavourable political and economic conditions, and continues to prosper today. To explain this fact, the Arcadian tradition, as described in Chapter 1, may be useful. According to this approach, the motivations underlying nature and animal protection are part of a value orientation that was first articulated in Romanticism but has since then combined with widening citizen interest in natural history, recreation and care for nature. In line with this view, we find that the origins of nature protection organizations are closely related to Romanticist ideas in most countries and that public support for nature protection increased as more people had time and money for pets, gardening and outdoor recreation. As elaborated in the chapter on France, among others, the emergence of nature protection was linked to the rise of new middle classes, which no longer depended on direct interaction with nature for their income and visited or even settled in the countryside with new interest. Whether the persistence of nature protection motives corroborates the biophilia hypothesis (see Chapter 1) remains open to debate. It is clear that nature appreciation persistently emerges among social categories whose members can afford it. On the other hand, it is equally clear that the sort of nature that is valued – wilderness versus cultural landscapes – and the amount of public and institutional support nature protection receives varies widely across different countries in accordance with varying cultural traditions.

Roles in Civil Society

Probably the most important role for the nature protection organizations and networks described in this book is converting societal interests in nature into actual nature protection measures, such as nature protection laws, designation of protected areas and species, and practical nature protection and management activities. In assessing the significance of this role, an important question is whose interests the nature protection organizations actually represent. For many of their supporters, it would be the interests of future generations and of 'nature for its own sake', rather than the personal interests of a specific group in society. For others, as for instance lovers of outdoor sports, nature protection may clearly represent a specific, personal interest. However, it is clear that in most Western countries the importance of nature protection is acknowledged by a great many citizens from various social categories. Representing and implementing their interests is an important and legitimate civil society role for nature protection organizations to play.

Another important civil society role of nature protection organizations and networks is educating and informing citizens. From the beginning, nature protection advocates have realized that preserving nature was not enough. Many nature protection organizations, such as the National Wildlife Federation in the USA and the German Nature Protection Ring, have also aimed to 'connect people with nature', in order to enrich their lives and build a long-term support base for nature protection. Work with schoolchildren and young volunteers has always been an important part of such efforts. WWF and many other organizations have special children's and youth organizations with educational goals. Education and information efforts are also directed to widely varying categories of adults through means such as visitor information centres in parks, educational campaigns, magazines and nature documentaries. Specific organizations and networks that specialize in public education, such as the Association for Environmental Education in the Netherlands, and the Ecole et Nature (School and Nature) network in France, have emerged in some countries.

Some of the country studies suggest that the importance of public education is growing and that new forms of education are emerging. In France, for example, such a development is described under the title of 'pedagogical activism'. In Norway, Bellona and Green Everyday Life are pursuing new and interesting strategies for informing citizens about environment and nature.

On a general level, apart from these specific roles, it is more difficult to say what the impact is of nature protection organizations and networks on the development of civil society. The other way round, the impact is beyond any doubt. The success of nature protection organizations has been strongly affected by the status of civil society. The fates of nature protection organizations under fascism in Italy and Germany, and under communism in the GDR and in Poland, dramatically demonstrate how vital the functioning of civil society is for the development of nature protection organizations.

To what extent have nature protection organizations and networks, in turn, strengthened civil society? In line with the analysis presented in the chapter on Norway, it appears that in the long run, the impact of nature protection organizations and networks on democracy and civil society has depended on the specific strategies they have deployed. In so far as they have relied on volunteer work, grass-roots activities and public debate, they may have contributed to developing civil society skills, widening the sphere of public debate and opening political institutions for input. This has been and remains the case for some of the nature protection organizations and for several of the environmental organizations that also worked for nature protection. On the other hand, many nature protection organizations have been primarily oriented to lobbying and consultation with government and business. Furthermore, the ongoing institutionalization of nature policy and management, along with the continuing professionalization of nature protection organizations, has created a certain distance between the lifeworlds of ordinary citizens and the work of nature protection organizations and networks. Finally, many nature protection organizations, including most of the large ones, are not democratically organized themselves. The broader impact of these organizations on civil society is probably limited.

It is because many of the larger and more powerful nature protection organizations miss these aspects of active, critical and democratic mobilization of citizens that it is hard to characterize nature protection organizations and networks as a social movement, in spite of their large public support base, a distinct role in representing societal interests, and a value orientation that to a significant extent is shared with the broader environmental movement.

THE ROAD AHEAD

Internationalization

Chapter 1 described how international nature protection organizations, such as WWF, FoE and Greenpeace, have successfully pushed for a broad set of international treaties and regulatory frameworks for nature protection worldwide and in Europe. The country studies make clear that both efforts to institutionalize nature protection and the activities of nature protection organizations at the national level have become deeply intertwined with international developments. In Europe, nationally based organizations, cooperating through the EEB and other networks, have influenced EU legislation, which, in turn, increasingly shapes national legislation and regulations. Working via Brussels has thus become an important way for nature protection organizations to influence their own national governments. This approach – and the resulting 'boomerang' effect – has proved especially important in Poland, and one could speculate that it is prevalent among other new EU members; however, the same phenomenon has also been observed in the older EU nations. Another prominent example of the interrelationship between international and national-level developments is biodiversity conservation. Promoted by IUCN, WWF and UNEP, the concept of biodiversity was adopted in the Convention on Biological Diversity at the 1992 UN Conference on Environment and Development in Rio de Janeiro. Since then, it has become a prominent concept in nature conservation, and it has influenced nature policy in many countries of the world, as was described in the chapters on Sweden and the Netherlands.

While most of the older nature protection organizations still have a strong national basis, many of the successful, recently established organizations are true multi-level organizations, with international, national and – in some cases – regional or local-level units. In addition to the WWF, FoE and Greenpeace, there is also Birdlife International, an organization originating from national bird protection organizations, which is increasingly active on international stages, and the International Fund for Animal Welfare (IFAW). The emphasis on activities, however, differs among these organizations (see also Chapter 1). WWF and IFAW have a strong international focus, both in activities and in the management of the organization. FoE, by contrast, is a rather loose network of national organizations, and in many countries – including England and the Netherlands – FoE has local chapters which have considerable autonomy *vis-à-vis* their national organization.

Despite the growing importance of work at the international level, support for organizations with a strong international character is remarkably uneven in the countries studied. While WWF and Greenpeace are among the largest nature protection organizations in the UK, the Netherlands and Germany, their support in Norway, France and Poland is quite weak relative to other nature protection organizations. In the USA, WWF is strong, but Greenpeace is, after a brief surge of popularity, weak in comparison to other nations. Weak support for these organizations in Norway, France and Poland may be related to a more general political orientation toward local or national-level politics. In France, nature protection is mostly locally based, and Norway is not a member of the EU.

In several countries, including Sweden and the Netherlands, WWF and other organizations are engaging in joint projects with business organizations and promoting market-based instruments, such as ecolabels. Given the increasingly internationalization of corporations, markets and product chains, these strategies tend to reinforce the internationalization of nature protection. The premier example of this trend is the international Forest Stewardship Council ecolabel for wood products, which was established with support from WWF and other nature protection organizations and has been heavily promoted in Sweden, Germany and the USA. In the USA, Conservation International and the Rainforest Alliance utilize corporate sponsorship and ecolabelling to focus directly on protecting regions with especially high biodiversity – the so-called hotspots – thereby involving producers and consumers worldwide as well as local NGOs in the targeted regions.

Future Challenges

Many of the authors in this book, in concluding their chapters, express the view that nature protection organizations need new strategies to successfully achieve their goals in the future. This is true not only for countries where nature protection and environmental organizations are coping with relatively unfavourable circumstances, such as Italy, Poland or the USA, but also for England, the Netherlands and Sweden, countries that have gone a long way towards what might be called the ecological modernization of nature protection (see Chapter 1). In view of the successful institutionalization of nature protection within these nations and the EU, and the well-established position of nature protection organizations internationally, calls for new strategies may seem ironic. They become more understandable, however, when one examines the challenges ahead. One useful way of thinking about this is to distinguish two possible future scenarios for nature protection.

The first scenario is an extension of national and international tendencies towards institutionalization, professionalization and cooperation with business organizations, which have been reported for all of the countries of this book, particularly with respect to the large nature protection organizations. In this scenario, nature protection organizations would increasingly function as civil society service organizations, providing services such as managing areas, lobbying for nature, consultancy and mediation, and providing education and information. To sustain their work, they would continue to make appeals to broad categories of citizens to support them via membership dues and contributions, thus providing the resources – money, political standing, and legitimacy – they need to operate successfully. Among the consequences of this scenario would be competition among the organizations for supporters and a tendency to avoid addressing highly controversial issues in order to retain their broad support and cooperative relationships with government and business.

This scenario fits well with actual developments, and at first glance, seems to contribute to the above-mentioned roles of nature protection organizations in civil society. Nevertheless, it is less clear that it can endure in the long term. Nature protection is becoming more and more intertwined with issues of environmental degradation, climate change, and with urban and rural development issues (including urbanization and urban sprawl, depopulation or gentrification of the countryside, and issues of transport and mobility). Moreover, the underlying threats to nature are increasingly based in unsustainable consumption on the one hand, and poverty and population growth on the other. Nature protection is thus less and less a matter of just protecting selected cultural landscapes or wilderness areas or implementing measures for species protection. Therefore it will become increasingly difficult to address nature protection within the context of pluralist or neo-corporatist political systems as merely one societal interest among many.

Given these developments, whether nature protection organizations will be able to effectively protect nature by restricting themselves to the first scenario remains debatable. It is also far from clear that nature protection organizations that hold controversial issues of consumption, industrialization and social justice at arm's length will be able to maintain the image of moral integrity and their public trust on which their influence and legitimacy are based.

In view of these issues, a second scenario, elements of which also emerge in many of the country chapters, warrants consideration. The keystones of this scenario are networking among environmental and nature protection organizations, grass-roots citizen participation, and tighter integration of issues of environment, nature protection, economic production and consumption, and social justice. Local knowledge and networks are prominent in this approach, and linking them to professional knowledge and institutional networks is a main challenge. In this scenario, voluntary action, consumer pressure, public protest, and positive and significant changes in lifestyle are much more relevant than large membership or high levels of donations. This scenario, it appears, would be more in line with the grass-roots activities of local organizations in France, the bottom-up strategies of FoE in England and the Netherlands, and Green Everyday Life in Norway than with the strategies of the National Trust, Greenpeace, or Conservation International.

These scenarios are not mutually exclusive. They may even reinforce each other in some ways. But this is not automatically so. As Chris Rootes argues in the chapter on England, the strategies of the two scenarios will have to be 'calibrated against each other'. This certainly is no easy task. Choices have to be made, not only by nature protection organizations themselves, but also by the citizens, companies and governments that allocate resources to them. It is our feeling at the end of this book that nature protection organizations and networks will only be able to fulfil their mission over another century if they succeed, more than most of them do now, in being part of a social movement.

REFERENCES

Finger-Stich, Andréa and Krishna B. Ghimire (1997), 'Local development and parks in France', in Krishna B. Ghimire and Michel P. Pimbert (eds), *Social Change and Conservation*, London: Earthscan, pp. 158–86.

Spaargaren, G. and A.P.J. Mol (1992), 'Sociology, environment, and modernity: ecological modernization as a theory of social change', *Society and Natural Resources*, **5**, 323–44.

Thomas, K. (1993), *Man and the Natural World: Changing Attitudes in England 1500–1800*, London: Penguin Books.

Index